WJEC EDUQAS GCSE (9-1)
GEOGRAPHY B

■ Alan Brown ■ Val Davis ■ Bob Digby ■ Andy Leeder

DYNAMIC LEARNING

HODDER
EDUCATION
AN HACHETTE UK COMPANY

Orders: Please contact Bookpoint Ltd, 130 Park Drive, Milton Park, Abingdon, Oxon OX14 4SE. Telephone: +44 (0)1235 827720. Fax: +44 (0)1235 400454. Email: education@bookpoint.co.uk. Lines are open from 9 a.m. to 5 p.m., Monday to Saturday, with a 24-hour message answering service. You can also order through our website: www.hoddereducation.co.uk

ISBN: 978 1 4718 5787 4

© Alan Brown, Val Davis, Bob Digby, Andy Leeder 2016

First published in 2016 by Hodder Education, An Hachette UK Company
Carmelite House, 50 Victoria Embankment, London EC4Y 0DZ
www.hoddereducation.co.uk

Impression number   10 9 8 7 6 5 4 3

Year   2020 2019

Cover photo © age fotostock/Alamy. Illustrations by Aptara, Inc and Barking Dog Art

Typeset in Trade Gothic LT Std, 10/13 pts, by Aptara Inc.

Printed in Dubai

A catalogue record for this title is available from the British Library.

CONTENTS

INTRODUCTION

How to use this book

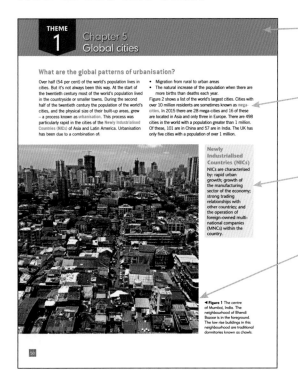

Each theme has a different colour so you can find your way around the book easily. Blue is used in Theme 1, purple in Theme 2 and green in Theme 3.

Important geographical terms are shown in **bold orange font**. You can check the meaning of these words in the glossary at the back of the book and expand your geographical vocabulary.

Geographical concepts are described in tinted boxes. You will find that these important concepts are mentioned in more than one chapter of the book.

Photographs show what real places look like. This photograph shows Mumbai – a unique place. But the photograph shows some features that are common in urban landscapes in many NIC cities. You should study the photographs carefully. What can you learn about NIC cities from this image?

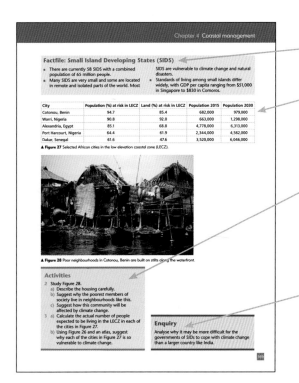

Factfiles make it easy for you to learn a few facts and figures about real places.

Maps, graphs and tables of data like this one provide us with evidence about the state of the world. Thinking like a geographer means that you need to look for patterns and trends in this evidence.

The activities will make you think carefully about the geographical information that has been presented in the photographs, maps, graphs and tables on the page. Doing them will help to build your geographical confidence and your ability to describe features, spot patterns and trends and explain why things happen.

Enquiries are longer activities. Some of them require further research, debate or discussion. Many will ask for your opinion and build your skills of analysis, evaluation and decision making. These tasks will encourage you to take an enquiry approach to learning – helping you to think like a geographer.

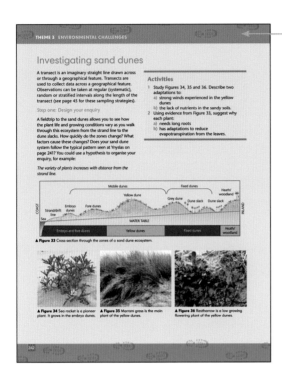

Fieldwork enquiries are described on pages which have a coloured border with footprints at the top and bottom of the page. Some pages focus on how to use specific fieldwork methods for collecting or representing data – like this page which describes the use of a transect to collect data in a sand dune ecosystem. Other fieldwork pages provide advice on preparing for fieldwork, sampling techniques, measuring flows, creating bi-polar surveys or using GIS in fieldwork.

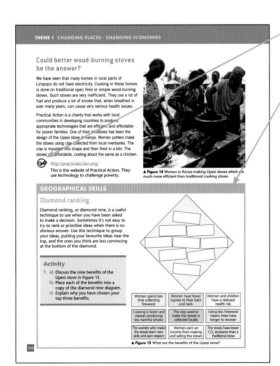

Weblinks will allow you to carry out further research or explore the interactive maps on sites that use Geographical Information Systems (GIS).

Geographical Skills panels describe how to carry out some important skills that are needed by geographers. These panels cover subjects like describing locations, drawing scatter graphs and reading hydrographs. The diamond nine panel, on page 108, describes a useful technique that will help with decision making.

CHANGING PLACES –
CHANGING ECONOMIES

▲ Wealth and poverty in the global city of Mumbai, India.

Introducing Cardiff

Cardiff is the largest city in Wales. It has a population of 350,000. Like many cities in the UK, Cardiff went through a period of rapid growth between around 1850 and 1920 as people moved into the city to find work in industries related to the sale of coal from Cardiff docks. Terraced houses were built to provide homes for these dock workers and many of these homes can still be seen today in the **inner urban** areas close to the city centre. The process of physical growth and population growth is known as **urbanisation**.

During the period 1930 to the mid-1980s Cardiff went through a second phase of growth. Better public transport and more widespread car ownership meant that people could live further from their place of work. The city began to spread outwards as new suburban housing was built. **Suburban sprawl**, as this process is called, filled in the spaces between the edge of the city and existing small villages such as Radyr and Whitchurch. These villages are now part of the urban area of Cardiff.

Between the mid-1980s and today Cardiff has gone through a third phase of growth. This time new housing was built on the old industrial sites once occupied by the dock-related industries in Butetown next to Cardiff Bay. These sites are known as **brownfield sites**. Because these sites are within the inner urban area of Cardiff the population of this zone has been rising, a process known as **re-urbanisation**.

GEOGRAPHICAL SKILLS

Describing locations

To describe a location means to be able to pinpoint something on a map. Describing a location on an Ordnance Survey (OS) map is easily done by giving a grid reference. However, describing a location on a map that has no grid lines requires a different technique.

First, you need to give a broad indication of the location by describing in which part of the map the viewer should be looking. Always use geographical terms such as 'in south Wales' rather than 'at the bottom of the map' or 'near to the Bristol Channel'.

Then, to describe the exact location, you should use another significant place on the map and give:
- the distance from that other place in kilometres
- the direction using points of the compass.

For example, on Figure 1, Bridgend is 28 km to the west of Cardiff.

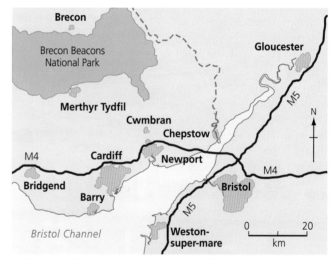

▲ **Figure 1** The location of Merthyr Tydfil.

Year	Population	Year	Population
1801	1,870	1931	226,937
1851	18,352	1941	No data
1861	48,965	1951	243,632
1871	57,363	1961	283,998
1881	96,637	1971	293,220
1891	128,915	1981	285,740
1901	164,333	1991	296,900
1911	182,259	2001	305,353
1921	222,827	2011	346,000

▲ **Figure 2** Population of Cardiff.

In 1841 87,000 tons of coal were shipped from Cardiff docks. By 1862 the docks were exporting 2 million tons of coal each year and by 1883 this figure had risen to 6 million. The maximum figure was 10.7 million in 1913. By 1946 it had fallen to 1 million tons.

In 1970 Bute East Dock was closed. In 1980 the M4 was completed to the North of Cardiff.

▲ **Figure 3** Some significant dates in Cardiff's development.

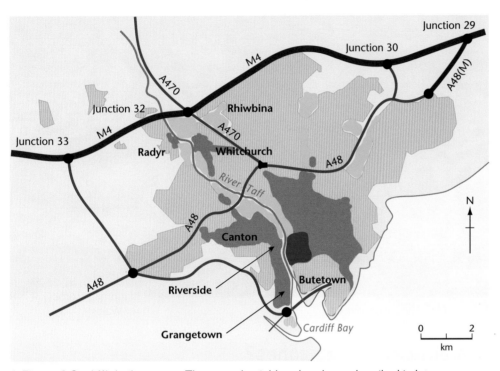

Key
— Main roads
━ Motorway
▨ Cardiff in 1920
▨ Cardiff's growth since 1920
▨ Area redeveloped since 1985
▨ Open spaces/parks
● City centre (CBD)

▲ **Figure 4** Cardiff's built up area. The named neighbourhoods are described in later pages.

Activities

1 Use Figure 1 to describe the location of each of the following places in relation to Cardiff:
    a) Brecon   b) Newport   c) Bristol

2 a) Select a suitable method to represent the information in Figure 2.
    b) Describe the changes in Cardiff's population carefully. In which decades did Cardiff's population rise most rapidly and in which did it decrease?
    c) Use the information in Figure 3 to create four labels for your graph. Your labels should help explain why Cardiff's population changed.

3 Study Figure 4. Describe how Cardiff changed between 1920 and the present day. Use the following specialist terms in your answer:

suburban sprawl   inner urban   re-urbanisation

Enquiry

How typical is Cardiff's pattern of growth? Research your own town or city to find phases of urbanisation and re-urbanisation. Compare it to what you have learned about Cardiff.

▲ **Figure 5** An aerial view of Cardiff taken from above Cardiff Bay.

Why does Cardiff have different urban zones?

Like other UK cities, Cardiff may be divided into several distinct neighbourhoods or zones. Each of these has distinctive features that give it character. These features may relate to the urban environment itself such as the age or style of houses or the presence of other land uses such as parks, shops, offices or factories. However, each neighbourhood is also defined by the community of people who live there. For that reason, geographers are interested in **socio-economic groups**. These are groups of people who have distinct social and economic characteristics. A number of factors influence which socio-economic group we belong to, including age, education, income, ethnicity and race. Over the next few pages we will examine several neighbourhoods in Cardiff including the suburban neighbourhood of Rhiwbina and the inner urban areas of Canton, Grangetown and Butetown. Your job is to identify what makes them special in terms of:

- the character of the urban environment
- the community of people who live there.

Activity

1 Study Figures 5 and 6.
  a) Match the following features to the labels A–D on Figure 5.
     i) Grangetown
     ii) River Taff
     iii) Millennium Stadium
     iv) Wales Millennium Centre
  b) Write a description, in no more than 100 words, of the urban environment you can see in Figure 5.

Activities

2 Study Figure 6. Identify the location of features a–d below by matching them to the following four-figure grid references:
1779   1873   1677   1876
   a) Open space in Llandaff
   b) Civic Centre, in the central business district (CBD)
   c) Cardiff Bay
   d) Hospital

3 a) Describe the location of:
   i)   Butetown
   ii) Grangetown
   iii) Rhiwbina
   b) Suggest the advantages and disadvantages of each location for local residents. Use grid references when describing evidence on the map.

4 Study the street pattern in each of the following grid squares. Suggest what this may tell you about the type and density of housing in these neighbourhoods.
1774   1877   1681   1783

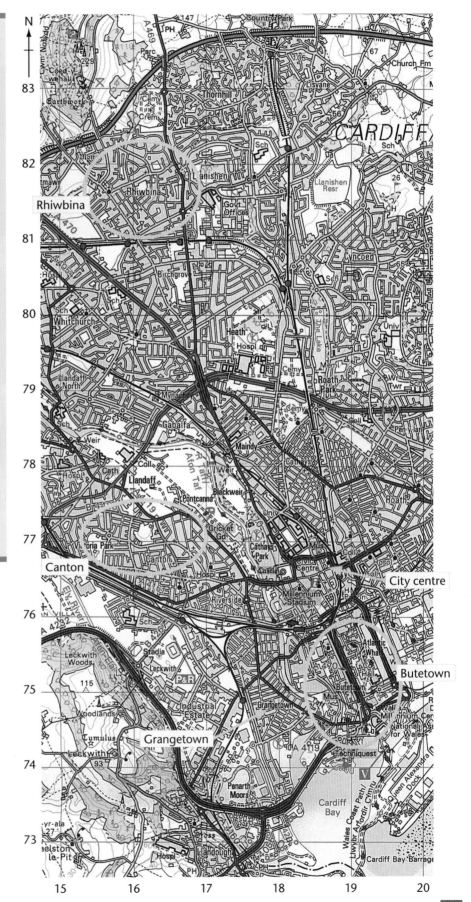

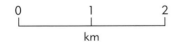

▶ **Figure 6** An Ordnance Survey extract showing central Cardiff. Scale 1:50 000.

How do Cardiff's suburbs and inner urban areas compare?

Cardiff has an inner urban area that still contains many terraced houses built in the period 1880–1914. This area includes neighbourhoods such as Canton and Grangetown (see Figures 4 and 6 for their location). To the north, west and east, Cardiff has a number of suburban neighbourhoods such as Rhiwbina. What are the physical and socio-economic characteristics of these neighbourhoods? How do they compare?

How might the park affect the value of properties in this neighbourhood?

▲ **Figure 8** Housing opposite Victoria Park in Canton.

How might street calming measures affect local children and elderly residents?

▲ **Figure 7** Typical housing in Grangetown.

▲ **Figure 9** Housing in Rhiwbina.

	Canton	Grangetown	Rhiwbina	Cardiff	Wales
Very good	57.4	48.2	44.4	50.4	46.6
Good	27.8	30.3	31.1	31.1	31.1
Fair	9.4	12.9	19.3	12.1	14.6
Bad	3.0	5.9	4.4	4.8	5.8
Very bad	2.4	2.6	1.9	1.6	1.8

◄ **Figure 10** General health of residents in selected wards of Cardiff. The 2011 Census asked people to describe their general health over the preceding 12 months as 'very good', 'good', 'fair', 'bad' or 'very bad'. The figures show the percentage who responded in each category.

	Canton	Grangetown	Rhiwbina
No formal qualifications	12	30	22
1 – 4 GCSEs any grade or equivalent	6	13	10
5 or more GCSEs, grade A – C or equivalent	9	10	16
Apprenticeship	3	3	5
2 or more A levels, or equivalent	9	8	8
Degree or higher, or equivalent	60	27	35

◄ **Figure 11** Qualifications of residents in selected wards of Cardiff (percentages of people aged 16 and over by their highest qualification).

Post code	Ward	Location	Very good health	% Residents in professional occupations	% Residents with a degree
CF24 1LR	Adamsdown	inner	48.5	14.5	28
CF10 5EB	Butetown	inner	49.3	20.1	33
CF5 5HJ	Caerau	suburb	39.1	5.4	10
CF5 1QE	Canton	inner	52.9	32.8	50
CF24 4NE	Cathays	inner	62.2	13.4	22
CF5 4LL	Ely	suburb	41.9	6.1	9
CF11 7AP	Grangetown	inner	53.2	13.0	22
CF14 5BL	Llanishen	suburb	47.1	19.5	31
CF23 8AN	Pontprennau	suburb	58.1	23.8	38
CF14 6RE	Rhiwbina	suburb	44.4	27.9	35
CF11 6LW	Riverside	inner	49.2	20.1	32
CF3 3JW	Rumney	suburb	43.6	9.2	13
CF24 2DQ	Splott	inner	44.4	17.0	26
CF14 1DB	Whitchurch	suburb	44.6	26.8	37

▲ **Figure 12** Data for selected inner urban and suburban wards in Cardiff.

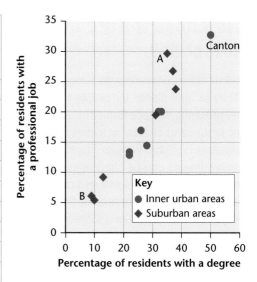

▲ **Figure 13** The relationship between % residents in professional occupations and % residents with a degree. This graph has been drawn using data from Figure 12.

Activities

1 A geography student wants to investigate the following enquiry question:

   'Do people with higher incomes live in suburban neighbourhoods of Cardiff?'

   Write down your prediction for this enquiry.

2 Study Figures 7, 8 and 9.
   a) Describe the type of housing in each photograph.
   b) For each photo, suggest one way in which the situation of the houses might affect the wellbeing of the local residents. The effect could be positive or negative. Elaborate your answer carefully using connectives like 'so'. An example is given below:

   Some houses in Canton overlook a park (simple statement) so residents can go for a jog (simple elaboration) which means that they can keep fit (further elaboration).

3 Use Figures 10 and 11 to compare the socio-economic characteristics of the three neighbourhoods. Prepare a short report that highlights the most significant differences. Include at least one graph.

4 Study Figure 13.
   a) Describe the relationship shown by this graph.
   b) Use Figure 12 to identify plots A and B on Figure 13.
   c) What does this graph tell you about the difference between inner urban and suburban neighbourhoods in Cardiff? Can you prove the prediction you made in activity 1?

Enquiry

Investigate the following enquiry question:
'Are house prices higher in neighbourhoods where there are more residents who have a degree?'

Figure 12 gives the post code for an address in each of the wards. Use a website such as zoopla to find average house prices in these areas and add them to a copy of Figure 12. Then draw a scatter graph like Figure 13 to answer the enquiry question.

How does the urban environment affect us?

Some urban environments have very mixed functions. They provide places for people to live and work as well as providing an opportunity for people to enjoy a mixture of leisure and cultural activities such as cinemas, theatres or clubs. With so many different features, these environments can be challenging and exciting places because people have different perceptions or feelings about the urban environment. For example, some people enjoy the excitement of a large sporting event. Others might find that meeting crowds of noisy and excited fans in the street outside the stadium is a frightening experience.

> How might the stadium give residents a better quality of life?

> What ought to happen to allow local residents to park more easily on match days?

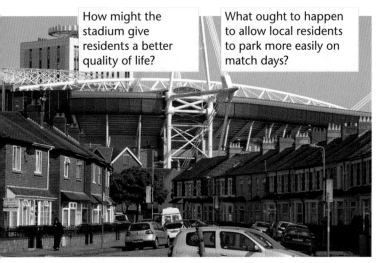

▲ **Figure 14** The Millennium Stadium is only a 5-minute walk away from these houses in Riverside, Cardiff.

Investigating spheres of influence

Each feature of the urban environment has a sphere of influence. This is an area within which local residents may be affected in either a good or bad way. A skate park, for example will provide benefits for teenagers in the local area. The noise from a busy road, however, may be a nuisance to people living close by.

Most features of the urban environment have the greatest effect on the people living closest to them. For example, town centre pubs and night clubs can be very rowdy places at closing time. Local residents complain about noise, bad language and drunken fights on the street, especially at the weekend. The worst affected properties are next to pubs. People in houses further away hear less of the noise. Geographers call this the 'friction of distance' and its effect is shown in Figure 15.

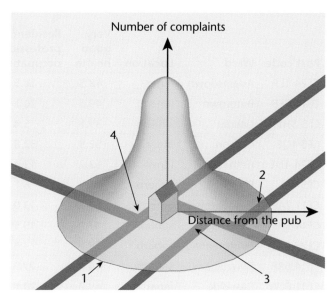

▲ **Figure 15** The sphere of influence declines with distance. In this case the graph shows complaints about a town centre pub. A similar graph could be drawn for other urban features. Not all effects are negative. Some features, such as an urban park, affect people in a positive way.

Activities

1 Study Figures 25, 14 and 15. Explain why the Millennium Stadium might affect people in Riverside in different ways to those living in Rhiwbina in the north of Cardiff.

2 Study Figure 15. Make a copy of the diagram and match each of the following statements to the correct numbered arrow.
   A The outer limit of complaints. Everyone living inside this line is within the sphere of influence.
   B People living in this neighbourhood are hardly ever disturbed by noise.
   C Most complaints about noise are from people living closest to the pub.
   D People living here sometimes complain about noise from the pub.

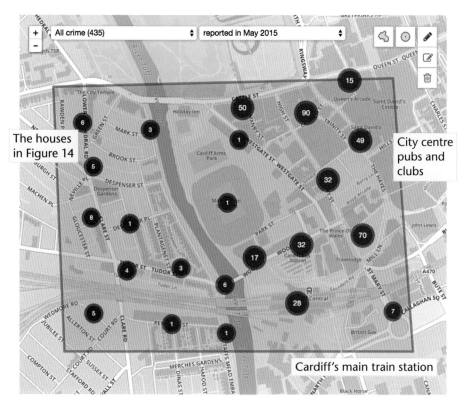

The houses in Figure 14

City centre pubs and clubs

Cardiff's main train station

◄ **Figure 16** Crime rates in central Cardiff (May 2015).

	Where would you want each of these urban features?				
	Next door	In the same street	In the same neighbourhood	In a different part of the town/city	In a different town/city
Take-away					
Premiership football ground					
Skate park					
Dual carriageway					
Secondary school					
Cemetery					
Petrol station					
Canal					
A & E (Accident and Emergency)					
Nuclear power station					
Sewage works					
Fire station					
Parks and gardens					

▲ **Figure 17** How do different features of the urban environment affect us?

Activity

3 a) Work in pairs to discuss the urban features listed in Figure 17. From the point of view of a teenager, sort the features into those that you consider would have a positive effect on quality of life and those that would have a negative effect.

b) Sort the list again, this time from the point of view of a retired couple. Is this list different to your first list? If so, why?

c) Make a copy of Figure 17 and place a tick to show where you would want each feature in your perfect urban environment. Use this table to explain why some urban features have a larger sphere of influence than others.

Enquiry

Use the website www.police.uk to research patterns of crime in your own town or city centre. How similar or different are they to the patterns shown in Figure 16?

Ethnic minorities in Cardiff

Cardiff is a multicultural city. Between 1800 and the 1930s economic migrants moved from other European countries and the countries of the British Empire to Cardiff. Many were sailors who worked on the ships that exported coal from South Wales. Most settled in Butetown, close to the docks, in an area that was then called Tiger Bay. Today, a total of 8 per cent of Cardiff's population are members of ethnic minorities. People have settled in the city from over 50 different countries. The two largest communities are descended from South Asian (India, Pakistan and Bangladesh) and Somali migrants.

The Somali population in Cardiff has a population estimated to be a little under 10,000. Most of them live in a relatively small neighbourhood within the inner urban area in the wards of Grangetown and Riverside. Somalis choose to live in this district to be close to other family members. The area has many shops that cater for the Muslim population such as halal butchers and fast food shops that sell food prepared using halal meat. The area has a number of mosques and Muslim cultural centres. This district also has a wide variety of different sized houses and flats for both rent and sale at a variety of prices.

▲ **Figure 18** A shop in Riverside, Cardiff selling halal meat.

GEOGRAPHICAL SKILLS

Describing distributions

To describe a distribution is to describe how similar things are spread across a map. Geographers are interested in the distribution of natural features such as glaciers, coral reefs and volcanoes; as well as human features such as settlements, hospitals or sporting facilities.

Describing a distribution requires you to do two things.

1   You need to describe where on the map the features are located. For example, of the ten parks marked on Figure 20, the majority are in the northern suburbs of the city and only four are within the inner urban area.

2   Describe any pattern the features might make. Distribution patterns usually fall into one of three types:
    ▪   Regular, where the features are more or less equally spaced.
    ▪   Random, where the features are scattered across the map at irregular distances from each other.
    ▪   Clustered, where the features are grouped together into only one part of the map.

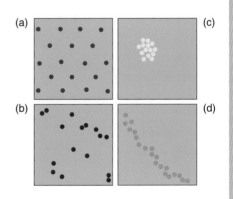
▲ **Figure 19** Distribution patterns.

In addition to this, some features make a linear pattern if they all fall along a line. Several parks in Cardiff make a linear pattern. The largest park follows the line of the River Taff as it enters the city in the north and flows southwards towards the city centre. The park makes a green corridor running north-south through the city.

The history of Somali migration to Cardiff

Somali migrants first arrived in Cardiff in the period 1880 to 1900. Many of them worked in the ships that were exporting coal from the docks in Butetown (which was then known as Tiger Bay). At this time Somali seamen settled in other UK ports, as well as Cardiff, such as the London docklands, Bristol, Hull and Liverpool. By 1945 there were around 2,000 Somali sailors and their families living in Cardiff. In 1991 a long civil war began in Somalia. Refugees from this conflict moved first to refugee camps in other African countries such as Kenya and Ethiopia. Eventually some of these people migrated to the UK where they joined the existing Somali community.

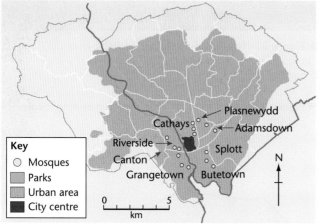

Key
- ○ Mosques
- ▨ Parks
- ▨ Urban area
- ■ City centre

0 ___ 5 km

▲ **Figure 20** Map showing the distribution of mosques in Cardiff. The white lines show the ward boundaries.

Ward	Black	Asian	Mixed ethnicity
Adamsdown	3.4	5.8	3.5
Butetown	13.4	8.1	8.3
Canton	0.8	4.7	1.8
Grangetown	4.2	13.2	3.8
Plasnewydd	1.5	9.5	1.7
Riverside	2.8	15.6	2.4
Splott	1.8	3.3	2.9

▲ **Figure 21** Wards with significant ethnic populations.

Activities

1 Match the four distribution patterns shown in Figure 19 to the following terms:

   random   regular   linear   clustered

2 a) Match the following geographical features to one of the four distribution patterns shown in Figure 19:
   - motorway service stations
   - high street banks in a large town
   - primary schools in a city

   b) Suggest why these features are distributed in this way.

3 Use Figure 20 to describe the distribution of mosques in Cardiff. Suggest what this map tells you about the distribution of the Muslim population of Cardiff.

4 Use the text on these pages to draw a timeline of Somali migration to Cardiff.

5 Explain why the Somali population of Cardiff is found in a relatively small area of the city. Make sure you give one historical reason and one social reason.

Enquiry

Do a web search for a ward map of Cardiff which shows the same ward boundaries as Figure 20. Use the data in Figure 21 to create three choropleth maps of the wards which have significant ethnic populations. What are the main similarities and differences between these three maps?

Zones of wealth and poverty

Like all other UK cities, Cardiff has some neighbourhoods where residents have, on average, high incomes while other neighbourhoods have residents with much lower average incomes. Sometimes, these neighbourhoods exist very close to one another. One example is Riverside, an inner urban area which stretches down the western bank of the River Taff, shown in Figure 22.

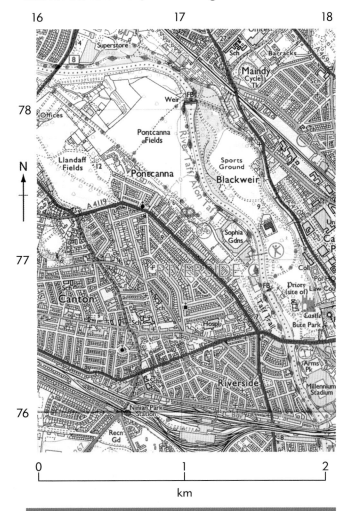

▲ **Figure 23** Houses in Pontcanna in RIV04, opposite Llandaff Fields (grid reference 164773).

◄ **Figure 22** Extract from an Ordnance Survey map. Scale 1:25 000.

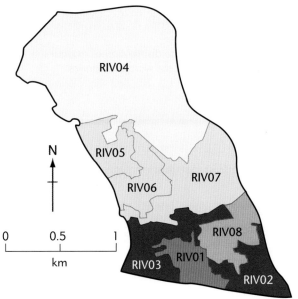

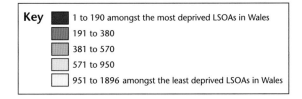

Key

■	1 to 190 amongst the most deprived LSOAs in Wales
▨	191 to 380
▦	381 to 570
☐	571 to 950
☐	951 to 1896 amongst the least deprived LSOAs in Wales

▲ **Figure 24** Deprivation in Riverside (2011). There are 1,896 Lower Super Output Areas (LSOAs) in Wales. The Welsh government has put all of these small districts into rank order of deprivation. The map shows five categories of deprivation (by rank order).

Activity

1   Study Figure 22.
   a) Match the following grid references to leisure features (i – iii) on the map:
      163776   178766   174770
      i)   Sport/leisure centre
      ii)   Llandaff fields (public park)
      iii) Bute Park (public gardens)
   b) Suggest how residents of Riverside may be affected by the sphere of influence of each of these features.

▲ **Figure 25** Houses in lower Riverside overlooking the River Taff and Millennium Stadium (in RIV02 grid reference 177763).

		Percentage of residents in:		
LSOA	Post code	very good health	professional occupations	elementary occupations
RIV01	CF11 6EW	46.5	15.8	18.2
RIV02	CF11 6AH	43.0	17.2	17.7
RIV03	CF11 6JQ	39.4	17.0	16.6
RIV04	CF11 9QJ	55.0	39.6	3.6
RIV05	CF11 9PW	57.6	38.3	4.4
RIV06	CF11 9DQ	56.1	36.0	6.2
RIV07	CF11 9LJ	57.4	40.6	6.2
RIV08	CF11 6LR	49.2	20.1	19.2

Figure 26 Selected factors that indicate standard of living or deprivation in Riverside (2011).

Ways of measuring wealth and poverty

Standard of living is a measure of the relative wealth of individuals or families. It can be measured using household income figures. A person's level of qualifications or job type can also be an indicator of income. Professional jobs, such as accountants or doctors tend to be well paid. Elementary jobs, such as labouring on a building site, tend to be low paid. In neighbourhoods where unemployment figures are high, or jobs are part time or low paid, the number of households living in poverty can be high.

Deprivation is a more complex way of measuring poverty. It takes into account factors such as income and job type. However, it also takes into account other factors such as people's health, community safety and the physical condition of the local environment.

LSOA	% Muslim faith
RIV01	33.2
RIV02	42.2
RIV03	20.8
RIV04	2.1
RIV05	3.4
RIV06	5.8
RIV07	7.8
RIV08	32.4

Figure 27 Percentage of the population of the Muslim faith in Riverside.

Activities

2 Describe the urban environment in Figures 23 and 25.

3 a) Use Figure 24 to describe the pattern of deprivation in Riverside.
   b) Use evidence from Figures 22, 23 and 25 to help explain the pattern on Figure 24.

4 Use the evidence in Figure 26 to investigate patterns of deprivation further.
   a) Select a graphical or mapping technique to display one or more of the columns of data.
   b) Compare your map or graph to Figure 24. What are the main similarities or differences?

5 Use the evidence in Figure 27 to investigate the distribution of the Muslim population within Riverside. Most Muslims in this neighbourhood are of South Asian or Somali descent.
   a) Represent the data in Figure 27 using a map or graph of your choice.
   b) Use evidence from pages 10 to 13 to suggest reasons for this pattern.

Enquiry

Does it surprise you that standard of living can vary so much within one small area? Work in groups to plan an investigation into standard of living and quality of life in a neighbourhood close to your school. What questions would you want answered? How would you structure your investigation?

Bi-polar surveys

Some features of the urban environment are easy to count and quantify. An example would be the number of cars passing along a street in ten minutes. However, fieldwork enquiries sometimes involve features that cannot be quantified so simply. People's perceptions of the urban environment are one example of something we might want to measure. Because perceptions vary a lot from one person to another we say they are subjective. So how do we assess perceptions?

▲ **Figure 28** Flats and neighbourhood shops in RIV07 (grid reference 169765) on Figure 22.

Activity

1 Study the urban environments in Figures 23, 25, 28 and 30.
 a) Use the bi-polar assessment in Figure 29 to calculate a score for each urban environment in these four photographs.
 b) Share your scores with at least four members of your class. Calculate a mean score for each photograph.
 c) Create a sketch map of Riverside using information from Figure 22. Plot the location of Figures 23, 25, 28 and 30 on your map. Choose a suitable method to represent your mean scores on this map.

Creating a simple bi-polar survey

Step 1 Choose categories for the bi-polar statements. These will depend upon the specific focus of your study, but may include factors such as presence/ absence of natural vegetation, street lighting, upkeep of building and condition of pavements. In some cases more personal attitudes may be investigated such as fear of crime or feelings of safety. Pairs of opposing statements are put at either end of a scale as can be seen in Figure 29. A bipolar scale has a range of values, for example, from -5 to +5. The positive and negative values indicate a person's perception of an environment. The zero is usually removed from the middle of the scale to discourage people from choosing the safe middle option.

Step 2 Choose the location for your survey. Your choice of location may be the result of a pilot study, having previously visited the area, or as a result of some previous knowledge of your study area. If you are unfamiliar with your site then you might use aerial photography (Bing Maps, Google Earth, for example) or an application such as Google Street View to help you choose your sites before going on the field trip. You could use secondary data (like Figures 26 or 27) from http://www.neighbourhood.statistics.gov.uk to help select your sites. If so, you would want to make sure that you visited at least 8 sites in Riverside, Cardiff, this is at least one in each LSOA.

Step 3 Collecting the bi-polar scores. The simplest method is to complete the survey yourself. However, in order to investigate differing perceptions you will need to compare your score with other people. These could be members of your class or members of the public. You can combine scores together to create a 'class score' or by calculating the mean score for each location. If so, these mean scores could then be represented on a base map of the area that you visited.

	+5	+4	+3	+2	+1	−1	-2	−3	−4	−5	
Attractive urban environment											Unattractive urban environment
Safe for pedestrians											Unsafe for pedestrians
Natural features nearby											No natural features nearby
Thriving communities with job opportunities											Declining communities with few job opportunities

▲ **Figure 29** An example of bi-polar statements.

Creating a more sophisticated bi-polar assessment

Here are three suggestions to try. In each case, think about the strengths and weaknesses of these assessments compared to a standard bi-polar survey.

1 **Different perceptions**   Conduct a standard bi-polar survey as yourself – a teenager. Then imagine what it might be like to perceive the urban environment as though you were someone else. Try doing the bi-polar survey again but imagining yourself as someone with limited mobility, for example, or as a single parent with a very young child. How would your perception change?

2 **Photo surveys**   Decide on five categories, or features, for your bi-polar survey. For example, open spaces, building design, pedestrian safety, leisure features and road traffic. Don't write opposing statements. Inspect your area carefully taking as many photographs as you can. Make sure you record where each photo was taken. Then choose the pair of photos that represent the best and worst examples of each category or feature.

3 **Weightings**   Not all of the categories or features recorded by a bi-polar survey have equal importance to people when they think about the quality of the environment. For example, you may decide that open space is a more important feature than road traffic or litter. Try ranking or weighting your bi-polar statements. For example, if you think the amount of open space is twice as important as litter then you should multiply your bi-polar scores for open space by a two. Discuss these weightings to get an agreement as a class or group. How might your weightings be different if you were an OAP rather than a teenager?

▲ **Figure 30** Flats, and neighbourhood shops in RIV02 (grid reference 179759) on Figure 22.

Enquiry

Write four new pairs of bi-polar statements. Use them to survey the neighbourhood around your school.
a) Conduct the survey as yourself.
b) Now imagine how another person might perceive this neighbourhood. Imagine yourself as:
    i) A single parent with a young child
    ii) An elderly resident
c) What are the strengths and limitations of this more sophisticated style of bi-polar survey in trying to collect different perceptions?

How can we create sustainable urban and rural communities?

Planners want to create **sustainable communities** in the towns and countryside of the UK. This means they have to consider how new housing, roads or other developments can be planned so that people and the environment benefit both now and in the longer term. It's relatively easy to see how new houses can be made more environmentally sustainable. Figure 1 shows some features of modern eco-housing.

▼ **Figure 1** Eco-homes at the Beddington Zero Energy Development (BedZED) in Surrey. BedZED was the first and largest carbo-neutral eco-community in the UK.

The buildings have 300 mm of insulation in the walls (most modern houses have 50 mm). This conserves heat energy so well that the homes need to be kept cool. These funnels direct fresh, cool air into the buildings.

Large windows on the south side of the building collect heat energy from the Sun – a technique known as passive solar gain.

Slate and tile roofs shed water quickly into storm drains. This can lead to problems of flash flooding. Roof gardens use up some rainwater and slow down the flow of run-off into the storm drains.

some affordable housing for people on lower incomes

a brownfield site rather than a greenfield site

jobs available locally

public transport available to everyone

A sustainable community has ...

some buildings designed for elderly or disabled people with wide doorways for wheelchair users and ground-floor bedrooms and bathrooms

local facilities for people of all ages, e.g. crèche, youth group, community centre

green technologies to reduce heating costs and carbon emissions

schemes to reduce car ownership such as increased parking costs

▲ **Figure 2** Possible features of a sustainable community.

Egan's Wheel

However, to build a sustainable community we need to consider other features of the urban or rural environment, as well as housing. Figure 3 explains the concept of the Egan Wheel. It shows the criteria we can use to judge a sustainable community.

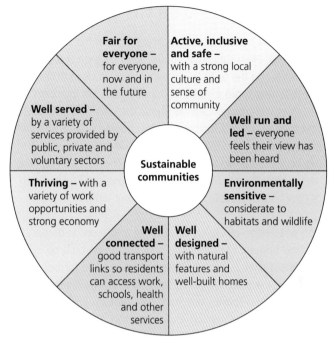

▲ **Figure 3** Egan's Wheel.

Egan's Wheel segments (clockwise):
- **Fair for everyone** – for everyone, now and in the future
- **Active, inclusive and safe** – with a strong local culture and sense of community
- **Well run and led** – everyone feels their view has been heard
- **Environmentally sensitive** – considerate to habitats and wildlife
- **Well designed** – with natural features and well-built homes
- **Well connected** – good transport links so residents can access work, schools, health and other services
- **Thriving** – with a variety of work opportunities and strong economy
- **Well served** – by a variety of services provided by public, private and voluntary sectors

Centre: **Sustainable communities**

Enquiry

How sustainable is Cardiff?

a) Design at least five pairs of bi-polar statements (see pages 14–15) that you could use to survey the sustainability of a community. You should use Figure 2 for some ideas.
b) Use your bi-polar survey to assess each of the images of Cardiff in Figure 4.

▲ **Figure 4** Evidence of sustainable urban communities in Cardiff.

Activities

1 Study the features of the eco-housing in Figure 1. Explain how each feature contributes to either environmental or economic sustainability.
2 Explain the main differences between an eco-home and a sustainable community.
3 Discuss Figure 3.
   a) For each feature in the diagram, suggest how it might be sustainable.
   b) Suggest at least two of the features that might be controversial. Which groups of people might come into conflict over these suggestions?
   c) Suggest at least two more features that you think are necessary in a new sustainable community.
4 Study the photographs in Figure 4.
   a) For each photograph, use Egan's Wheel to identify the element of sustainability that is being met.
   b) Choose one of these photographs. Write a 50-word caption that explains how the feature in the photo is contributing to a sustainable community.

Should we build on the green belt?

A lot of new housebuilding took place after the Second World War. New suburban homes were built on the edges of UK cities and the term 'suburban sprawl' is used to describe the resulting rapid growth of the suburbs. UK planners at the time were so concerned about the loss of countryside that they prevented further loss by creating wide green belts around many UK cities. Green belts currently occupy 13 per cent of total land area in England. They contain smaller towns and villages, farmland and countryside. The building of new homes is restricted on green belt land.

The population of the UK is growing and there is demand for new homes. Should these new homes be built on greenfield sites – land that has not been used for building before? Or should homes be built on brownfield sites – land that has had a former use such as a factory, warehouse, dock or quarry and which is now unused or derelict? New housebuilding on greenfield sites may be opposed by local people who are concerned that new housing will spoil the rural character of their local community. Protests about local planning issues are commonly called NIMBYism – which stands for Not in My Back Yard.

City	Ratio
Oxford	15.0
Cambridge	14.8
London	14.0
Brighton	12.2
Reading	10.1
Milton Keynes	8.0
Birmingham	7.3
Nottingham	6.8
Swansea	6.7
Derby	6.2
Liverpool	5.8

▲ **Figure 6** The cost of housing compared to average local wages (2014).

> Oxford's employers, who include BMW Mini, schools, hospitals and the university, are finding it difficult to recruit workers because of the high cost of housing.

> Over 50 per cent of the workforce commute into the city. In Oxford, new building on greenfield sites leap-frogs the green belt. This means that families who occupy the new housing in places like Bicester have a particularly long commute to work into Oxford. The pressure on our roads and public transport is not sustainable.

> Oxford's universities have an international reputation for excellence in both research and teaching. We need cheaper housing so we can recruit the best research workers. These researchers are the reason for so many high-tech firms locating here.

▲ **Figure 7** Members of Oxford City Council explain why building on the green belt may be necessary.

New homes in Oxford?

Where demand for houses is greater than supply, the price of homes has risen rapidly. Research in 2014 suggests that house prices are particularly high in Oxford. In 2014, average wages in Oxford were £26,500 per year. At the same time, the average cost of a house was £426,720, which is 15 times the average wage.

Oxford City Council believes that Oxford needs between 24,000 and 32,000 homes to be built by 2031. Controversially, it would like to build many of these within the green belt. South Oxford District Council has opposed the plan. It recognises that new homes are needed but doesn't want them built on green belt land.

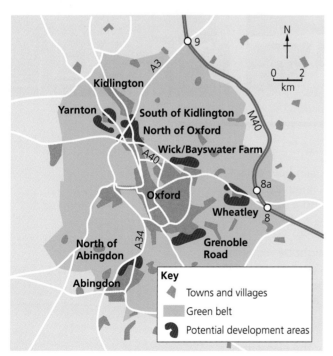

▲ **Figure 5** Development areas suggested by Oxford City Council that are within Oxford's green belt.

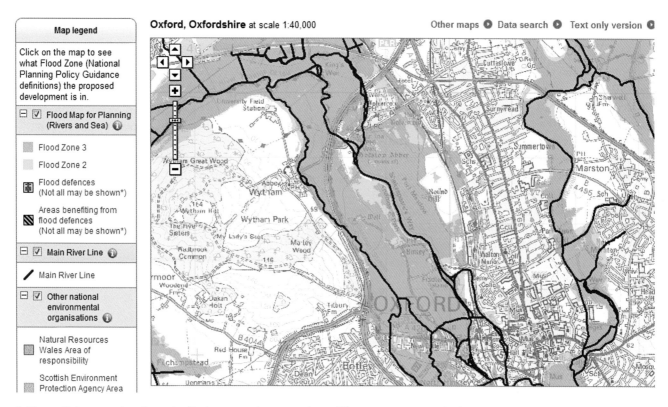

Oxford, Oxfordshire at scale 1:40,000   Other maps ⊙ Data search ⊙ Text only version ⊙

Map legend

Click on the map to see what Flood Zone (National Planning Policy Guidance definitions) the proposed development is in.

☐ ☑ Flood Map for Planning (Rivers and Sea) ⓘ

Flood Zone 3

Flood Zone 2

Flood defences (Not all may be shown*)

Areas benefiting from flood defences (Not all may be shown*)

☐ ☑ Main River Line ⓘ

/ Main River Line

☐ ☑ Other national environmental organisations ⓘ

Natural Resources Wales Area of responsibility

Scottish Environment Protection Agency Area

▲ **Figure 8** A screenshot from the Environment Agency website. The city centre is in the bottom right corner of the shot. Notice the open space to the north-west of the city which forms a green corridor along the River Cherwell. Urban ecosystems like this can provide many benefits – some are explored on page 238.

Activities

1 Write a 200-word press release which explains why Oxford City Council thinks it is necessary to build in the green belt. Use Figure 7.
2 Study Figure 6.
   a) Choose a suitable technique to represent this data.
   b) Use an atlas to analyse the pattern shown by this data.
3 a) Describe the location of the development site at Wheatley. Use Figure 5.
   b) Use Figure 9 to list two reasons why you think the development should go ahead.
   c) Give two reasons why you think the development should not go ahead.
   d) Suggest two different groups of people who might object to this development.
4 a) Use Figure 8 to describe the areas of Oxford that are vulnerable to flooding.
   b) Explain why it is important to maintain green corridors of land that have not been developed within cities like Oxford.

The development will extend the village of Wheatley. The village will lose its distinctive character.

The site is alongside the A40 so access into Oxford is easy.

The land is open countryside and has never been built on before.

The land is sloping and poor quality farmland used for grazing.

Steep slopes on some of the site will make the building of homes expensive.

▲ **Figure 9** Features of the proposed development site at Wheatley.

Enquiry

How important is the green belt?

Design a survey to investigate people's views of house building on green belt land. How could you design the sampling strategy (see page 45) to ensure that the views of different groups of people are included?

Does the UK need to build more new homes?

In the financial year 2012–13 there were 135,500 new homes built in the UK. That was the lowest amount since 1945. It's not enough. As the population of the UK increases we need more homes. If too few are built, demand is greater than supply and the price of buying a new home rises faster than people's wages. The government wants to see an extra 240,000 homes being built every year. But where should these new homes be built? The greatest demand is in the south east of England. The economy is strongest in the south east, so this is an area where many younger people are moving to from other parts of the UK and from other EU countries.

Activities

1 Study Figure 10.
   a) Draw proportional bars on graph paper to represent the growth of population in each region.
   b) Cut out the bars and stick them onto an outline map of the UK.
   c) Explain why this representation of Figure 10 is more useful than a simple bar graph.
2 Describe the location of the Thames Gateway development.

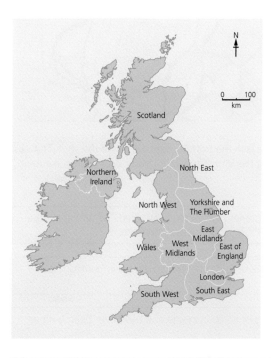

Region of the UK	Population increase (1,000s)
Northern Ireland	135
Scotland	247
Wales	163
North East	63
North West	307
Yorkshire and The Humber	336
West Midlands	355
East Midlands	374
East of England	491
London	955
South East	683
South West	384

◀ **Figure 10** Population increase in the regions of the UK (2001–2012).

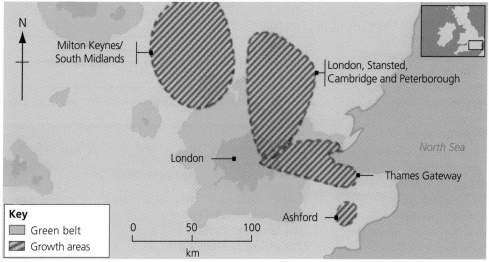

Key
Green belt
Growth areas

◀ **Figure 11** The key areas for new homes in the south east of the UK.

Are new garden cities the answer?

In 2014 the UK Government announced that three new **garden cities** would be built in England. Each would have about 15,000 new homes. The first garden cities were built in the 1930s at a time when there was a lot of new housebuilding. These towns had a lot of open space – hence the name. The new garden cities will feature high quality homes, lots of green space, and access to local jobs and services. They will be built at:

- Bicester, near Oxford
- Northstowe, in Cambridgeshire
- Ebbsfleet, in the Thames Gateway (Kent).

Ebbsfleet, in Kent, is part of the Thames Gateway region. This region is well connected to London – it is only 20 minutes by rail from Ebbsfleet. The UK Government is keen to see new housebuilding in the Thames Gateway – perhaps as many as 90,000 new homes by 2030. It has committed £200 million to help fund the Ebbsfleet Development Corporation that will oversee the project and pay for new infrastructure in Ebbsfleet, such as roads.

The proposed garden city of Ebbsfleet will be designed as though it were a cluster of smaller traditional villages. Each 'village' will have its own primary school that is within walking distance of all homes in its catchment. Each 'village' will also have green open space, allotments, sports pitches and a community building for the use of groups of local residents. Building at Ebbsfleet has begun. It is expected that between 3,000 and 5,000 homes will be built between 2015 and 2020.

> The Thames Gateway is low lying and some parts are at risk of coastal flooding (see pages 164–5). The cost of new sea defences could be £500 million.

> Much of the development land in the Thames Gateway is brownfield. Part of Ebbsfleet will be built on a disused quarry.

> Neighbouring small villages will become part of the new, larger town. They may lose their distinctive character.

> A new bus service, called Fastrack, will run every 5–10 minutes during the day between Ebbsfleet and other towns in the Thames Gateway.

> The government wants the Thames Gateway to be a low-carbon region. It hopes that people will work locally.

▲ **Figure 12** Aspects of development in the Thames Gateway.

▲ **Figure 13** Existing homes on the edge of an area of scrubland that has been identified as the possible site of the new Ebbsfleet garden city. Part of this site is a disused quarry.

Activity

3 Use information about the Thames Gateway and Ebbsfleet to complete a table like the one below. You will write more in some boxes than others.

	Arguments for building new homes in Ebbsfleet	Arguments against building new homes in Ebbsfleet
Economic		
Environmental		
Social		

Enquiry

Do the new garden cities sound as though they will be sustainable communities?

Use Figure 3 (page 17) to help you to justify your ideas.

Urban renewal

During the 1970s and 80s, it became unfashionable to live in the inner urban areas of many UK towns and cities. People didn't really want to live in areas of older inner-city housing, especially in the docks and waterfront areas of the UK's ports like Butetown in Cardiff or Salford Quays in Manchester.

However, these once run-down or derelict **brownfield sites** have been redeveloped with new homes and businesses. People are moving back into the inner-city – a process known as re-urbanisation.

Urban renewal in Ipswich

▲ **Figure 14** A view of Ipswich waterfront from one of the blocks of flats.

Ipswich is one of the fastest growing towns in the UK. Like many of the towns and cities in the south east, Ipswich is partly growing through natural population increase but also through significant inward migration of people.

Ipswich Waterfront development is the biggest urban renewal project in the east of England. The site was formerly an industrial dock area with warehouses and factories, but it had become increasingly derelict since the 1970s. Ipswich Borough Council worked in partnership with a number of developers to renew this brownfield site. Old warehouses have been refurbished and turned into shops, restaurants and flats. A range of new buildings has been constructed for homes, leisure use and education. Sadly, due to the economic crash of 2009, the project has not been entirely successful. Cranfield Mill, a 23-storey block remained unfinished in 2015. The development company owed money to the banks and could not afford to complete the building. Ipswich Council hopes to buy the building and work with a new building firm to complete the project. When finished, it will contain 300 flats, offices, shops and restaurants.

Activities

1 Study Figure 14. Write a 100-word description of this distinctive urban landscape.
2 a) Represent the data shown in Figure 15.
  b) What factors create the need for so many new dwellings in Ipswich?

	Population			Estimated number of new dwellings required
	2001 Census	2021 (predicted)	Change	
Suffolk as a whole	670,200	733,600	+ 63,400	61,700
Ipswich	117,400	138,700	+ 21,300	15,400

▲ **Figure 15** Population growth of Ipswich and housing need.

Some derelict sites were contaminated by waste from their former industrial use. For example, the Orwell Gasworks Quay was the site of a town gasworks where coal had been converted to gas. The land was polluted and it cost up to £270,000 per hectare to remove the waste and make it safe.

Anglo-Saxons lived here in the seventh century so archaeological surveys had to be carried out. Remains of historical value had to be conserved. This cost £1.2 million per hectare.

The ground is mainly soft sands and gravels deposited at the end of the ice age. This means that the foundations for new buildings had to be driven deep into the ground, which was expensive.

The site is next to a tidal estuary. Flood defences had to be built to protect central Ipswich from tidal floods. These cost £53 million. They protect 10 hectares of brownfield land which could not have been redeveloped without these flood defences.

Buildings of historical interest, such as old warehouses, had to be conserved and modernised. This was more expensive than building new homes and offices.

Building on greenfield sites on the edge of Ipswich may have been cheaper but it leads to urban sprawl. As our towns grow larger, this creates more transport problems as people have to commute further to work.

If we fill in the empty spaces in our towns and cities with pockets of new housing then the city doesn't grow any larger and people can live close to their work and leisure facilities in the city centre.

▲ **Figure 16** Advantages and disadvantages of developing the waterfront sites in Ipswich.

The location is superb. I can walk to my office in the town centre in minutes and I no longer need to use my car during the week.

I have all the entertainment I need on my doorstep. The bars are lively at night and on a sunny day you can sit and watch the activity in the marina whilst enjoying a coffee with friends.

▲ **Figure 17** The views of residents.

▲ **Figure 18** The medieval street pattern, narrow roads and old sewers are under pressure as the waterfront development has created more traffic in this area of the inner city.

Activities

3 Study Figures 16, 17 and 18. Use information from these resources to complete a table like the one below. You will write more in some boxes than others.

	Advantages of using brownfield sites	Disadvantages of using brownfield sites
Economic		
Environmental		
Social		

4 Use Figure 3, page 17, to explain why developing a brownfield site is often more sustainable than developing a greenfield site.

Enquiry

For a new housing or other urban development close to your school, design a table which has two columns featuring positive and negative aspects of the scheme. Try to consider social, economic and environmental factors when you review the successes and failures of the scheme.

How does commuting link urban and rural areas?

Towns and cities are closely linked to their surrounding rural areas. One of these links is the daily flow of commuters. Many commuters live in the region surrounding the city and travel into the city each day to work. A much smaller number of commuters travel in the opposite direction, leaving their home in the city to work in a nearby town. Almost 11.3 million people in the UK travel between their home in one local authority and their workplace in a different local authority each day of the working week.

Large cities, like London, Manchester or Cardiff, have many more jobs available than their surrounding region. Consequently, they act as magnets – pulling in young families of working age. But, as we saw on pages 18–19, not everyone can afford house prices in our cities. It's often cheaper to live in a smaller town and commute into the city. That's partly why our roads are getting more congested and why the length of the average commute is getting longer.

As cities have grown and traffic has become busier, so some wealthy city residents have decided to move out of the city. Selling a small house in the city centre can release enough cash to buy a pretty cottage in a village in the countryside – somewhere like Cowbridge in Figure 21. With so few houses for sale in this type of village, demand exceeds supply and house prices rise, making it difficult for local people to buy a house.

Factfile: Commuting

- Average commuting times in the UK are going up. In 2003 it was 45 minutes. By 2015 the average commute had risen to 54 minutes.
- 616,000 people commute into the City of London each week day.
- 1.8 million people in the UK (one in ten UK commuters) travel for over three hours a day. These are so-called 'extreme commuters'.

Area of UK	Average commuting time (minutes)
London	74.2
South East	56.4
East of England	56.0
South West	44.8
Wales	41.0

▲ **Figure 19** Average UK commute times.

The difference in house prices between a city and its surrounding region.

Fast rail links.

The rising cost of fuel and the rising cost of rail fares.

The availability of good 3G and 4G signals and free Wi-Fi on train services.

The affordability of fuel-efficient cars.

Flexible working hours that allow workers to begin the working day any time between 7am and 10am.

▲ **Figure 20** Factors that affect commuting.

◄ **Figure 21** Cowbridge High Street. Cowbridge is a small market town in the Vale of Glamorgan approximately 11km from Cardiff. The average house price (2014–15) in this post code was £385,000.

Activities

1 For each factor in Figure 20, suggest how it may affect patterns of commuting.
2 a) Suggest why London has the longest commute times in the UK.
  b) Explain why the length of the average commute in the UK is increasing.
3 Study Figure 21. Suggest why people who work in Cardiff may want to live in Cowbridge.
4 Explain why house prices in Cowbridge are higher than average for Wales.

Factfile: Cardiff city region

- Half the population of Wales, 1.49 million people, live within 32 km of Cardiff city centre.
- Cardiff is the largest city in Wales, with a population of 350,000.
- The city has a workforce of 189,000. Of these, 166,000 people work in the service sector.
- Almost 78,000 people commute into Cardiff each weekday.
- About 33,900 people commute out of Cardiff each weekday.
- It is estimated that 80 per cent of commuters to Cardiff travel by car.

www.zoopla.co.uk/house-prices

Use this website to find the average house price in the last 12 months in any postcode area.

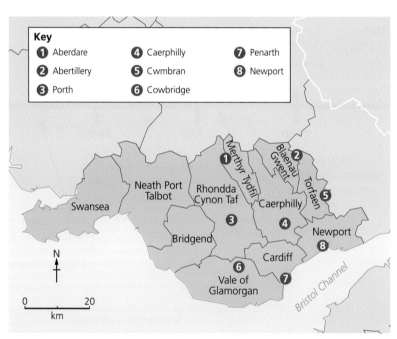

Key
1. Aberdare
2. Abertillery
3. Porth
4. Caerphilly
5. Cwmbran
6. Cowbridge
7. Penarth
8. Newport

▲ **Figure 22** Map of Cardiff and the surrounding local councils.

Local council	Total workplace population	Daily commuters to Cardiff	Daily commuters from Cardiff
Vale of Glamorgan	37,300	20,600	4,700
Rhondda Cynon Taf	71,500	20,400	3,800
Caerphilly	56,500	15,100	3,200
Newport	70,200	6,900	6,700
Bridgend	62,900	5,400	ND
Merthyr Tydfil	21,900	2,300	ND
Torfaen	35,400	1,900	1,900
Monmouthshire	43,200	1,700	ND
Swansea	111,400	1,600	ND
Neath Port Talbot	45,200	1,500	ND
Blaenau Gwent	19,200	1,000	ND
Cardiff	217,000	0	0
Other		4,500	13,700

ND: Means there is no data for these commuter flows. They are likely to be small.

▲ **Figure 23** Commuting patterns in and out of Cardiff.

Activity

5 a) Make a simple copy of Figure 22.
  b) Use the data in Figure 23 to make a choropleth (see page 105) of daily commuters to Cardiff.
  c) Describe the patterns shown by your map.
  d) Describe another technique that could be used to represent this data.

Changes to the rural population

Counterurbanisation is the word we use to describe the process of change that involves population movement from urban areas to the countryside. This change is complex and it's not just about numbers. It's also about who moves, where they move to, and the impacts of this movement on rural communities. What is more, not all of the movement is in one direction. While some people want to move to rural areas, others want to move out.

The UK countryside is often beautiful and rural homes sometimes have stunning views. It is usually peaceful, without the noise, crowds and busy traffic of the city centre. Rural communities are often closely knit and very supportive of one another. These features attract people to move to the countryside. Many move while they are still working in the city. They become commuters, travelling each day or, perhaps, living in the city in the week and in their rural home at the weekend. Cowbridge, in the Vale of Glamorgan, is a commuter village.

Other people move to the countryside and set up a business from home or telework. Teleworkers use mobile technology and the internet to use their home as an office. Many more move to the countryside when they retire. Bishop's Castle, in Shropshire, is one such place. However, remote rural areas, like South Shropshire, don't appeal to everyone. Many teenagers living in this area move to cities elsewhere in the UK when they leave school. The lack of jobs, leisure facilities, shops, theatres and cinemas in the countryside are push factors, while the chance to go to university and the greater choice of jobs are pull factors for moving to a city. In addition, the cost of buying a house in the countryside is likely to prevent young people on lower incomes from staying in a rural area.

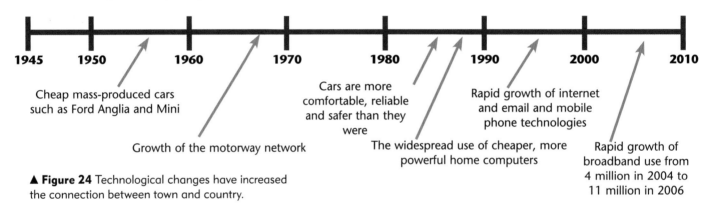

1945   1950   1960   1970   1980   1990   2000   2010

Cheap mass-produced cars such as Ford Anglia and Mini

Growth of the motorway network

Cars are more comfortable, reliable and safer than they were

Rapid growth of internet and email and mobile phone technologies

The widespread use of cheaper, more powerful home computers

Rapid growth of broadband use from 4 million in 2004 to 11 million in 2006

▲ **Figure 24** Technological changes have increased the connection between town and country.

▲ **Figure 25** The beautiful countryside of South Shropshire attracts people who want to work from home or retire to the countryside.

	Sundorne, Shrewsbury (%)	Bishop's Castle (%)	England (%)
Age 75 and above	7.4	10.4	7.8
Age 65 to 74	7.7	13.5	8.6
Age 45 to 64	25.9	30.6	25.4
Age 30 to 44	19.2	16.7	20.6
Age 20 to 29	12.4	8.5	13.7
Age 16 to 19	6.3	4.5	5.1
Age 10 to 15	8.2	6.9	7.0
Age 0 to 9	12.9	9.0	11.9

▲ **Figure 26** Population structure (per cent) in Bishop's Castle (rural Shropshire) and Sundorne (urban Shropshire).

How are rural areas changing?

Newcomers to a rural area often commute to a full-time job outside the rural area, whereas local residents may work locally. Commuters may do their shopping in a large retail park on the edge of the city where they work because by the time they get home, the village shops have closed for the day. The result is that, as a village attracts more commuters, its shops may get fewer customers. Village pubs close and are converted to homes, bus services are axed, and local shops and banks may also close. The rise of internet banking has also badly affected small rural branches of high street banks.

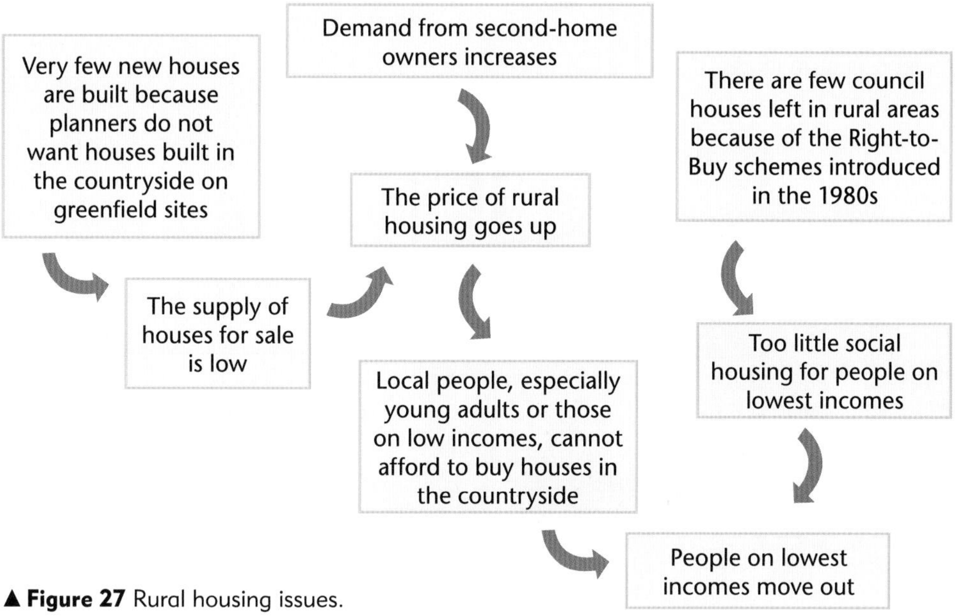

Demand from second-home owners increases

Very few new houses are built because planners do not want houses built in the countryside on greenfield sites

There are few council houses left in rural areas because of the Right-to-Buy schemes introduced in the 1980s

The price of rural housing goes up

The supply of houses for sale is low

Local people, especially young adults or those on low incomes, cannot afford to buy houses in the countryside

Too little social housing for people on lowest incomes

People on lowest incomes move out

▲ **Figure 27** Rural housing issues.

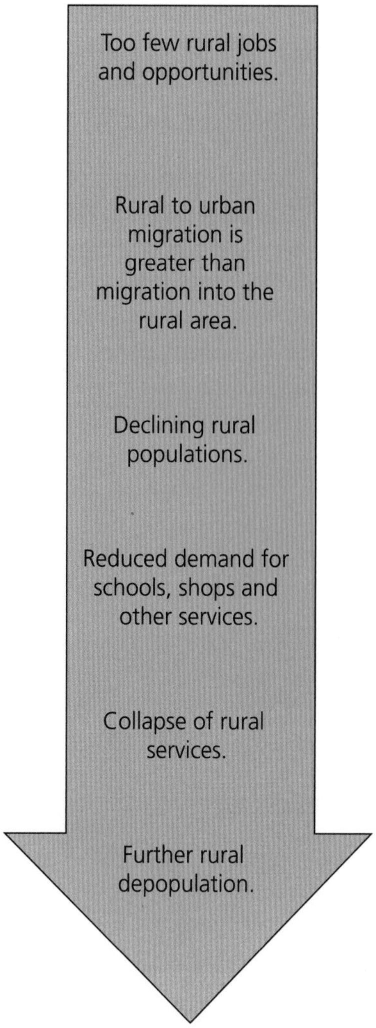

Too few rural jobs and opportunities.

Rural to urban migration is greater than migration into the rural area.

Declining rural populations.

Reduced demand for schools, shops and other services.

Collapse of rural services.

Further rural depopulation.

▲ **Figure 28** How rural depopulation creates unsustainable communities.

Activities

1. Study Figure 24. Use it to explain how technology has allowed:
   a) greater commuting
   b) greater use of the countryside for leisure
   c) more opportunities to move to the country and work from home.
2. Study Figure 26.
   a) How could you represent this data to make easy comparisons?
   b) Describe two significant differences between Bishop's Castle and Sundorne.
   c) Suggest how these differences may affect services in Bishop's Castle.
3. Give two different reasons for the closure of some rural banks and building societies.
4. Explain how closures of services can be both a cause and an effect of rural depopulation.
5. Study Figure 27. Identify two main causes for the lack of affordable housing in rural areas.

Enquiry

Who is moving in and who is moving out of rural areas?

a) Make a copy of the table below.
b) Add push and pull factors to explain the movements in and out of rural areas like Shropshire.

Retired professional moving out of larger towns and into the countryside		Young adult moving out of the countryside and into larger towns	
Push factors	Pull factors	Push factors	Pull factors

Retail catchments

The **catchment area** of a shop is the area from which it gets its customers. Retail catchment areas vary in size, depending on the type of shop and the goods it sells. Small shops selling convenience goods and services tend to have relatively small catchment areas. By contrast, larger supermarkets, shops that sell comparison goods and shops selling specialist goods tend to have larger catchments.

Types of goods

Convenience goods are low-cost items that consumers buy frequently. Convenience goods include things such as groceries sold by supermarkets. **Comparison goods** are more expensive items that consumers buy less often such as clothes, TVs and washing machines.

▲ **Figure 1** District shopping centre in Cowbridge Road, Cardiff.

Activity

1 Study Figures 1 and 2. Put the shops in Figure 1 into rank order according to the probable size of their catchment areas.

Concepts of range and threshold

Range is the distance that a consumer is willing to travel to buy a product. Items such as a newspaper, milk or a loaf of bread are relatively cheap and there is no real benefit to the consumer in shopping around for them. So, bread and milk have a short range because consumers tend to buy them from a shop that is close to home or their workplace. On the other hand, consumers are prepared to travel some distance to shop for comparison goods where they might shop around and grab a bargain. So, an item like a new TV or washing machine has a much larger range than a loaf of bread.

Threshold is the minimum population size needed to create demand for an item or service. Threshold population depends on the value of the product and how often that item or service is purchased. Hairdressers, newsagents and grocery stores all have low population thresholds because consumers buy these low-cost products and services frequently. Specialist shops, such as car dealerships, however, have very large threshold populations because consumers buy new cars infrequently.

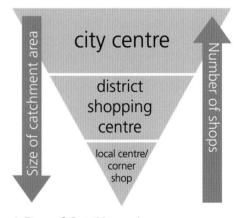

▲ **Figure 2** Retail hierarchy.

Competing retail catchments

Larger towns tend to have a wide variety of shops so they have a larger retail catchment area than a smaller town or village. This means that shops in some smaller town centres struggle to compete with shops in larger neighbouring towns or cities where consumers will find more choice.

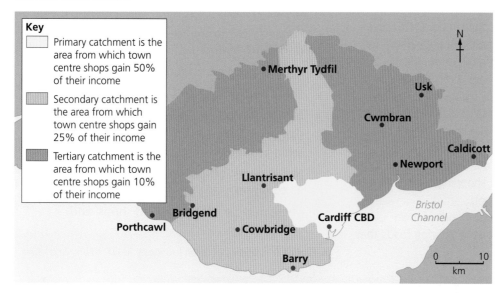

Key

Primary catchment is the area from which town centre shops gain 50% of their income

Secondary catchment is the area from which town centre shops gain 25% of their income

Tertiary catchment is the area from which town centre shops gain 10% of their income

◀ **Figure 3** Retail catchment area of Cardiff city centre (based on sales of non-bulky comparison goods such as shoes, clothes and books).

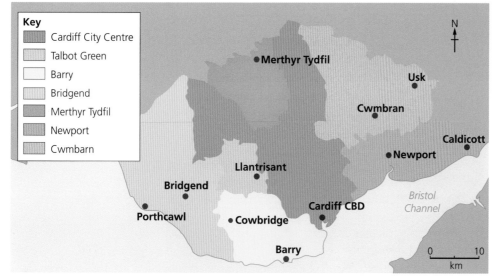

Key

Cardiff City Centre

Talbot Green

Barry

Bridgend

Merthyr Tydfil

Newport

Cwmbarn

◀ **Figure 4** Dominant retail catchment areas.

Activities

2 Study Figure 3. Use the scale line to describe the approximate area of the primary catchment.

3 a) Describe the shape and location of the secondary catchment in Figure 3.
   b) Suggest how transport networks and neighbouring shopping centres may have influenced this shape.

4 Compare Figures 3 and 4. Which other town centres are likely to perceive Cardiff as a threat?

Enquiry

Design an enquiry to investigate the retail catchments of the two towns that are closest to your school.

a) What questions might you pose about catchment, range and threshold?
b) What sampling methods might you use to investigate the competing retail catchments?

Where does retailing occur in UK towns and cities?

The **Central Business District (CBD)** is the traditional town centre location for a wide range of shops and services. Roads spread out from the CBD like arteries in the human body. These arterial roads give shops in the CBD access to a large catchment area and threshold population. By comparison, district shopping centres located in the suburbs of a larger city tend to have a much smaller range of shops. These are usually convenience stores such as small supermarkets, cafés or hairdressers whose catchment area is the immediate neighbourhood. Two other shop locations are common in the UK:

- Shopping centres, or malls, are usually located in the town or city centre. Covered shopping centres have a variety of shops under one roof.
- Retail parks are usually located in out-of-town locations close to arterial roads or the ring roads that circle our towns and cities.

- Consumers can visit several shops, usually chain stores, while under one roof.
- Large department stores may be a feature of this location.
- Limited parking can be a problem, especially on busy roads.
- Parking close to the shops may be expensive or difficult to find.
- Large surface car parks are usually free.
- Good road links makes access easy.
- Shops catering for ethnic groups.
- Large supermarkets and superstores selling furniture or electrical items are common.
- Newsagents, off-licences and takeaways are all common.
- There may be a lot of 'pound shops' and charity shops.

▲ **Figure 6** Features of retail locations in UK towns and cities.

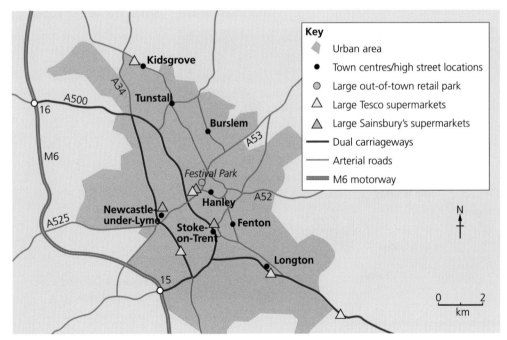

▲ **Figure 5** Map of retail locations in Stoke-on-Trent and Newcastle-under-Lyme.

Activity

1 Study Figure 5.
   a) Describe the distribution of (i) Tesco and (ii) Sainsbury's supermarkets.
   b) Suggest reasons for these locations.
   c) Tesco has a number of smaller 'Express' stores in this area. Predict where they might be located. Justify your prediction.

www.aldi.co.uk/storelocator

This page on the Aldi supermarket site allows customers to search for their nearest store using an interactive map. Tesco, Morrisons, Sainsbury's and Asda have similar sites. Use a search engine to search for the supermarket and add the words 'store locator'.

▲ **Figure 7** Festival Park, an out-of-town retail park in Stoke-on-Trent.

Activities

2 Consider how the site and location of Festival Park might give advantages to retailers there.
   a) Use Figure 5 to consider the advantages of this location.
   b) Use Figure 7 to consider the advantages of this site.
3 Discuss the advantages and disadvantages for the consumer of each retail location before completing the following table. Figure 6 will give you some ideas.

Retail location	Advantages	Disadvantages
Town centre high street locations		
Town centre shopping centres		
District/suburban shopping centres		
Out-of-town retail sites		

4 Use Figure 8 to compare vacancy rates across these three locations. Can you suggest why they might vary so much?

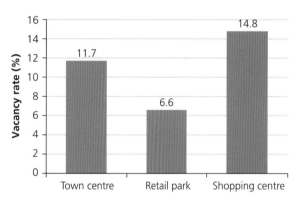

▲ **Figure 8** UK shop vacancy rates. This graph shows the percentage of empty shops in three different locations (2015).

Enquiry

How well are the smaller towns, such as Burslem and Tunstall, served by the supermarket chains?

a) Use the Aldi, Asda and Morrisons store locators on the internet to find the location of other supermarkets in the area covered by Figure 5. You could create a sketch map to show all supermarket locations.
b) Analyse the pattern made by the supermarkets on your sketch map. How well do you think independent grocers and butchers are coping in this urban area?

How is technology changing how and where we shop?

In the past ten years there has been a rapid increase in the number of people who buy their clothes, furniture, groceries, music or books online. Clothes are the most popular item that is bought online, followed closely by household goods such as furniture, computers or TVs. However, it's not just the online sales of goods that affect our high street shops. We also like to pay for our train journeys, flights and holidays online, with 37 per cent of all travel arrangements now being made online rather than in a high street travel agent. Managing your bank account online is easy and more convenient than visiting a high street bank. Consequently, as more people bank online, more high street banks have closed their branches.

Factfile: Online shopping

In 2014 almost three-quarters (74 per cent) of all adults reported buying goods or services online. This has risen from 53 per cent in 2008.

About 50 per cent of online browsing for retail items in 2015 was on mobile devices (up from 42 per cent in 2014) and about 25 per cent of purchases are made using mobile devices.

	2011	2012	2013	2014
Food	74.4	86.8	97.8	109.2
Department stores	34.1	41.6	54.1	60.7
Textiles, clothing and footwear	62.8	75.1	85.4	100.1
All online sales	483.0	556.9	643.0	718.7

▲ **Figure 10** Weekly online sales (£ million).

I run a small business selling antiques. I have a shop in a small town and I also have a website. Sales in the shop and website have declined over the last 10 years. I have noticed that a lot of the antique shops that I visit to buy items for my business have closed. I think the main reason is the rise of online auction websites. It's so easy to sell second hand items on one of these sites. You don't need to pay the bills for a shop like rent, electricity or business rates.

I live in a rural area of mid Wales. I was really quite annoyed when my bank closed its local branch. It forced me to start banking online. I admit that banking online is convenient. I can check my account whenever I want. But I worry about online security and the internet connection where I live isn't brilliant. Also, if I need advice, it's a 25 mile round trip to see my bank manager!

▲ **Figure 9** Points of view on the rise in online services.

Activities

1 Study Figure 10. Draw a series of graphs to show how each type of shopping has changed.
2 List the positive and negative impacts of online shopping for goods and services. Consider the social, economic and environmental impacts.
3 Use Figures 11 and 12.
   a) Describe each graph and compare the similarities and differences.
   b) Suggest how Tesco might use this information.
   c) Suggest how you could use this information if you were doing fieldwork into consumer shopping patterns.

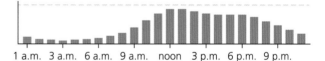

1 a.m. 3 a.m. 6 a.m. 9 a.m. noon 3 p.m. 6 p.m. 9 p.m.

▲ **Figure 11** Footfall in Tesco Extra in Hanley on Fridays.

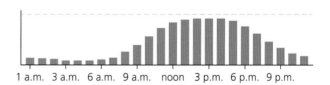

1 a.m. 3 a.m. 6 a.m. 9 a.m. noon 3 p.m. 6 p.m. 9 p.m.

▲ **Figure 12** Footfall in Tesco Extra in Hanley on Saturdays.

www.google.co.uk
Use the Google search engine to search for 'Tesco' and the name of your nearest town. The search engine will display footfall for each day of the week for its stores that are open for 24 hours a day.

24-hour opening and online groceries

The way we shop is changing. We expect to be able to go shopping 24/7 – either from the comfort of home, or by visiting a large store that is open 24 hours a day. The rise of 24-hour shopping for groceries has created a new set of logistical problems for the supermarkets. How do you get perishable goods to the customer quickly and efficiently? The answer is to have effective distribution services that can take advantage of the UK's motorway network. Morrisons has a total of 143 acres of warehouse space – similar in size to 81 football pitches.

Morrisons' expansion into the south of the UK

Morrisons is the UK's fourth largest supermarket chain. It has 500 supermarkets and 150 smaller 'M' convenience stores. The company began in Yorkshire and up until 2004 most of its stores were in the north of England. At that point the company bought Safeway and expanded its stores into locations in the south of England. It needed to improve its distribution system so that it could supply its new stores. Two new distribution centres were built in Sittingbourne (in the south east) and Bridgwater (in the south west).

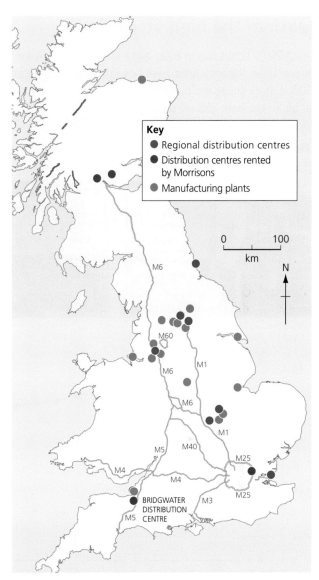

▲ **Figure 13** Morrisons' regional distribution centres and manufacturing plants.

Factfile: Morrisons

1889 – William Morrison begins selling eggs and butter on a market stall in Bradford.

1961 – Morrisons' first supermarket opens in Bradford.

1988 – The first distribution centre opens close to Junction 41 of the M1 motorway to allow Morrisons to expand beyond Bradford.

2004 – Morrisons buys Safeways.

2011 – Morrisons opens a new distribution centre at Bridgwater in Somerset.

Enquiry

Conduct a survey within your class and at home to find out the online shopping habits in your area. Discuss the questions you need to ask collectively, to enable you to build up a picture of who is buying online and what they are buying.

Activities

4   Use Figure 13 to compare the pattern made by Morrisons' distribution centres and its manufacturing plants.
5   Using Figure 13:
   a)   Describe the location of the Bridgwater Distribution Centre.
   b)   Explain why Morrisons chose this location for a new distribution centre after 2004.

Death of the high street?

During 2015 about one in every eight shops in the UK (or 13 per cent) was vacant at any one time. Vacancy rates have been particularly high since the economic recession of 2008. Empty shops are bad for business. Shoppers have less choice and empty shops can be an eye-sore and off-putting for visitors. So it's a concern if vacancy rates are high.

▼ **Figure 14** Empty shops in Burslem, Stoke-on-Trent. Burslem had a higher shop vacancy rate than anywhere else in the UK in 2014 and 2015.

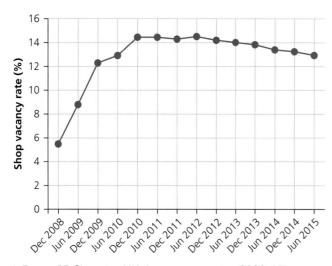

The convenience of online shopping from the comfort of home

Online shopping gives consumers more choice to look for bargains

The difficulty and cost of parking in town centres

The success of large out-of-town retail parks where parking is free

Large supermarket chains such as Tesco can offer more choice and often at lower prices than smaller high street shops

▲ **Figure 15** Changing UK shop vacancy rates (2008–15).　　▲ **Figure 16** Why are town centres in decline?

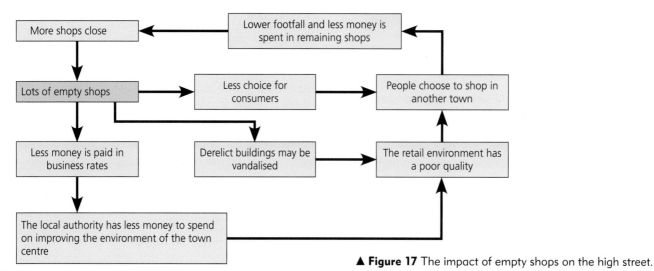

▲ **Figure 17** The impact of empty shops on the high street.

Where are the UK's vacant shops?

The vacancy pattern is not even across the UK. There is a North–South divide, with more empty shops in the North of England and Wales than in the South. Five of the highest vacancy rates in 2015 were in the West Midlands with Burslem (29.4 per cent) and Hanley (27.7 per cent) being in the top three (see Figure 5 page 30). Cobham in Surrey, where Chelsea FC has its training ground and where several Premiership footballers live, is one of the UK town centres that has fewest empty shops.

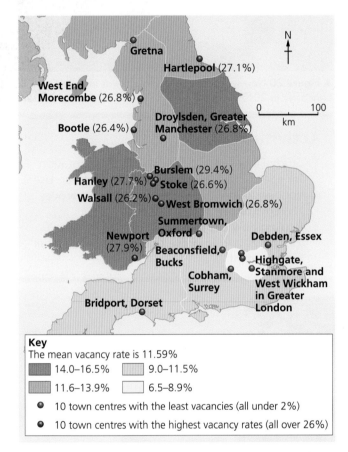

Key
The mean vacancy rate is 11.59%

- 14.0–16.5%
- 11.6–13.9%
- 9.0–11.5%
- 6.5–8.9%
- 10 town centres with the least vacancies (all under 2%)
- 10 town centres with the highest vacancy rates (all over 26%)

▲ **Figure 18** Vacancy rates in the UK's towns with the highest and lowest percentages of empty shops (2015).

Enquiry

'The death of the high street is due to changes in technology such as online sales.'

To what extent do you agree with this statement?

Factfile: Vacant shops

Twenty per cent of vacant shops have been empty for more than three years.

The total number of vacant shops in the UK could create five city centres the size of Manchester.

	Burslem	Cobham	England overall
All people of working age claiming a key benefit (%)	34.0	5.0	15.0
People claiming incapacity benefits (%)	18.0	2.0	7.0
Properties in Council Tax Band A (%) (A is the cheapest band)	75.5	1.0	24.8
Properties in Council Tax Band G (%) (G is one of the most expensive)	0.1	19.7	3.5

▲ **Figure 19** Selected socio-economic statistics for Burslem and Cobham.

Activities

1 Explain why shopping centres in some towns are in decline. Use Figure 16 and elaborate on each statement.
2 Using Figure 18, describe the distribution of towns that have:
   a) High vacancy rates
   b) Low vacancy rates.
   c) To what extent is it true that there is a North–South divide?
3 What are the impacts of high vacancy rates on our town centres? Divide the impacts into the following categories:
   a) social
   b) economic
   c) environmental.
4 a) Explain why a few empty shops can lead to other shops closing.
   b) Suggest three ways that local authorities might try to solve the problem of shop vacancies.
5 Study Figure 19.
   a) Compare the socio-economic statistics for Burslem and Cobham.
   b) Use these statistics to suggest why Burslem has a higher vacancy rate than Cobham.
   c) Use Figure 5 (page 30) to suggest additional reasons for Burslem's high vacancy rate.

The high street fights back

The past 20 years have seen high streets in UK towns and cities undergoing rapid change. Town planners and high street retailers have had to adapt to threats from both out-of-town retailing and online shopping. The high street has fought back to improve the quality of the urban environment for shoppers. A variety of strategies have been used to win back high street shoppers. Some schemes have provided safer streets for pedestrians by restricting access for cars or adding more CCTV cameras. Local councils have worked with developers to create covered shopping malls where it doesn't matter if it's raining outside!

The city centre of Lancaster has recently been improved with new paving in some pedestrianised streets and better street furniture using high quality, strong materials. Changes to road layouts meant that old signposts were confusing. New wayfinding (or signage) information has been installed for shoppers and visitors to the town. A camera was also installed to measure footfall – the number of pedestrians in key locations. It proves that 185,000 people use the city centre each week and that Wednesday is the most popular day – which is market day. This would seem to prove that people still like to shop from independent traders as well as the big chain stores.

▲ **Figure 20** New wayfinding information was installed in Lancaster in 2015.

Activities

1 Study Figure 21 carefully. Write an annotation for each of the features that has a number. Use your annotation to explain how this improves the environment for shoppers.
2 Explain how the features shown in Figures 20, 21 and 22 can improve the quality of the retail environment.

▲ **Figure 21** The high street environment in Lancaster.

▲ **Figure 22** French market in Oswestry.

| Pedestrianised shopping streets |
| Traffic calming such as ramps and pinch points |
| Permitting street entertainment such as buskers |
| Improving signs and wayfinding information for pedestrians |
| Providing street furniture such as flower beds and benches |
| Reducing the cost of short-stay parking |
| Creating park-and-ride schemes |
| Special high street events such as French or Christmas markets |
| Allowing pop-up shops to sell from vacant shops |

▲ **Figure 23** Strategies to improve the high street.

Enquiry

What are the best strategies for improving the retail environment?

Study the strategies in Figure 23.

a) Make a diamond nine diagram (like the one on page 108) and place the strategies in the diagram, putting those that you think are essential at the top of the diagram.
b) Justify your choice of the top three strategies by explaining how they will benefit the experience of shoppers and improve the economy of the high street.

Investigating flows of shoppers

You can measure the flow of shoppers through a retail environment with pedestrian counts. Do this by counting the number of people moving past a specific point over a set period of time. This could be one minute or longer, depending on how busy the location is.

Top tips for a successful survey

1 Choosing locations for your survey is important. Keep away from busy junctions and locate yourself midway along streets to build up an idea of the flows of people along these routes.

2 Using categories can provide you with more information. For example, you can categorise by age group and/or as male/female etc. This might prove useful as certain groups might be attracted to different retail functions.

3 Record the direction that people are walking. Your results can be represented using proportional arrows. The bigger the arrow, the greater the flow.

4 To map pedestrian flows across a town, you will need to record the results of several surveys. Use a systematic sampling technique to choose your locations – see page 45.

5 The number of pedestrians changes throughout the day so you could conduct your survey at different times of the day.

Does each town centre need its own distinct identity?

Each town's **identity** is created by the mixture of features that give it its own character. A town's identity is what gives it its unique sense of place. Many are concerned that a town loses its identity when locally owned independent shops are replaced by shops that are part of a national chain.

Timpson – dry cleaning and key cutting		Bailey's – café and bakery
Radio – café		Age UK – charity shop
VACANT		
Shades – curtains/fabrics		Cascade – amusement arcade
The Flower Gallery – florists	Bailey Street	
The Oak Furniture Shop – beds and furniture		Pound Stretcher – discount shop
Polka Dot – travel agent		
RJ Christian – jewellers		Card Factory – greeting cards
The Works – book shop		Specsavers – opticians

▲ **Figure 24** A simple way to record shops. Note that the photographs in Figure 25 were taken in the same street.

Clone town

The clone town survey is part of a national survey to identify the number of independent shops that are left in the UK's high streets. It is a measure of the range of different types of shop (diversity) and of the proportion of independent shops compared to chain stores (identity). Follow these steps to calculate a 'clone town' score.

Step 1 Use a recording sheet like Figure 27 to survey between 40 and 60 shops.

Step 2 Find the total number of **types** of shop in your survey and the total number of **independently** owned shops in your table.

Step 3 Multiply the total number of independently owned shops by 75, then divide this by the total number of shops in your survey.

Step 4 Add the total number of types of shop to the figure you found in Step 3. This gives your clone town score. Scores below 50 are clone towns. Scores above 65 have a good diversity of shops and enough independent shops to give the town identity.

▲ **Figure 26** Clone town score.

▼ **Figure 25** Shops on Bailey Street, Oswestry, Shropshire. Bailey Street is pedestrianised. It has not been photographed on Google Street View

Type of shop	Independently owned	Part of a chain
Food (butcher, baker, supermarket)		
Newsagent/tobacconist		
Books/stationery		
Department/catalogue store		
Pub/bar		
Off-licence		
Professional e.g. insurance/accountancy		
Estate agent		
Healthcare/pharmacy/optician		
Household goods (furniture, kitchen)		
Clothes/shoes		
Cinema/theatre		
Electronic/IT, e.g. phones, computers		
Pets/pet supplies/vet		
Hair salon/beauty treatment		
Toys/sports/cycling/outdoor leisure		
Car accessories/petrol		
Builders merchant/DIY store		
Florist/garden centre		
Dry cleaning/launderette		
Travel agent		
Camera/photo processing		
Post Office		
Other, e.g. betting, amusements, antiques, charity shops, jewellers		
Total		

▲ **Figure 27** Clone town survey recording sheet.

Activities

1 Study Figure 25.
   a) Identify one feature that gives this street an identity.
   b) Using Figures 24 and 27 to help you create a tally chart for the shops in Figure 25. In your tally chart, you should identify:
      i) the number of independently owned shops
      ii) the number of different types of shop.
2 Use Google Street View to complete a virtual clone town survey of Oswestry. You can add your results to the tally chart, Figure 27. This means that you will need to classify between 25 and 45 shops.
3 Discuss the features that give your local town centre an identity of its own.
   a) List three features of the built environment and three features of the human environment that create identity.
   b) To what extent do you agree that it is important for town centres to have their own identity? Why does this issue seem to be important?

Enquiry

Create an enquiry that could be used to investigate perceptions of identity in your own town centre. Your plan should include:

a) An overarching enquiry question.
b) Your sampling strategy.
c) Ideas for how you would gather both quantitative and qualitative data (see page 45).

How do leisure activities damage the natural environment?

Millions of people enjoy leisure activities in the UK countryside. Walking, jogging and cycling are all popular activities that are good for your health. Being outside in the fresh air can make you happier, too. But are leisure activities good for the countryside? Too many visitors can cause problems, with litter, parking and footpath erosion all being issues that need careful management. These issues become acute when the number of visitors exceeds the **carrying capacity** of the location and an activity begins to damage the landscape or ecosystem. Too many people trampling through the sand dunes, for example, can kill the plants and increase the

risk of an erosional scar known as a blow-out (see page 244).

Carrying capacity is most likely to be exceeded at the UK's **honeypot sites**. Like bees around a pot of honey, these sites attract the largest numbers of people because they are:
- exceptionally beautiful or interesting
- accessible by road and within easy reach of people living in larger towns or cities.

The majority of the UK's natural honeypot sites occur in either one of the UK's Areas of Outstanding Natural Beauty (AONBs) or one of our National Parks.

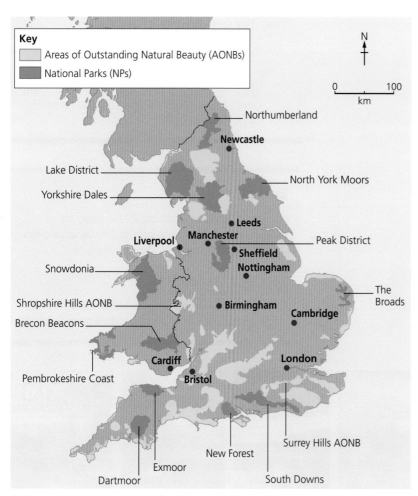

Key
Areas of Outstanding Natural Beauty (AONBs)
National Parks (NPs)

N

0   100
km

Northumberland
Newcastle
Lake District
North York Moors
Yorkshire Dales
Leeds
Liverpool Manchester
Peak District
Sheffield
Nottingham
Snowdonia
The Broads
Shropshire Hills AONB
Birmingham
Brecon Beacons
Cambridge
Cardiff
London
Pembrokeshire Coast
Bristol
Surrey Hills AONB
New Forest
Exmoor
South Downs
Dartmoor

▲ **Figure 1** The location and distribution of Areas of Outstanding Natural Beauty (AONBs) and National Parks in England and Wales. AONBs are selected because of their exceptional scenic qualities.

Activity

1 Study Figure 1.
   a) Describe the location of Shropshire Hills AONB.
   b) List five urban areas that all within 100 km of the Peak District National Park.
   c) Which National Park is furthest from any large city?

Enquiry

What are the distinctive landscapes of one National Park?

a) Research one UK National Park.
b) Choose five photographs to summarise the distinctive landscapes of this National Park.
c) Write a 500-word article that would attract visitors to this National Park.

How might visitors damage an upland honeypot site?

The Stiperstones is a rocky ridge in the Shropshire Hills AONB. This AONB is within easy driving distance of the towns and cities of the West Midlands. The hills are not large. The summits of most are around 400 m above sea level and slopes are not too steep so they are accessible to walkers and cyclists of all abilities and ages.

The soils on the Stiperstones are particularly thin. In fact, rocky outcrops called **tors** stick out along the backbone of the ridge. People walk up to the top to climb over the tors and admire the view. But trampling along the same routes has damaged the vegetation and led to erosion of the soil. You can see the scars made by footpath erosion in Figure 2.

◄ **Figure 2** Footpath erosion is not a widespread problem in the Shropshire Hills AONB but it is a localised problem on the Stiperstones ridge.

▼ **Figure 3** Causes of footpath erosion.

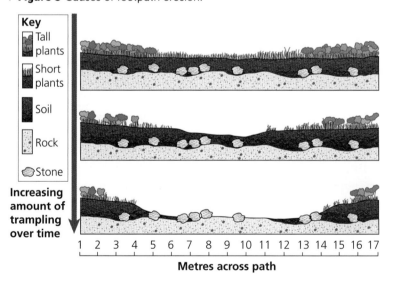

Key
- Tall plants
- Short plants
- Soil
- Rock
- Stone

Increasing amount of trampling over time

1 2 3 4 5 6 7 8 9 10 11 12 13 14 15 16 17
Metres across path

Activities

2 a) Make a copy of Figure 3.
   b) Add a suitable label for each stage of the diagram.
   c) Copy the statements and put them in order to show why the path gets wider over time.
3 a) Why should walkers keep to the path in Figure 2, even though the path is already damaged?
   b) Suggest why it is difficult to repair environments like the one in Figure 2.

| Plants die | Soil is exposed to rainwater | Soil is eroded by rain splash and gulley erosion |

| The path becomes wider and wider | Plants are short and stunted where they have been trampled |

| Walkers avoid the central muddy section of path so walk at the edge | Stones are exposed as soil is eroded |

Investigating the impact of trampling – the use of controls

Figure 4 clearly shows the difference in vegetation between areas that have been heavily trampled by visitors and areas that have not been walked across. However, as Figure 3 (page 41) suggests, people walk through the vegetation on either side of the path to avoid walking on the uneven stones. This leads to an enquiry question:

Are some species of plants more vulnerable to damage than others?

If so, you might find that there are a lower percentage of some plants growing immediately next to the path because they have been damaged by trampling. To find out you would need to set up a control – an experiment to find the average amount of each species of plant. This is what you would do:

Step one

Use a quadrat to measure the percentage of various plants in an area at a distance away from the path that appears to be unaffected by trampling. A quadrat is a metal or plastic grid – usually about half a metre across. You can estimate the percentage of each plant in each quadrat. Take at least five control measurements in different places and then calculate the mean percentage of each plant in these areas.

Step two

Set up a transect (see page 242) across the footpath. You will need to start and end the transect several metres away from the eroded section of path so that you sample the plants on the edge of the trampled area. Each quadrat will need to be 2 m apart along the transect.

Vegetation	Quadrat									
	1	2	3	4	5	6	7	8	9	10
Bilberry	30	10	0	0	0	0	0	10	20	35
Heather	60	70	70	0	20	0	70	80	80	65
Other plants	10	20	10	0	0	0	30	10	0	0
Bare soil/ rock	0	0	20	100	80	100	0	0	0	0

▲ **Figure 5** Percentage of each type of vegetation in each quadrat. Each quadrat was 2 m apart.

Vegetation	Quadrat				
	1	2	3	4	5
Bilberry	30	10	40	25	55
Heather	60	80	60	60	40
Other plants	10	10	0	15	5
Bare soil/rock	0	0	0	0	0

▲ **Figure 6** Percentage of each type of vegetation in the control quadrats.

Enquiry

How does trampling affect different species of plant?

a) Use the data in Figure 6 to calculate the mean percentage of each plant in the control.
b) Choose a suitable technique to represent the data in Figure 5. See page 243 to see how to draw a kite diagram.
c) What conclusions can you draw about the effect of trampling on bilberry and heather plants at the edge of the path?

◄ **Figure 4** Footpath erosion on the Stiperstones and the natural vegetation of bilberry and heather on either side.

How is the Shropshire Hills AONB managed?

AONBs are managed carefully to ensure that special and unique qualities of the landscape, wildlife and cultural heritage are recognised and conserved. The work is done by a small team of full-time staff and a large number of volunteers. Each of the UK's AONBs produces a five-year management plan and identifies action points that need to be met.

Activity	Per cent
Walking/hiking	57
General sightseeing	18
Visiting relatives/friends	8
Other	5
Visiting an attraction	4
Cycling	3
Shopping	2
Visiting an historic site	1
Eating out	1

▲ **Figure 7** Main activities undertaken by visitors to the Shropshire Hills AONB (percentages of 196 people who were surveyed).

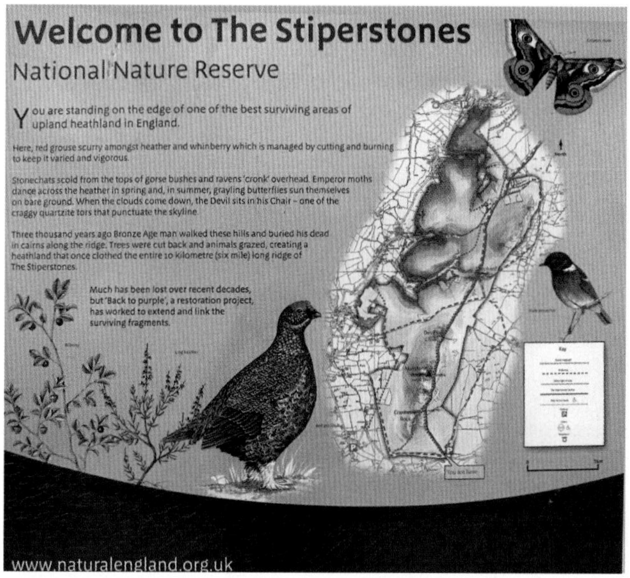

▲ **Figure 8** An interpretation board at the Stiperstones.

Establish a programme of photography at key locations as a means of monitoring landscape change.

Promote local food by a variety of means including press, leaflets, exhibitions and events such as food fairs.

Provide and improve outdoor education for schools and support for in-school activities.

Develop new initiatives to encourage the creation of more woodland.

Develop guidance on how renewable energy can be developed in the area with minimum impact on the AONB's special qualities.

Develop a programme to promote cycling opportunities in the Shropshire Hills.

Improve and upgrade interpretation facilities for visitors.

Develop training opportunities which support conservation land management.

Continue to provide visitor information at the Shropshire Hills Discovery Centre.

▲ **Figure 9** Selected action points in the 2014–19 Shropshire Hills AONB management plan.

Activities

1 Choose an appropriate technique to represent the data in Figure 7.
2 a) Discuss the nine action points in Figure 9.
   b) Make a diamond nine diagram (like the one on page 108) and place the action points in the diagram, placing those that you think are essential at the top of the diagram.
   c) Explain why you have chosen your top three action points. You should explain how your chosen action points will help to conserve or recognise: landscapes, wildlife or heritage of local communities.

Enquiry

How should the Shropshire Hills management plan change its priorities?

The colours in Figure 9 represent the priorities given by the Shropshire Hills AONB management plan. The yellow represents essential actions and green are aspirations. Repairing footpaths is an aspirational action point. Do you agree with these priorities? Explain your reasoning.

Investigating leisure use of a honeypot site

Box Hill, in the Surrey Hills AONB, is a beautiful area of woodland and chalk grassland covering 486 hectares. Most of Box Hill is designated a Site of Special Scientific Interest (SSSI) and Special Area of Conservation. London is nearby so Box Hill is a popular destination for walkers and cyclists out on a day trip from the capital.

Developing an enquiry question

Imagine you are about to go on a fieldtrip to Box Hill. Your enquiry will need an enquiry question, but before you can set a suitable enquiry question, you need to get a feel for the place and the issues it faces. Using the internet to read about Box Hill and visitors to Surrey Hills AONB or using Google Maps or Google Street View are all good places to start.

Then you can begin to make a list of possible enquiry questions. A good enquiry question should not be too broad or it will be very difficult to analyse. For example:

What impact do visitors have on the environment at Box Hill, Surrey?

This question can be broken down into smaller sub-questions to help to give it structure:

1 *What do we know about the visitors to Box Hill?*

2 *What is the environment of Box Hill?*

3 *How have visitors affected the environment of Box Hill?*

▲ **Figure 10** The location of Box Hill in the Surrey Hills AONB.

Investigating the concept of place

Place is a geographical concept which is used to describe what makes somewhere special, unique or distinct. AONBs like the Surrey Hills are created to identify and conserve the features that make them unique. These might include many different features of the human and physical environment such as landscape features and landmarks, local styles of building, local ecosystems or local historical or cultural features. But you don't have to be in an AONB to be able to identify a sense of place. It is the combination of geographical features that creates an identity for any place.

Activities

1 Use Figure 10 to describe the location of Box Hill.
2 Suggest two separate reasons why it so popular with day trippers from London.
3 Study the enquiry question about Box Hill: *What impact do visitors have on the environment at Box Hill, Surrey?*
   a) Suggest one way the enquiry question could be amended so that you can investigate whether visitors have an impact on businesses in the Surrey Hills AONB.
   b) How would you amend the sub-questions?

Enquiry

What features give the Surrey Hills AONB a sense of place?

a) Research the Surrey Hills. What are the physical and human features that give it a unique identity?
b) How would you go about designing an enquiry into what gives your local area a sense of identity? What quantitative and qualitative data could you collect?

Sampling strategies

A sample is a set of data that provides us with a good understanding of what is happening without having to record everything. The sample must be representative – a fair reflection of the whole. It is essential that the sample is not biased. There are three main sampling strategies and these are shown in Figure 12. In addition, sampling can sometimes be 'opportunistic'. Opportunity sampling means that the sample has been chosen because it is convenient and easily or safely available. For example, sample points along a river are usually chosen because access into the river is permitted (the landowner has agreed) and safe. The problem with this type of sampling is that it isn't fair or unbiased so your sample may not be representative.

▲ **Figure 11** The zig-zag is a popular cycling route on Box Hill, Surrey. It was used in the 2012 Olympic Games.

What's the difference between quantitative and qualitative data?

Geographers can collect all sorts of different kinds of data during a fieldwork enquiry but it will always fall into one of two categories:

Quantitative data is information that can be measured and recorded as numbers. Counting traffic, measuring the width and velocity of a river, or measuring the size of pebbles on a beach are all examples of quantitative data.

Qualitative data is information that is not numerical. You can collect qualitative data in a wide variety of ways such as by taking photographs, field sketches, videos or audio recordings. Interviewing people to find their opinions or perceptions about an issue is also an example of qualitative data collection. Using a bi-polar technique (pages 14–15) is a way to try to make the collection of opinions more quantitative.

	Random sampling	Systematic sampling	Stratified sampling
What is it?	Every sample point has an equal probability of being sampled.	Data is collected at regular intervals. These intervals can be in time or space (distance).	Proportional samples are taken from separate groups or strata.
How might you use it?	To investigate how busy a country park is, select a range of locations across the park; put the names of all locations in a bag and pull out five. Carry out pedestrian counts at each of these sites.	To investigate how tourist impact changes as you move further away from a visitor centre, you might carry out litter counts and environmental impact surveys every 100 m away from the centre.	When carrying out a questionnaire, make sure that you sample appropriate numbers from different age groups based on data from the census, i.e. 20% aged 0–18, 25% aged 19–45, 35% aged 45–65 and 20% aged 66+.
Advantages (+) and Disadvantages (−)	(+) Removes bias completely in the selection of sites. (−) Survey sites may be clustered together so you do not get an even spread of locations.	(+) Covers a range of locations and provides an even spread over the whole survey area. (−) If samples are too far apart you may miss important variations.	(+) Provides a true representative sample. (−) You will need information on the size of each group before you start.

▲ **Figure 12** Sampling strategies.

Using questionnaires

Questionnaires are a quick way of capturing people's opinions or recording their behaviour. However, questionnaires are subjective. You cannot guarantee that people have been honest in their response to you. You can either ask closed or open questions. To set closed questions you will need to create some possible answers – people then select one of these responses. Closed questions are quick and easy for people to complete and the results are easy to represent later. However, respondents are limited to the options that you have already chosen on their behalf. Open questions allow people to answer freely in any way they choose. They can be very useful in that they can allow people to respond freely about the subject, but it can be harder to analyse the answers.

1 How far have you travelled to get to Box Hill?			
0–5 miles	6–20 miles	21–50 miles	More than 50 miles
10	23	17	5

2 How did you travel here?			
Walked	Public transport	Car	Other
2	3	50	0

3 Which locations on Box Hill have you visited?						
Visitor's Centre	Viewpoint	Broadwood's Tower	Labelliere's Grave	Stepping Stones	Burford Spur	Other
36	51	15	23	12	16	8

4 What activities are you taking at Box Hill?
5 How long have you been at Box Hill today?

▲ **Figure 13** Visitor questionnaire for Box Hill.

Impact score on a scale 0–5 (0 is low 5 is high)						
Site	Distance from visitor centre (m)	Footpath erosion	Noise	Litter	Space (busyness)	Total score
1	0	5	4	3	4	16
2	100	5	2	4	3	14
3	200	4	1	2	2	9
4	300	3	1	2	2	8
5	400	2	1	1	1	5
6	500	1	0	1	1	3
7	600	1	2	2	3	8
8	700	0	1	0	1	2
9	800	0	0	1	0	1

▲ **Figure 14** Environmental impact assessment scores.

Activity

1 Study Figure 13.
  a) Identify one closed and one open question.
  b) Amend one of the open questions to make it closed.
  c) Suggest two further questions that would support the investigation title.
2 Study Figure 14.
  a) What type of sampling was used to collect this data?
  b) Represent the data using two different techniques.
  c) What are the strengths and limitations of each technique?

Processing and presenting evidence

You can process data in various ways. For example, by calculating:

- totals and percentages
- averages (mean, mode or median)
- maximum, minimum and interquartile ranges (see page 119).

Your data needs to be represented using appropriate techniques to help you identify any patterns or trends. Here are some questions to consider when choosing a technique:

- Is the data expressed as actual values or percentages? You could use block charts for actual values and pie charts to show percentages.
- Is the data discrete or continuous? A block graph should be used to represent discrete data, whereas a line graph should be used for continuous data.
- Does the data tell you something about different places? If so, could you locate your blocks or pie charts on a base map?
- Have you got two sets of data that are related to one another? If so, would a scatter graph (page 75) show a relationship?

Analysing the evidence

Analysis means studying the data and identifying any patterns or trends. For example:

- Is the data increasing, decreasing or consistent throughout your surveys?
- Is there any data that does not follow the pattern? These are anomalies. Can you explain why this might this be?
- How does the data relate to sites on the ground? Does the data show a spatial pattern? In other words, can you see patterns that vary over space?

You should also consider how your evidence compares to the patterns that you expected when you take into account your wider geographical understanding. For example, most visitors to Shropshire Hills AONB are day trippers who live locally – 56 per cent live in Shropshire. Does the evidence collected at Box Hill match this general pattern?

Drawing conclusions

The most important thing to do in your enquiry is to attempt to answer the question you posed at the start. In order to do this, you must draw together all the evidence you have collected to make your final assessment.

Evaluating your enquiry

Evaluation means assessing the strengths and weaknesses of each step of the enquiry process. Your evaluation could involve taking the following steps:

Step 1 Did I ask the correct question at the beginning? Was I able to collect the right type of data to allow me to draw conclusions?

Step 2 Was my data representative and reliable? If you used questionnaires, did you get enough responses to properly represent the opinions of the public? If you used data from the internet, or another source, can the source be trusted or could the information be biased?

Step 3 Was the enquiry well planned? Be aware that not collecting enough data, running out of time, and not putting in appropriate effort is not human error but poor planning. In what ways could I improve my enquiry if I repeated it?

Step 4 Are there any further questions that need to be answered? How might the enquiry be extended?

Activity

3 Your enquiry question was:
   What impact do visitors have on the environment at Box Hill, Surrey?
   Using Figure 14, what conclusions can you draw?

Enquiry

For a leisure or honeypot site that you are familiar with:

a) Develop a question that you might study.
b) What data might you collect?
c) What sampling strategies will you use? Why?
d) What analysis and presentation techniques might you use?

What are the impacts of major sporting events?

Leisure activities don't only take place in the countryside at honeypot sites. Urban locations regularly host sporting events such as football matches. These have economic and environmental impacts on local communities – good and bad. Noise and parking issues may create negative impacts for locals. These negative effects usually decline very rapidly with distance as you can see in Figure 15 on page 8. However, sporting events can also create positive economic multipliers – benefits for local businesses that spread, like ripples in a pond, through the local community. These benefits are increased when the sporting event is a large one, such as a major tournament. In this case, the investment in infrastructure such as stadia, training facilities and local transport can have a positive legacy – a long-lasting impact that will benefit people for years to come.

What were the impacts of the Rugby World Cup 2015?

The 2015 Rugby World Cup was hosted by England. Matches were played in 13 different venues across England and Wales. The economic benefits were estimated to be huge. Around 16,000 people were directly employed as a result of the tournament, for example, in construction, ticket sales and stadia staff. Another 6,000 people gained valuable experience as volunteers. But the benefits don't stop there. Many more people gained indirect employment as a result of the tournament. These are people already working as, for example, taxi drivers, hotel cleaners and bar staff, who gained extra work as a result of the huge influx of visitors. For example, it is estimated that the sale of food and drinks to the supporters generated £32 million, including £13 million from foreign visitors. Rugby supporters were thought to have spent £16 million in London on food and drink, and a further £7 million in Cardiff.

Venues	(£ millions)
Newcastle	93
Leeds	53
Manchester	45
Leicester	59
Birmingham	56
Milton Keynes	56
Gloucester	48
Cardiff	316
Landon	1,203
Exeter	39
Brighton	46

◄ **Figure 15** Location of the Rugby World Cup 2015 and above is the estimated (direct and indirect) benefit to the local economy.

Visitors spend money in the local economy, for example, in hotels and on food and drink so …

Stadia are improved so …

Increased participation in sport so …

The country is seen by foreign tourists as an interesting destination so …

▲ **Figure 16** Examples of benefits to the host nation of a major sporting event.

24 the average number of nights spent by Australian fans in the UK

173 the average amount spent each day (in pounds) by Australian fans

85 million the amount spent (in pounds) on improvements to infrastructure

41,000 the total number of jobs supported directly and indirectly

466,000 total number of international visitors to the tournament

869 million the total amount of money (in pounds) spent by international visitors

◄ **Figure 17** The Rugby World Cup 2015 in numbers.

▲ **Figure 18** Posters outside the Principality (Millennium) Stadium, Cardiff. The posters were designed by Visit Wales which promotes Wales as a tourist destination. Each poster used a well-known rugby phrase to advertise the attractions of Wales.

Activities

1 Study Figure 15.
   a) Describe the distribution of the stadia that were used to host the Rugby World Cup 2015.
   b) Suggest why the organisers used so many different stadia.
2 Complete each of the statements in Figure 16 to explain the benefits of this type of tournament.
3 Give examples of jobs created both directly and indirectly by sporting events.
4 Study Figure 18. Suggest why Visit Wales used these particular images of Wales.
5 Summarise the benefits of the Rugby World Cup 2015 for each of the following:
   a) taxi drivers in Cardiff
   b) children aged 10–15
   c) large hotels in London.

Enquiry

How has the Rugby World Cup benefited the UK economy?

Use the data in Figure 15 to create a map with located proportional symbols to represent the economic benefits of the tournament across the UK.

What are the global patterns of urbanisation?

Over half (54 per cent) of the world's population lives in cities. But it's not always been this way. At the start of the twentieth century most of the world's population lived in the countryside or smaller towns. During the second half of the twentieth century the population of the world's cities, and the physical size of their built-up areas, grew – a process known as **urbanisation**. This process was particularly rapid in the cities of the **Newly Industrialised Countries (NICs)** of Asia and Latin America. Urbanisation has been due to a combination of:

- Migration from rural to urban areas
- The natural increase of the population when there are more births than deaths each year.

Figure 2 shows a list of the world's largest cities. Cities with over 10 million residents are sometimes known as **mega-cities**. In 2015 there are 28 mega-cities and 16 of these are located in Asia and only three in Europe. There are 498 cities in the world with a population greater than 1 million. Of these, 101 are in China and 57 are in India. The UK has only five cities with a population of over 1 million.

Newly Industrialised Countries (NICs)

NICs are characterised by: rapid urban growth; growth of the manufacturing sector of the economy; strong trading relationships with other countries; and the operation of foreign-owned multi-national companies (MNCs) within the country.

◀ **Figure 1** The centre of Mumbai, India. The neighbourhood of Bhendi Bazaar is in the foreground. The low-rise buildings in this neighbourhood are traditional dormitories known as chawls.

1990		2015		2030	
Tokyo, Japan	32.53	Tokyo, Japan	38.00	Tokyo, Japan	37.19
Osaka, Japan	18.39	Delhi, India	25.70	Delhi, India	36.06
New York–Newark, USA	16.09	Shanghai, China	23.74	Shanghai, China	30.75
Ciudad de México (Mexico City)	15.64	São Paulo, Brazil	21.07	Mumbai, India	27.80
São Paulo, Brazil	14.78	Mumbai, India	21.04	Beijing, China	27.71
Mumbai, India	12.44	Ciudad de México (Mexico City)	21.00	Dhaka, Bangladesh	27.37
Kolkata, India	10.89	Beijing, China	20.38	Karachi, Pakistan	24.84
Los Angeles–Long Beach–Santa Ana, USA	10.88	Osaka, Japan	20.24	Cairo, Egypt	24.50
Seoul, South Korea	10.52	Cairo, Egypt	18.77	Lagos, Nigeria	24.24
Buenos Aires, Argentina	10.51	New York–Newark, USA	18.59	Ciudad de México (Mexico City)	23.86

▲ **Figure 2** The world's ten largest mega-cities, population in millions.

What will happen next?

The world's urban population is expected to rise from 3.9 billion (in 2014) to 6.0 billion by 2045. The largest urban growth is expected to be in India, China and Nigeria where an extra 404 million, 292 million and 212 million urban dwellers will be added respectively by 2050. The fastest growing cities are not mega-cities but those with a population under 500,000. Many of the world's fastest growing cities are expected to be in sub-Saharan Africa and Asia.

Region	1990–1995 (%)	2015–2020 (%)	2045–2050 (%)
Sub-Saharan Africa	4.09	3.83	2.78
East Asia (including China)	3.28	1.91	-0.06
South Asia (including India)	2.95	2.40	1.37
Western Europe	0.78	0.47	0.12
South America	2.43	1.16	0.36

▲ **Figure 4** Average annual rate of change of the urban population (per cent).

Year	Population Mumbai, India	Population Kinshasa, DRC
1950	2.86	0.20
1960	4.06	0.44
1970	5.81	1.07
1980	8.66	2.05
1990	12.44	3.68

▲ **Figure 3** Population (millions) of Mumbai, India and Kinshasa, Democratic Republic of Congo (DRC).

Enquiry

What is the geographical future for urban areas around the world?
a) Represent the data in Figure 4. A good way to do this would be to draw proportional bars on an outline map of the world.
b) Use your map to write a 200-word report. Make sure that you contrast the rates of urban growth in different regions of the world.

Activities

1 Write definitions for the following terms:
  urbanisation   mega-cities   NICs
2 Study Figure 2.
  a) Choose a suitable graph to present this data.
  b) Describe what has happened to the distribution of the world's largest cities.
3 Study Figure 3.
  a) Draw a pair of line graphs to represent the growth of these two cities.
  b) Describe the similarities and differences of these two graphs.
4 Is rapid urbanisation a good thing? Predict the possible consequences of rapid population growth in a city such as Kinshasa, which is in a Low Income Country (LIC). You should consider advantages and disadvantages.

So what are global cities?

All cities have a regional influence. They interact with the area that surrounds them, for example:

- attracting daily commuters to work
- providing specialist services such as hospitals and universities
- acting as transport hubs for rail networks or regional airports.

However, some cities have greater influence than others. **Global cities** are those cities which interact with other places at the global scale. Figure 5 illustrates some of these global connections. The Globalisation and World Cities Research Network has identified over 300 cities that have inter-connections with other parts of the globe. The UK has 13 global cities. London is ranked first, but the next highest in the UK is Manchester at 78th; Cardiff is in 248th place. Figure 6 shows those global cities that have the most important global connections.

Globalisation

The process of **globalisation** connects places economically, socially, politically or culturally. Global cities play an important role in this process. Cities have always been connected by trade and migration. However, as communications and transport improve, the process is accelerating. It's as though the world is shrinking as it becomes better connected and places become less isolated.

Migration and culture:
Global cities attract economic migrants from all over the world. Migration leads to cultural diversity. More than 100 languages are spoken in 30 of London's 33 boroughs. The 2011 Census showed that 22 percent of London's residents do not speak English as their main language. That's just over 1.7 million people.

Finance and trade:
The world's most important global cities are financial centres. Banks have their head offices here. Dealers working at financial markets like FTSE buy and sell commodities on the world markets.

Transport hubs:
The top global cities are all well-connected to the rest of the world by major airports or ports. These allow the flow of people, tourists and trade. About 1,400 flights take off or land at London's Heathrow airport every day.

Governance and decision-making:
Business managers in one city can make decisions that affect people worldwide. For example, Tata is an Indian MNC with its headquarters in Mumbai and businesses in over 100 countries. Politicians and civil servants can also have worldwide decision-making roles. The UN employs 41,000 people. 6,389 are based in their headquarters in New York.

Ideas and information:
Many of the world's global cities are the home for major broadcasting companies. Newspapers, TV stations and filmmakers are based in global cities. BBC World News is an international TV channel broadcasting 24 hours a day to over 300 million households in 200 countries.

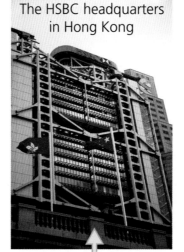

The HSBC headquarters in Hong Kong

Global cities

The United Nations headquarters in New York City

New Broadcasting House in London

▲ **Figure 5** How global cities connect to the rest of the world.

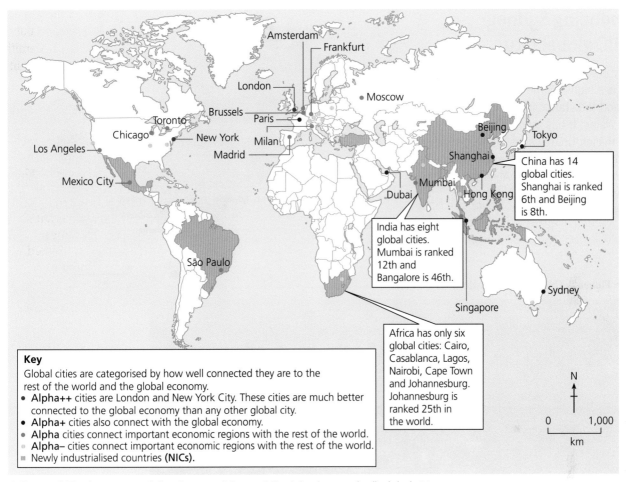

▲ **Figure 6** The location and distribution of the world's alpha (top-ranked) global cities.

Key

Global cities are categorised by how well connected they are to the rest of the world and the global economy.
- **Alpha++** cities are London and New York City. These cities are much better connected to the global economy than any other global city.
- **Alpha+** cities also connect with the global economy.
- **Alpha** cities connect important economic regions with the rest of the world.
- **Alpha–** cities connect important economic regions with the rest of the world.
- Newly industrialised countries (**NICs**).

China has 14 global cities. Shanghai is ranked 6th and Beijing is 8th.

India has eight global cities. Mumbai is ranked 12th and Bangalore is 46th.

Africa has only six global cities: Cairo, Casablanca, Lagos, Nairobi, Cape Town and Johannesburg. Johannesburg is ranked 25th in the world.

Year	Population
1950	8.36
1960	8.19
1970	7.51
1980	7.66
1990	8.05
2000	8.61
2010	9.70
2020	10.85
2030	11.47

▲ **Figure 7** Population (millions) of London, the top-ranked global city.

Activities

1 Explain the difference between mega-cities and global cities. Make sure that you give examples of cities that fall into both categories by using Figures 2 and 6.
2 Study Figure 6.
   a) Describe the distribution of the world's alpha++ and alpha+ cities.
   b) What percentage of global cities shown on Figure 6 are located in NICs?
   c) Suggest why there are so many global cities in India and China.
3 a) Use the data in Figure 7 to draw a line graph of London's population growth.
   b) Use your graph to estimate the year in which London became a mega-city.
   c) Compare and contrast London's population growth to that of Mumbai and Kinshasa (shown in Figure 3).

Enquiry

Why do you think London is the world's most important global city? Make a list of ten ways that London is:
a) connected to other parts of the UK
b) interconnected with other parts of the world.

Introducing Sydney: an HIC global city

Sydney is the largest city in Australia, which is a high-income country (HIC) and the state capital of New South Wales. It has a population of 4.5 million (2015) so is not a mega-city. Nevertheless, Sydney is a very important city within Australia, the Pacific region and within the international economy.

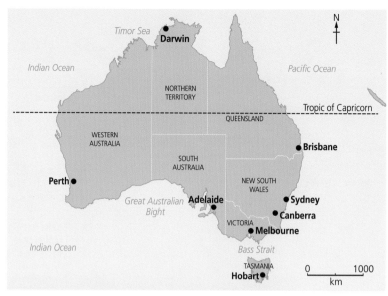

► **Figure 8** The location of Sydney.

▲ **Figure 9** Sydney Harbour. The CBD of Sydney is in the top centre of the photograph.

Sydney is built on either side of a large natural harbour. Sydney Harbour Bridge and Sydney Opera House are two distinctive urban landmarks that are recognised worldwide. The CBD is built on the south side of Sydney Harbour and the suburbs sprawl to the north, south and west as much as 20 km from the city centre.

Sydney is a relatively modern city. It grew rapidly during the second half of the twentieth century, largely as a result of international migration. This is one of the reasons that Sydney is regarded as an important global city.

Year	Population
1950	1.69
1960	1.14
1970	2.89
1980	3.25
1990	3.63
2000	4.05
2010	4.36
2020	4.73
2030	5.30

▲ **Figure 10** The population (millions) of Sydney.

Why is Sydney a global city?

As we shall see, Sydney is one of the world's most multicultural cities. People of different nationalities share ideas, cultures, languages and food. Sydney is an alpha+ city. That means it's very well connected to the rest of the world, especially the Pacific and South East Asian regions:

- The headquarters of 76 per cent of all of Australia's domestic and foreign-owned banks are located in the city. Approximately 155,000 people are employed in banking and finance in the city.
- Sydney has seven of Australia's top ten visitor attractions – including the Sydney Harbour Bridge and Sydney Opera House. The city attracts over 2.8 million foreign visitors a year.
- Sydney generates approximately 65 per cent of the wealth of New South Wales and 20 per cent of Australia's wealth.
- The city's reputation for a youthful and well-educated workforce is attracting foreign-owned multinational companies that specialise in ICT and media.
- Sydney's universities attract over 50,000 international students each year.

Immigration to Sydney

Up until the 1970s most of Sydney's migrants came from the UK, Ireland and other European counties such as Italy and Greece. At this time, Australia had relatively few cultural or economic ties to Asia or the Pacific. Sydney really became a global city during the 1970s

when it began to accept large numbers of refugees from the conflict in Vietnam. Since then, Sydney has welcomed immigration from a large number of Asian and Pacific countries. It sees immigration as an opportunity rather than a threat. Immigrants are mainly young adults and they come to Sydney with a wide range of workplace skills that can help Sydney develop its workforce and its economy.

Country of birth	2001	2011
United Kingdom	154,795	155,065
China	80,627	146,853
India	33,625	86,767
New Zealand	74,521	77,297
Vietnam	61,020	69,405
Philippines	45,657	61,122
Lebanon	51,060	54,215
Korea (Republic of)	25,150	39,694
Italy	45,619	39,155
Hong Kong	35,772	36,804
South Africa	24,044	31,681
Fiji	24,797	29,598

▲ **Figure 11** Migrants in Sydney by country of birth.

Activities

1. a) Describe the landscape in Figure 9 in 100 words.
   b) Suggest three reasons why tourists from the UK are attracted to Sydney.
2. a) Describe the location of Sydney.
   b) Give three examples of connections between Sydney and the rest of Australia.
   c) Give three examples that explain why Sydney is an important global city.
3. a) Draw a line graph to show the growing population of Sydney.
   b) What is Sydney's population likely to be in 2025?
   c) Compare the growth of Sydney to that of Kinshasa (Figure 3, page 51). Use this evidence to suggest why Sydney is likely to face different challenges to those faced by Kinshasa in the future.
4. Study Figure 6 on page 53 and Figure 11. Suggest why Sydney's location gives it advantages compared to European cities when it comes to globalisation.

Enquiry

How is immigration to Sydney changing?

Use Figure 11 to analyse trends (over time) and patterns (over space). A good way to help visualise these trends and patterns would be to:

a) draw pairs of blocks (one to represent origin of migrants in 2001 and the other representing migrants in 2011)
b) locate these bars on an outline world map.

Patterns of migration and wealth

Average incomes in Sydney vary considerably. The lowest incomes are in the suburb of Cabramatta in Fairfield, where the average annual income is Au$39,000. By contrast, average annual incomes in the coastal suburb of Mossman are Au$123,000. Why do these large differences exist?

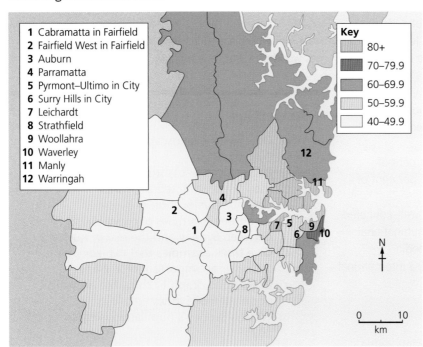

1 Cabramatta in Fairfield
2 Fairfield West in Fairfield
3 Auburn
4 Parramatta
5 Pyrmont–Ultimo in City
6 Surry Hills in City
7 Leichardt
8 Strathfield
9 Woollahra
10 Waverley
11 Manly
12 Warringah

Key
80+
70–79.9
60–69.9
50–59.9
40–49.9

◀ **Figure 12** Average annual incomes in Greater Sydney (Au$, 1,000s).

Pyrmont-Ultimo

Pyrmont–Ultimo is an inner urban area close to Sydney's central business district (CBD). This area, close to the waterfront of Sydney Harbour, was once an important dock area. The dock industries declined after World War Two and the area became run-down and derelict. A regeneration programme in the 1990s transformed the area. People moved back in, a process known as **re-urbanisation**. The population rose from 900 in 1990 to over 11,000 today. It's a vibrant, multicultural area with a large Chinese-born population (22 per cent).

Parramatta

Parramatta is located in the western part of Greater Sydney, 23 km from the city centre. This suburb makes a major contribution to the Sydney economy. Several government offices have relocated here since 2000, including the New South Wales Police Force Headquarters. Parramatta is a large, multicultural suburb which has attracted many migrants from India in the past 15 years.

Cabramatta

Cabramatta is a suburban area located 30 km to the south west of Sydney's city centre. This suburb grew rapidly during the 1970s when it received migrants who had fled the war in Vietnam. Today 35 per cent of Cabramatta's population were born in Vietnam and around a third of all Sydney's residents who were born in Cambodia live in this suburb.

Activities

1 Describe the income patterns shown on Figure 12.
2 Compare the population of the inner urban area of Pyrmont–Ultimo to each of the two suburban areas. Identify three key differences.

Percentage of the population who were born in:	Pyrmont–Ultimo	Parramatta	Cabramatta–Lansvale	Greater Sydney
South East Asia	10.6	6.4	44.5	5.3
North East Asia	17.9	9.9	5.3	5.6
Southern and Central Asia	3.1	10.7	0.5	3.7

▲ **Figure 13** Asian immigration into Pyrmont–Ultimo, Parramatta and Cabramatta.

Occupations	Pyrmont–Ultimo	Parramatta	Cabramatta–Lansvale	Greater Sydney
Professional occupations (%)	37.0	22.5	10.5	25.5
Labourers (%)	4.1	10.5	21.6	7.3
Working age population 15–64 (%)	86.4	68.7	67.9	68.0
Total fertility rate*	1.0	2.2	2.0	1.9
Average wage (Au$)	61,536	51,194	39,311	57,612

▲ **Figure 14** Selected census data for Pyrmont–Ultimo, Parramatta and Cabramatta–Lansvale.
*See page 60 for an explanation of fertility rate.

Region of Sydney	Neighbourhood	Percentage speaking a language other than English	Average income (Au$)
Fairfield	Cabramatta	80.1	39,311
Fairfield	Fairfield West	69.8	41,615
Parramatta	Auburn	71.0	44,401
Parramatta	Parramatta	48.4	51,194
City and Inner South	Pyrmont–Ultimo	41.5	61,536
City and Inner South	Surry Hills	25.4	64,496
Inner West	Leichardt	15.1	82,800
Inner West	Strathfield	50.8	52,005
Eastern Suburbs	Woollahra	11.3	99,527
Eastern Suburbs	Waverley	21.4	75,668
Northern Beaches	Manly	12.3	80,624
Northern Beaches	Warringah	16.1	65,442

▲ **Figure 15** Average incomes in selected neighbourhoods of Sydney.

Activities

3 Use evidence from Figures 14 and 15 to identify the best neighbourhood to set up a small software business. Give reasons for your choice.

4 Use the information on pages 56–7 to design an investigation into patterns of incomes in Sydney.
   a) Set an enquiry question or hypothesis using data in Figure 15.
   b) Predict the outcome of your investigation.
   c) Use the data in Figure 15 to draw a scatter graph (see page 75).
   d) What conclusions can you draw from this evidence?

www.transport.nsw.gov.au/
This is the New South Wales government transport site.

Enquiry

Sydney is a large city with sprawling suburbs. What is Sydney doing to try to improve transport systems for commuters into the city centre? Use the Weblink to help your research.

Introducing Mumbai: an Indian mega-city

Mumbai is India's largest city with a population of 18.4 million in 2015. The city of Greater Mumbai is built on a low-lying island in the Arabian Sea. As the city has grown, it has sprawled northwards and eastwards across Thane Creek to form a large metropolitan region. 465 km of suburban railway links central Mumbai to its suburbs on the mainland. However, there are only four rail crossings onto the island and this creates congestion for Mumbai's daily 7.5 million commuters.

Activities

1 Use Figure 16 to draw a sketch map of Mumbai. Include the city centre, CST, airport, container port and Navi Mumbai.
2 Explain why the site of Greater Mumbai has contributed to the problems of traffic congestion.

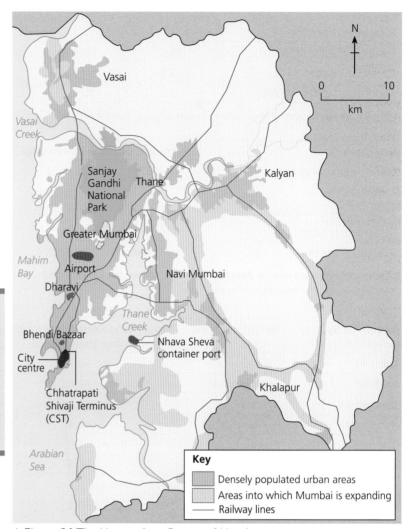

Key

	Densely populated urban areas
	Areas into which Mumbai is expanding
——	Railway lines

▲ **Figure 16** The Metropolitan Region of Mumbai.

◀ **Figure 17** Crowded platforms in Chhatrapati Shivaji Terminus (CST) in Mumbai's city centre. Double platforms allow passengers to board trains quickly from each side.

Transport issues – an inevitable consequence of rapid growth?

Large cities like Mumbai need efficient **mass transit** (or rapid transit) systems so that commuters can get into work quickly and safely. Mumbai's rail system is one of the busiest in the world. At peak times, trains carry three times the number of passengers they were designed for. People hang from doorways and even ride on the train's roof. Overcrowding is more than just uncomfortable – it is dangerous. People die when they fall from trains or are hit when they are crossing the tracks. At least nine people are killed every day on Mumbai's railways. How can the system be improved? Trains run every three minutes at peak times. It may not be possible to add any more trains without risking accidents.

Encourage businesses to offer flexi-hours instead of regular 9 a.m.–5 p.m. hours.
Reserve more seats on trains for elderly passengers.
Improve toilet facilities.
Prevent people from travelling on the roofs of trains.
Remove fast food kiosks and other vendors from all platforms.
Increase platform length.
Improve ventilation in carriages.
Demolish informal housing next to railway tracks.
Fit proper doors to all trains so passengers cannot travel half-in and half-out.

▲ **Figure 18** Possible ways to improve Mumbai's rail system.

◄ **Figure 19** Many people live dangerously close to Mumbai's railways in informal housing.

Activities

3 a) Discuss the ideas in Figure 18. Explain the best ways to improve the following:
  i) rail safety
  ii) passenger comfort
  iii) train times.
  b) Use the diamond nine technique (described on page 108) to rank all nine ideas. Which three do you think should be given the highest priority to improve services? Justify your choice.

4 Study Figure 19.
  a) Describe the buildings in this neighbourhood.
  b) Suggest three ways that people who live here are affected by the quality of their environment.

5 Explain why demolishing informal housing next to railway lines could:
  a) improve rail safety
  b) improve train times.

Why has Mumbai grown?

We saw on page 51 how quickly Mumbai's population has grown. Like other Indian cities, Mumbai has grown due to a combination of natural increase and rural to urban migration.

Natural increase of Mumbai's population

Natural increase is the growth of population that occurs when there are more births than deaths. Natural increase has been the main reason for Mumbai's growth during the twentieth century. One simple way to investigate this is to examine average family size, a statistic which is known as fertility rate. If women, on average, have more than two children, then the population will grow. Fertility rates in Mumbai tend to be slightly lower than in rural areas of Maharashtra. In 2007, the fertility rate was:

• 2.2 in rural areas of Maharashtra
• 1.8 in urban areas of the state.

Year (or period)	Fertility rate
Average 1974–1982	4.03
Average 1984–1990	3.45
Average 1994–2000	2.60
2004	2.20
2010	2.00
2013	1.80

▲ **Figure 20** Changing fertility rates in Maharashtra.

What push/pull factors explain rural to urban migration in Maharashtra?

India's rail system has some of the lowest fares in the world. It costs only 250 rupees (about £2.50) to travel from Kolkata to Mumbai. Cheap rail travel is one pull factor that encourages migration to Mumbai. People living in rural areas of India are attracted by the jobs and better training opportunities available in cities such as Mumbai. Poverty, the poor standard of housing, health care and sanitation are all push factors that can force people to move away from rural areas.

Activity

1 a) Select a technique to represent the data in Figure 20.
   b) Describe the trend in fertility. What does this suggest about the reasons for population growth in Mumbai?
   c) Suggest why fertility is lower in urban areas of Maharashtra.

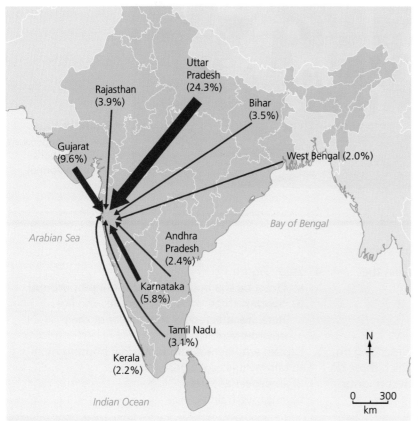

◄ **Figure 21** Migrant flows into Mumbai from other Indian states.

Factfile: Why do people move to Mumbai?

Out of 1,000 people who were interviewed about why they moved to Mumbai:

- 538 moved because of marriage
- 187 moved because a family member/parent moved
- 173 moved to find work
- 35 moved to improve their education/attend university.
- 62% of males gave work or business related reasons.
- 80% of females moved to marry or accompany a family member.

◄ **Figure 22** Where do migrants to Mumbai come from?

- from rural areas within Maharashtra
- from rural areas outside Maharashtra
- from urban areas within Maharashtra
- from urban areas outside Maharashtra

Name of Indian state	Number of households	Number of households with no bathroom	Number of households with a computer
Maharashtra	23,830,580	3,478,681	3,174,031
Uttar Pradesh	32,924,266	14,761,001	2,664,447
Gujarat	12,181,718	3,967,358	1,077,510
Karnataka	13,179,911	1,807,662	1,692,253
Rajasthan	12,581,303	5,595,753	869,923
Bihar	18,940,629	11,849,779	1,334,565
Tamil Nadu	18,493,003	6,625,321	1,956,630
Andhra Pradesh	21,024534	6,910,308	1,763,555
Kerala	7,716,370	1,097,456	1,214,644
West Bengal	20,067,299	12,869,502	1,668,757

▲ **Figure 23** Selected data for the Indian states which are the source of Mumbai's migrant population.

GEOGRAPHICAL SKILLS

Calculating percentages from raw data

The census data in Figure 23 is **raw data**, meaning data that has not been processed. It would be interesting to see whether poverty in Uttar Pradesh is a push factor. For example, are there more households in Uttar Pradesh than Maharashtra that do not have a bathroom? To make a comparison we need to process the raw data to find the percentage of homes that have no bathroom. You do this by dividing the number of households with no bathroom by the total number of households in that state and then multiplying by 100. For Uttar Pradesh this would be:

14,761,001 ÷ 32,924,266 = 0.4483

0.4483 × 100 = 44.83%

Activities

2 a) List five facts about the origin of Mumbai's migrants.
   b) In African countries, most migrants only move short distances. To what extent is this true in India?

3 Describe the main push and pull factors for migration to Mumbai.

Enquiry

Is poverty a push factor in rural to urban migration?

a) Process the data in Figure 23 into percentage figures.
b) Draw a scatter graph to show the percentage of migrants (shown in Figure 21) on the vertical axis and the percentage of households with no bathroom on the horizontal axis.
c) Comment on the trend shown by your scatter graph. What conclusions can you draw?

What are Mumbai's housing problems?

Overcrowding, poor sanitation and homes that are in danger of collapse, flooding or fire – these are some of the issues facing the urban poor of Mumbai. There are three types of housing where occupants are at risk because of the poor conditions:

- **Chawls** are a type of four- or five-storey tenement building. Families live in single rooms arranged along a corridor. Basic toilet facilities are shared by the tenants on each corridor. Many chawls were built between 1920 and 1956. They are overcrowded and poorly ventilated. But they are affordable.

- **Squatter homes**, also known as **slums** in India, are simple single or two-storey buildings built without planning control. Sanitation is very poor: 73 per cent of residents share communal latrines.
- **Pavement dwellers**, many of whom are children, live in huts which narrow the pavement. Pavement dwellers pay rent to criminals who control the pavements. The structures are illegal and may be demolished by the authorities.

Opinions vary about how these issues can be solved. Some people believe that **self-help** projects can improve housing or sanitation. Others think that **wholesale clearance** and redevelopment are the best solutions. Which is the most sustainable solution?

◀ **Figure 24** Traditional chawl tenements in Bhendi Bazaar that will be demolished.

▼ **Figure 25** Market traders in Bhendi Bazaar.

Activities

1 Use Figure 16 on page 58 to describe the location of Bhendi Bazaar.
2 Suggest how each of the following might affect the safety and health of local residents:
   a) Overcrowding in the chawls.
   b) Having to share toilet facilities.
   c) Insecurity of tenure for pavement dwellers.
3 Study Figure 3 on page 17. It shows Egan's Wheel. Explain how each of the following elements of sustainability might be met by the redevelopment of Bhendi Bazaar:
   a) housing and built environment
   b) social and cultural
   c) economy.

Is wholesale clearance and redevelopment the answer?

Bhendi Bazaar is a mixed area of chawls and 1,250 shops and stalls. It is estimated that 20,000 people live here. The chawls are old and overcrowded. There is no proper waste disposal system and water is only supplied for a few hours each day. An ambitious plan will demolish 250 buildings and replace them with 17 high-rise tower blocks. Work started in 2010 and some families have already been moved temporarily into a new tower block in a neighbouring district.

The new development is planned to be sustainable:
- There will be a mixture of houses and shops so people can continue to work locally.
- Wide roads and tree lined pavements will replace narrow alleyways.
- There will be open spaces for parks, green spaces and play areas.
- Mosques will be retained and enhanced.
- Car parking and connections to public transport are planned.

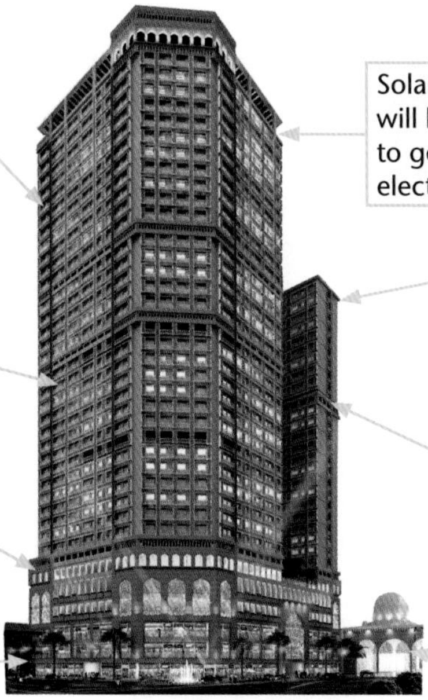

The aspect of the buildings will make the best use of natural light and ventilation in each home

Solar panels will be used to generate electricity

◀ **Figure 26** Sustainable features of the new multi-storey buildings at Bhendi Bazaar.

Rainwater harvesting

Sewage treatment and water recycling to flush toilets

Air-source heat pumps will use natural heat in the atmosphere to heat water in the tower-block

CCTV will improve safety for tenants

Wide, tree-lined pedestrian areas

Good lighting of communal areas

Activity

4 a) Discuss the strengths and limitations of this redevelopment scheme.
   b) Can you suggest three different ways it could be improved?

My home in Bhendi Bazaar has already been demolished and I now live in the 'transit' housing while I wait to be permanently rehomed. Life is much better here. We have moved into a furnished room. It has a carpet, curtains and a cupboard. There is a small kitchen with hot water and a washing machine. It is so much cleaner and quieter here! My children can play cricket in the open space in front of the tower block. We even have internet connection.

Mariya, tenant of the temporary 'transit' block

Large fire engines cannot get into districts with chawls like Bhendi Bazaar or squatter settlements like Dharavi. We need to buy mini-fire tenders to get into the narrow, congested alleyways. We also need to build new fire stations across the city. Mumbai has only 33 fire stations. It needs at least 100 fire stations to meet global standards.

Aziz, city planner

I am a street vendor and I sleep in front of one of the shops. Tenants will get a new home. But I am fearful that I will get nothing. There are thousands of pavement dwellers like me who make a living in the street market. If I can no longer live and work here I may have to go back to my village in Uttar Pradesh.

Taha, a second-hand wristwatch seller

In 2015 a fire quickly spread through Kalbadevi which is another congested neighbourhood of chawls. Widening of roads is crucial to make the area safer. I understand that the clearance of Bhendi Bazaar will allow them to widen the roads from the current width of 6 to 8 metres to up to 16 metres.

Mohammed, a firefighter

▲ **Figure 27** Opinions on the redevelopment of Bhendi Bazaar.

Urban and economic change in Mumbai

India is undergoing rapid economic and urban change. Its economy grew by around 6 per cent each year between 2005 and 2015 at a time when most European countries were struggling to grow their economies at all. A large group of young, professional, well-paid men and women is creating urban and economic change in India. This **emerging middle class** is an economic powerhouse. Many are young graduates who left rural lives behind when they went to university in a city like Mumbai. They then stayed in the city to begin a career in manufacturing or a service job in, for example, IT. In 2015 a team manager of software developers can earn over £5,000 a year in India. That's four times the average salary of an Indian worker. Higher wages mean that the middle classes can afford to buy consumer goods and luxury items. These items have to be manufactured then retailed in Indian cities. That creates jobs. Alternatively these goods are imported, creating jobs for city traders, bankers, hauliers and dock workers in a city like Mumbai. That's more jobs.

	2000	2014
Percentage of people working in farming	67	49
Percentage of people working in manufacturing	18	30
Percentage of people working in services	15	21

▲ **Figure 28** Changing employment in India.

	2000	2014
Percentage of GNI from agriculture	25	18
Percentage of GNI from manufacturing	30	24
Percentage of GNI from services	45	58

▲ **Figure 29** Where India's Gross National Income (GNI)* comes from.
*See page 72 for an explanation of GNI.

Activities

1 a) Use Figures 28 and 29 to create a series of graphs that show how patterns of work are changing in India.
   b) Analyse these graphs. In particular, what do you notice about the changes in manufacturing?
2 Explain how each of the following is creating urban growth in India.
   a) Low ages in rural occupations.
   b) University education.
   c) Demand for consumer goods.
   d) The emerging middle class.

◄ **Figure 30** Rohit Suri, vice-president of Jaguar and Land Rover India, which is a subsidiary company owned by Tata Steel. He is posing with a Jaguar F-type in Mumbai when the car was launched in 2013.

Why is Mumbai considered to be a global city?

Mumbai's economy is well connected to other locations both within India and abroad:

- The Hindi film industry, also known as Bollywood, is based in Mumbai and is thought to employ 175,000 people.
- Tata Steel, which employs people in over 100 countries, has its headquarters in Mumbai.
- Nheva Sheva is India's largest container port. Goods made in India can be shipped to Felixstowe in the UK, via the Suez Canal, in 19 days. Container ships from Kolkata, on India's east coast, take 28 days. This gives Mumbai a clear advantage in its global rankings.
- Mumbai International Airport is well placed to fly business people between Europe, the Middle East and Asia. London is nine hours, Dubai three hours and Hong Kong six hours by air.

Activities

3 Study Figure 32.
  a) Describe the location of:
     i)   Mumbai
     ii) Kolkota
     iii) Chennai
  b) Compare the distribution of Tata's sales offices to its projects.
4 a) Use a suitable technique to represent the data in Figure 31.
  b) Suggest what this tells you about the value of Bollywood to people living and working in Mumbai.
5 Explain why the location of Mumbai has given the city an economic advantage over Kolkata and Chennai in its global rankings.

▶ **Figure 31** Global film: figures for the world's four largest film making nations.

Film producer	Gross box office revenue (US$ billion)	Number of films produced per year	Number of tickets sold per year (millions)
USA	10.8	476	1,358
China	2.74	745	470
Japan	2.45	554	155
India	1.59	1,602	2,641

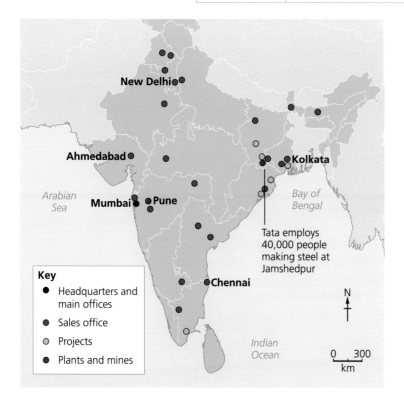

Tata employs 40,000 people making steel at Jamshedpur

Key
- ● Headquarters and main offices
- ● Sales office
- ○ Projects
- ● Plants and mines

▲ **Figure 32** The location and distribution of Tata Steel in India.

Enquiry

How important is Tata to the UK economy? What does Tata make in the UK and how many people do they employ?

Mumbai: formal or informal occupations?

Mumbai has a thriving economy. There are jobs in central and state government; banking and financial industries; the IT industry; textile manufacturing; jobs related to the sea port; and the Hindi movie industry. These are all **formal occupations** which receive a regular wage. Rules ensure that people are paid a minimum wage and measures are taken to keep workers safe. However, Mumbai's economy also has a very large **informal sector**. Street vending, rickshaw driving and recycling waste are all examples of informal jobs. These jobs are not regulated by the state. You don't necessarily need a qualification to do them and you probably don't pay tax. However, informal jobs have no paid holidays, pensions or sickness benefits and there are no rules to protect your health and safety at work.

Factfile: Minimum wages

Many formal jobs in Mumbai have a protected minimum wage. The table below gives some examples of monthly minimum wages:

Job	Monthly minimum wage (Indian rupees)	Equivalent in British £
A skilled worker in a bakery	9,352	92
A semi-skilled worker in a court of law	9,076	89
Unskilled worker in a hotel/restaurant	8,152	80
Unskilled worker in a film studio	7,580	74
Skilled pottery worker	6,073	59

Heads:	Tails:
1 I am a welder on a construction site. My employer has given me a six-month contract so …	I inhale dangerous smoke and fumes from the kiln.
2 I sell food on the street. I don't have a permit for a market stall so …	I can progress in my career.
3 I work in the family business making pottery. My work isn's checked by city officials so …	I know I will be able to pay my rent and pay my children's school fees.
4 I work for a large bank and I get regular training so …	I don't have much time to rest and I am always tired.
5 I am a young mother. I spend a lot of time each day caring for my children so …	sometimes I am hassled by the police and get moved on.

▲ **Figure 33** The consequences of formal and informal work.

Activity

1 a) Copy the statements in Figure 33, matching the opening 'head' to the correct 'tail'.
   b) Now decide whether each statement describes an advantage or disadvantage of formal or informal work. Complete a copy of the table below.

Statement	Advantage/Disadvantage	Of formal/informal work
1	Advantage	
2		
3		Informal
4		
5		

   c) Summarise the main benefits of formal work and informal work to the worker.

Dharavi: India's recycling miracle?

Mumbai is a city of huge contrasts between rich and poor. It is said to have the third most expensive office space in the world. It is also home to millions of people living in poverty. Informal housing occupies 7 per cent of Mumbai but houses 60 per cent of its population so they are extremely overcrowded. These slums develop on unwanted land: on marshland that is vulnerable to flooding during the monsoon or alongside busy railway tracks where trains travel at 50 kmph.

Dharavi is a neighbourhood in central Mumbai that is home to perhaps 700,000 people. Some people see Dharavi as a slum and a problem, with:

- long queues for toilet blocks and municipal water taps
- narrow alleyways with open sewers that are a health risk
- flimsy buildings that leak in the monsoon rains
- poor air quality from all of the small factories.

Other people see Dharavi as a model sustainable community for people on low incomes. People live in low-rise self-built homes close to where they work so the population here does not require complex and expensive urban transport. The residents are hard-working and most people work in informal occupations. Family-run businesses make pottery, tan leather or sort and recycle rubbish. There are an estimated 15,000 single room factories, employing around a quarter of a million people. Together they contribute around £700 million to Mumbai's economy each year. **Ragpickers**, as the recyclers are known, recycle 80 per cent of Mumbai's waste. In the UK we manage to recycle about 20 per cent of our household waste.

Activities

2 Study Figure 35. Explain why poverty in the informal sector may prevent India from:
   a) developing greater wealth in the economy
   b) improving education, training and healthcare facilities.
3 a) Describe the economic, social and environmental benefits and problems of the informal economy in Mumbai. In a second pen, write down problems that exist.
   b) To what extent do benefits exceed the problems?
4 Use Figure 3 on page 17 to discuss the sustainability of Dharavi. Explain the argument that Dharavi is a sustainable urban community.

▲ **Figure 34** A young ragpicker in Dharavi, Mumbai. Sorting recycled plastics is an example of an informal occupation.

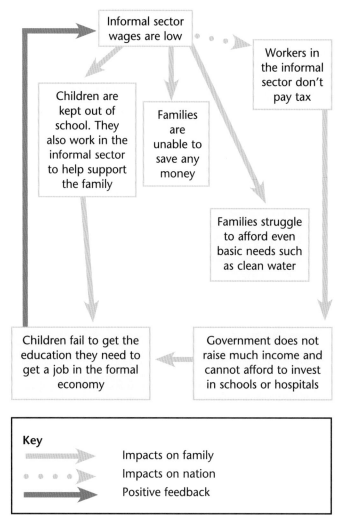

Informal sector wages are low

Workers in the informal sector don't pay tax

Children are kept out of school. They also work in the informal sector to help support the family

Families are unable to save any money

Families struggle to afford even basic needs such as clean water

Children fail to get the education they need to get a job in the formal economy

Government does not raise much income and cannot afford to invest in schools or hospitals

Key
Impacts on family
Impacts on nation
Positive feedback

▲ **Figure 35** The relationship between the informal sector and the wider economy.

How should Mumbai's slums be improved?

In 2003 the Vision Mumbai Report suggested that US$10 billion of public money and US$30 billion of private investment should be spent to improve quality of life and boost the city's economy. Vision Mumbai recommended:

- Improving roads and reducing congestion on trains.
- Clearing away slum housing and building 1.1 million low-cost homes. This would reduce the percentage of people living in slum housing from 60 per cent to between 10 and 20 per cent.
- Improving air quality, sanitation and water supply.
- Creating jobs in construction, tourism and retail.

Vision Mumbai is run by the Mumbai Transformation Support Unit which co-ordinates local authorities, property developers, the state government and the World Bank. This type of project is known as **'top-down' development** – where big decisions are made by public officials and business leaders.

Activities

1 a) List the four main aims of Vision Mumbai.
   b) Suggest how ordinary people in Mumbai will benefit from each of these aims.
2 a) Discuss the potential advantages and disadvantages of top-down developments like Vision Mumbai.
   b) Suggest three reasons why Dharavi should be cleared and redeveloped.

The redevelopment of Dharavi

Dharavi's location next to Mumbai's financial district makes it worth US$10 billion. Since 2007, large parts of Dharavi have been demolished and redeveloped. Property developers have been given the land by the City. In return, they must provide affordable homes in high-rise flats but they are also allowed to build offices and luxury apartments for the middle classes, for which they can make a profit.

Enquiry

How should Dharavi be redeveloped? Discuss the following points of view before recommending what you would do.

- Mumbai needs to invest in basic infrastructure, including modern waste collection.
- Dharavi is a sustainable urban community. It needs support not demolition.
- Dharavi is built on valuable land. It should be redeveloped as high-rise apartments for the emerging middle classes.

▲ **Figure 36** A potter in Dharavi, Mumbai. There are 2,000 families who make pottery in Dharavi.

Self-help schemes

Finance is a major problem for business people working in the informal sector. They have low incomes and few savings. Women in particular have difficulty borrowing money. High street banks won't lend them money and borrowing money from a money lender means paying back huge interest repayments. That's where **micro-credit** schemes can help. By joining a micro-credit scheme, informal workers can begin to save small amounts of money, take small loans, improve their businesses, and pay the money back at a reasonable rate. This type of **self-help** scheme doesn't need powerful decision makers or lots of money like a top-down development project. It comes from grassroots level.

The Grameen Bank was the first non-government organisation (NGO) to provide micro-credit. There are now many NGOs who provide micro-credit working in India. The Vandana Foundation is one such NGO which supports self-help projects in India, including in Dharavi and other slums in Mumbai. They support a number of different projects, including:
- micro-credit loans with low interest repayments
- enterprise training for small businesses
- financial literacy training
- after-school clubs for children
- free diagnostic health camps in Mumbai's slums.

Activities

3 Define the term micro-credit.
4 a) Suggest why micro-credit schemes loan money to the poorest members of society.
    b) Explain why women are reluctant to borrow money from money-lenders.
    c) Describe the benefits of micro-credit. Identify social and economic benefits.
5 Suggest why some people object to slum clearance and prefer self-help schemes.

Meet Pushpalata Chittikindi who runs a small business in Dharavi

I am the main breadwinner in our house and life used to be a struggle. My first job in Dharavi was making metal buckles for a nearby factory.* I could work from home but I also had to look after my young children and do all the housework. It was hard work and I often felt exhausted but at least I was earning some money.

A friend suggested that I should take out a loan so I could buy my own machine to make the buckles. But I was terrified I would never be able to pay back the moneylenders. Then somebody told me about Vandana. At first I was worried about paying back the money but the interest was low. I soon started to make Rs250 (about £2.50) a day but the work was very physical and I still felt exhausted.

I spoke to an advisor at Vendana and she suggested that I tried a different business. So I started making biscuits and snacks. It was a huge success and I paid back the loan within one year. I sold them from home at first but the business has grown so much I now rent a small shop.

* It is common for women to make small items for factories from home. They get paid a **piece rate** which means they are paid for each piece they make.

My family make pottery. We burn cotton, waste oil and waste cloth in our kilns which emit harmful gases. I am worried about our health. We need lpg (gas) cylinders, but no one is ready to address this problem.

Potter in Dharavi

I work in one of 20 family businesses which tan leather in Dharavi. About 5,000 other businesses in Dharavi use our leather. Leather tanning makes a lot of chemical waste. I don't suppose the Dharavi Redevelopment Project will have space for us in their plans.

Leather tanner in Dharavi

Mumbai does not have a formal system of waste collection. Without the ragpickers, solid waste and domestic rubbish would not be collected or recycled. Mumbai would have to invest in a European style rubbish collection system with dustbin lorries. Can you imagine them collecting from Mumbai's narrow streets?

Local politician, Mumbai

▲ **Figure 37** Views on the redevelopment of Dharavi.

What do we mean by development?

Development means 'change'. It ought to mean 'change for the better'. But how do we know if a country is developing for the better? To do this, we need **indicators** of development – that is, data to show how much a country changes between one year and another.

The most common indicators are economic. These show whether people's wealth increases or their poverty decreases. This is explored in more detail on pages 72–3. However, development can also be measured using social indicators, for example, health, education or equality. These indicators are explored in more detail on pages 74–5. This chapter looks at these measures to identify whether the gap between the richest and poorest countries is closing.

Development is ...

- reducing levels of poverty
- increasing levels of wealth
- bringing benefits to all, not just to the wealthiest in a society
- reducing the gap between richest and poorest
- creating equal status and rights for men and women
- creating justice, freedom of speech and the right to vote (democracy) for everyone
- making everyone safe from conflict or terrorism
- making sure that everyone has their basic needs of food, water and shelter
- making sure every child has the right to a good standard of education and actually gets it.

▲ **Figure 1** Different ways of seeing development.

▲ **Figure 2** Development is ...

▲ **Figure 3** Development is ...

Activities

1 Study Figure 1. Work in pairs to discuss this list.
   a) What are the advantages and disadvantages of each of these statements as a definition of development?
   b) Are there other statements that you would include in Figure 1?
   c) Choose the five statements that you think are the best definitions of development. Join with another pair and justify your choice.
   d) Working in fours, produce a joint definition of development. Each member must contribute and agree with the statement.

2 Working on your own, explain which aspects of human development are illustrated by Figures 2 and 3. Complete the caption for each figure.

Changes to average life expectancy

Since 1980, life expectancy has increased in almost every country of the world, as shown in Figure 4. The map represents countries according to what has happened to their life expectancy since 1980. The greater the increase in life expectancy, the bigger the country appears:

- Countries with large populations and the biggest improvements to life expectancy are the largest on this map.
- Countries with an already large life expectancy appear smaller, because they have less room for improvement.

Some of the biggest improvements have been in poorer countries. For example, in Cambodia, average life expectancy has increased from 54 years (in 1980) to 68 (in 2015).

Population and health

In most wealthy countries primary health care is generally very good and people have long life expectancy. However, as a country's population ages, the causes of death also change:

- Deaths in countries with low life expectancy tend to be caused by infectious disease (e.g. HIV/AIDS, malaria), and conditions caused by dirty water (e.g. diarrhoea, which particularly affects children). These deaths are reducing quickly, as global organisations such as UNICEF vaccinate against infectious disease, and as campaigns to get rid of malaria have some success.

- Deaths in wealthier countries with the longest life expectancy are most commonly caused by diet and lifestyle. The main causes of death are heart disease (deaths from which could be reduced by improved diet and exercise), cancer (caused by smoking and poor diet) which together account for over 80 per cent of deaths.

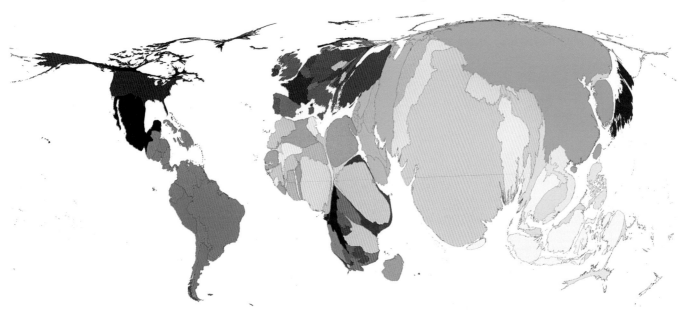

▲ **Figure 4** Increase in global life expectancy, 1980–2013.

Activities

3 Study Figure 4. Describe the distribution of countries which have most improved life expectancy.

4 Suggest reasons why life expectancy has increased in some countries more than others.

5 a) Explain why not all people in wealthy countries have healthy diets.

   b) Explain what effect these diets might have on health data.

Enquiry

How and why does health vary across the globe?

a) Research the phrase 'main causes of death in the world's poorest and wealthiest countries'.

b) Choose one major cause of death that is preventable and explain how the number of deaths could be reduced.

Using economic indicators to measure development

The wealth of a country is usually measured by its economy, or how much money it makes. This is measured by **Gross National Income (GNI)** per person. The GNI per person (often called 'per capita') of a country is calculated as follows:

Step 1 Add up the value of goods and services produced by people living in that country and by people overseas who are still citizens of that country. For example, the total earnings for Malawi in 2014 were US$4.26 billion.

Step 2 Divide this figure by the number of citizens of that country. For example, the total number of citizens in Malawi in 2014 was 16.8 million. By dividing Malawi's GNI by its population we can see that the average per capita GNI was about US$250.

US$250 sounds very little, and it is! Remember, it is an average, so some people earn more while others earn less. However, although this gives a per capita figure for Malawi, it is a bit misleading. Prices are cheaper in Malawi than in many countries, so US$250 will buy more there than in, for example, the UK.

To take account of this, the World Bank changes its data to **Purchasing Power Parity (PPP)**. This converts GNI into a figure that describes what that money will buy in local prices. For Malawi, the GNI per capita figure in PPP in 2014 was US$780, over three times more than GNI, because prices there are three times cheaper.

The World Bank divides the world's 215 countries by GNI per capita into one of three categories: High Income Countries (HICs), Middle Income Countries (MICs) and Low Income Countries (LICs). The Middle Income Countries are then separated into upper and lower incomes. These are shown in Figures 5 and 6.

These income groups help to describe the level of development of a country, that is, how far it has developed, and how it compares to others.

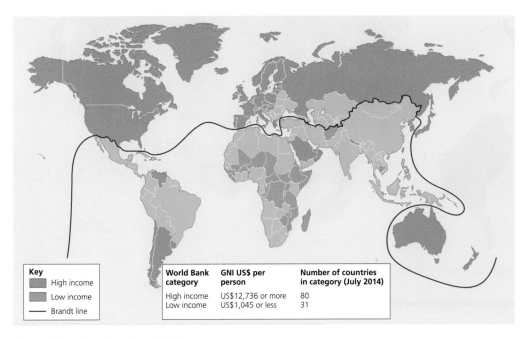

Key		World Bank category	GNI US$ per person	Number of countries in category (July 2014)
	High income	High income	US$12,736 or more	80
	Low income	Low income	US$1,045 or less	31
—	Brandt line			

◀ **Figure 5** The world's High and Low Income Countries. Colours on this map indicate GNI per capita.

The North–South divide

Figure 5 shows a clear 'gap' between the wealthiest and poorest countries of the world. This 'gap' was first identified in a report over 35 years ago by a German politician, Willy Brandt. His report drew a line, later known as the Brandt Line, which separated rich countries from poorer ones.

- The line showed that most wealthy countries were in the northern hemisphere, so these became known as the 'global north'. The line loops around Australia and New Zealand in the southern hemisphere so that they could be included in the 'north'.
- Poorer countries became known as the 'global south' because most were in the southern hemisphere.

The line dividing these groups became known as the 'North–South divide'. Other people call it the 'development gap'. Whichever term is used, is it still relevant to divide countries like this in the 21st century?

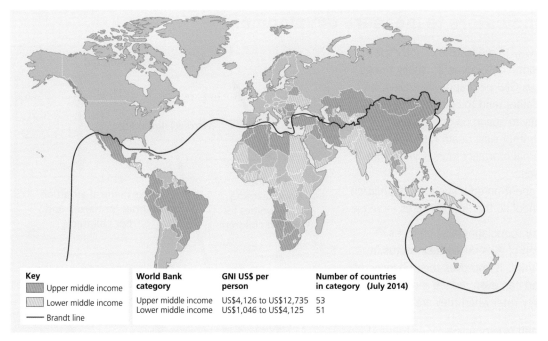

▲ Figure 6 The world's Upper Middle and Lower Middle Income Countries. Colours on this map indicate GNI per capita.

Key

	World Bank category	GNI US$ per person	Number of countries in category (July 2014)
Upper middle income	Upper middle income	US$4,126 to US$12,735	53
Lower middle income	Lower middle income	US$1,046 to US$4,125	51
—— Brandt line			

▲ Figure 7 How do you see the world?

Enquiry

Do you think that there is an argument for re-drawing the Brandt Line in the 21st century? If so, where should it go? Explain your answer.

Activities

1 Use Figure 5.
   a) Describe the distribution of the world's High Income Countries (HICs).
   b) Identify examples of HICs which i) do, and ii) do not fit the Brandt 'North–South divide' from 1980.
2 Now repeat questions 1a and 1b – but this time for the Low Income Countries (LICs).
3 Use Figure 6.
   a) Describe the distribution of the world's Upper Middle Income Countries.
   b) Describe the distribution of the world's Lower Middle Income Countries.

   c) Identify which of these Upper and Lower Middle Income Countries are i) north of the Brandt Line, ii) south of the Brandt Line.
4 Study Figure 5 and Figure 6. Explain which you think describes the world as it is today – the Brandt division into two categories of country, or the World Bank division into four categories.
5 Study the cartoon in Figure 7.
   a) Describe the two characters – what each is doing and how each is dressed.
   b) Explain who the two characters represent, and why.

Using social indicators to measure development

Money is not the only way to measure a country's level of development. Economic development usually brings social change too. So as GNI per capita increases, a number of social indicators tend to change as well.

- There is more money to spend on doctors and hospitals. As health improves, death rates fall, as do infant and maternal mortality rates. Overall, life expectancy increases.
- As more money is spent on education, more children spend longer in school so that literacy rates increase.

As these changes occur, population also changes. Improving the education of girls raises their status in society, as Figure 8 shows. It improves their chances of formal employment and can even reduce the size of their own family (their fertility rate) when they are adults.

In a few countries wealth is very unevenly distributed, so increased wealth makes little difference to the majority of the people. For example, in an oil-rich country such as Nigeria, almost all wealth goes to a few wealthy families and companies. Figure 9 shows how Nigeria's GNI is higher than many countries in the table, but this does not seem to have benefited its population. It's a matter of who gets the wealth and how it is spent.

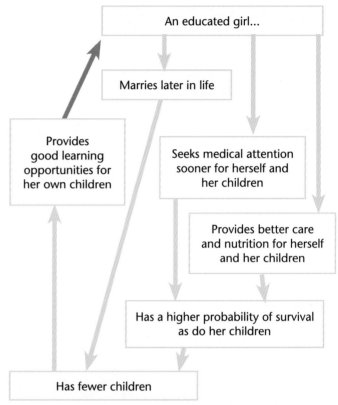

▲ **Figure 8** The advantages of improving education for girls.

Country	GNI in US$ (PPP)	Life expectancy	Infant mortality rate	Maternal mortality rate	HDI
Bangladesh	3,340	71	33	170	0.558
India	5,760	66	41	190	0.586
Nepal	2,420	68	32	190	0.540
Pakistan	5,100	67	69	170	0.537
Sri Lanka	10,270	46	8	29	0.750
Ghana	3,960	61	52	380	0.573
Malawi	780	55	44	510	0.414
Mozambique	1,170	50	62	480	0.393
Nigeria	5,680	52	74	560	0.504
Sierra Leone	1,830	74	107	1,100	0.374
Tanzania	2,530	60	36	410	0.488
Uganda	1,690	59	44	360	0.484
Zambia	3,860	58	56	280	0.561

| Selected South Asian countries |
| Selected sub-Saharan African countries |

▲ **Figure 9** Table of GNI and social development indicators for selected countries in South Asia and sub-Saharan Africa.

Life expectancy: the average number of years a person can expect to live when they are born.
Infant mortality rate: the number of children per 1,000 live births who die before their first birthday.
Maternal mortality rate: the number of mothers per 100,000 who die in childbirth.

The Human Development Index (HDI)

The United Nations (UN) developed the **Human Development Index (HDI)** as a different way of showing a country's level of development. The HDI gives a single figure per country, between 0 and 1. The closer the figure is to 1, the better. HDI is calculated using an average of four development indicators:

- Education – average length of schooling in years.
- Education – literacy (as a percentage of the adult population).
- GNI per capita (PPP) in US$.
- Life expectancy in years.

GEOGRAPHICAL SKILLS

Using scatter graphs to compare data

Is economic development related to improved health care and education? It is possible to answer this question by analysing data, using graphs. Before starting, it helps to make a prediction, or **hypothesis**, such as 'Countries with lowest GNI have low HDI indicators'.

Testing this hypothesis needs two sets of data that are related – known as **bivariate data**. In this case, the data are GNI per capita (PPP) and HDI. Find these columns of data in Figure 9. These data are known as **variables**.

To test their relationship, you should draw a scatter graph. Follow these steps:

- **Step 1** Draw the graph axes. The scale on the vertical axis should be for the data that you are trying to find out about – in this case, HDI. We want to know whether HDI is affected by GNI. HDI is what we call the **dependent variable**.
- **Step 2** The **independent variable** is GNI – we want to test to see whether it affects HDI. This goes along the horizontal axis.
- **Step 3** Label the axes 'HDI' (vertical) and 'GNI' (horizontal).
- **Step 4** Plot the points for each country. These are called 'scatter points' and the graph is therefore called a **scatter graph**.
- **Step 5** Your points should look like the one in Figure 10. There is a pattern to the plotted data – a line has been plotted to help you to identify this. This is known as a **line of best fit**. It does not join up points, but follows their general trend. There should be the same number of points on each side of the line of best fit.
- **Step 6** In this case, the best fit line shows that as one indicator increases – (GNI) so does the other (HDI). The hypothesis has been proved correct!

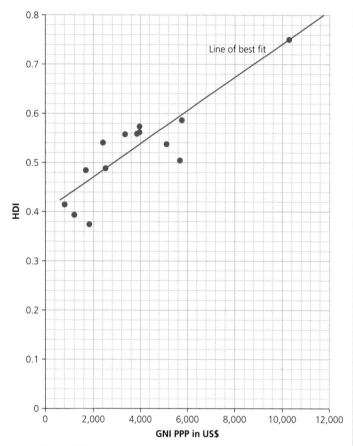

▲ **Figure 10** A scatter graph to test the relationship between HDI and GNI using data in Figure 9.

Activities

1. Using Figure 8, explain why countries that invest in girls' education often find that
   a) birth rates fall, and
   b) the health of their population improves.
2. Using the guidance for the graph in Figure 10, draw a scatter graph to investigate the relationship between GNI and life expectancy. Add a line of best fit and describe what your graph is telling you.

Enquiry

What should Nigeria do to reduce inequality?

a) In pairs, devise hypotheses to test the relationship between any two other pairs of data shown in Figure 9.
b) Draw a scatter graph with a best fit line to investigate this relationship.
c) Describe what your graph is telling you.
d) Based on what you have found out, write a 400-word report to the Nigerian government about why you think more money should be invested in health and education, and what benefits the government would get in return.

What is globalisation?

Economic development is now closely linked to the process of globalisation. Globalisation means the free flow of goods, people, ideas, and money. Together, these are making a complex global web of interdependence, linking people and places in distant continents. Few people in the world are now untouched by it. But what impacts does globalisation have on trade, culture, companies and communications?

Example: local people demonstrating about falling water levels in their wells after a soft-drink company opened a bottling plant in Kerala, India.

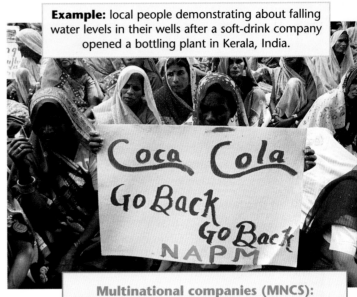

Example: avocados grown in Mexico are flown to UK supermarkets. This improves customer choice but food air miles have an impact on carbon emissions.

Multinational companies (MNCS): Large companies manufacture and sell their products in almost every country in the world.

Communications: The growth of fibre and satellite communication technology has increased global connections via smart phones, the internet and satellite television.

The factors that drive globalisation

Trade: Improved technology and cheap aviation fuel mean that fresh food can be flown from distant places to our supermarkets.

Culture: Western styles of music, TV and film are released throughout the world at the same time.

Example: films made in Hollywood, USA, advertised in an Asian street. But will local styles of music and entertainment survive?

▲ **Figure 11** The impacts of globalisation.

Activities

1 In pairs, study the four impacts of globalisation in Figure 11. Draw a spider diagram with four arms – labelled Trade, Culture, Multinational companies (MNCs), and Communications. For each 'arm', write in one colour pen the advantages that globalisation brings. In a second colour pen, write the disadvantages. Use examples where you can (e.g. of products, or films and music).

2 Based on your spider diagram, write about 200 words on whether you believe globalisation brings more advantages or disadvantages.

3 Based on the data and images on pages 76–77, create a display to show the growth of the economies of Newly Industrialising Countries, and their influence. Include details about:
   a) their largest companies
   b) movement of their populations across the world
   c) the ways in which new technologies have helped this growth
   d) the ways in which they now influence global culture.

How do newly industrialised countries benefit from globalisation?

Newly industrialised countries (NICs) such as India and China have benefited from globalisation with rapid economic growth. In the 1990s, they offered cheap labour so their manufacturing industries boomed. Their economies have benefited from changes in technology (e.g. container shipping) and from investment of capital by their governments and by multinational companies (MNCs). Now they are becoming centres of the world's largest companies – just look at how rapidly the growth of companies in Asia now puts them in the Forbes 'rich list' of the top 2,000 companies.

> **Flows of people:** Indian migrants work in many parts of the world, earning money which is often sent home to the family in India. In 2013, 734,000 people who were born in India lived and worked in the UK.

> **Flows of ideas and culture:** The Hindi movie industry based in Mumbai (known as Bollywood) produced over 1000 films in 2013. These films are extremely popular in South Asia and, with the growth of satellite TV, are easily accessible in other parts of the world.

Rank	Country of birth of resident UK population (2013)	Population (1,000s)
1	India	734
2	Poland	679
3	Pakistan	502
4	Republic of Ireland	376
5	Germany	297
6	South Africa	221
7	Bangladesh	217
8	United States of America	199
9	China	191
10	Nigeria	181

Forbes Top 2000 Companies List			
Rank in 2015	Rank in 2008	Country	Number of companies
1	1	United States	579
2	4	China (with Hong Kong)	232
3	2	Japan	218
4	3	United Kingdom	94
5	8	South Korea	66
6	5	France	61
7	10	India	56
8	6	Canada	52
9	-	Taiwan	47
10	7	Germany	45

	Mobile subscriptions (millions)	Mobile subscriptions (% population)	3G/4G subscriptions (% population)
World	6587.4	93	27
China	1246.3	92	33
India	772.6	62	3
United States	345.2	110	92
Indonesia	285.0	115	18
Brazil	272.6	137	55
Russia	237.1	165	29
Japan	137.1	108	85
Nigeria	128.6	76	8
Vietnam	127.7	144	20
Pakistan	126.1	70	-
Bangladesh	116.0	75	22
Germany	113.6	139	56
Philippines	109.5	113	17
Mexico	102.7	95	16

> **Foreign investments:** Indian companies, such as Tata are very successful in the world economy. In 2015, India's companies had taken it from 10th to 7th in the Forbes Top 2000 companies.

> **Improved communication technologies:** India and China dominate the global communications market with over 2 billion customers! India produces thousands of IT and software graduates from its universities each year.

▲ **Figure 12** Examples of India's interdependence with the world economy.

Globalisation: Nike are just doing it

Every year, the Forbes Directory researches and puts a value on every major company in the world. It publishes a Top 100 called 'The World's Most Valuable Brands', which tries to put a value on brand names. It also groups them by category, such as technology or clothing. In 2015, the most valuable clothing company in the world was Nike. Forbes valued its 'brand', that is to say the value of the name if it were to be sold, at US$26 billion. Most people immediately associate the 'swoosh' logo as Nike, and their 'Just do it' slogan is also an asset. Nike's global sales in 2014 were US$28 billion, that's bigger than the gross national income (GNI) of some countries! US$9 out of every US$10 the company earned came from merchandise with Nike logos.

Nike is a multinational company (MNC) because it operates and sells in over 140 countries around the world. 41 of these countries manufacture Nike products, as Figure 13 shows. In 2014, it employed 48,000 people directly worldwide. It provided jobs for 20 times this number in factories which are under contract to make Nike products. This process is known as **outsourcing**, where companies work for Nike for a period of time under a signed contract. It gives Nike one big advantage – that it can negotiate on price. In 2012, China was Nike's biggest source of outsourced workers. By 2015 China had lost its place to Vietnam, because China's currency has increased in value, which made its products more expensive.

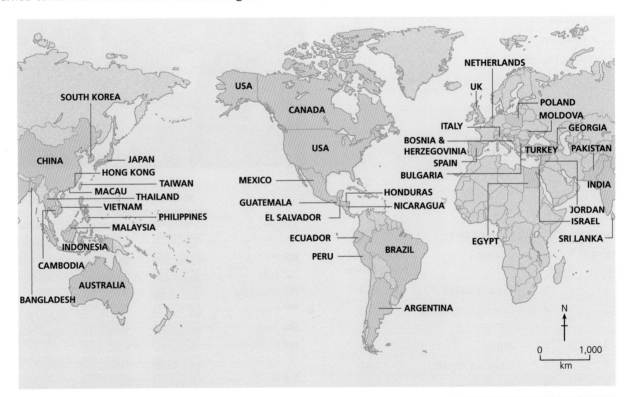

Japan: 1960s A factory making training shoes opened in Japan because labour was so cheap at the time. It was probably one of the world's first outsourced factories.

Taiwan and South Korea: 1970s Nike opened up its manufacturing here, using local companies who were contracted to make sportswear.

China: 1980s Nike began production here, taking advantage of cheaper labour in China as labour in South Korea and Japan became more expensive.

Thailand and Indonesia: late 1980s South Korean-owned companies making Nike products moved their manufacturing into Thailand and Indonesia in search of cheaper labour.

Vietnam: 2010s Now that China's currency is worth more, it is cheaper to make many items in Vietnam, so Vietnam has become the largest producer. Companies working for Nike in Vietnam employed over 140,000 more people between 2012 and 2015. China lost 43,000 jobs in the same period.

USA: today The location of Nike Head Office: Nike World Campus in Beaverton, Oregon. All research and development, and new product design is done in the USA.

▲ **Figure 13** World map showing the countries in which Nike manufactures its products.

Although small amounts of Nike clothing are made in the USA and Europe, almost all factories are located in Asia (Figure 14). Most factories employ a majority of women because pay is rarely equal for women compared to men. In Vietnam, the largest producer, many workers are migrants from rural areas. Workers live in hostels owned by the factory.

Manufacturing country	Manufacturing workers 2015	Workers + or -
1 Vietnam	341,204	Up 143,000
2 China	228,732	Down 43,000
3 Indonesia	186,425	Up 60,000
4 Sri Lanka	33,587	Up 13,000
5 Thailand	31,770	Down 20,000
6 India	28,165	Down 4,000
7 Honduras	26,090	Up 16,000
8 Brazil	20,935	No data
9 Bangladesh	15,090	No data
10 Pakistan	14,899	Up 4,400
Global total	1,016,657	

▲ **Figure 14** Nike's ten largest manufacturing countries by number of employees.

Activities

1 a) Represent the information in Figure 14 using a suitable map or graph.
   b) What are the strengths and limitations of your chosen technique?
2 Suggest why Nike contracts companies to do its work instead of opening its own factories.
3 Explain the risks for Nike manufacturing overseas.
4 Why do many countries such as Vietnam want to attract MNCs such as Nike?
5 a) Using Figure 15, calculate the percentage of a US$65 pair of trainers that goes to
   i) the country of manufacture
   ii) the USA
   iii) the retailer.
   b) Calculate the percentage of US$65 that consists of profit.

Nike and outsourcing

The company we know as Nike began in 1964 when Phillip Knight, a former athlete, began manufacturing training shoes in Japan, because of its cheap labour, and importing them to the USA. But all management operations and decisions – from design to finance and marketing – operate from the USA. The jobs in Nike's Asian and Central American companies are low-paid and unskilled. You can calculate from Figure 15 just how much of a US$65 pair of trainers goes to the manufacturing country, and how much goes to the headquarters in the USA.

	Cost
Production labour	$2.50
Materials	$9.00
Factory costs	$3.25
Supplier's operating profit	$1.00
Shipping costs	$0.50
Cost to Nike	**$16.25**
Nike costs (Research and development, promotion and advertising, distribution, admin.)	$10.00
Nike's operating profit	$6.25
Cost to retailer	**$32.50**
Retailer's costs (rent, labour, etc.)	$22.50
Retailer's operating profit	$10.00
Cost to consumer	**$65.00**

▲ **Figure 15** Where the money goes: breakdown of a US$65 pair of Nike training shoes.

Enquiry

What are the common features of MNCs?

Compare Nike with a company of your choosing, such as Apple, L'Oréal or Coca-Cola. For your chosen company, research:
a) Where it manufactures in different parts of the world.
b) Their methods of outsourcing.
c) Who they use as outsourced workers.
d) The benefits and problems that each company gets from outsourcing.

What are the benefits and problems brought by MNCs?

The benefits for companies who outsource their manufacturing overseas are clear. If labour costs are low, then a product can be made more cheaply and the price of the product falls. American, European and Asian consumers gain through cheaper goods. Job done.

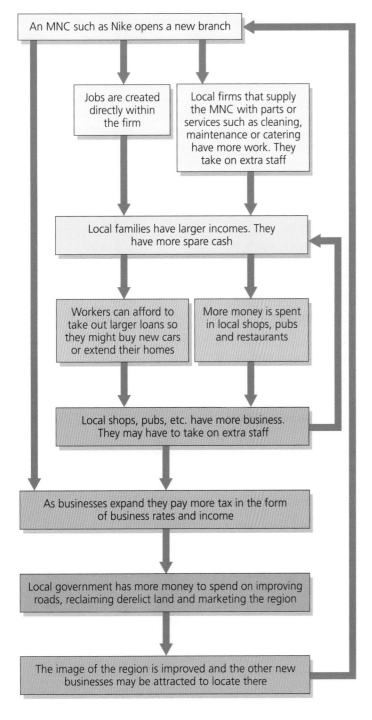

An MNC such as Nike opens a new branch

Jobs are created directly within the firm

Local firms that supply the MNC with parts or services such as cleaning, maintenance or catering have more work. They take on extra staff

Local families have larger incomes. They have more spare cash

Workers can afford to take out larger loans so they might buy new cars or extend their homes

More money is spent in local shops, pubs and restaurants

Local shops, pubs, etc. have more business. They may have to take on extra staff

As businesses expand they pay more tax in the form of business rates and income

Local government has more money to spend on improving roads, reclaiming derelict land and marketing the region

The image of the region is improved and the other new businesses may be attracted to locate there

▲ **Figure 16** The multiplier effect – how investment brings growth that builds on itself.

But what about the countries, like Vietnam, in which MNCs such as Nike operate? Do they gain as well? These are the **host countries** in which MNCs invest. In theory, host countries should gain, as after all, factories bring jobs. In theory, investment brings even more jobs. People move closer to a factory, which is usually in a city, to work. In turn, this means a demand for housing, which in turn leads to shops and services to cater for the working population. These have to be built, which creates a huge increase in employment in the building industry. New networks develop for transport services and energy and water supplies known as **infrastructure**. The process creates an upward spiral known as the **multiplier effect**.

So is there a downside to MNC investment?

Many NICs have few workers' rights (e.g. maximum working hours) and no minimum wage. The governments of these countries think a minimum wage might put companies off from investing there. Thailand introduced a minimum wage of US$10 a day in 2013. Within two years, Nike had cut the number of jobs there by a third. As wages increase in one country, an MNC might decide to move production to another country where wages are lower. Wage levels in 2015 were as low as US$1 a day in Indonesia.

Activities

1 Copy and complete the following table to show the advantages and disadvantages brought by MNCs such as Nike for:
   a) the host countries
   b) the MNC.

	Advantages	Disadvantages
For the host country (e.g. Vietnam)		
For the MNC (e.g. Nike)		

2 Explain why, in spite of disadvantages, an NIC might decide to attract investment from MNCs such as Nike.

3 In pairs, decide whether you think Nike should have invested in Vietnam in 1995. Explain your reasons.

Nike in Vietnam

Nike began producing sportswear in Vietnam in 1995. Vietnam was one of the world's poorest countries. But its people had a reputation for hard work from other companies who had already invested there. Costs were much lower:

- There were no trade unions, or strikes for higher pay, so wages were low.
- The Communist government was keen to develop exports.

Getting to know Vietnam

Vietnam has become one of South East Asia's most rapidly industrialising and growing countries. It has a Communist government which is keen to raise the standard of living through the growth of manufacturing and services. The government began to open up opportunities for investment by overseas companies in the mid-1990s. It began by welcoming travel companies and overseas tourists. More recently a programme of industrialisation has rapidly increased Vietnam's GNI and other economic indicators (shown in Figure 17).

	Vietnam 2000	Vietnam 2014
GNI per person (in US$) PPP	2,070	5,350
Where GNI comes from (%)	Agriculture: 26 Industry: 33 Services: 41	Agriculture: 22 Industry: 40.3 Services: 37.7
Percentage of people by occupation	Agriculture: 67 Industry and Services: 33	Agriculture: 48 Industry: 22.4 Services: 29.6
Value of exports (US$)	11.5 billion	147 billion
Export goods (in rank order)	Crude oil, seafood, rice, coffee, rubber, tea, garments, shoes	Clothing, shoes, electronics, seafood, crude oil, wooden products, machinery, rice

▲ **Figure 17** Comparing the economy of Vietnam in 2000 and 2014.

Enquiry

What should Nike do? Write a letter to the chief executive of Nike to show how you feel about reports of abuses in NICs such as Vietnam or Indonesia.

Nike became Vietnam's largest foreign employer with ten factories employing 40,000 people. In 2015, it employed 300,000 people. But Nike made mistakes in the late 1990s:

- All its sub-contracted companies in Vietnam were South Korean and Taiwanese, so all profits went overseas, instead of Vietnam.
- Factories gained reputations for sweatshop conditions. There were stories of abuse of workers.

The Vietnamese government attacked Nike for its practices. Nike found itself in the newspapers every day. Some stories were later found to be false, but by then the stories had reached overseas. The harm was done. Nike told the Vietnamese government that if attacks continued, it would leave. The criticism stopped.

Many pressure groups have tried to persuade Nike to improve workers' conditions. Many consumer groups want to see fair treatment for workers overseas. Pressure from groups such as the 'Boycott Nike' campaign in the early twenty-first century also came from US Congress. Nike now argues they have improved factory conditions, working hours and wages. Their workers live in hostels which are high quality, and there are agreements to restrict working hours. Nike now publishes data about all of its suppliers on its website, nikebiz.com.

▼ **Figure 18** Photo showing protestors in the USA against Nike.

Why have NICs emerged so quickly?

If you're wearing anything from a supermarket budget range of clothing, it's worth looking at the label to see where it has come from. Almost all budget items have been made in factories in Bangladesh. Bangladesh is a typical example of an NIC. Its economy doubled in size during the decade up to 2014, making it one of the fastest-growing economies in the world.

Figure 19 shows countries that are usually classified as NICs. Four of the world's five most populated countries are in the list (China, India, Indonesia and Brazil). Between them, they have nearly 40 per cent of the world's population. This means they have huge numbers of workers. They also have huge numbers of increasingly wealthy consumers, which means they are important markets for products as their GNI increases.

Every NIC wants investment from industry because manufacturing creates jobs and increases GNI. In 2014, the Bangladeshi clothing industry employed 5.5 million people and earned over US$28 billion in GNI for Bangladesh. The attractions for companies are twofold:

- NIC government policies have encouraged overseas MNCs to invest in factories. This is called **foreign direct investment**. In Bangladesh, most investment has been in the clothing industry. To help companies, Bangladesh has created export processing zones. These mean their exports to the EU or USA are duty-free, which reduces their price.
- Large supplies of cheap labour. In 2015, average wages in Bangladesh were 95 per cent lower than those in the EU and the USA.

Country	GDP per capita (PPP) 2014 in US$	GDP growth rate during 2014 (%)
Bangladesh	3,340	4.8
Brazil	15,900	0.1
China	13,130	7.4
India	5,760	7.4
Indonesia	10,250	4.8
Malaysia	23,850	6.0
Mexico	16,710	2.4
Philippines	8,300	6.0
Thailand	13,950	2.4
Turkey	19,040	2.9
Vietnam	5,350	5.4

▲ **Figure 19** Economic data for countries classified as NICs.

Social impacts

Increased GNI leads to improvements in education and health, and therefore life expectancy. Together, these form the basis of the HDI figures which have improved, some hugely, between 2000 and 2014, as you can see in Figure 20.

Country	HDI 2000	HDI 2014	Percentage improvement
Bangladesh	0.453	0.558	23.2
Brazil	0.682	0.744	9.1
China	0.591	0.719	21.7
India	0.483	0.586	21.3
Indonesia	0.609	0.684	12.3
Malaysia	0.717	0.773	7.8
Mexico	0.699	0.756	8.2
Philippines	0.619	0.660	6.6
Thailand	0.649	0.722	11.2
Turkey	0.653	0.759	16.2
Vietnam	0.563	0.638	13.3

▲ **Figure 20** Improvements in HDI 2000–14 for the world's NICs.

Enquiry

Should consumers in the UK buy clothing that has been made in Bangladesh?

a) Survey your year group with three questions about their attitudes towards buying low-cost clothing (for example, their attitudes towards sweatshops and child labour).

b) Collate the results and present them in a short report.

c) Explain the possible reasons why people still buy clothing produced in such conditions.

Activities

1 Describe three features of NICs listed in Figure 19.
2 Explain why low wages and sweatshops make buying low-cost brands of clothing controversial.

Economic impacts

Employment in Bangladeshi clothing factories is controversial. People in the UK ask whether it is right that clothing should be produced in this way. The main arguments are these:

- Poverty is common in Bangladesh, so there is no shortage of people willing to work long hours for a low wage. Are factories taking advantage?
- Although conditions have improved, there are many sweatshops deliberately employing women, who can be paid less.
- Bangladeshi laws mean that children can work in factories from the age of 14.
- Many workers begin work at 7 a.m. and finish 12 hours later – six days a week. Factory workers say that the usual minimum wage is £25 a month. Sewing-machine operators earn £40 a month, about 15p an hour. But a living wage in Bangladesh should be £160 a month!

'This trade has provided employment to over 3 million impoverished Bangladeshis, the vast majority of them women, and transformed the economic and social landscape of the country. Since 1971, the poverty rate has plummeted from 80 per cent to less than 30 per cent, GNI growth has averaged 5–6 per cent for over 20 years, and the garment industry has had a lot to do with it.'

▲ **Figure 21** The view of the textile industry from Bangladeshi journalist Zafar Sobhan.

Activities

3 Suggest why Figures 21 and 22 take different views of the clothing industry in Bangladesh.
4 Make a large copy of the table below. Using Figures 20, 21, 22 and 23, explain the economic, social and environmental impacts of rapid industrial growth in NICs.

	Advantages	Disadvantages
Environmental		
Economic		
Social		

▶ **Figure 23** Sewers working in a factory in Bangladesh that makes items for Ikea.

Environmental impacts

One of the reasons that many companies are attracted to NICs is that they have far more relaxed environmental and planning laws. In the EU, pollution laws are very strict. By locating in countries such as Bangladesh, companies can often reduce costs by not having to comply with strict pollution or building regulations. As a result, factories working in the textile industry may discharge waste water into open drains and ditches. You can tell which colours are trendy in the fashion design studios of Europe simply by looking at the waste water in the ditch! The impacts of poor construction can be very serious. In 2013 the Rana Plaza building in Bangladesh collapsed, killing 1,100 people – mainly young women who were working in a clothing factory.

'**The collapse of the Rana Plaza building is, to date, the deadliest disaster in the history of the garment industry worldwide.**

Some 3,639 workers toiled in five factories housed in the Rana Plaza building producing clothing for US, Canadian and European clothing labels and retailers.

Eighty per cent of the workers were young women, 18, 19, 20 years of age. Their standard shift was 13 to 14 and a half hours, from 8:00 a.m. to 9:00 or 10:30 p.m., toiling 90 to 100 hours a week with just two days off a month. Young 'helpers' earned 12 cents an hour, while 'junior operators' took home 22 cents an hour, $10.56 a week, and senior sewers received 24 cents an hour and $12.48 a week.'

▲ **Figure 22** Report from the Institute for Global Labour and Human Rights on conditions in the Rana Plaza building.

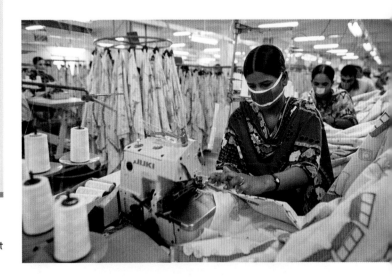

Tata, an Indian MNC

The Tata Group is an Indian MNC. Its headquarters are in Mumbai. In 2013–14, Tata earned US$103 billion from its 100 companies. Those earnings mean that:

- Tata is the world's 60th largest company (four places below Tesco).
- If it were a country, Tata would be the world's 61st largest economy!

Of Tata's earnings, 67 per cent came from outside India. Its companies employ 580,000 people worldwide. It owns subsidiary companies, including steel makers, car manufacturers, chemicals, energy and hotels. In the UK, Tata owns 38 companies, employing 50,000 people.

Its UK subsidiaries include:

- Jaguar Land Rover
- Tetley Tea
- Tata chemicals, which is based in Nantwich, Cheshire.

How do MNCs grow?

Every MNC started small and grew. This happened through:

- Sales growth – e.g. Apple, whose product range has moved from desktop computers to a range of electronic products.
- Mergers, by consolidation (merging with companies making similar products, to give more market share) or creating a conglomerate (building a range of different products as a safety net in case one fails).

Getting to know India

India has the world's second largest population, after China. Its population of 1.27 billion people is 17.5 per cent of the global total. Its economy grew by 7 per cent per year on average from 1997, and had quadrupled in size by 2015! India is now one of four NICs that have real global economic power – Brazil, Russia, India and China are known as the **BRICs**.

One reason for India's growth is its willingness to develop a globalised economy, combining a huge population and economy with the world's major MNCs. Its economy has grown because of globalisation – global flows of people, ideas and investment have helped India.

	India, 2000	India, 2014
GNI per person (in US$) PPP	2,000	5,760
Where GNI comes from (%)	Agriculture: 25 Industry: 30 Services: 45	Agriculture: 17.9 Industry: 24.2 Services: 57.9
Percentage of people by occupation	Agriculture: 67 Industry: 18 Services: 15	Agriculture: 49 Industry: 20 Services: 31
Value of exports (US$)	36.3 billion	342.5 billion
Export goods (in rank order)	Clothing, precious stones, engineering goods, chemicals, leather goods	Petroleum products, precious stones, vehicles, machinery, iron and steel, chemicals, pharmaceutical products, rice, clothing

▲ **Figure 24** India's economy in 2000 and 2014.

◄ **Figure 25** The Tata steel works at Port Talbot, South Wales. There has been a steel plant here since 1902. In 2015, Port Talbot and its sister plant at Llanwern employed 5,000 people.

Tata Steel and the global steel industry

Tata Steel is the steel-making subsidiary of Tata Group. Tata Steel employs over 80,000 people making steel in countries all over the world including India, China, Thailand and Australia. In 2006 Tata bought Corus – a large steel-making company with plants in the UK and Holland. Buying European factories meant that Tata could sell steel more easily to buyers in Europe. Tata's steel is used in the car industry as well as in construction of steel-framed buildings and rail tracks. Since 2006 Tata has spent £3 billion improving steel making in Europe.

In the winter of 2015–16 steel makers in the UK reached a crisis point. Cheap steel, imported from China, was being sold for less money than it cost to make it in Europe. China is able to make steel cheaply because it has lower labour costs than Europe. Another reason is the cost of energy. Steel making uses huge amounts of energy and the Chinese government keeps the cost of energy low to protect its steel industry. The EU could protect its own steel industries (including Tata) from these cheap imports by placing a tariff, or tax, on Chinese steel. In 2016 the EU tariff on Chinese steel is just 16 per cent whereas the USA charges a 236 per cent tariff on Chinese steel. You can read more about tariffs on page 93.

Steel makers in the UK struggled to sell their steel. SSI, a Korean MNC, was forced to close its steel plant at Redcar, in Teesside, with the loss of 2,200 jobs. Tata claimed that its UK steel plants were losing £1 million every day. At first, Tata announced that it would lay off some of its 15,000 UK workforce. Then, in March 2016, Tata decided to sell the UK part of its steel-making business. If no one could be found to buy the business, it was feared that parts of South Wales and Yorkshire would go into a spiral of economic decline – the opposite of the multiplier effect that is shown in Figure 16 on page 80.

> If Tata closes its steel making in the UK and a buyer cannot be found, 15,000 British workers will lose their jobs. It's not just the people employed directly by Tata – another 25,000 people work in jobs that supply Tata with parts and services. All of these jobs are at risk.

Institute for Public Policy Research

> China makes more steel than it needs and it is dumping its own unwanted steel on the European market. The EU could make this steel more expensive for European buyers but the EU's tariff of 16 per cent is too low. We have been arguing that it should be increased to protect our own steel makers but the UK government has opposed this plan.

Spokesperson for the European Steel Association

> The UK government has created this problem by refusing to agree to an increase in the EU tariff on cheap Chinese steel. They are too concerned about keeping on good terms with China in the hope that China will import more British-made products in the future.

Stephen Kinnock, MP in South Wales

> The cost of energy is between 20 and 40 per cent of all of our steel-making costs. If the government agreed to subsidise our energy costs we would be able to make a cheaper product and sales would increase.

Spokesperson for the UK steel industry

▲ **Figure 26** Viewpoints on the global steel crisis.

Activities

1 Give one reason why Tata bought Corus in 2006.
2 Explain why Chinese steel is cheaper than European steel.
3 Give one advantage and one disadvantage of globalisation for the UK steel industry.
4 Study Figure 16 on page 80. Draw another flow diagram to show how the region around Port Talbot, South Wales, could be affected if the steel industry closes.

Enquiry

What might happen to the UK steel industry?

- Use evidence from Figure 26 and your own research to suggest what would happen to the UK steel industry if:
  a) EU tariffs on Chinese steel were increased
  b) the UK Government subsidised energy costs for the UK steel industry.
- What do you think the UK Government could have done, if anything? Justify your choice.

What are the positive and negative impacts of globalisation?

The process of globalisation has had many impacts on how we live our lives. Many of these impacts are positive. Think, for example, about the choice of foods from around the world that each of us can experience by simply visiting our local supermarket or cafes and restaurants on our high streets. We can choose Chinese, Indian, Mexican, French or Polish – and that's just a few of the options! The explosion of different kinds of food is a direct result of globalisation. Our food is influenced by cultures from all over the world – it is one example of the **globalisation of culture** which has spread ideas about food, music, art, architecture, religion and even language, right around the world.

Another impact of globalisation has been the **globalisation of consumer products**. Thanks to multi-national companies (MNCs) we can now drink the same brand of coffee or cola, and eat the same brand of burger, whether we are in America, Europe, Africa or Asia. Coca-Cola and Starbucks are good examples of successful global consumer products.

▲ **Figure 27** Customers at Camden Lock Market, London, can buy food that represents cultures from all over the world.

Impacts on culture

We have seen that globalisation is driven by travel and migration; the growth of MNCs and sharing ideas through the internet, film and TV media. Two key drivers of the spread of western culture are the USA and the UK, the leading English-language speaking countries in the world. BBC programmes are shown on almost every airline, and 'Top Gear' is the world's most popular TV programme, shown in 104 countries! British TV companies lead the world in selling successful formats overseas. Over 30 countries broadcast their own versions of 'Strictly Come Dancing', 'Pop Idol', 'Britain's Got Talent' and 'Come Dine With Me'. Whilst these TV programmes may be popular with many, some people see them as a threat to their own local culture. Some think there is a danger that global music or TV brands will swamp music or drama that represents local or minority cultures, languages, histories and art forms. The UN has warned that half of the world's 6,000 different languages could die out by 2100 if nothing is done to protect them. Perhaps the world would be a more boring place if we aren't able to conserve a wide variety of different cultures – like the musicians shown in Figure 28.

▲ **Figure 28** Malian hunter musicians. Their traditional music dates back to the seventh century and has had a major influence on modern African pop.

Coca-Cola in India

Coca-Cola first opened a bottling plant in India in 1993. In the first ten years, Coca-Cola invested US$1 billion in their Indian business. By 2008 it employed 6,000 people, with a further 125,000 people indirectly employed in jobs such as distribution, e.g. lorry drivers. By 2015, it had 24 separate manufacturing locations (see Figure 29).

▲ **Figure 29** Map of Coca-Cola manufacturing locations in India.

Coca-Cola is one of many foreign-owned MNCs investing in India. Their investments are examples of global interdependence because:

- money spent by an American company creates jobs in another country
- manufacturing and distribution are done locally, not in the USA
- profits go back to the home country, i.e. the USA, where most decision making takes place.

Problems faced by Coca-Cola

However, not all has gone well. Large companies often face opposition, and Indian protest groups are unhappy with the way in which big MNCs sometimes operate. They claim that big business ignores the needs of poorer communities and disadvantaged groups. In the case of Coca-Cola, there have been protests against the soft drinks firm. Most protests have been by local people (see Figure 30) claiming that their wells are running dry as the company takes water out of the ground for the production of soft drinks. Some have complained about pollution from factories.

Coca-Cola deny that they have caused any such problems and are trying hard to win over local people by getting involved in local community aid projects to improve the company's image.

▲ **Figure 30** Local people protesting about falling water levels in their wells after Coca-Cola opened a bottling plant in Kerala, India.

Activities

1 Explain the difference between the terms 'globalisation of consumer products' and 'globalisation of culture'.
2 Explain the possible benefits of conserving traditional music, art forms and minority languages in the modern, global world.
3 Using Figure 29, describe the distribution of Coca-Cola manufacturing locations in India.
4 Suggest what benefits are created by foreign MNCs locating in India for:
   a) local people
   b) Coca-Cola themselves.
5 Outline two objections from Indian communities about local bottling plants.

Enquiry

Has globalisation been good or bad for India?

In a table, summarise the advantages and disadvantages of economic and cultural globalisation for India.

What are the other impacts of globalisation?

For some countries, globalisation is an opportunity. For HICs such as the UK, globalisation is the chance for goods to be manufactured overseas more cheaply than at home. For LICs and NICs, it is a chance to expand manufacturing industries, which leads to greater employment and an increase in GNI.

There is a third, small group of countries who see globalisation as a chance to enter the world stage. These include the oil-rich states of the Middle East, such as the United Arab Emirates (UAE) and Qatar (shown in Figure 31). They know that their oil cannot last forever, and are looking for ways to diversify (or broaden) their economies for when it runs out. Although each of these states is small, they have big ambitions.

- Emirates Airline, run from Dubai in the UAE, started in 1985, but by 2014 was the world's largest airline.
- Dubai has been the world's single-largest international passenger airport since 2014 (see Figure 32). There is a plan to develop its second airport, Al Maktoum, to accommodate 200 million people, by far the world's biggest, by 2025.
- Qatar will be host city for the 2022 World Cup.

The role of international migration

In developing big projects, both the UAE (population 9 million) and Qatar (2 million) have acute labour shortages because of their small populations. Almost all workers have had to be recruited from overseas.

- 90 per cent of Dubai's population now consists of **guest workers** from countries such as India, Bangladesh, and Vietnam.
- In Qatar in 2014, there were 1.4 million migrants working in construction in the tiny Gulf state, 400,000 migrant workers from Nepal alone. Many were working on the new football stadia for 2022.

Migration therefore provides economic benefits for the UAE and Qatar and for the migrants who work there. Conditions for many professionals who go to live and work in either location are very good. Subsidised housing and tax-free incomes are big advantages. Air conditioning helps living in 40–50°C of heat!

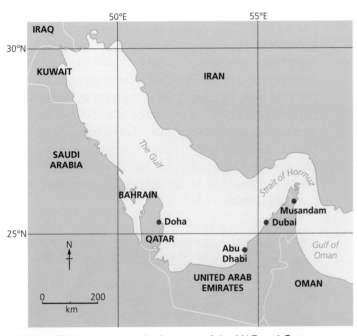

▲ **Figure 31** Map showing the location of the UAE and Qatar.

▲ **Figure 32** Dubai's international airport – part of its grand design to be the world's major air 'hub'.

Activity

1 Find the UAE and Qatar in an atlas. Using the atlas map and Figure 31, explain the advantages and disadvantages that each possesses as host countries for:
   a) global airlines
   b) the World Cup football tournament
   c) migrants from overseas.

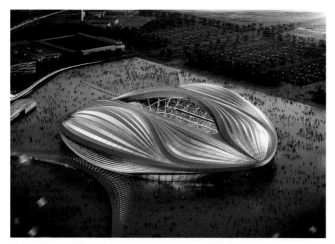

▲ **Figure 33** Image of the future: the Al-Wakrah stadium, one of the new football stadia being built in Qatar ready for 2022.

Jobs in the Middle East create opportunities for migrant workers and their families who often remain in their home country. Many migrant workers to the Middle East come from countries with high unemployment, like the former teacher from Uzbekistan in Figure 34 who moved to Dubai. He found better-paid work at Dubai's international airport. However, there's a cost to family life because his wife is still in Uzbekistan. She is unable to get a visa to the UAE. Like many who work overseas, her husband sends a large part of his income home. These are known as **remittance payments**.

My dear friend

My work here is ok and, of course, you are absolutely right, it pays much more than teaching in Uzbekistan. It really is a tragedy! How I miss teaching! If I was paid as much as I am paid now … the teachers in Uzbekistan can only dream about it. I am working at the airport as a check-in and boarding agent. I am at the Transfer Desk, we check-in transit passengers. Things are fine. I don't know how long I might stay with the company. Because it's a job with much stress, one day I am afraid I might get fed up. But so far so good. I have to be tolerant.

My best wishes to you

Akram

▲ **Figure 34** Email from a migrant worker from Uzbekistan in Dubai employed at the airport.

The downside of international migration

However, there is a negative side to migration in both the UAE and Qatar.

1 **Exploitation**. Once in the UAE, many migrants (both legal and illegal) are on the bottom rung of the work ladder. Many construction workers in Qatar have found they receive only low wages and no protection from exploitation. Many work long hours, seven days a week. In 2014, the Guardian newspaper reported that migrant workers from Nepal, India, and Sri Lanka were dying in their hundreds, killed in workplace accidents. The Qatari government confirmed that 964 workers from Nepal, India and Bangladesh had died there in 2012 and 2013.

2 **Abuse and harassment**. In a few cases, migrant workers have been the victims of harassment or racial abuse and violence. In 2014, Human Rights Watch claimed that women domestic workers were trapped in abusive conditions, similar to slavery. There are 146,000 migrant domestic workers in the UAE.

Activities

2 Draw up a list of advantages and disadvantages of working and living in the Middle East for:
   a) the Middle Eastern countries themselves
   b) the workers
   c) the countries from which they have moved.
3 In pairs, draw up a list of the Strengths, Weaknesses, Opportunities, and Threats offered by globalisation for those who live and work in the UAE and Qatar.

Enquiry

How great is the issue of migrant abuse?

In pairs, research examples from the Middle East or Asia of exploitation, or worker abuse, or illegal migration. The BBC News website is a useful place to start your research.

What are the impacts of globalisation on the UK?

London, 4 August 2012, during London's 2012 Games. The cheering in London's Olympic Stadium reaches a deafening roar, as Team GB wins its sixth Olympic Gold medal that day. The winner is Mo Farah, Somalian by birth but a British citizen. Earlier, Jessica Ennis-Hill also won gold, daughter of a Jamaican-born father and British mother. It's one of the upsides of globalisation. The UK is lucky enough to be the home of choice for migrants who contribute to its sporting and cultural history.

▲ **Figure 35** Mo Farah, Somalian by birth, but winning gold for Team GB in London's 2012 Games.

Year	Population (millions)
1965	54.3
1970	55.6
1975	56.2
1980	56.3
1985	56.6
1990	57.2
1995	58.0
2000	58.9
2005	60.4
2010	62.8
2014	65.0

◀ **Figure 36** The UK's increasing population.

The impacts on the UK population

Globalisation has brought a migration revolution to the UK. In 2014, 15 per cent of the UK working population was born overseas, and net migration into the UK was 318,000. By July 2015, the UK's population had reached 65 million, an increase of 6 million in 14 years, and the fastest growth in UK population history.

There have been two causes of this growth:
- **Net immigration**, mostly of young working adults aged 18–35. This is partly caused by the UK's membership of the EU, whereby anyone in the EU is free to move to and work in any EU member state.
- A higher **birth rate**, partially caused by immigration of women of childbearing age (15–44) and also due to rising fertility among UK-born women.

The UK Government believes that immigration benefits the UK. Like many HICs, the UK has an **ageing population**, with a smaller proportion of people of working age. Ageing populations are expensive because of pension and health costs. Governments need increased taxation from working people to pay for these.

Activity

1. a) Draw a line graph using Figure 36 to show the UK population. Extend the x-axis to 2050.
   b) Using the graph, calculate:
      i) when the UK population will reach 70 million
      ii) the size of the UK population in 2050.

www.ons.gov.uk/ons/interactive/uk-population-pyramid---dvc1/index.html

An interactive population pyramid for the UK showing change between 1971 and 2085.

▲ **Figure 37** Canary Wharf in London, where the knowledge economy is most concentrated.

The impacts on the UK economy

The globalised UK economy has led to higher immigration. Its manufacturing economy declined in the 1970s and 1980s, and was replaced by a growing service economy. Now, two groups of workers migrate to the UK for jobs here. Half of these are **highly skilled**.

- Many come to take up well-paid jobs in the UK's **knowledge economy**. These are jobs requiring expertise in, for example, finance and banking, law, and IT. Between them, people in these jobs produce 35 per cent of all UK exports.
- The majority of these jobs are in the city of London, where banks, law firms, shipping and biotechnology companies need employees recruited from the world's most highly qualified people.
- London now 'imports' experts from overseas, as there are not enough in the UK.

The other half are **unskilled workers**. There is plenty of work:
- Many dirty, difficult and dangerous jobs are rejected by UK workers.
- The lifestyle of many British families is sustained by unsocial hours jobs ranging from childcare to house cleaning and pizza delivery.
- Jobs filled by immigrants in sectors such as farming, construction, hotels, restaurant and tourism, which suffer from seasonal shortages of labour.

The social and cultural impacts

With 37 per cent of its population born overseas, London has the world's second largest urban immigrant population, after New York. Immigration is much debated by politicians and newspapers.
- Some journalists and politicians claim there are too many migrants: that migrants take jobs from local people and strain services such as schools and housing. In fact, the impact on services is more than made up by taxes paid by migrants.
- Others emphasise benefits of immigration. Many believe that the UK is improved by migrant skills and cultural contributions. They claim that diverse friendships, varied restaurants, and the cultural impact on British sport, music and media more than make up for any problems.

Activities

2 Suggest the likely reasons why UK manufacturing jobs declined after the 1980s.
3 Draw a spider diagram to show economic benefits to the UK of:
   a) skilled migrants
   b) unskilled migrants.
4 Draw and complete a table to show possible benefits and problems for the UK economy if:
   a) the UK reduced immigration
   b) the UK left the EU.

How far has trade hindered economic progress in LICs?

The theory says that trade is good for all. If no country can produce everything it needs, then trade makes sure everyone has all they want. Speaking in the 1960s, Martin Luther King (seen in Figure 38) reminded us that countries rely on each other for goods and services.

Since he spoke, larger, faster and more fuel-efficient aircraft and container ships move goods around the world. Globalisation brings everything from strawberries in December to the latest smart phones from China. Increasingly, countries rely on goods traded with others. Trade is made easier where partnerships have been agreed between countries. These trading partnerships are known as **trade blocs**. The European Union (EU), G20 and APEC are all examples.

> Before you finish eating breakfast this morning, you've depended on more than half the world.

Shop in any UK supermarket and you can buy ingredients for hot drinks: tea, coffee, or chocolate! Each is likely to have come from Malawi (tea and coffee) or Ghana (cocoa beans, the basis of all chocolate). Goods from overseas are known as **imports**. For both Malawi and Ghana, the European Union (EU) is its biggest customer.

Figure 39 shows that the trade of each country is different to that of the UK:
- UK earnings (US$834 billion) are 50 times those of Ghana (US$16 billion), and 640 times those of Malawi (US$1.3 billion).
- Ghana and Malawi's largest exports are either foods or minerals. These haven't been processed, like tea (leaves) or cocoa beans, so they are known as **raw materials**.
- More than half of their imports are **manufactured goods**.
- The UK, by comparison, exports a huge range of manufactured goods. Manufactured goods are worth more: a wooden chair is worth more than a piece of wood.
- The UK is also a global banking centre, so financial services earn over a third of its exports, e.g. interest charged on loans, and shares sold overseas.

◀ **Figure 38** Martin Luther King, the American civil rights leader.

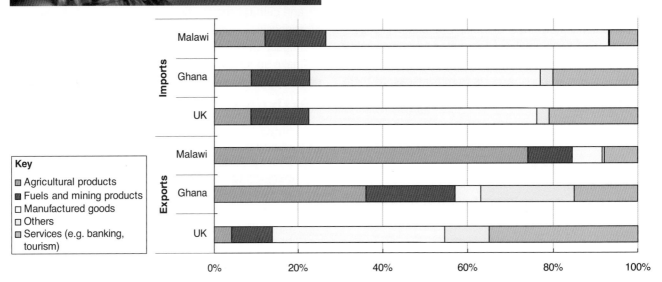

Key
- ▣ Agricultural products
- ▪ Fuels and mining products
- ▢ Manufactured goods
- ▢ Others
- ▣ Services (e.g. banking, tourism)

▲ **Figure 39** Comparing trade data for Malawi, Ghana and the UK in 2013.

Free trade

Developing countries rely on trade to increase their GNI. Since the 1980s, the world has moved towards **free trade**, that is, trade without limits, duties or controls. Each country within a trade bloc has a free trade agreement with other countries in the bloc, or is working towards a free trade agreement. Countries can export as many goods as they wish. This is good for producers who export goods and services. The disadvantage of free trade is that a country can find itself swamped by cheap imports from other countries, with job losses in its own producing industries.

To avoid this, some countries protect themselves from cheap imports in one of three ways:
- Placing **quotas** that restrict the amount of imports each year.
- Placing an **import duty** or **tariff** on imports. This is a tax on imports to make them more expensive.
- Paying a **subsidy** to businesses so that their own goods can be sold at a lower price.

Free – but fair? Fair trade and Ghana

Ghana joined the World Trade Organization (WTO) in 1995. The WTO exists to promote free trade between its members. Until it joined, Ghana's government had paid farmers a subsidy to encourage them to grow food for Ghana's cities.

It sounds fine. But WTO rules are that farmers cannot be subsidised, even though the USA and EU (who are members of WTO) pay subsidies to their own farmers. These subsidies make American and European food cheaper. Farmers in Ghana suffer because of imports of subsidised EU food:
- Ghana's tomato farmers find it hard to sell their produce, because imported EU tomatoes are cheaper, and factories canning Ghanaian tomatoes have closed.
- Ghana's rice growers have been affected by cheap imported rice from the USA.

▲ **Figure 40** Tomato selling in Ghana. Most farmers sell at street markets.

Enquiry

Are subsidies fair? Write a 300-word letter to the WTO, arguing why either a) subsidies to EU and US farmers should be allowed to continue, or b) subsidies should be abolished.

Activities

1 In pairs, research the internet to find out where breakfast items come, e.g. cereal, orange juice, tea, coffee.
2 Using Figure 39, compare Malawi's and Ghana's trade with that of the UK as follows: a) export value, b) import value, c) type of goods exported, and d) type of goods imported.
3 Using the data in Figure 39, identify three priorities that would improve trade for Ghana and Malawi.
4 Explain the advantages and disadvantages of farm subsidies for:
   a) consumers in Europe
   b) tomato growers in Ghana.

How does trade help to create global inequality?

Farming in sub-Saharan Africa tends to be of two types:

- Small, subsistence plots, where farmers trade very little and consume most of what they produce. Almost 90 per cent of Ghana's cocoa is grown on smallholdings. These are small farms of under three hectares. About 2.5 million smallholders in Ghana grow cocoa as their main crop.
- Plantations in which single crops are grown are known as a monoculture (the production of a single item). In Malawi, almost all tea is grown on large plantations.

Each country exports most of its coffee or tea to earn foreign currency.

Most tea and cocoa beans are exported to the EU, as Figure 41 shows. The main importing countries are the Netherlands, Germany, Belgium and France. The beans are ground into cocoa powder in these countries. Some of this powder is then re-exported to other EU countries where the chocolate is made. The main producers of chocolate are in Belgium, Germany, Ireland, the UK and Austria. 90 per cent of Malawi's tea is sold either to the UK or to South Africa.

What decides the price of commodities?

Tea and coffee are examples of raw products known as commodities. Commodity prices depend on global supply and demand. Traders buy tea and cocoa beans on the London Stock Exchange. If prices of cocoa beans from Ghana are too high, dealers shop around and buy from whichever country is cheapest. The pressure on prices is downwards. The same is true for tea.

Figure 42 also shows how production of cocoa beans varies from year to year. Production depends on weather conditions, pests and diseases. In 2010 production was lower in all countries. In that year, global prices rose because supply was short. When demand is high, the price for cocoa beans is high. Figure 43 summarises how price can be decided by supply and demand.

Producing country	1,000s of tonnes 2010	1,000s of tonnes 2012
Cote d'Ivoire	1,610	1,650
Indonesia	574	936
Ghana	490	879
Nigeria	212	383
Brazil	180	253
Cameroon	129	256
Ecuador	94	133
Mexico	37	83
Total (all eight countries)	3,326	4,573

▲ **Figure 42** The world's top producers of cocoa beans (1,000s of tonnes).

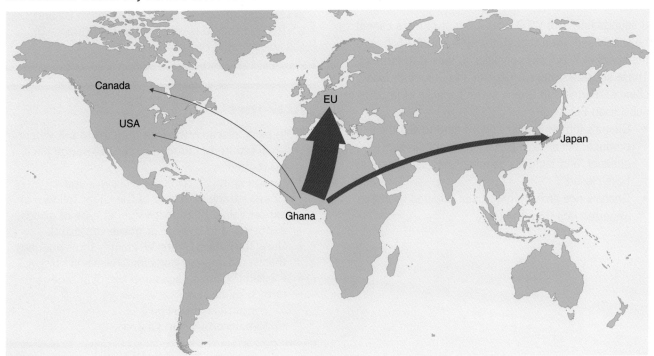

▲ **Figure 41** Typical flow of exports of cocoa from Ghana.

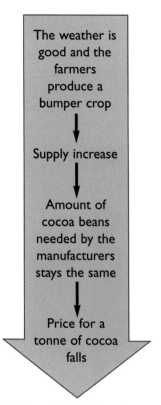

The weather is good and the farmers produce a bumper crop

↓

Supply increase

↓

Amount of cocoa beans needed by the manufacturers stays the same

↓

Price for a tonne of cocoa falls

▲ **Figure 43** Supply and demand.

▶ **Figure 44** How a) cocoa and b) tea vary in price on global markets.

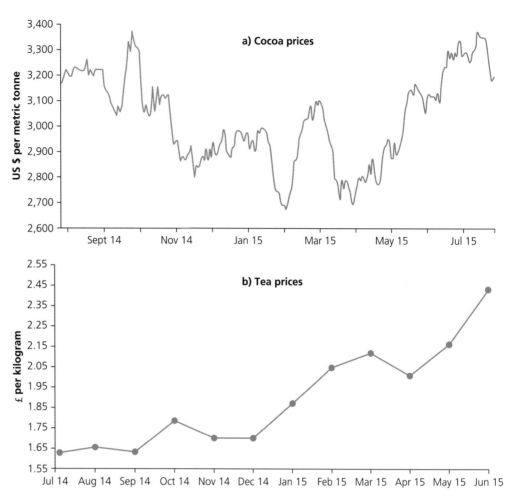

a) Cocoa prices

b) Tea prices

Activities

1 Use Figure 42.
   a) Choose a suitable technique to illustrate the data.
   b) Compare the amount of cocoa grown in Ghana with that grown in other countries.
   c) If the EU imports more tea or cocoa from other producers, what would happen to the price of tea or cocoa in Malawi and Ghana?

2 Study Figure 43. Make a similar flow chart which starts with the following statement: 'A disease in many cocoa or tea plantations means that the harvest is poor.'

3 a) Using Figure 44, compare the cocoa price with that of tea on the global markets between 2014–15.
   b) Identify the highest and lowest prices of i) cocoa and ii) tea.
   c) Explain the problems faced by farmers with such variable prices.

4 Look at Figure 45. Suggest what will happen to the price of tea and cocoa on the world market based on each of these future scenarios.

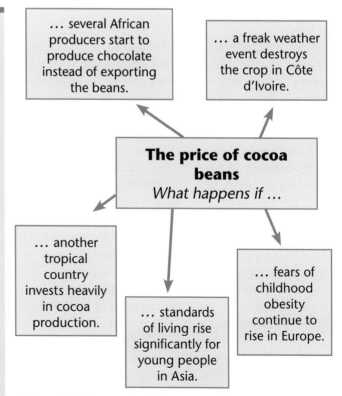

... several African producers start to produce chocolate instead of exporting the beans.

... a freak weather event destroys the crop in Côte d'Ivoire.

The price of cocoa beans
What happens if ...

... another tropical country invests heavily in cocoa production.

... standards of living rise significantly for young people in Asia.

... fears of childhood obesity continue to rise in Europe.

▲ **Figure 45** A futures wheel for cocoa and tea.

Is fair trade the way forward?

One of the ways in which Low Income Countries (LICs) can increase wealth is by developing manufacturing industries to process their raw materials. Why doesn't Ghana develop its own cocoa processing or make chocolate?

There would be a number of processes: making cocoa powder or butter, and then adding ingredients to make chocolate. Each stage would **add value**, boosting the economy. Each would create jobs, and chocolate would earn more money for Ghana than raw cocoa beans.

▲ **Figure 46** Thornton's chocolate – made in Britain using raw cocoa products.

The trade barrier

In fact, chocolate is made in Europe, the world's biggest market for chocolate. The manufacturers import cocoa beans or partly processed cocoa powder. It's cheaper that way because of import **tariffs** – or duties charged on imports. Import on cocoa beans in the EU are lower than those on processed cocoa. In 2015, the EU charged a 7.7 per cent tariff on cocoa powder imports and between 8 per cent and 18 per cent on chocolates, but zero per cent on raw cocoa beans. This is a process known as 'tariff escalation': the duty gets higher the more the item is processed. By the time VAT (value-added tax) is added to the finished product, a £1 bar of chocolate may be £1.25 instead. It would make Ghanaian chocolate expensive, and people would buy cheaper products instead. Similarly, Japan and the USA have no duty on unprocessed cocoa beans but charge large tariffs on imported chocolate of up to 65 per cent.

So Ghana has little option but to export cocoa beans, and loses the opportunity to develop its own manufacturing economy.

Where does fair trade fit in?

The idea that trade should be 'fair' is not new. The Fairtrade Foundation was established in 1992 to issue the Fairtrade Mark to products meeting particular international standards. These standards, and the Fairtrade Mark, guarantee a better deal for farmers and workers in developing countries to improve their standard of living.

It works like this:
- Farmers receive a payment that is agreed and stable – not like the variable prices on pages 94–5.
- Communities also receive an additional payment called a Fairtrade Premium to be used for local projects.
- One of Fairtrade's aims is to develop a long-term partnership with farmers, so they can plan, knowing how much they will earn.

It's not just about cocoa, Fairtrade deals with a range of foods, including bananas, coffee, tea, sugar, and flowers.

The Kuapa Kokoo co-operative of cocoa farmers

Kuapa Kokoo is a co-operative of cocoa farmers in Ghana. It sells part of its cocoa bean crop to Divine Chocolate Ltd in the UK who make Fairtrade chocolate products such as Divine and Dubble. The main benefits of this are:

- Farmers receive US$2,000 per tonne for their cocoa, or about 10 per cent more than the usual price on the world market.
- Farmers receive training to help them deal with pests or diseases, such as black pod, that affect the cocoa crop.
- Members of the co-operative can borrow small amounts of money from a **micro-credit** bank to invest in improving their farms.

- Farmers elect a trusted member of the village to weigh and record their cocoa beans. This makes trading more official and people more accountable, and raises the status of women who have been elected.
- Kuapa Kokoo are shareholders in Divine Chocolate Ltd. Profits from the sale of chocolate are invested in projects in Ghana.

The co-operative also receives an extra Premium of US$200 per tonne that is then used to fund community projects such as the well in Figure 47. Other projects include village schools, corn mills, and toilet construction.

▲ **Figure 47** The Premium is used by the producers for community projects such as this village well.

Activities

1 Use the terms 'add value', 'processing', 'tariffs', 'manufacture' to explain why the EU, and not Ghana, makes chocolate.
2 Explain three differences that belonging to a Fairtrade organisation can bring farmers.
3 Draw and complete a table to show the economic, social and environmental impacts of Fairtrade on communities in Ghana.
4 In pairs, discuss whether 'all trade should be fair trade'. Feed back your ideas to the class. Make sure you justify your decision.

Enquiry

Are Fairtrade products more expensive? Use two UK supermarket websites to research whether Fairtrade bananas, coffee, tea and chocolate are more expensive than non-Fairtrade products.

Investigating long-term aid

Why give aid? Who gives it and what is it for? We are all familiar with the TV appeals after there has been a natural disaster such as a major earthquake. Such aid is known as **emergency aid**. However, most aid is, in fact, planned over long periods of time to tackle poverty and improve health and education. This type of aid is known as long-term or **development aid**. One example can be seen in Malawi, an LIC in southern Africa.

Getting to know Malawi

Malawi was one of sub-Saharan Africa's poorest countries in the 1970s, and it remains so. Although keen to develop manufacturing and services, there are several barriers:

- It is landlocked (it has no coast) which raises the costs of transporting goods to the coast for export.
- It exports little compared to other countries.
- It has suffered major impacts from deaths caused by HIV/AIDS.

	Malawi 2000	Malawi 2014
GNI per person (in US$) PPP	490	780
Population living below poverty line (%)	54	53
Where GNI comes from (%)	Agriculture: 37 Industry: 29 Services: 34	Agriculture: 30.1 Industry: 18.5 Services: 51.3
Percentage of people by occupation	Agriculture: 86 Industry and services: 14	Agriculture: 90 Industry and services: 10
Value of exports (US$)	0.5 billion	1.3 billion
Export goods (in rank order)	Tobacco, tea, sugar, cotton, coffee, peanuts, wood products	Tobacco (53%), tea, sugar, cotton, coffee, peanuts, wood products, clothes

▲ **Figure 48** Comparing the economy of Malawi in 2000 and 2014.

Activity

1 Use data in Figure 48 to provide evidence that Malawi is an LIC.

Providing development aid to Malawi

Middle Shire is a district in southern Malawi named after a local river, the Shire. The river is vital to this part of Malawi, because it provides most of Malawi's hydro-electric power (HEP). It's an agricultural region. Most families are **subsistence farmers**, growing crops such as maize or cassava. Others work on large sugar cane and cotton plantations.

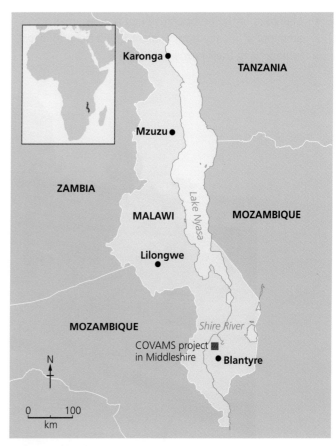

▲ **Figure 49** Map showing the location of the COVAMS project in Middle Shire.

But Middle Shire has a problem. It is affected by **soil erosion** during the intense rainy season each year. Between 1990 and 2005, Malawi lost 13 per cent of its forest due to land clearance for farming. Two pressures have caused this:

- A rapidly rising population. The population of Middle Shire has doubled since 1980, so farmers have cut down forest to grow more food.
- Tobacco, Malawi's most valuable export, has suffered falling prices because of global over-production and falling consumption in HICs of the world. So, if farmers are to earn the same income, they must grow more tobacco.

▲ **Figure 50** An agricultural training scheme in Malawi.

COVAMS – saving the soil

A project in Middle Shire aims to save soils and re-plant trees. It's known as Community Vitalization and Afforestation in Middle Shire (COVAMS), a ten-year aid project funded by the Japanese government. It is designed to build **capacity**, which means it aims to allow Malawi to increase food and jobs. The project uses several methods to prevent soil erosion:

- Explain to communities what causes soil erosion.
- Build rock, wood and bamboo barriers across streams to prevent soil loss during rainy seasons.
- Train villagers how to conserve soil and plant trees.
- Train farmers to plough around hillsides, following the contours rather than ploughing up and down the hills, which increases surface run-off.
- Build terraces into hillsides to reduce surface run-off.
- Supply fast-growing tree species from local nurseries to speed up **reafforestation**.

This approach uses **intermediate technology**, teaching local people skills in using local materials to provide low-cost solutions to problems. It has had three impacts:

- By 2011, 75 per cent of households in Middle Shire had taken part.

- Crop yields improved dramatically.
- With less soil erosion, water quality improved in the dams, so Malawi produces more HEP.

Why do countries give aid?

Malawi benefits from aid, especially long-term projects such as COVAMS. But Japan also benefits for the following reasons:

- **Diplomacy and good relations.** Aid improves relations between countries, and enables the Japanese to influence politicians in southern Africa.
- **Tactics.** Japan is keen to become a member of the UN Security Council, and needs the support of African countries.
- **Economics.** Sub-Saharan Africa countries have averaged 5 per cent annual economic growth during the 21st century. Japan sees opportunities to sell more Japanese products in Malawi if it invests in Malawi.

Enquiry

Analyse the impacts of COVAMS. Create a table to show the economic, social and environmental impacts of COVAMS on Middle Shire.

Activities

2 In pairs, design a flow diagram to show causes, processes and effects of soil erosion.
3 Explain why it is important to train Malawian farmers about how to prevent soil erosion.
4 Write a five-minute script for local radio in Middle Shire to tell people about the COVAMS project.

Emergency aid – the Ebola outbreak 2014–15

The villages of coastal West Africa rarely make the news in the UK. However, in March 2014, some of the world's poorest LICs: Guinea, Sierra Leone, and Liberia, shown in Figure 51, were under the media spotlight. The reason was Ebola, one of the world's deadliest diseases. A lethal strain of Ebola had appeared in these countries. First discovered in 1976, this was the most serious outbreak to date.

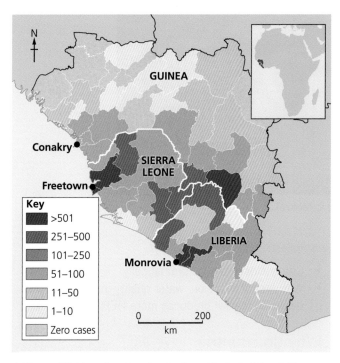

Key
- >501
- 251–500
- 101–250
- 51–100
- 11–50
- 1–10
- Zero cases

0   200
km

▲ **Figure 51** Map showing deaths from Ebola in West Africa.

Activities

1 Use Figure 51 to describe the location and distribution of the largest number of deaths during the Ebola outbreak.
2 Using data in Figure 52, explain how poverty and vulnerability are connected.

Country	GNI per capita (US$ PPP)	HDI score (and ranking out of 187)	Doctors per 1,000 people	Infant mortality
Guinea	1,140	0.392 (179th)	0.1	53.4
Sierra Leone	1,830	0.374 (183rd)	0.02	71.7
Liberia	820	0.412 (175th)	0.01	67.5
UK	38,370	0.892 (14th)	2.8	4.4

▲ **Figure 52** Poverty indicators for the three most-affected countries.

What is Ebola?

Ebola is a virus (the same sort of illness as flu and a common cold, but much more serious). It spreads by direct contact, including water molecules from someone sneezing. Because of this, it poses a danger to health workers as well as patients.

Ebola's symptoms are like flu, but rapidly become more serious. Symptoms begin between 2 and 21 days after infection. It begins with a fever and headache, joint and muscle pain, sore throat, and muscle weakness. Diarrhoea, vomiting, a rash, stomach pain and reduced kidney and liver function follow. The patient bleeds internally, and from the ears, eyes, nose or mouth. Ebola is fatal in about 40 per cent of cases, though that is falling. The earlier that treatment is given, the better the chances of survival. During 2015, treatment became possible and death rates fell.

Poverty and vulnerability

Before the outbreak, over half of Liberia's population lived below the **poverty line**. Ebola made this worse.

This part of West Africa contains some of the world's poorest countries, as Figure 52 shows. Poverty makes people **vulnerable**:

- They are less well fed or able to resist disease.
- Living conditions, e.g. lack of sanitation, make the spread of disease likely.
- They are likely to carry on working because they cannot afford not to, and so treatment often comes too late.
- They have no savings, and cannot afford private medical care.

Many people lost friends and relatives, as well as jobs, savings (after paying for health care) and a season planting crops. Oxfam found that incomes of three-quarters of the population fell, and 60 per cent said they hadn't had enough food in the past week. To cope, many had to borrow money, reduce meals each day, or miss meals to allow children to eat.

Oxfam's response to the Ebola outbreak

Oxfam raised money to fight the outbreak, together with the Red Cross and the French charity Médecins Sans Frontières. They organised emergency fundraising campaigns, and during 2014–15 spent £28m in the countries affected.

In total, Oxfam helped 3.2 million people. They had two main roles:
- Supporting medical care with water, sanitation and cleaning equipment.
- Working with communities to raise awareness of the disease and help with treatment, safe burials and tracing contacts.

▲ **Figure 53** An ambulance driver in protective clothing is disinfected with chlorine after returning from transporting an Ebola victim to a treatment centre in Freetown, Sierra Leone (2014).

Medical care

Health care helped doctors in diagnosing, isolating and treating those affected. Oxfam provided funding for:
- Building medical facilities and equipping them, e.g. facemasks, boots, gloves and soap.
- Providing infrastructure for dozens of health centres in Sierra Leone and Liberia, e.g. water tanks and pipes.
- Building community hand-washing stations.
- Providing teams to carry out contact tracing.
- Safe burial of the dead, providing kits containing e.g. masks, overalls, boots, gloves, body bags.

Working with communities

In Liberia, Oxfam:
- provided financial support to 15,000 families
- built and repaired toilets and water points in 400 schools
- trained teachers and students in good hygiene to improve community health and reduce the risk of future outbreaks.

Enquiry

Evaluate how far you think Oxfam's efforts were successful in the Ebola outbreak. Use evidence to justify your decision.

Factfile: Ebola 2014 to 2015

Total number of cases: 27,741

Deaths: 11,284

Death toll by country:

- Liberia: 4,808
- Sierra Leone: 3,949
- Guinea: 2,512
- Nigeria: 8
- Mali: 6
- USA: 1

In 2014, there was a separate outbreak of Ebola in the Democratic Republic of Congo, killing 43 people. However, this was a different strain, and not linked to the outbreak in West Africa. In July 2015, a new vaccine against Ebola was announced.

Activities

3 Using the Ebola Factfile, calculate the percentage of:
   a) those infected who died
   b) deaths in each country affected.
4 a) Create a table to show the economic, social and environmental impacts of Ebola.
   b) Decide which impacts were greatest and explain why.
5 Using Figure 53, explain why treating Ebola is more expensive than many other diseases.
6 Design a poster to assist Oxfam's campaign to either a) make people more aware of Ebola and its symptoms, or b) improve public hygiene to prevent further spread of Ebola.

Chapter 7
Problem-solving exercise: Rural development in South Africa

Investigating rural to urban migration to Johannesburg, South Africa

Johannesburg is South Africa's largest city and also the top-ranked global city in the whole of Africa. Johannesburg is located in Gauteng Province which is rich in mineral deposits including gold, coal, iron, nickel, aluminium and platinum. Johannesburg is connected to other global cities such as London and New York by flows of money and trade – especially trade in minerals.

The neighbouring province of Limpopo is very rural. Johannesburg is connected to Limpopo by rural to urban migration – young people hope they will find a better job and a better standard of living by moving to the city. Consequently, Johannesburg is growing quickly. According to the South African census, its population grew from 3,226,055 in 2001 to 4,434,827 in 2011.

▲ **Figure 1** The stock exchange, Johannesburg, where traders buy and sell commodities such as minerals on the world market.

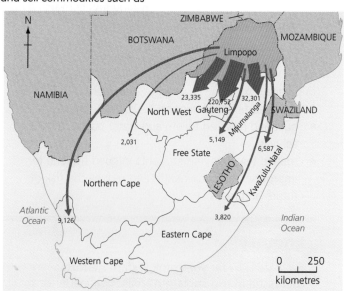

▲ **Figure 2** Average annual migration from Limpopo Province during 2011–16.

Activities

1 Describe two ways in which Johannesburg is connected to other places.
2 Study Figure 2. Copy and complete the following sentences to describe migration from Limpopo.

   Most migrants move *short/long* distances.

   The number of migrants who move to Gauteng is *20/24/28* times greater than the number of migrants who move to Western Cape.

What are the push/pull factors for rural to urban migration in South Africa?

People living in rural areas such as Mutale, which is a municipality in northern Limpopo, are attracted by the jobs and better opportunities available in Johannesburg. Unemployment and low wages are a problem in Johannesburg. Youth unemployment in Johannesburg is 31.5 per cent, which is very high. But youth unemployment in Mutale is an astonishing 62.2 per cent. Lack of money, poor job opportunities and poor access to basic facilities such as clean water and electricity are all push factors that can force people to move away from rural areas such as Mutale.

Percentage of households with:	Mutale	Johannesburg
Flush toilet connected to the sewerage system	3.8	87.1
Pit toilet	92.6	6.0
Connection to a safe water supply	63.0	92.0
Electric or gas stove	44.9	86.6
Television	66.6	83.8
Computer	7.7	33.6
Motor car	15.6	38.2

▲ **Figure 3** Comparing standard of living between Mutale (in Limpopo) and Johannesburg.

	Jan	Feb	Mar	Apr	May	Jun	Jul	Aug	Sep	Oct	Nov	Dec
Average daytime temperature °C	31	31	30	29	27	25	25	28	30	30	31	31
Average precipitation (mm)	54	79	66	28	4	15	10	13	9	36	71	94

▲ **Figure 4** Climate data for Mutale, Limpopo.

http://tellmaps.com/mapsalive

Uses a **Geographical Information System (GIS)** to display an online atlas of South Africa. It uses data from the most recent census which can be displayed in either map or graph form.

Province	Percentage in poverty	Population (est. 2015)
Limpopo	78.9	5,726,800
Eastern Cape	70.6	6,916,200
Mpumalanga	67.1	4,283,900
KwaZulu-Natal	65.0	10,919,100
Northern Cape	63.0	1,185,600
Free State	61.9	2,817,900
North West	61.4	3,707,000
Western Cape	35.4	6,200,100
Gauteng Province	33.0	13,200,300

▲ **Figure 5** Percentage of people living in poverty in each province of South Africa.

Activities

3 Use Figure 5 to calculate how many people live in poverty in:
   a) Gauteng
   b) Limpopo.
4 a) Draw a sketch map of South Africa's provinces. Use Figure 2 as your guide.
   b) Use data from Figure 5 to draw a choropleth showing poverty in South Africa.
5 a) Use Figure 4 to draw a climate graph for Mutale (see page 185).
   b) Suggest why this climate pattern makes farming in Mutale difficult.
6 Outline the push and pull factors that might be the reason for migration from Mutale to Johannesburg. Use evidence from Figure 3.

Enquiry

What other rural to urban migration flows occur in South Africa? Eastern Cape is the most rural part of South Africa. Where do rural migrants from this province go to? Use the tellmaps website to investigate these patterns.

Investigating patterns of uneven development in Limpopo

Many of South Africa's development problems are a legacy of the policy of apartheid which was enforced between 1948 and 1993. This policy segregated (or separated) black Africans from white and mixed-race South Africans. White South Africans controlled government decision making. The rural economy of large parts of Limpopo was neglected. Apartheid ended in 1993 when a democratically elected government took control but poverty and unemployment remain in many rural areas. The South African government recognises the need to improve the rural economy through schemes such as:

- Improvements to safe water supplies and extension of the electricity grid.
- The development of Limpopo's coal fields to create electricity.
- Training and grants for farmers who work on small farms.
- Creating jobs through tourism.

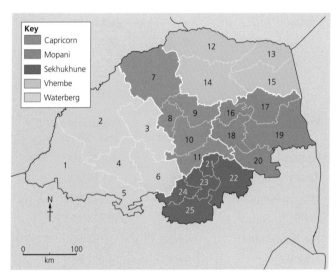

▲ **Figure 6** Percentage of the population who have access to piped water and electricity in the districts of Limpopo.

▲ **Figure 7** A traditional home in Venda, Limpopo. This home does not have mains electricity or piped water. The solar panel on the roof provides power for lighting. Cooking is done on an open fire.

Map reference	District	Population	Population with piped water (%)	Households with electricity (%)
8	Aganang	131,164	59	15
19	Ba-Phalaborwa	150,637	83	63
5	Bela-Bela	66,500	85	61
7	Blouberg	162,629	45	19
25	Elias Motsoaledi	249,363	47	69
24	Ephraim Mogale	123,648	70	54
21	Fetakgomo	93,795	36	15
17	Greater Giyani	244,217	44	45
16	Greater Letaba	212,701	45	50
22	Greater Tubatse	335,676	31	21
18	Greater Tzaneen	390,095	45	54
11	Lepelle-Nkumpi	230,350	52	34
2	Lephalale	115,767	67	70
14	Makhado	516,031	43	28
23	Makhuduthamaga	274,358	32	25
20	Maruleng	94,857	48	29
4	Modimolle	68,513	86	52
3	Mogalakwena	307,682	63	31
9	Molemole	108,321	56	39
6	Mookgophong	35,640	91	56
12	Musina	68,359	76	57
13	Mutale	91,870	27	8
10	Polokwane	628,999	71	43
1	Thabazimbi	85,234	71	53
15	Thulamela	618,462	42	33

Enquiry

Does Limpopo suffer multiple deprivation? Use Figure 6 to test the following hypothesis:

'The districts with the lowest connection to piped water also have the lowest percentage of households with electricity.'

Activities

1 Describe the home in Figure 7. Suggest how the lack of mains electricity and piped water could affect the well-being of the people who live here.
2 Study Figure 6.
   a) Describe the location of:
      i) Mutale
      ii) Lephalale.

b) Is lack of piped water just a rural problem? How many people **do not** have access to piped water in:
   i) Mutale
   ii) Polokwane (Limpopo's largest city).

GEOGRAPHICAL SKILLS

Using choropleth maps

A **choropleth** is a coloured or shaded map. Darker colours or darker shading represent higher values on the map. Choropleth maps are useful for showing patterns. You don't need to know pinpoint locations for your data. A choropleth may be drawn when you have data for each area or district on a map. There are two factors to consider when you draw a choropleth.

1 How many colours or shades should you use? Too many and patterns will be difficult to see. However, if you have too few then any small differences between areas will be lost.
2 If the data is available for different sized areas, which data set should you choose? This question is illustrated by Figures 8 and 9.

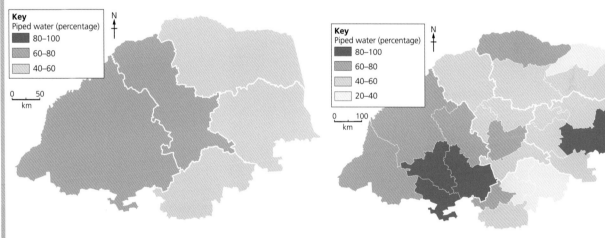

▲ **Figure 8** Choropleth map showing piped water (percentage) to districts of Limpopo.

▲ **Figure 9** Choropleth map showing piped water (percentage) to municipalities of Limpopo.

Activity

3 a) Describe the pattern shown on Figure 8.
   b) Describe the pattern shown on Figure 9.
   c) Which of these two maps is more useful to a geography student who is studying patterns of deprivation across Limpopo? Explain your answer.

Coal mining and energy generation

The government of South Africa aims to ensure that at least 90 per cent of people have access to grid electricity by 2030. One way it may achieve this is by developing its coal mining industry. The province of Limpopo contains huge deposits of coal. Approximately 44 per cent of South Africa's coal reserves are in Waterberg. At the moment there is one large open cast coal mine, where coal is blasted from rocks at ground level. The Grootageluk Coal Mine, in Lephalale, employs 2,000 people. It is operated by Exxaro which is a South African company. The coal is processed and sent to the Medupi and Matimba power stations.

The Medupi power station is still under construction. When completed, the power station will have six boilers, each powering an 800-megawatt turbine. This will make it one of the largest coal-fired power stations in the world.

Now there are plans to develop a new open cast coal mine in Makhado in northern Limpopo. The mine will be operated by Coal of Africa (CoAL) which is an Australian MNC. This coalfield has reserves of 188 million tonnes. Some of the coal will be exported to Mozambique, the rest will be used to generate electricity in South Africa.

Limpopo's coal could be converted to oil products in a new petro-chemical processing plant. If this happened it could employ over 20,000 people in the province.

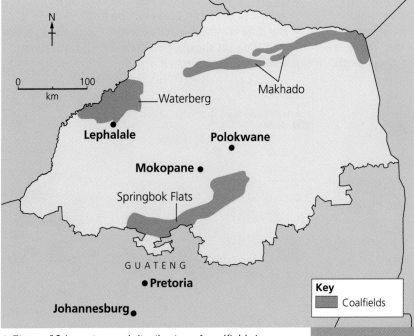

▲ **Figure 10** Location and distribution of coalfields in Limpopo.

Activity

1 Describe the location of the Waterberg coalfield.

▶ **Figure 11** Construction of the Madupi Power Plant in Lephalale (2015).

What are advantages and disadvantages of developing the Waterberg coalfield?

Farming, ecotourism and game reserves are the largest employers in Limpopo. However, most jobs in these industries are low skilled and poorly paid. Unemployment is high; as much as 37 per cent in Makhado. By comparison, jobs in mining and petro-chemical industries are highly skilled and well paid. The development of the Makhado coalfield will require a new railway and improvements to roads. These improvements to infrastructure may encourage further industrial developments.

Limpopo Province has a semi-arid climate and largely unspoilt savanna ecosystem which is a major tourist attraction. Mining is a noisy, dirty industry that generates a lot of waste. The coal has a high carbon and sulphur content. The waste heaps from the mine are prone to bursting into flames and the fumes pollute the air. The biggest environmental issue is the use of water. The extraction of coal and its processing use a lot of water in a region where many homes do not yet have piped water. Furthermore, the dumping of coal waste can lead to the pollution of natural stores of groundwater.

	Jan	Feb	Mar	Apr	May	Jun	Jul	Aug	Sep	Oct	Nov	Dec
Average daytime temperature °C	30	29	28	26	24	22	22	24	28	29	29	29
Average precipitation (mm)	96	83	65	25	10	14	3	3	3	37	111	93

▲ **Figure 12** Climate data for Waterberg, Limpopo (average 1991–2000).

The most important issue that the participants are concerned about is the water that the coal mining needs in order to extract the coal from the ground.

Looking at the information given at that meeting, a lot of water is needed: water from the ground, rain water and surface water, which includes water from existing dams like the Nzhelele Dam, Vondo Dam and Nandoni Dam, including the Vhembe/ Limpopo River.

Presently communities are battling on a daily basis to get water for household purposes and farmers in the area need water for agricultural purposes as well.

If a licence were to be granted to Coal of Africa now, we will face an unforeseen damage to the ground water through contaminated water seepage back into the water table.

Fountains will go dry, rivers will run dry, plants, animals and human beings alike will die. The environmental damage will be extreme because of adverse impact on the ecosystem and the good health of everyone living in it. Please be informed that water is already a depleting precious resource in the area where the mining is going to take place.

▲ **Figure 13** An open letter written by Moses Mudau to the Minister for Water and Environmental Affairs about the proposal to develop the Makhado mine.

Activity

2 a) Use Figure 12 to draw a climate graph for Waterberg.
  b) Explain why the following may oppose coal mining in Waterberg:
   i) local families who have no piped water
   ii) owners of game reserves.

Enquiry

Should coal be used to generate more electricity in Limpopo?

Consider the advantages and disadvantages of developing coal mining and coal-fired electricity generation in Limpopo. Use the information on pages 106–7 to complete a table like the one below:

	Advantages	Disadvantages
Social		
Economic		
Environmental		

Could better wood-burning stoves be the answer?

We have seen that many homes in rural parts of Limpopo do not have electricity. Cooking in these homes is done on traditional open fires or simple wood-burning stoves. Such stoves are very inefficient. They use a lot of fuel and produce a lot of smoke that, when breathed in over many years, can cause very serious health issues.

Practical Action is a charity that works with local communities in developing countries to produce appropriate technologies that are efficient and affordable for poorer families. One of their initiatives has been the design of the Upesi stove in Kenya. Women potters make the stoves using clay collected from local riverbanks. The clay is moulded into shape and then fired in a kiln. The stoves are affordable, costing about the same as a chicken.

http://practicalaction.org/

This is the website of Practical Action. They use technology to challenge poverty.

▲ **Figure 14** Women in Kenya making Upesi stoves which are much more efficient than traditional cooking stoves.

GEOGRAPHICAL SKILLS

Diamond ranking

Diamond ranking, or diamond nine, is a useful technique to use when you have been asked to make a decision. Sometimes it's not easy to try to rank or prioritise ideas when there is no obvious answer. Use this technique to group your ideas, putting your favourite ideas near the top, and the ones you think are less convincing at the bottom of the diamond.

Activity

1 a) Discuss the nine benefits of the Upesi stove in Figure 15.
   b) Place each of the benefits into a copy of the diamond nine diagram.
   c) Explain why you have chosen your top three benefits.

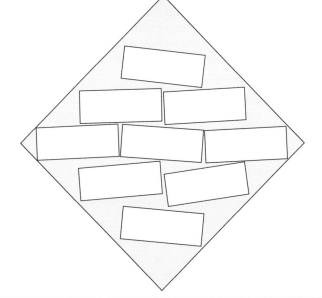

Women spend less time collecting firewood	Women have fewer injuries to their back and neck	Women and children have a reduced health risk
Cooking is faster and cleaner, producing less harmful smoke	The clay used to make the stoves is collected locally	Using less firewood means trees have longer to recover
The women who make the stoves learn new skills and earn respect	Women earn an income from making and selling the stoves	The stoves have lower CO_2 emissions than a traditional stove

▲ **Figure 15** What are the benefits of the Upesi stove?

Creating more jobs in ecotourism

There is an urgent need to **diversify** the rural economy of Lephalale. This means creating a variety of new jobs that are not necessarily connected to farming. The semi-arid climate makes farming difficult and incomes are low. One option is the creation of jobs in **ecotourism** which is a form of small-scale tourism that benefits wildlife.

South African and foreign tourists already visit a number of sites in Limpopo. Most visit the Kruger National Park in the east of the province. The Waterberg Biosphere Reserve in Lephalale is another popular destination. The Reserve contains 75 mammal species (including the big five: lion, elephant, buffalo, leopard and rhino) and 300 species of bird. About 80,000 people live in the reserve. Tourists to Waterberg create jobs in a variety of ways. Tourists pay to stay with local families or in luxury lodges which employ cleaners, cooks and bar staff. Local people are employed to act as tour guides and wardens in the reserve.

▲ **Figure 16** A darted buffalo that after medical checks will be sold to a breeder, is lifted onto a stretcher to the back of a truck on a private farm near Lephale (19 September 2014).

Enquiry

'The Upesi stove is a sustainable solution for rural homes in Limpopo that are not connected to the electricity grid.' How far do you agree with this statement? Consider the arguments for and against.

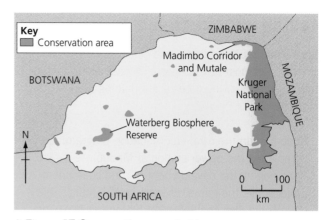

▲ **Figure 17** Conservation areas in Limpopo.

Poaching or hunting?

Game ranching is one way in which wealthy landowners are creating new incomes and managing wildlife. It involves the capture of wild animals, such as the buffalo in Figure 16, and the transfer of these animals as breeding stock to wildlife reserves where they can be protected from illegal poaching. In this way, the population of these wild animals has gradually been rising.

A limited amount of hunting by tourists is then allowed. The main income comes from tourists who pay large sums of money to shoot antelope, buffalo and other wild animals. The meat is sold in South Africa, generating more income. This money is then used to pay for conservation projects such as breeding programmes, habitat conservation and anti-poaching patrols.

Activities

2 Use Figure 17 to describe the distribution of conservation areas in Limpopo.
3 Explain what it is meant by the phrase 'diversify the rural economy'.
4 Explain how a new ecotourism project would:
   a) improve standards of living for local people
   b) conserve wildlife.
5 Discuss the arguments for and against the hunting of wild animals in South Africa.

Making your decision

Step 1 The first thing to do is to decide which of the schemes has most advantages and least disadvantages. Which of the following ideas are you going to recommend?

- Speeding up the rural electrification programme by completing the power station at Madupi.
- Encouraging the development of rural ecotourism projects like the game reserves in Waterberg.
- Developing new coalfields like the one at Makhado and creating more mining and industrial jobs.
- You could suggest a combination of these approaches or ideas of your own, such as improving the supply of piped water.

Step 2 You now need to **justify** your plan. This means explaining why you think your plan will be successful.

Key questions to ask yourself	Comments
How does my plan meet the needs of particular groups of people?	Will the women and children who do chores such as collection of firewood and cooking benefit?
Does my plan improve quality of life?	Will people have healthier and happier lifestyles as a result of your plan?
What are the advantages of my plan for the rural economy or the environment?	Does your plan create jobs for unemployed young men? Will wildlife be conserved?
Is my plan sustainable? In other words, will it create lasting benefits?	Will people be happier to stay in Limpopo as a result of your plan? Will your plan slow down rural to urban migration?

Your decision

How should the South African government try to improve life in rural Limpopo?

a) Recommend one or more of the schemes described in this chapter.
b) Justify your descision.

Considering sustainability

The aim of this problem-solving exercise is to create a rural development plan that will be sustainable. In other words, you need to prove that your plan will have lasting benefits. You could structure your answer around two headings:

1. The benefits that might be created in the first few months of your plan. These are the short-term benefits or advantages.

   For example:

Short-term benefits

If the rural electrification project was speeded up in the Mutale region, the benefits in the immediate future or short-term benefits would be …

[Consider health benefits for women, and educational benefits for children.]

2. The benefits that might be created over the next ten or more years. These are the long-term benefits.

   For example:

Long-term benefits

If this region had better water and electricity supplies it would be more appealing to foreign tourists. Such people expect to be able to have hot showers and air conditioning. So, in the longer term (over the next ten years or so) the benefits of rural electrification would be …

If you want to take the justification of your decision one stage further, why not apply Egan's Wheel to your answer? See page 17 for details of Egan's Wheel. You could use three or four different 'spokes' of the wheel as subheadings to structure your decision.

▲ Beach replenishment at Hythe, Kent.

River processes

▶ **Figure 1** A number of different river processes are evident in this river.

From the moment water begins to flow over the surface of the land, gravity gives it the power to erode the landscape. The gravitational energy of the flowing water enables the river to **transport** its **load** of boulders, gravel, sand and silt downstream. Where energy levels are high, the main river process is erosion. At other times of the year, or in other parts of the river where energy levels are lower, the main process is **deposition**.

Erosion occurs where the river has plenty of energy so, for example, where the river is flowing quickly or when

the river is full of water after heavy rain. Rivers that are flowing across gentle slopes (such as the river in Figure 1) tend to flow with greatest force on the outer bend of each curve (or **meander**). Water is thrown sideways into the river bank, which is eroded by both **hydraulic action** and **abrasion**. The bank gradually becomes undercut. The overhanging soil slumps into the river channel where this new load of material can be picked up and transported downstream by the flowing water.

Transportation process	Sediment size or type	Typical flow conditions	Description of the process
Solution	Soluble minerals such as calcium carbonate	Any	Minerals are dissolved from soil or rock and carried along in the flow
Suspension	Small particles e.g. clay and silt	Suspension occurs in all but the slowest flowing rivers	Tiny particles are carried long distances in the flowing water
Saltation	Sand and small gravels	More energetic rivers with higher velocities	The sediment bounces and skips along
Traction	Larger gravels, cobbles and boulders	Only common in high energy river channels or during flood events	The bed load rolls along in contact with the river bed

▲ **Figure 2** The transportation of sediment.

Erosional processes

Hydraulic action – water crashes into gaps in the soil and rock, compressing the air and forcing particles apart

Abrasion – the flowing water picks up rocks from the bed that smash against the river banks

Attrition – rocks carried by the river smash against one another, so they wear down into smaller and more rounded particles

Corrosion – minerals such as calcium carbonate (the main part of chalk and limestone rocks) are dissolved in the river water

▲ **Figure 3** Four processes of river channel erosion.

The process of deposition occurs where the river loses its energy. For example, where a river enters a lake and its flow is slowed by the body of still water. Deposition also occurs in very shallow sections of a river channel where friction between the river bed and the water causes the river to lose its energy and deposit its load. The process of deposition creates layers of sand and gravel that are often sorted by sediment size because the coarsest sediment is deposited first.

▲ **Figure 4** The river channel, which flows from the left, has split into a number of smaller distributaries as it flows into a lake. Derwent Water, the Lake District.

Activities

1 Study Figure 1. Use evidence from the photograph to suggest what river processes are occurring at A, B and C.
2 Draw four diagrams or cartoons to illustrate the ways in which a river transports material.
3 Study Figure 4 and explain how erosion, transportation and deposition have each played a role in the formation of this landform.
4 Study Figures 1 and 4. Use evidence in these photos to explain the difference between abrasion, hydraulic action and attrition.

Distinctive landscapes of upland rivers

The river in Figure 5 shows typical features of a river flowing over steeper gradients. Much of the force of the water is directed downwards. **Vertical erosion** cuts into the river bed. The river cuts a narrow valley with steep V-shaped sides. The flow of water within the river channel also swings from side to side, creating some sideways erosion. Over time this process means that the V-shaped valley is cut, or incised, into the hillside to form **interlocking spurs** rather like the teeth of a zip.

Rivers flowing over steep gradients have enough energy to erode and transport a large quantity of material. The load on the river bed here is large and angular. The rocks of the river bed may show evidence of abrasion in the form of smoothly cut potholes or scour holes. As a river flows downstream, the process of attrition gradually reduces the overall size of the load.

▲ **Figure 5** Ashes Hollow, Shropshire is a typical V-shaped valley.

Activities

1 Study Figure 5. Describe how each of the following features was formed:
   a) V-shaped valley sides
   b) large angular boulders in the stream bed
   c) interlocking spurs
2 Study Figure 6. Describe the process that created the features on this river bed.

▲ **Figure 6** Scour holes on the bed of the River Wye, mid Wales.

Enquiry

Do waterfalls only occur in the upland regions of the UK? Use the web link on this page to investigate the interactive map.

a) Describe the location of the UK's waterfalls.
b) What proportion is located in upland regions – over 400 m above sea level?

 http://www.world-of-waterfalls.com/europe.html
An interactive map showing the location of waterfalls across the UK.

How are gorges and waterfalls formed?

High Force is a waterfall in the upland section of the River Tees. Below the waterfall is a narrow valley with almost vertical sides. This feature is known as a **gorge**. The rocks here are alternating layers of dolerite, which is an igneous rock, and limestone. The dolerite is very resistant to erosion whereas the limestone is eroded more easily. It is the geology of this landscape that has caused the waterfall and gorge to form.

As the river plunges over the dolerite, it pours onto the softer limestone below. A combination of hydraulic action and abrasion erodes this rock relatively easily, creating a **plunge pool**. The river water is slightly acidic so the limestone is also eroded by corrosion. Abrasion at the back of the plunge pool undercuts the layers of dolerite. Eventually this overhang will fracture and the rocks will fall into the plunge pool where they are broken up by attrition. So each step is gradually cut back and the waterfall retreats backwards along the river's course. It is this process of **retreat** that has cut the gorge.

▼ **Figure 7** How the waterfall and gorge at High Force are formed.

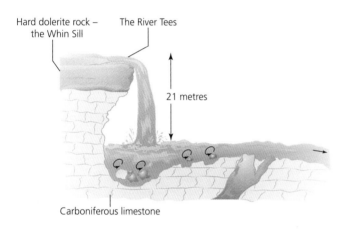

Hard dolerite rock – the Whin Sill

The River Tees

21 metres

Carboniferous limestone

1. Acidic water flowing from Cross Fell can corrode the limestone.

2. A 'cap rock' of dolerite is resistant so erosion is relatively slow.

3. An overhang of jointed limestone is susceptible to collapse and retreat.

4. Hydraulic action and corrosion attack the limestone.

5. Abrasion deepens the plunge pool.

6. Attrition breaks down the eroded rock fragments.

7. Fragments of dolerite swirl around in hollows to create pot-holes by abrasion.

8. Small outcrops of dolerite create an irregular river bed of rapids and smaller waterfalls.

▲ **Figure 8** High Force waterfall on the River Tees.

Activity

3 a) Make a copy of Figure 7.
   b) Add the labels below Figure 7 to relevant places on your diagram
   c) Explain why the retreat of the plunge pool has, over thousands of years, created a gorge. You could draw a series of diagrams to show this.

How are river meanders formed?

Rivers flowing over gentle gradients tend to swing from side to side. The water flows fastest on the outside of the bend of each meander. This causes erosion of the banks rather than the bed, a process known as **lateral erosion**. The slower flowing water on the inside of each bend loses energy and deposits its load. The material is sorted, with the larger gravel being deposited first, then the sand and finally the silt. This process creates a river beach or **point bar**. Meandering rivers such as the Greatham in Figure 12 flow across a wide **floodplain**. This flat landform has been created over many thousands of years by the processes of lateral erosion and deposition.

Activity

1 Use Figure 11 to:
   a) Give the six-figure grid references for
      i) one river cliff
      ii) one point bar.
   b) Describe the relief in square 3208.

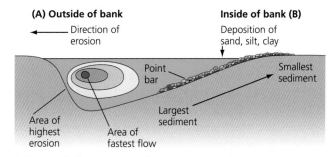

▲ **Figure 9** Cross-section through a meander.

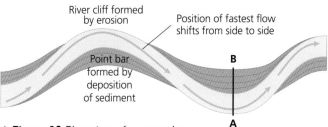

▲ **Figure 10** Plan view of a meander.

▼ **Figure 11** Meanders on the River Tees, near Hurworth-on-Tees, 10 km west of Yarm. Scale 1:25 000.

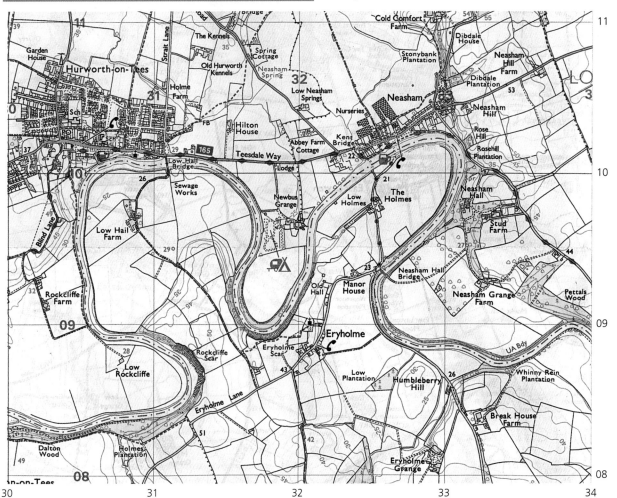

The estuary of the River Tees

The River Tees flows through an estuarine landscape for its final few kilometres before it reaches the North Sea. This distinctive landscape is made up of several features that include:

- Natural landforms such as floodplains, meanders and **ox-bow lakes** which are old meander loops that have been detached from the river channel by erosion.
- Habitats such as mud flats and salt marshes which attract wading birds.
- Wide, flat flood plains that have been drained and used for large industrial buildings.

The landscape of the river channel in the estuary is constantly changing as the flow of water changes:

- The power of the tide varies daily and throughout the year.
- The **discharge** of the river is also variable, depending on the amount of precipitation in the catchment.

Where the water is at its stillest, in the narrow creeks of the salt marsh, silt and mud from the river are deposited. The mixing of river water with salt water from the sea encourages deposition of mud particles. The mud flats between the creeks are covered at high tide and exposed at low tide.

▲ **Figure 12** The estuarine landscape close to the mouth of the River Tees.

Activities

2 Meanders erode laterally, or sideways, over time.
   a) Draw a sketch map showing the course of the river in Figure 11.
   b) Draw a second sketch showing the course of the river after erosion and deposition have altered the shape of the river meanders. Justify your prediction.
   c) Identify an area of the map where one of the meander bends could, in time, form an ox-bow lake.

3 Use what you have learned in this chapter to:
   a) Create labels for the features at points A to D on Figure 12.
   b) Compare the river features and processes in Figures 5, 8 and 12.

Investigating downstream changes

Rivers can change in shape and character as they flow downstream. It is possible to pose geographical questions about these changes. For example, when investigating change at the small scale:

How does river velocity change across a point bar and how does this affect sediment size?

Or, when investigating change at a larger scale:

How do cross-sectional area and river velocity change as you move downstream?

Choosing sample sites

The UK's rivers vary from just a few hundred metres in length to rivers like the River Severn which, at 369 km, is the UK's longest river. In an enquiry about how a river changes as it flows downstream it is important to make sure that your sample points are far enough apart to show change. For a river that is 10 km long you could either collect data at 1 km, 5 km and 10 km, or at 3 km, 4 km and 5 km. The first sampling strategy would provide a representative sample of the whole of the river, whereas the second would only provide evidence of small-scale changes in just one short section of the river.

Activity

1 Explain why sampling at 3 km, 4 km and 5 km would not be representative of change along a whole river that is 10 km in length.

Calculating cross-sectional area

To measure the cross-section of a river channel you will need to set a horizontal line across the river and carefully measure down from this line to the ground. This is shown in Figure 13 where the horizontal yellow line represents the survey line from X to Y and the four vertical lines represent the first four measurements. Collect data when the river is low but take measurements for the dry land on either side of the river. Then, when your results are plotted on a graph, you can estimate the amount of water in the river when the river channel is full and about to flood.

Step 1 Stretch a tape measure at right angles across the river from one bank to the other, keeping it parallel to the surface of the water.

Step 2 Divide the width of the river by 10. This will create 11 equally spaced survey points. For example, in a river that is 4 metres wide you will record the depth every 40 cm (1/10th) of the way across. This is an example of systematic sampling (see page 45).

Step 3 At each survey point measure the depth of the river. Make sure that your depth and width readings are both recorded in the same units (for example, both in metres).

Cross-sectional area (CSA) in square metres = width (m) multiplied by mean depth (m).

▼ **Figure 13** Sample sites on a meandering river.

Survey site	1	2	3	4	5	6	7	8	9	10	11
Distance from bank (m)	0	0.4	0.8	1.2	1.6	2.0	2.4	2.8	3.2	3.6	4.0
Distance from survey line to ground (m)	0.25	0.68	0.71	0.65	0.67	0.64	0.58	0.52	0.48	0.33	0.22
Depth of water (m)	0	0.28	0.31	0.25	0.27	0.24	0.18	0.12	0.08	0	0

▲ **Figure 14** Depth measurements taken in the river in Figure 13 at 0.4 m intervals.

Activity

2 Use Figure 14.
   a) Plot the profile of this river on graph paper. Remember to work downwards from your horizontal axis.
   b) What is the mean water depth?
   c) Calculate the cross-sectional area.
   d) If water levels rose by 20 cm, what would be the new cross-sectional area?

How do I calculate range, median and interquartile range?

The flow of water in the river channel has enough energy to transport sediment. As the water speed slows, for example, in shallow water on the point bar, energy is lost and sediment is deposited.

To test whether this process is happening in your river, you will need to sample some pebbles and record their size. Students collected a sample of 11 pebbles from sites A, B and C in Figure 13. Their aim was to discover how the size and range of pebbles changed across the point bar.

To calculate the range, median and interquartile range, you need to put your data into rank order. The data for site A is shown in Figure 16 in rank order.

Site	Pebble sizes (mm)										
A	45	52	12	67	34	75	42	81	65	40	24
B	44	37	28	56	61	43	38	28	35	42	36
C	37	34	26	40	24	35	29	42	38	18	20

▲ **Figure 15** Pebble sizes (mm) collected at random at sites A, B and C in Figure 13.

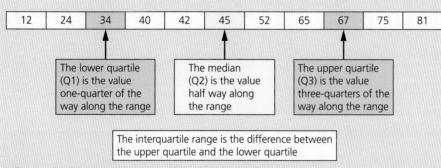

12	24	34	40	42	45	52	65	67	75	81

The lower quartile (Q1) is the value one-quarter of the way along the range

The median (Q2) is the value half way along the range

The upper quartile (Q3) is the value three-quarters of the way along the range

The interquartile range is the difference between the upper quartile and the lower quartile

▲ **Figure 16** Pebble sizes for site A arranged in rank order.

Activity

3 Use Figure 15.
   a) For each sample site, calculate the:
      i)   range
      ii) median
      iii) interquartile range.
   b) What conclusions can you draw from these results?

How are river landscapes affected by geology?

Climate, geology and human activity all play an important part in the river landscapes of the UK. The **porosity** and **permeability** of the rocks beneath our feet help to determine how much water we see in the UK landscape. **Porous** rocks have tiny spaces known as pores between the grains of rock. Porosity is a measure of how much water can be stored in these pore spaces. Rocks such as sandstones can hold water in their pore spaces as a **groundwater store**. Permeability is a measure of how easily water can travel through a rock. **Permeable** rocks

allow water to pass through them. Water easily travels through the vertical and horizontal joints and cracks that are common in permeable rocks such as sandstone and limestone. **Impermeable** rocks have few pore spaces or joints so water tends to flow over them on the surface of the land. Most igneous rocks, such as granite and metamorphic rocks such as slate, are impermeable. Clay, which is a sedimentary rock, is also impermeable. In regions where the geology is impermeable, water can be stored at the surface. Lakes and rivers are natural **surface stores** of water. Rivers can be dammed to control flooding and create reservoirs for water supply. There are 168 large dams (defined as being more than 15 m high and holding at least 3,000,000 cubic metres of water) in the UK.

▲ **Figure 1** The River Elan flows through an upland area of Wales. Rocks are impermeable and soils are thin.

▲ **Figure 2** The Penygarreg reservoir and the Craig Goch dam in the Elan Valley.

	Jan	Feb	Mar	Apr	May	Jun	Jul	Aug	Sep	Oct	Nov	Dec
Aberystwyth	97	72	60	56	65	76	99	93	108	118	111	96
Cwmystwyth	192	139	158	108	97	116	116	135	151	187	206	213
Birmingham	74	54	50	53	64	50	69	69	61	69	84	67
Norwich	55	43	48	41	42	58	42	54	47	68	70	53

▲ **Figure 3** Monthly precipitation totals for UK weather stations along a west–east transect through Wales and England.

Activities

1 Using Figures 1 and 2, suggest **two** different ways that human activity has affected the landscape of the River Elan.

2 a) Describe the landforms visible in Figure 1 or 2 and the processes that formed them (see page 113).

3 Study Figure 3.
   a) Draw four precipitation graphs.
   b) Describe how precipitation changes from west to east across Wales and England.
   c) Give two reasons why the Elan Valley may have been chosen to build the Craig Goch Dam.

Where are the water stores and flows in a drainage basin?

Very little precipitation falls directly into rivers. Most falls elsewhere within the **drainage basin** which is the area of land that is drained by the river and its **tributaries**. Figure 4 shows flows of water through a typical drainage basin. Water either flows over the surface as **overland flow** or flows into the soil – a process known as **infiltration**. Once in the soil, water moves slowly downhill as **throughflow**. Some water percolates deeper into the ground and enters the bedrock where it continues to travel as **groundwater**

flow. Rates of infiltration, throughflow and groundwater flow will depend on a number of factors which include the:
- size and shape of the drainage basin and the steepness of its slopes
- amount of rainfall throughout the year and the intensity of rain storms
- amount and type of vegetation cover
- permeability and porosity of the soil and underlying rocks.

▼ **Figure 4** Stores and flows of water in a natural drainage basin.

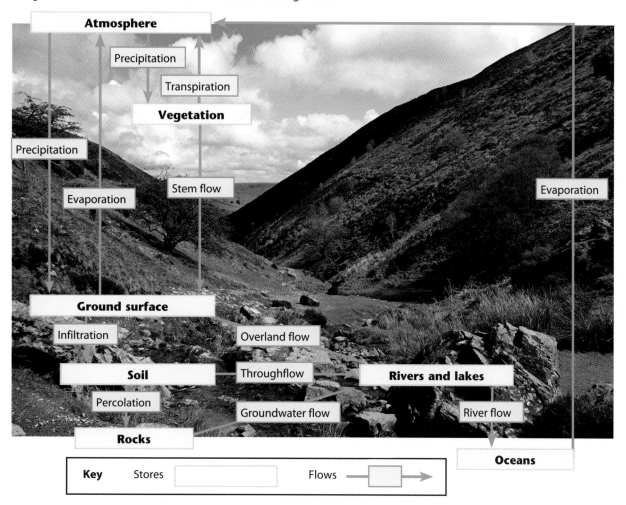

Activities

4 Use Figure 4 to name:
  a) three surface stores of water
  b) two places water is stored below the surface.

5 Suggest why precipitation falling into a drainage basin of impermeable rocks is likely to reach the river much more quickly than rainwater falling in an area of porous rocks.

How does geology affect flows and stores of water in the drainage basin?

Geology is a major influence on how quickly water flows through a drainage basin. It also influences the amount of water that can be stored within the drainage basin. The amount of water in a river is its **discharge** and this is measured in cubic metres per second, or **cumecs**. The annual pattern of a river is known as its **annual regime**. Study Figures 5 and 6. They show the annual regime in 2004 for two rivers that have similar sized catchment areas. However, the geology of the two drainage basins is quite different and this affects the flow of water through each basin.

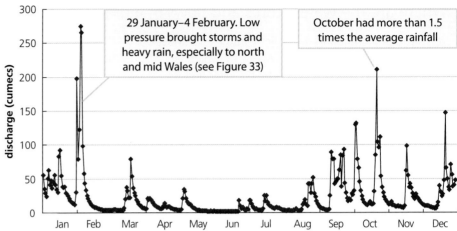

29 January–4 February. Low pressure brought storms and heavy rain, especially to north and mid Wales (see Figure 33)

October had more than 1.5 times the average rainfall

▲ **Figure 5** Hydrograph for the River Dyfi, Wales (2004).

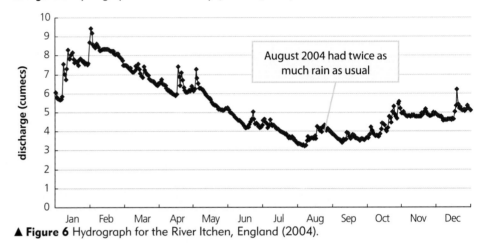

August 2004 had twice as much rain as usual

▲ **Figure 6** Hydrograph for the River Itchen, England (2004).

Factfile

River	River Dyfi	River Itchen
Location	West Wales	South East England
Total average rainfall	1,834 mm	838 mm
Geology	100% impermeable rocks	90% chalk which is porous
Size of drainage basin (above the gauging station)	471 km²	360 km²
Landscape	Steeply sloping hills and mountains reaching a maximum of 907 m above sea level	Rolling hills. Maximum height 208 m above sea level
Land use	60% grassland (sheep pasture); 30% forest; 10% moorland	Mainly arable (cereal) farmland with some grassland
Human factors affecting run-off	There are virtually no human influences on run-off	Run-off is reduced by some abstraction for water supply. Some water is used to recharge groundwater in the chalk aquifer

▲ **Figure 7** Factfile on the River Dyfi and River Itchen.

Activities

1 Compare Figures 5 and 6. Describe:
   a) one similarity
   b) three differences.
2 Use Figure 7 to suggest how each of the following factors may have affected the flow:
   ▪ rainfall
   ▪ total geology
   ▪ landscape
   ▪ land use.
3 Imagine you work for a water company. Suggest how each river could be used for water supply.

The abstraction of water

Some bands of porous rock can hold huge quantities of water. These groundwater stores are also known as **aquifers**. Examples are chalk and some types of sandstone. Water that enters an aquifer is **recharge**; water that leaves an aquifer is discharge. When water is taken from either a surface or groundwater store, we say the water is **abstracted**. If water is taken from a store faster than it can be recharged then **over-abstraction** is taking place. The last significant drought in the UK was in 2005 and 2006. Low precipitation during the winter months failed to recharge some aquifers. Water levels dropped in rivers in the south east of England.

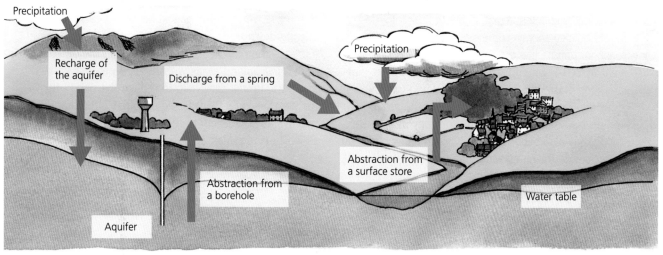

▲ **Figure 8** A cross-section to show how water moves between surface and groundwater stores.

▶ **Figure 9** Major aquifers in the UK. Located bar graphs indicate the percentage of water supply that comes from groundwater supply. The remainder will come from surface stores (rivers and reservoirs).

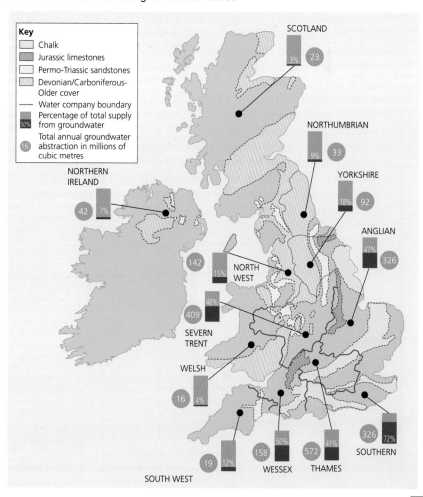

Activities

4 Define the following terms:
 ▪ discharge
 ▪ abstraction
 ▪ over-abstraction.
5 Use Figure 9.
 a) Make a table of the 12 water companies and put them in rank order by the percentage of their water supply that comes from groundwater.
 b) Describe the distribution of water companies that take less than 10 per cent of their supply from groundwater. What does this tell you about rock type in these regions?
 c) For each company, calculate the actual amount of water that is abstracted from groundwater stores.

Why do rivers flood?

In the UK we experience two types of flood:

- **Flash floods**, like the Boscastle flood event of 2004, when high volumes of rain fall in a very short period of time, causing a sudden rise in river levels. Flash floods sometimes occur in the summer in the UK when the ground is hard and baked dry. With these soil conditions, the rainfall is so intense that it cannot soak into the ground quickly enough so runs overland instead.

- Seasonal floods, like the Somerset Levels flood event of 2014, when river levels rise due to seasonal variations in rainfall. These types of flood usually occur after a long period of rain, when the ground is already saturated and cannot absorb any more water. Floods may also occur in the UK when snow melts but the ground is frozen so water cannot infiltrate the soil.

Do human actions increase flood risk?

Flooding occurs when water cannot infiltrate the soil. Paving over the soil creates an impermeable surface and reduces infiltration, so the growth of urban areas increases the risk of flooding. It is thought that paving over front gardens to create parking spaces may increase the risk of flash floods in urban areas. Vegetation helps to remove water from the soil before it reaches a river so cutting down trees or leaving fields bare in winter can increase the risk of seasonal floods. On the other hand, replanting upland areas with trees, a process known as **afforestation**, may help to reduce the risk of floods further downstream. It is thought that afforestation in mid Wales could help to reduce floods at Shrewsbury or Bewdley (see pages 134–5).

GEOGRAPHICAL SKILLS

How do you analyse a hydrograph?

A flood **hydrograph** shows the discharge of a river over the period of a flood. The example in Figure 10 shows how a small river might respond to a flood event. The blue bar represents a sudden downpour of rain, like the one at Boscastle in 2004. In this example it takes two hours for overland flow from the drainage basin to reach the river channel. At this point the amount of water in the channel rises rapidly and reaches its maximum or **peak discharge**. The time between the peak rainfall and the peak discharge is known as **lag time**. The lag time and height of the peak discharge depend on the features of the drainage basin. In drainage basins where infiltration is reduced, the lag time will be shorter and the peak discharge larger. For example, urban drainage basins have a lot of tarmac and concrete which are impermeable surfaces. Artificial storm drains have to be installed to quickly remove surface water otherwise urban streets would flood after each rainfall event. Some of these factors are illustrated in Figures 11 and 12.

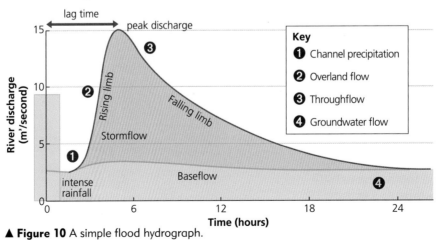

▲ **Figure 10** A simple flood hydrograph.

Activity

1 Use Figure 11 to explain how cutting down a large forest could affect lag time and peak discharge in a nearby river.

▶ **Figure 11** Forests reduce overland flow and throughflow.

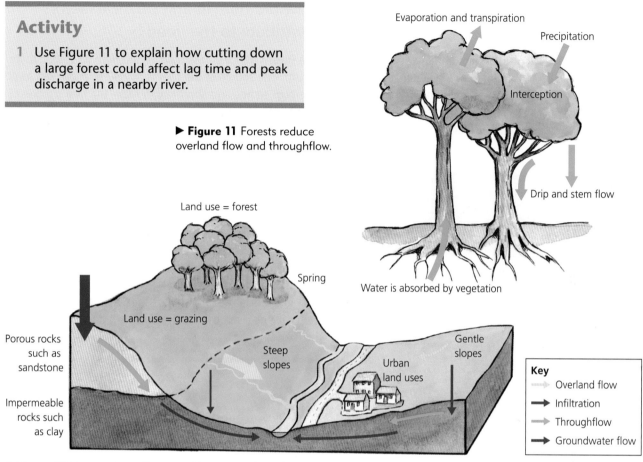

▲ **Figure 12** Factors that influence infiltration and overland flow in the drainage basin.

Activities

2 Study Figure 10.
   a) Use times and discharge figures from the hydrograph to describe:
      i)   the shape of the rising limb and the lag time
      ii) the shape of the falling limb and baseflow.
3 Use Figures 4, 10, 11 and 12 to help you copy and complete the following table.

Drainage basin factor	Impact on infiltration	Impact on overland flow and throughflow	Impact on lag time
Steep slopes			
Gentle slopes			
Porous rocks			
Impermeable rocks			
Urban land uses			
Planting more trees			

Enquiry

Can you predict the response of different drainage basins to a sudden downpour of rain?

a) Sketch a pair of flood hydrographs to show the difference between similar sized drainage basins – one of which has urban land uses and one of which has lots of forests
b) Draw a second pair of hydrographs to compare the response of rivers in a drainage basin that has porous rocks compared with one that has impermeable rocks.
c) Discuss your hydrographs with a colleague. Justify the shapes on your hydrographs. Make sure you can explain why you have predicted the shape of the rising and falling limbs and the possible length of the lag time.

Why did the River Valency flood?

The drainage basin of the River Valency, in Cornwall, normally gets 100–120 mm of rainfall during August. But in just four hours on the afternoon of 16 August 2004, 200 mm of rainfall fell causing a flash flood. The force of water rushing through the town caused the collapse of 5 buildings. Thankfully nobody was killed.

▲ **Figure 13** The River Valency in its upper course close to Tresparrett (Grid square 1491).

How did human and physical factors contribute to the flood?

The River Valency is less than 10 km from its source to its mouth. The source of the river is at 280 m above sea level. The high source and short length make the river's gradient rather steep. The total size of the drainage basin is around 26 km². The rocks of the drainage basin are mainly slates, which are impermeable. The river has a number of small tributaries which all flow through steep V-shaped valleys.

There are no large towns in the drainage basin. Boscastle itself covers less than 1 km². The upland part of the drainage basin is used for grazing. Some of the valleys are wooded. Trees help to remove some water from the soil before it reaches the river. However, during flood events, tree branches that are overhanging the river can be broken off. These branches then restrict the flow of water in the river, especially if they get caught against the piers of bridges.

Activities

1. Make a sketch of Figure 13.
2. Label three features that help to explain why this river floods so easily.

GEOGRAPHICAL SKILLS

Using geographical terms

You should always try to use the correct technical terms when you are writing a geographical report. Using geographical terms will improve your communication skills because their correct use will:

- make your writing more accurate and concise
- give your writing the correct scientific style and tone.

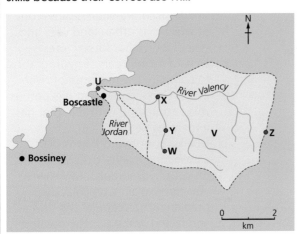

▲ **Figure 14** The drainage basin of the River Valency.

Activity

3. a) Make a sketch of Figure 14.
   b) Match the following key terms to features U, V, W, X, Y and Z on Figure 14.
      - Catchment area
      - Source
      - Tributary
      - Confluence
      - Watershed
      - Mouth.
   c) Write a simple definition for each of these terms.

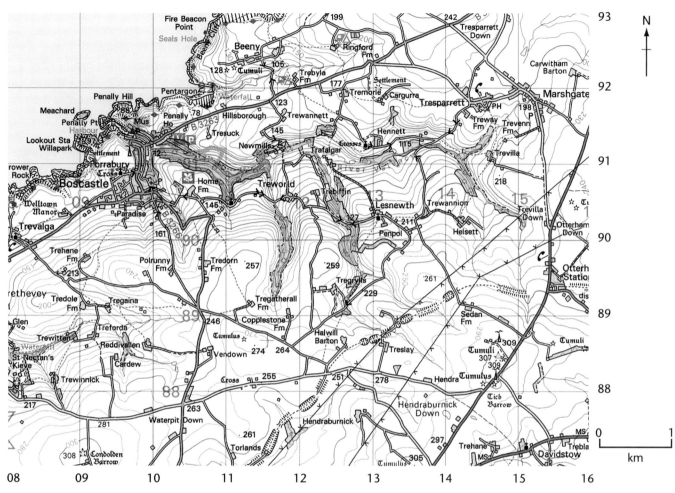

▲ **Figure 15** An Ordnance Survey extract of the catchment area of the River Valency. Scale 1:50 000.

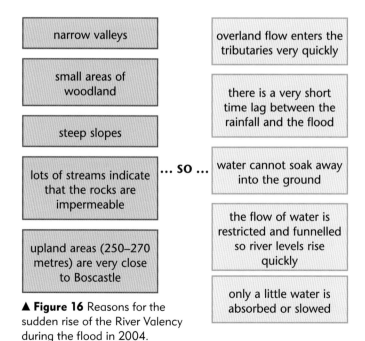

▲ **Figure 16** Reasons for the sudden rise of the River Valency during the flood in 2004.

Enquiry

Analyse the factors that led to the Boscastle flood of 2004.

a) Match the pairs of statements shown in Figure 16 to make five sentences that help to explain how the character of this drainage basin led to the flooding in 2004.

b) Use the OS map to find five different grid squares which provide evidence for your five sentences. For example, you could choose 0989 to match with 'upland areas are very close to Boscastle … so …'

c) Using Figure 14 as a simple outline, draw your own sketch map of the drainage basin of the River Valency. Add your five statements to appropriate places on the map as annotations.

127

How should rivers be managed?

In the UK it is the responsibility of the Environment Agency to warn people about flood hazards and to reduce the risk of both river and coastal floods. They estimate that in England and Wales around 5 million people live in areas that are at risk of flooding.

How has the River Valency been managed since the 2004 flood?

After the flood of 2004, the Environment Agency was responsible for designing a flood defence scheme for Boscastle. The defences cost £4.6 million and took two years to complete (2006–8). Many of the important features of this scheme are shown in Figure 18. One of the main features has been to widen and deepen the river channel so that it can carry more water. Making this kind of physical alteration to the river channel is known as **hard engineering**. It involves artificially controlling the course of the river.

Engineers were aware that during the flood, the road and foot bridges in the town became blocked by large branches that had been washed downstream. They decided to deepen the river bed under the main bridge and to replace the other two bridges with new structures. These new bridges have much wider spans so it is more difficult for them to become blocked with debris.

The National Trust owns a large part of the lower section of the valley of the Valency. In the past, the river was straightened and dredged so that its water could be used to power water mills. The National Trust and Environment Agency are now restoring parts of the river to take on a more natural form. For example, just before it enters the town the river has been given a wider, shallow channel. This should slow the flow of water and encourage deposition of gravel in a natural **braided** pattern. During another large flood, this 'natural' section of river would help trap boulders and other load before it entered the town where it could cause damage. Using the natural features of a river in this way is known as **soft engineering**.

▲ **Figure 17** The section of river between the main bridge and the harbour has been lowered by 75 cm. The river has also been widened.

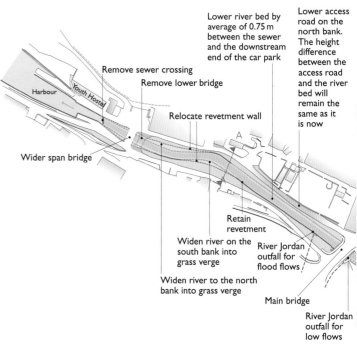

▲ **Figure 18** A plan of the Boscastle flood defences designed by the Environment Agency and built 2006–8.

◀ **Figure 19** Workmen using a JCB to dig out the rocky bed of the river under the main bridge during 2007.

◀ **Figure 20** One of the new footbridges and a view east along the widened river. The car park is behind the building in the left of the photo.

Activities

1 Use Figure 18 to describe the flow of the River Valency through Boscastle.
2 Use Figure 18 to explain why the Bridge Walk shops were at risk during the 2004 flood.
3 Explain how each of the following features shown in Figure 18 will reduce the risk of future floods:
   a) lowering the river bed
   b) widening the river channel
   c) removal of trees next to the river
   d) replacing two of the bridges with wider spans.
4 Use Figures 17–20 to give examples of different types of:
   a) hard engineering
   b) soft engineering.

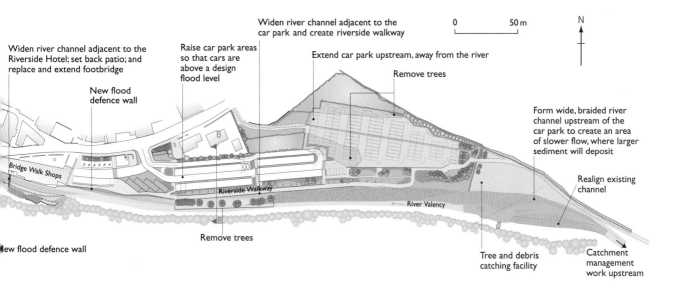

Widen river channel adjacent to the Riverside Hotel; set back patio; and replace and extend footbridge

Widen river channel adjacent to the car park and create riverside walkway

Raise car park areas so that cars are above a design flood level

Extend car park upstream, away from the river

0   50 m

N

New flood defence wall

Remove trees

Bridge Walk Shops

Riverside Walkway

B

B

River Valency

Form wide, braided river channel upstream of the car park to create an area of slower flow, where larger sediment will deposit

Realign existing channel

New flood defence wall

Remove trees

Tree and debris catching facility

Catchment management work upstream

The distinctive landscape of the Somerset Levels

The Somerset Levels is a distinctive flat landscape covering 250 square miles. The Levels are only 8 m above sea level and much of this landscape would be flooded twice a month by high spring tides if it wasn't for flood defences at the coast. The Romans built flood defences and they dug ditches to improve the drainage. Over the years, rivers have been dredged and water pumped out, changing the wetland into productive farmland used for livestock and arable crops. Some wetland remains and is conserved as nature reserves. The flat land of the Somerset Levels is vulnerable to:

- coastal flooding by high tides and storm surges, for example in 1919
- river flooding after prolonged periods of rain, for example in 2014.

What caused the 2014 floods?

High rainfall totals over the winter of 2013–14 saturated the soils with water. More rainfall during January and February 2014 ran overland into the already flooded rivers. At each high tide, the rivers backed up because flood water couldn't escape quickly into the Bristol Channel. Local people claimed that the rivers and drainage ditches of the Levels hadn't been cleared of silt and mud since the 1990s. This reduced the capacity of the river channels to hold water. Overhanging trees slowed down the rivers' discharge.

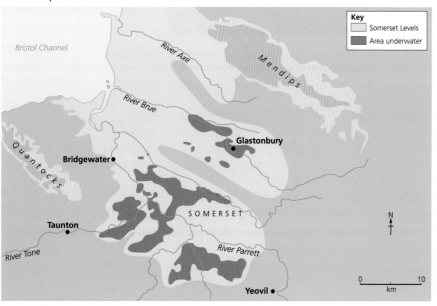

▲ **Figure 21** Map showing the location of the Somerset Levels and the flooding of 2014.

www.metoffice.gov.uk/public/weather/climate-historic/#?tab=climateHistoric

This website gives access to historic weather data from 40 weather stations across the UK including Yeovilton in Somerset.

http://nrfa.ceh.ac.uk

This is the National River Flow Archive. You can view and download discharge data for many UK rivers. Use this data to create hydrographs like Figure 22.

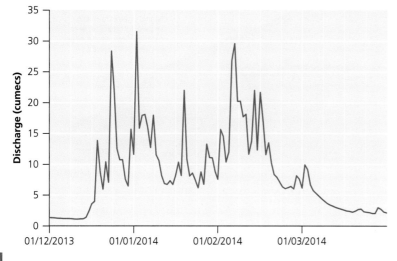

◄ **Figure 22** Discharge in the River Tone at Bishops Hull (December 2013 to end March 2014).

Activity

1 Use Figure 21 to:
   a) Describe the drainage patterns in the Somerset Levels
   b) Estimate the proportion of the Levels that were flooded in 2014.

Year	Tidal/coastal	River
1885	✓	
1919	✓	
1968		✓
1981	✓	
1990	✓	
2005		✓
2007		✓
2008		✓
2012		✓
2014		✓

▲ **Figure 23** Historic flood events in the Somerset Levels.

Year	Month	Precipitation (mm)
2013	Jun	25.7
	Jul	40.4
	Aug	15.2
	Sep	67.6
	Oct	115.8
	Nov	42.9
	Dec	121.4
2014	Jan	166.4
	Feb	131.2
	Mar	38.4
	Apr	62.2
	May	59.6
	Jun	79.0
	Jul	56.8
	Aug	74.6
	Sep	3.2
	Oct	99.8
	Nov	108.0
	Dec	34.8
2015	Jan	75.4
	Feb	41.8
	Mar	22.0
	Apr	25.8
	May	55.2

▲ **Figure 24** Monthly precipitation totals at Yeovilton (2013–15).

▲ **Figure 25** Large areas of the Somerset Levels were under water for weeks in 2014.

Activities

2 a) Explain why the 2014 floods happened. You should be able to identify physical and human factors.
   b) Study Figure 23. What is happening to the frequency of floods in the Levels?
   c) Suggest two different reasons that might explain this frequency pattern.
3 Use Figure 22 to describe the discharge pattern of the River Tone.
4 a) Draw a graph to represent the monthly precipitation patterns at Yeovilton shown in Figure 24.
   b) How unusual was the rainfall pattern during the period November 2013 to February 2014?
   c) Compare your completed graph to Figure 22. Use these two graphs and your understanding of tidal movements to suggest reasons for the peaks in discharge.

Enquiry

Analyse winter discharge patterns of rivers in the Somerset Levels. Use the National River Flow Archive website for your investigation. How do patterns in the last winter compare to Figure 22? Suggest reasons for any similarities or differences.

How should we react to the Somerset floods?

During January and February 2014, the local authorities, Environment Agency and UK Government reacted to protect people from the floods. The immediate responses to the flooding were:

- Thirteen large pumps from Holland were used to remove 7.3 million tonnes of water per day from the flood plain. The pumps worked day and night for six weeks. The fuel to run the pumps cost £1.5 million.
- Residents of flood-damaged homes were given emergency help and insurance advice.
- Teams were brought in to start emergency repairs to infrastructure such as rail and road networks, electricity supplies, telephone systems and sewers.
- Livestock was rescued and moved to other areas.

In mid-2014 the UK Government announced a £100 million recovery programme for the Somerset Levels. The aims of the Somerset Levels and Moors Flood Action Plan are shown in Figure 27.

The Somerset Levels and Moors Flood Action Plan

Medium-term aims – up to 2020

- A dredging operation on the Rivers Parrett and Tone costing £6 million.
- Embankments will be built around vulnerable villages. £180,000 was spent protecting the ten houses in Thorney. Ten other sites will be identified and protected by the year 2020.
- Raising the height of the A372 road and repairing 44 km of damaged roads.
- Better preparation and planning to protect residents and business owners. Ideas such as stored sand bags, knowledge of the location of vulnerable people, emergency livestock movement and improved communication systems would be developed.

Longer-term aims – up to 2035

- Building a flood barrier at Bridgwater by 2024. The estimated cost is £32 million. This would reduce the impact of high tides that prevent flood water from escaping from the Levels.
- Investigate the costs and benefits of building a £16 million flood storage scheme upstream from Taunton. This would capture and hold back rainwater from draining into the River Tone. A large-scale tree-planting programme in the upper catchment would be part of this scheme.

▲ **Figure 27** The Somerset Levels and Moors Flood Action Plan.

▲ **Figure 26** Pumps from Holland were used to pump water back into Somerset's rivers from the floodplain.

▶ **Figure 28** Dredging and bank stabilisation on the River Parrett.

Factfile: Impacts of the floods

- Half of all businesses in Somerset were affected either directly or indirectly by flooding.
- Damage to residential property cost up to £20 million.
- Costs to local government, the police and rescue services totalled £19 million.
- The rail line between Taunton and Bridgewater was closed for four weeks, costing the local economy £21 million.
- Over 80 roads were submerged for weeks with a cost of £15 million to the local economy.

Enquiry

Who should pay for the Somerset Levels and Moors Flood Action Plan? Discuss the responsibility of the following groups before making your recommendation:

- Those directly affected by flooding.
- All the residents of Somerset.
- The tax payers of the UK.

Activities

1 Draw and label a sequence of simple cross-sectional diagrams to show how dredging of the rivers would make them more efficient and reduce the risk of flooding.
2 Evaluate the arguments for and against continued dredging of rivers in the Levels.
3 Use the information on pages 132–3 to analyse the Somerset Levels and Moors Flood Action Plan. Do this by completing a table like the one below:

	Advantages	Disadvantages
Economic		
Social		
Environmental		

Our computer models suggest that the dredging programme will make the rivers 90% effective in flushing out flood water. Currently the silt build up since 2009 makes them only 60% efficient.

Ashley Gibson, Somerset Water Management Partnership

Part of the blame must be down to the Environment Agency. Why on earth did they cut back on the dredging programme in the first place?

Ian Liddell-Grainger, MP

Dredging has an impact on the habitat in and around the river. The fish are severely disturbed during dredging and the water is murky for days after. Reed beds alongside the river are ripped up so birds and small mammals lose habitat.

Royal Society for the Protection of Birds

It would have been cheaper to maintain the rivers properly instead of cutting back the dredging process in 2009. The clean-up and all the repairs will cost the tax payer millions.

National Farmers Union

I would urge the authorities not to take dramatic action until they have considered the impact of climate change and sea level rise. A 12 cm rise in sea level could easily make the proposed Bridgwater barrage a waste of money.

Lord Krebs, Climate expert

I object to paying an extra £25 a year in local taxes to fund flood prevention. The council should not allow building on flood plains. I have heard that over 900 homes have been built on vulnerable land in Somerset since 2001.

Resident of Glastonbury not affected by the flood

The Environment Agency are taking a lot of the blame for reducing the dredging programme in recent years but government cutbacks in public spending required them to lose 1,700 jobs. We can't have it all ways.

Western Morning News

We must allow the rivers to flood naturally. Some of the wetland habitats are unique. Sometimes nature needs to come before economics and people.

The Somerset Wildlife Trust

▲ **Figure 29** Different views from stakeholders on what should be done.

How is the River Severn managed?

The River Severn is Britain's longest river. A serious flood in 2000 prompted flood defences to be built at Frankwell, Shrewsbury. These included earth embankments, concrete flood walls and demountable flood barriers. These flood defences were completed in 2004 at a cost of £4.6 million. The demountable barriers (seen in Figure 30) are made of aluminium panels. They can be slotted together before the flood arrives. The demountable barriers successfully held back 1.9 metres of flood water during a flood in February 2004 and 74 properties were protected. But not everywhere is protected. Land uses in Shrewsbury have been zoned. Land uses that have a low value, such as car parks and playing fields, are not protected. These zones provide safe areas for water to be 'stored' during a flood event, as shown in Figure 30.

Demountable defences | Car park | A section of new flood wall | The river channel is behind the trees

▲ **Figure 30** A total length of 700 m of flood embankments and walls has been built where the river enters the town to prevent floods in Shrewsbury. A further 155 m of river bank is protected using demountable defences.

▲ **Figure 31** Guildhall and Frankwell car park, SY3 8HQ, the same location as shown in Figure 30.

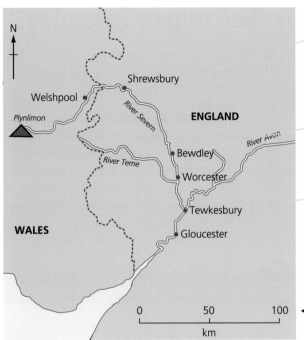

Shrewsbury: Flood damage in 2000 (severe), 2002, 2004 and 2007 (severe) and in 2014. Major flood defences were constructed in the spring of 2004. A further £20 million for extended flood defences for Shrewsbury was announced in February 2015, the work will be completed by 2020.

Bewdley: Flood damage in 2000 and 2002. Severe flooding was avoided in 2004 and again in 2014 by the use of demountable flood barriers.

Tewkesbury: Both Tewkesbury and **Gloucester** were badly affected by floods in 2000 and 2007. A five year multi-million pound flood prevention scheme protected both towns when the River Severn rose to dangerous levels in 2012. Only isolated villages downstream from Tewkesbury suffered any damage in 2012 and 2014.

◄ **Figure 32** Historic floods (2000–15) on the River Severn.

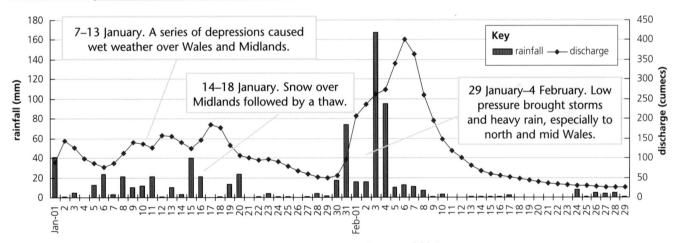

▲ **Figure 33** Flood hydrograph for the River Severn at Bewdley (January–February 2004). Rainfall data is for Capel Curig, North Wales.

Activities

1 Describe the course of the River Severn.
2 Suggest why planners might prevent the building of new homes on the flood plain of the River Severn.
3 Suggest why local residents might prefer demountable barriers to walls and embankments.
4 Explain why flood zoning is used in Shrewsbury. Consider the economic and environmental benefits.

Enquiry

How do weather events affect seasonal flood patterns?

a) Carefully describe the shape of the flood hydrograph between 29 January and 29 February. Use Figure 10 on page 124 to help your description.
b) Describe how each of the three weather events described in the labels affected the flow of the river. Focus on the time lag as well as the gradient of each rising limb.
c) Suggest how the Environment Agency uses rainfall data from Wales to warn householders in Bewdley about future flood events.

Virtual Preparation for your fieldwork enquiry?

The starting point for every good enquiry is a good enquiry question or hypothesis. In order to ask the most useful and searching questions, you need to do some preparation – ideally by exploring your study area in a virtual environment before the fieldtrip. Google Street View is often a good place to start. If you are investigating communities that are vulnerable to river flooding, then Street View will allow you to explore the area and identify different land uses close to the river. It should help raise some questions in your mind, such as

what land uses are common close to the river? A virtual visit will help you prepare for your sampling strategy too by helping to identify accessible sites.

The Environment Agency operates a simple geographic information system (GIS) that shows flood hazards in both river and coastal communities. Follow the Weblink below and click on 'Find out if you're at risk' within the 'Prepare for a flood' section. You can now search the atlas using postcodes. You could use this site to prepare for an enquiry into flood hazards.

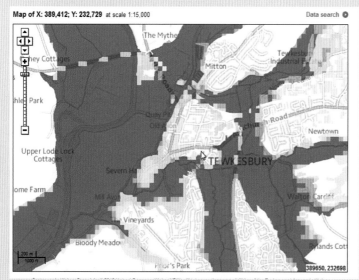

www.gov.uk/check-if-youre-at-risk-of-flooding

The Environment Agency GIS that shows flood hazards

◀ **Figure 34** A screenshot for the Environment Agency flood maps GIS. It shows that central Tewkesbury is at risk of being surrounded by water from the rivers Avon and Severn during a flood.

Activity

1 Discuss the following questions. All are possible starting points for an enquiry into flood risk.
   a) How would you go about answering each question?
   b) Which question might create the most interesting and useful enquiry? Justify your choice.
      ▪ How often does the river flood here?
      ▪ How many homes are at risk of flooding?
      ▪ How is land used in the flood risk zone?
      ▪ What is the relationship between land use and frequency of flooding?

Enquiry

How vulnerable to flooding are different towns along the River Severn?

Use the following postcodes to examine the flood risk to towns along the River Severn (the postcodes are in order, going from source to mouth):

SY16 2LN   SY21 7DG   SY3 8HQ
DY12 2AE   GL20 5AP

a) For each town identify:
   i)   the extent (area) that is at risk
   ii) which main roads are at risk of flooding
   iii) whether residential areas are at risk or not
   iv) whether the town has any flood defences.

b) Based on your findings, suggest which of these towns most needs new flood defences.

Should we change our approach to river and floodplain management in the future?

In 2004, the UK Government commissioned a scientific report on the future of river and coastal floods in the UK. The scientists considered how climate change and growing populations might affect the risk of flooding by the year 2080. The main findings of the 'Foresight Report' are:

- The number of people at high risk of flooding could rise from 1.5 million to 3.5 million.
- The economic cost of flood damage will rise. At the moment flooding costs the UK £1 billion a year. By 2080 it could cost as much as £27 billion.
- One of the main causes of the extra flood risk is climate change. The UK's climate is likely to become stormier with more frequent heavy rain. Sea level rises will increase the risk of coastal floods.

- About 10 per cent of the UK's housing is already built on the floodplains of rivers and these homes are at risk of river floods. Hundreds of thousands of new houses will be built in the next 20 years and many of these could also be at risk.
- River floods could cause massive health risks if the flood water contains untreated sewage or chemicals that have been washed off farm land.
- Towns and cities will be at risk of flash floods, even if they are not built near a river. Drains that are supposed to carry away rainwater will not be able to cope with sudden downpours of rain. This kind of flooding could affect as many as 710,000 people.

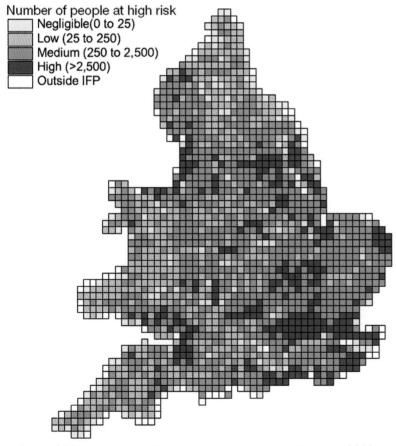

Number of people at high risk
- Negligible(0 to 25)
- Low (25 to 250)
- Medium (250 to 2,500)
- High (>2,500)
- Outside IFP

▲ **Figure 35** Number of people at risk of river and coastal floods in 2080, assuming that carbon dioxide emissions remain high.

Activities

1 Use Figure 35 to describe the distribution of areas where there are high numbers of people at risk of flooding.
2 Outline how future floods are likely to affect people living:
   a) in coastal areas
   b) close to rivers
   c) in towns and cities.
3 What are the main reasons for extra flood hazards in the future?

What should be done to reduce the risk of future floods?

Householders should be encouraged not to pave over their gardens. Paving and tarmac are impermeable. Rainwater goes straight down into storm drains and into the river rather than soaking slowly into the soil. Advice needs to be given so that gravel and permeable surfaces are used instead of tarmac. We also need to replace old storm drains which are too old and small to cope with heavy rain storms. However, motorists won't like that because it will mean digging up urban roads!

Planner

The scientists who wrote the 'Futures Report' into flooding identified that poor land management had increased the risk of river floods. For example, over the last 50 years farmers in upland areas of England and Wales have added drains to their fields to improve the amount of grass that can be grown. However, these field drains have had an effect on the flow of rivers further downstream. We are involved in a scheme to restore the old peat bogs in upland Wales. Between 2006 and 2011 we are going to block a total of 90 km of old land drains on the hills close to Lake Vyrnwy. We are using bales made from heather to block the drains. This will slow down the overland flow and force water to soak back into the soil. Not only will this help reduce the risk of floods but it will also improve the moorland ecosystem and will help to protect rare birds of prey like the merlin and hen harrier.

Spokesperson for RSPB

Hard engineering schemes, like the flood walls and embankments in Shrewsbury, speed up the flow of water. These schemes may funnel water along to the next community living further downstream and actually increase their risk of flooding. What we need to do is to return river valleys to a more natural state. We should use floodplains as temporary water stores so that flooding can occur away from built-up areas.

River scientist

Homes can be made more flood proof with measures such as putting plug sockets higher up the walls and replacing wooden floors and carpets with tiles.

House builder

I'm really pleased with the new flood defences. My property has flooded in the past but was protected during 2007. The Shrewsbury flood defence scheme cost £4.6 million but I think it was worth it.

Resident in Shrewsbury

We need to build an extra 3 million homes in the UK by 2020. Almost half of them are in the Midlands and the south of England which are the same areas hit by flooding in 2007. Some of these houses will have to be built on greenfield sites. However, we should restrict building on floodplains in the future.

Government housing minister

▲ **Figure 36** Alternative points of view on solving the flood problem.

▼ **Figure 37** The movement of water through upland drainage basins in mid Wales was altered when field drains were added. The size of the arrows is in proportion to the amount of each flow.

a) The natural system

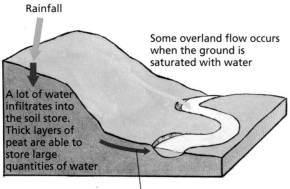

Rainfall

Some overland flow occurs when the ground is saturated with water

A lot of water infiltrates into the soil store. Thick layers of peat are able to store large quantities of water

Throughflow: water moves slowly through the soil and enters the river several hours or days after the rainfall

b) Field drains were added to improve drainage

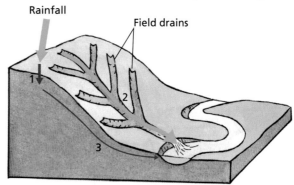

Rainfall

Field drains

Activity

1 Study Figure 37.
   a) Make a copy of the second diagram.
   b) Add labels that explain water flows at 1, 2 and 3.

   c) Explain how the differences in the two diagrams would affect the flow of water in the river downstream.

Enquiry

You have been asked to advise Tewkesbury Council on flood prevention. What do you think should be done to prevent future floods in the town?

a) Use what you have learned in this chapter, and the points of view in Figure 36 to complete a copy of the table.

Possible solution	Short-term benefits and problems	Long-term benefits and problems	Who might agree and disagree with this solution
Building flood defences like those in Shrewsbury			
Restoring bogs and moorland in mid Wales by blocking drains			
Tighter controls on building on floodplains and paving over gardens			
Allowing rivers to flow naturally and spill over onto the floodplain			

b) Now you need to recommend your plan. What do you think should be done and why do you think your plan will work? Use the following table to plan your answer.

Key questions to ask yourself	My answers
Is my plan realistic and achievable?	
Which groups of people will benefit from my plan?	
How will the environment be affected?	
Why is this plan better than the alternatives?	

Investigating the impacts of flooding

It's not safe to do fieldwork during a river flood. However, it is possible to do fieldwork in an environment that is at risk of flooding – as long as the fieldwork is done when the river is in low flow conditions. Your fieldwork enquiry might try to assess flood risk, or the impacts of flooding, by posing a question like one in the box below.

> Which areas of this town are at the greatest flood risk?
>
> What might be the social, environmental and economic impacts of a flood here?
>
> Does this town need better flood protection?

Designing your enquiry

Imagine you are about to investigate the risk of flooding – somewhere like Shrewsbury in Figure 38. This site is at risk of flooding because it is located next to the river and there are no flood defences here.

You will need to collect data from at a number of different survey sites. First, you will need to record the distance (from the river) and height (above the river bank) of each site. You may be able to use an app on your phone to do this – alternatively you can use a large-scale OS map. Before you begin, you will need to design data collection sheets so that data is recorded in the same way at each site. Your data collection sheet will be easier to use if it contains closed questions (see page 46) and boxes that you can tick. Study Figure 38 carefully. Apart from distance and height, what other data do you think you could collect?

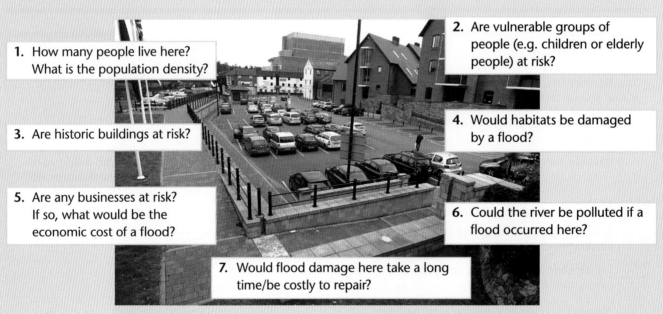

1. How many people live here? What is the population density?

2. Are vulnerable groups of people (e.g. children or elderly people) at risk?

3. Are historic buildings at risk?

4. Would habitats be damaged by a flood?

5. Are any businesses at risk? If so, what would be the economic cost of a flood?

6. Could the river be polluted if a flood occurred here?

7. Would flood damage here take a long time/be costly to repair?

▲ **Figure 38** Questions to ask yourself when investigating flood risk. The photograph shows a car park in Shrewsbury that is next to the River Severn.

Activity

1 a) Discuss the questions posed around Figure 38. Add three more questions that could be investigated during fieldwork into flood risk.

b) Use Figure 38 to design a data collection sheet. Think about how you might record each of the following using closed questions and ticked boxes:
- land use
- population density
- habitats
- vulnerable groups of people

Using GIS to identify flood-prone areas

Figure 40 is a screenshot from a website which uses information from the Environment Agency to identify flood-prone locations. The blue shading varies from high risk (shown in darker blue) to very low risk (shown in very pale blue). In order to carry out an enquiry into flood risks in an urban area like Shrewsbury, you would collect data along transects. Each transect would begin at the edge of the river and move through areas of decreasing flood risk. In Shrewsbury, transects of 300 m would be long enough to cross a range of risk levels. Ideally, the transects should be straight, but will have to follow roads and pathways in built-up areas. Stop and record information every 25 m along the transect route.

 www.checkmyfloodrisk.co.uk

This site displays flood risk information provided by the Environment Agency.

Location	Postcode	Description
Dingle Gardens	SY1 1JL	Public open space and ornamental gardens
Coleham Primary School	SY3 7EN	A primary school for around 400 children
Shrewsbury Abbey	SY2 6BA	A historic building. There has been a church on this site since 1083
Asda, Shrewsbury	SY3 7ET	A large supermarket
Frankwell Quay car park	SY3 8HQ	A large car park close to the town centre
Greenhous West Mid Showground	SY1 2PF	A flat open space that is used for agricultural shows, antique fairs and car boot sales
Travis Perkins	SY1 2PP	A large shop selling building materials

▲ **Figure 39** How many of these locations in Shrewsbury are at risk of flooding? What might the impact of a flood be at each location?

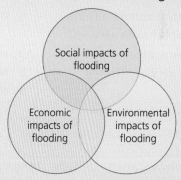

▲ **Figure 40** Screenshot from the checkmyfloodrisk website showing a flood risk map of Shrewsbury.

Activity

2 Imagine your local town is flooded.
   a) Write a list of all the possible impacts of the flood. Think about the different stakeholders: property owners, tenants, schools, businesses, customers, commuters, and how each would be affected.
   b) Draw a large Venn diagram with three circles like the one shown below. Work with a partner to fit the impacts on your list into the diagram.
   c) Classify your list of impacts as short-term, medium-term or long-term.

Social impacts of flooding

Economic impacts of flooding

Environmental impacts of flooding

Enquiry

Which parts of Shrewsbury are at risk of flooding?

Use www.checkmyfloodrisk.co.uk to search the postcodes in Figure 39. For each site:

a) Is the site at risk of flooding? If so, what is the level of risk?
b) What might the impact of a flood be at each location? Does this site contain land uses or groups of people who are particularly vulnerable to flooding?

Using GIS to process flood enquiry data

Step 1 Be safe. Do not go near the river if there is immediate risk of flooding.

Step 2 Decide what information to collect and what scores to use. Figure 41 shows an example of a data collection sheet.

Step 3 Stop at each survey site, every 25 m along the transect, and record:

a) The latitude and longitude and the altitude of the site (using your phone app).

b) A score (out of 10) for each possible impact of a flood.

Step 4 Total the mark (out of 30 in this example) for the social, environmental and economic impacts at each site.

Transect 1

Location .... Altitude ....

Latitude .... Longitude ....

Social impact		Environmental impact		Economic impact	
Number of people affected		**Pollutants entering environment**		**Type of economic activity**	
Many	10	Toxic/hazardous	10	Large retail	10
Some	5	Some pollution	5	Small retail	5
None	0	None	0	None	0
Vulnerability of people affected (e.g. elderly, children)		**Destruction of/damage to habitats**		**Number of people employed**	
Many vulnerable groups affected	10	Many habitats affected	10	Many people (30+)	10
Some vulnerable groups affected	5	Some habitats affected	5	Some (1–30)	5
None	0	Few habitats affected	0	None	0
Disruption to community life (e.g. schools/health services)		**Damage to built environment**		**Level of impact on business**	
Vital service affected	10	Historic buildings affected	10	Complete shutdown	10
Non-vital service affected	5	Modern buildings affected	5	Some activities continue	5
None	0	None	0	None	0
Total social impact score		**Total environmental impact score**		**Total economic impact score**	

▲ **Figure 41** Example data collection sheet.

Transect and Location	Latitude	Longitude	Altitude	Total social impact Score	Total environmental impact Score	Total economic impact Score

▲ **Figure 42** Table to collate results.

Activity

1 a) Use Figure 41 to score the impacts of a flood on some places you know well, for example, your school, the street you live in, some buildings in your local town centre.

b) Compare your scores with that of a friend for the same places. How do they compare?

c) If you have different scores, you will have to explain how you decided on that score. Try and convince them why your score is the right one, but be prepared to compromise!

Representing data using GIS

Step 1 Collate your results in a spreadsheet. Once you have input all your data, including latitude and longitude, save it as a .csv file.

Step 2 In your internet browser, visit ArcGIS Online and click on 'MAP' at the top of the screen.

When ArcGIS Online is showing the map, drag and drop the .csv file onto the map. The GIS will automatically recognise the latitude and longitude data and locate your data on the map. The GIS will also select one category (shown as an 'attribute' in ArcGIS)

from the data set and present that data using located proportional circles (see Figure 43).

Step 3 The category or drawing style can be changed on the menu on the left of the screen (see Figure 43).

- Change category being displayed using (1) Chose an attribute to show.
- Change the way in which the data is displayed using (2) Select a drawing style.

Step 4 Click on 'Done'. The menu on the left-hand side of the screen will change. Clicking on any of the data points on the map will display a pop-up box displaying all of the data collected at that point.

▲ **Figure 43** Screenshot of the ArcGIS Online map showing social impact scores.

www.arcgis.com

ArcGIS online is a cloud-based GIS platform where you can view existing data and add your own content. Your school will need to subscribe to the site before you can use it.

Enquiry

Use www.checkmyfloodrisk.co.uk to identify a local area at risk of flooding. Choose the location for your transects and identify the social, environmental and economic impact data you wish to record. Carry out the fieldwork enquiry and record the information in a .csv file. Upload onto www.arcgis.com and add the Environmental Agency Flood Risk layer.

a) Where are areas of highest/lowest impact?
b) Consider the following statement: 'The economic impacts of flooding are always the most significant.'

Use your data to discuss the validity of this statement. Remember to justify your answer.

How do waves erode our coastal landscapes?

Waves provide the force that shapes our coastline. Waves are created by friction between wind and the surface of the sea. Stronger winds make bigger waves. Large waves also need time and space in which to develop. So, large waves need the wind to blow for a long time over a large surface area of water. The distance over which a wave has developed is known as **fetch**, so the largest waves need strong winds and a long fetch.

The water in a wave moves in a circular motion. A lot of energy is spent moving the water up and down. So waves in deep water have little energy to erode a coastline. However, as a wave enters shallow water, it is slowed by friction with the sea bed. The water at the surface, however, surges forward freely. It is this forward motion of the breaking wave that causes the erosional processes described in Figure 3.

Activity

1 Make a copy of Figure 1 and add the following labels in appropriate places.
- Waves in deeper water
- Circular motion
- Breaking wave
- Water thrown forward
- Friction with the sea bed.

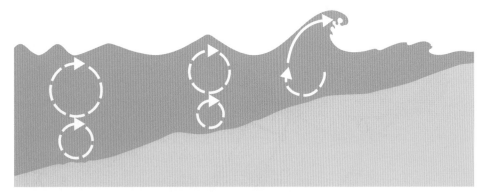

▲ **Figure 1** The motion of water in a wave.

vertical joints in the wave-cut platform

The repeated pounding of large waves at the foot of a cliff can cause enormous damage through the process of hydraulic action and abrasion. The repeated hammering effect of the waves on this narrow zone creates a **wave-cut notch**. Cliffs that are already weakened by joints or cracks can suddenly collapse in a rock fall which is a type of **mass movement**. The collapse causes the line of the cliffs to **retreat** inland. The **wave-cut platform** in Figure 2 has been formed by the gradual retreat of the cliffs.

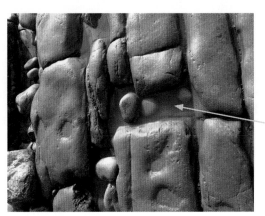

pothole

▶ **Figure 2** The rocky wave-cut platform of the Glamorgan Heritage Coast.

Erosional processes

Hydraulic action – waves crash against the cliff, compressing the water and air into cracks and forcing the rocks apart.

Abrasion – waves pick up rocks from the sea bed or beach and smash them against the cliffs.

Corrosion – minerals such as calcium carbonate (the main part of chalk and limestone rocks) are slowly dissolved in sea water.

Attrition – sand and pebbles are picked up by the sea and smash against one another, wearing them down into smaller and more rounded particles.

▲ **Figure 3** Four processes of coastal erosion.

A huge mass of rocks overhang the notch. This will be the next section of cliff to collapse

Horizontal bedding planes and vertical joints in the rock are lines of weakness that can be eroded rapidly by hydraulic action

A recent rock fall. This debris will break the force of the waves so, for a while at least, the cliff behind will be protected from the battering of the waves

Waves use pebbles from the beach to erode a notch at the foot of the cliff through the process of abrasion

▲ **Figure 4** Evidence of erosion in limestone cliffs on the Glamorgan Heritage Coast.

Activities

2   Study Figures 2 and 3.
 a) Use the correct erosion terms to complete the annotations below.
  ▪ Joints in the rock are widened in the process of .... which is when ....
  ▪ Boulders on the beach are rounded because ....
  ▪ This pothole has been scoured into the rock by ....
 b) Make a simple sketch of Figure 2 and add your annotations (above) to the sketch.

3   Consider Figure 4 and its annotations.
 a) Write a list (or draw a timeline) that puts the events acting on this cliff in the correct sequence.
 b) Make another list (or timeline) suggesting what will happen to this cliff in the next few years.
 c) Over the next 100 years this coastline will retreat by about 20–40 metres. Draw a story-board to show how this process of retreat creates the rocky wave-cut platform in front of the cliff.

Erosion and coastal flooding during extreme weather events

During the winter of 2013–14, several low pressure systems rolled over the UK, bringing wind and rain. The storms caused flooding in many areas of the UK, including Somerset. High winds and waves battered the UK coastline. Erosion is more rapid during these extreme weather events, as you can see in Figure 5.

The storm surge of December 2013

Low pressure in the atmosphere has the effect of raising sea levels. When air pressure falls by 1 millibar (mb), sea levels rise by 1 cm. So, a deep depression of 960 mb will cause sea levels to rise by 50 cm. Strong winds create large waves that are pushed in front of an advancing area of low pressure, creating even higher water levels. This effect is known as a **storm surge**, and is shown in Figure 6.

▲ **Figure 5** Rapid coastal erosion of the cliffs at Hemsby, during the 2013 storm, caused the collapse of seven homes.

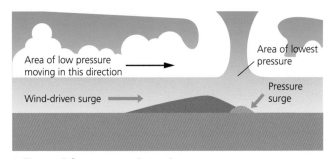

▲ **Figure 6** Storm surge due to low pressure.

1,000 sandbags were distributed to home-owners in Aldeburgh, Suffolk.	In the Humber region, 400 homes were affected by flood water.
Seven houses were destroyed in Hemsby, Norfolk when the cliff beneath them collapsed into the sea.	In Great Yarmouth, Norfolk, residents of 9,000 homes were advised to evacuate overnight.
The sea wall was breached at Jaywick, Essex. Firefighters and 10 rescue boats helped to evacuate 2,500 homes.	Boston, Lincolnshire was flooded; 223 people were evacuated from their homes.
In Kent, 200 homes were evacuated in Faversham and another 70 in Seasalter.	The sea wall at Scarborough, Yorkshire, was damaged.

▲ **Figure 7** The locations affected by the 2013 storm surge.

If a storm approaches the coast at high tide, an event that happens twice a day, then the risk of flooding is increased. The UK's North Sea coastline is particularly vulnerable to storm surges. The southern part of this sea is shallow and shaped like a funnel. When low pressure travels southwards across the North Sea, the bulge of the storm surge can increase in height as water is forced through this shallow funnel.

During December 2013, coastal communities along the North Sea coast faced the worst storm surge since 1953. Some of its effects are shown in the Figures 5 and 7. Nevertheless, the Environment Agency said 800,000 homes had been protected by:
- accurate weather forecasts that gave time for people to evacuate their homes
- coastal defences that held back some of the storm surge.

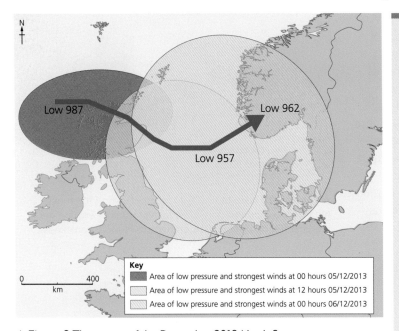

▲ **Figure 8** The course of the December 2013 North Sea storm.

Key
- ▨ Area of low pressure and strongest winds at 00 hours 05/12/2013
- ▨ Area of low pressure and strongest winds at 12 hours 05/12/2013
- ▨ Area of low pressure and strongest winds at 00 hours 06/12/2013

Low 987
Low 962
Low 957

0   400
km

Activities

1 Explain why the shape of the North Sea increases the risk of storm surges in Essex, Kent and the Thames Gateway areas.
2 a) Make a sketch map of Figure 7.
  b) Use an atlas to add the eight labels describing the effects of the storm surge to the correct locations on your sketch.
3 Use Figure 8 to describe the location of areas affected by the storm as it moved across the UK.
4 Analyse Figure 9.
  a) At what times was high tide expected on 5 December?
  b) At what time did the storm surge reach Lowestoft?
  c) How much higher was the storm surge than the expected height of high tide?

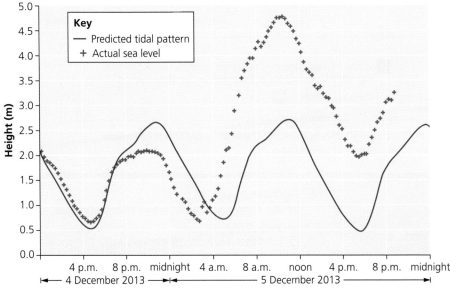

▲ **Figure 9** Sea levels at Lowestoft, Suffolk, during the storm surge.

Key
— Predicted tidal pattern
+ Actual sea level

Enquiry

How did the 2013 storm surge compare to the 1953 event?

Use the internet to research the main causes and effects of the 1953 North Sea storm surge.

a) Compare the causes.
b) Compare the effects.

How are coastal processes affected by geology?

On a map, the blue line showing the coastline of the UK looks like a fixed and permanent feature. In reality, beaches and estuaries are a constantly changing environment as the tide moves in and out. Even solid cliffs can suddenly collapse when they are battered by storms like the one in December 2013.

Coastal retreat is particularly rapid on some sections of the North Sea coast of England. In the East Riding of Yorkshire, cliffs are retreating at an average of 2 metres per year. This is due to geology. The cliffs here, and in North Norfolk, are made of layers of sand, silt and clay deposited at the end of the ice age (see page 190). These young sedimentary rocks have not been compacted as much as older rocks and they are unconsolidated – which means the grains of sediment are not 'glued' together very well. This makes them much less resistant to erosion than older sedimentary rocks such as the carboniferous limestone cliffs seen in Figures 2 and 4 on page 144–5.

▲ **Figure 10** The extent of the ice sheet during the most recent glacial period. The UK's fastest rates of erosion are in the East Riding of Yorkshire and North Norfolk coastlines.

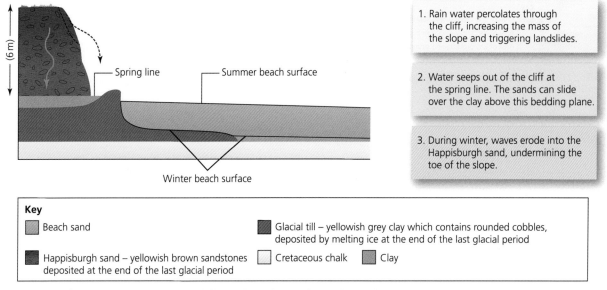

1. Rain water percolates through the cliff, increasing the mass of the slope and triggering landslides.

2. Water seeps out of the cliff at the spring line. The sands can slide over the clay above this bedding plane.

3. During winter, waves erode into the Happisburgh sand, undermining the toe of the slope.

Key

- Beach sand
- Happisburgh sand – yellowish brown sandstones deposited at the end of the last glacial period
- Glacial till – yellowish grey clay which contains rounded cobbles, deposited by melting ice at the end of the last glacial period
- Cretaceous chalk
- Clay

▲ **Figure 11** Cross-section through the cliffs at Happisburgh, North Norfolk. These cliffs are made of loosely compacted layers of sand, silt and clay deposited at the end of the ice age.

Activities

1 Use Figure 10 to:
 a) Describe the extent of the ice sheet across the UK.
 b) Explain why parts of the UK's North Sea coast are vulnerable to erosion.

2 a) Make a copy of Figure 11.
 b) Add the annotations 1–3 to suitable places on your diagram.
 c) Use the diagram to explain why the rock type and structure of the cliffs at Happisburgh make them vulnerable to erosion and mass movement.

Figure 11 helps to explain why the cliffs at Happisburgh in Norfolk are not very resistant to erosion by waves. Once the toe of the slope has been eroded by the sea, the whole slope becomes unstable. It is then at risk of mass movement – a process by which the whole cliff face can slide or slump onto the beach. The chance of slumping is increased by periods of heavy rain which adds mass to the cliff. Rain water also erodes small V-shaped notches called **gulleys** in the upper slopes of the cliff.

After the 1953 storm surge, a lot of money was spent building better coastal defences along the North Sea coast, including at Happisburgh. However, the erosion here has continued and a succession of coastal defences has failed to protect the village at the top of the cliff. In 2009, a trial programme called Pathfinder offered £11 million to help 15 coastal communities cope with erosion by moving away from danger rather than build more coastal defences. The Happisburgh Pathfinder scheme is the largest, costing £3 million.

 www.northnorfolk.org/pathfinder

This site describes the Pathfinder scheme in North Norfolk

Wooden barriers known as revetments that should break the force of the waves before they reach the toe of the cliff

D

C

B

A

The remains of a concrete slipway that have collapsed during a landslide

▲ **Figure 12** The coastline at Happisburgh in 2011.

Activities

3 Historical records show that the cliffs here retreated by 250 m between 1600 and 1850. What is the average rate of erosion per year?
4 Read the following annotations and decide where they fit best on Figure 12.
   ▪ Waves have eroded the toe of the cliff here
   ▪ The vegetation on this slope proves that it hasn't slumped for several months
   ▪ Concrete blocks on the beach may protect the cliff from wave erosion
   ▪ Evidence of gulley erosion by rain water on these slopes.

Enquiry

How should we respond to erosion when it threatens villages like Happisburgh?

a) Use the Weblink to discover how the Pathfinder project works.
b) Debate whether any other actions would have been sustainable.

Cliff landforms in resistant rock types

We have seen that young sedimentary rocks such as those at Happisburgh have a weak structure which makes them vulnerable to erosion. By contrast, older sedimentary rocks are compacted and consolidated, meaning they are more resistant to erosion. Limestone coastlines, like those in Figure 13, tend to form almost vertical cliffs. However, bedding planes and joints in the rock are lines of weakness in these cliffs. These lines are more easily eroded than the massive blocks of stone in between them. Erosion along these lines can lead to the formation of caves, **sea arches** and **stacks**.

▲ **Figure 13** The Green Bridge of Wales, Pembrokeshire. A natural sea arch formed in a carboniferous limestone cliff.

▼ **Figure 14** Durdle Door, a natural arch, on the Jurassic coastline.

Headlands and bays on the Jurassic Coast

The Jurassic coastline of Dorset is made up of alternating bands of sandstone, limestone and clay. The sandstones and limestones are quite resistant to erosion and make tall, almost vertical cliffs. The clays are much more easily eroded. Figure 15 shows how these bands of rock lie parallel to the coast.

Where the sea has been able to erode a hole through the resistant limestone, it has then scoured out a shallow, rounded bay (known as a **cove**) in the much less resistant clays behind. This has created a very distinctive landscape of cliffs, arches and coves. Figure 15 shows an arch and Figure 16 shows a cove.

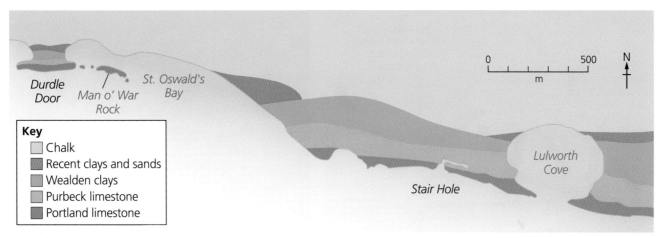

▲ **Figure 15** Alternating bands of chalk, Whealdon clay and Purbeck limestone in Dorset.

▲ **Figure 16** Man o'War Rocks and St Oswald's Bay on the Jurassic Coast near Lulworth.

Beach and sand dune processes

Beaches are dynamic environments. In other words, the energy of the wind and waves is constantly moving sediment around and changing the shape of the beach. Where the waves approach the beach at an angle, some of the sediment is transported along the coastline in a process known as **longshore drift**. However, most sediment is simply moved up and down the beach. Each wave transports sediment up the beach in the **swash** and back down again in the **backwash**. All of this movement uses a lot of the wave's energy, so a wide, thick beach is a good natural defence against coastal erosion.

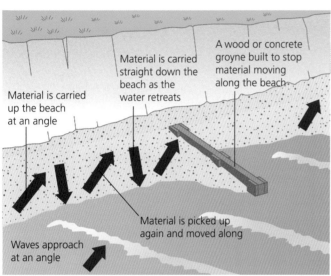

Material is carried straight down the beach as the water retreats

A wood or concrete groyne built to stop material moving along the beach

Material is carried up the beach at an angle

Material is picked up again and moved along

Waves approach at an angle

▲ **Figure 17** Transport of sediment by the process of longshore drift.

▲ **Figure 18** The beach at Borth seen from the cliffs to the south of the pebble ridge.

The sand and pebbles on a beach usually come from the local environment. Neighbouring cliffs may supply some sediment if they are being actively eroded by wave action. A lot of finer silts and sands are transported to the coast by rivers. This sediment is then deposited in the estuary or on an **offshore bar** at the mouth of the river. It will be washed onshore by the swash of the waves and deposited on the beach.

At Borth, on the Ceredigion coast, there is a pebble ridge making a **spit** on the southern side of the estuary. These pebbles came from cliffs to the south. Figure 20 shows the processes that are supplying and transporting material on this coastline.

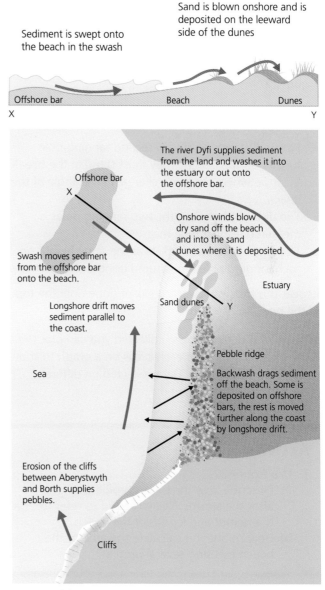

▲ **Figure 19** The sand dunes at Ynyslas seen from Aberdyfi on the north side of the Dyfi estuary.

Sand is blown onshore and is deposited on the leeward side of the dunes

Sediment is swept onto the beach in the swash

Offshore bar   Beach   Dunes

X   Y

The river Dyfi supplies sediment from the land and washes it into the estuary or out onto the offshore bar.

Offshore bar

X

Onshore winds blow dry sand off the beach and into the sand dunes where it is deposited.

Swash moves sediment from the offshore bar onto the beach.

Estuary

Longshore drift moves sediment parallel to the coast.

Sand dunes

Y

Pebble ridge

Sea

Backwash drags sediment off the beach. Some is deposited on offshore bars, the rest is moved further along the coast by longshore drift.

Erosion of the cliffs between Aberystwyth and Borth supplies pebbles.

Cliffs

▲ **Figure 20** The transport of beach sediment at Borth and Ynyslas on the Ceredigion coast.

Activities

1 Describe the landforms seen at A, B and C on Figures 18 and 19.
2 Study Figures 17, 18 and 20. Use an annotated diagram to explain the formation of the pebble ridge on which the village of Borth is built.

Enquiry

Interpret the landscape in Figure 19. How have erosion, transportation and deposition all helped to make this landscape? Write a story-board to explain the evolution of this landscape.

Investigating landscape change

The coastline is a constantly changing landscape. Change can be very gradual and occur over many decades. Change over long periods can be measured by comparing primary fieldwork data with historical photographs or maps. However, the shape of a beach profile (its cross-sectional shape) can sometime change overnight. For example, rapid change occurs when beach sediment is eroded or deposited by an extreme storm event. Rapid change to a beach profile may be recorded by comparing measurements taken on two separate days.

Collecting primary evidence of a beach profile

The size and shape of beaches can be recorded by taking beach profile measurements, as shown in Figure 21.

- Person A stands at a safe distance from the edge of the sea holding a ranging pole.
- Person B stands holding a second ranging pole further up the beach. They must stand at the break in slope where there is a change in the angle of the beach.
- The distance between the two ranging poles is measured using a tape measure.
- The angle between markers at the same height on each ranging pole is measured using a clinometer.

Repeat this process at each break of slope until the top of the beach is reached.

When all the data has been collected you can plot the distances and angles for each break on a graph to show the profile of the beach. Data collected on different dates can then be compared.

▲ **Figure 21** How to carry out a beach profile.

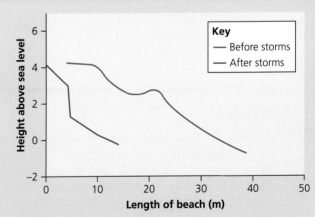

▲ **Figure 22** Beach profiles for different dates at Slapton Sands, Torcross.

Activity

1 Use Figure 22.
  a) Describe how the beach profile changed after the storms. You will need to refer to the height and length of the beach.
  b) How might you calculate the area of the beach by using several profiles?

Investigating the concept of place

Coastal locations provide an opportunity to investigate how people think about the environment – whether it be the physical environment of a natural coastal landscape, or the human environment of a seaside resort. This will involve collecting qualitative data (see page 45) by using, for example:

- bi-polar surveys (see page 14)
- and questionnaires (see page 46).

Place

Place is a geographical concept which is used to describe what makes somewhere special, unique or distinct. Each place includes many different features of the human and physical environment such as landscape features and landmarks, local styles of building, ecosystems and habitats, or local historical and cultural features. Each of these features may be relatively common across the UK. However, it is the unique combination of these geographical features that creates an identity for any one place.

Posing questions for an enquiry

Study Figure 23, it shows the seaside resort of Rhyl on the North Wales coast. How do people of different ages think about this place: what features do they like and dislike? What words would they use to describe the unique or special features of this place? How many would be positive and how many would be negative? Do tourists to Rhyl have the same ideas about this place as local people? You could use a mixture of open and closed questions to investigate these ideas. If you record the approximate age of each person you could then sort your results to see whether younger people have a different view of the place than older people. Or whether tourists have a different view to local people.

▲ **Figure 23** Like many UK seaside resorts, Rhyl has an ageing population and suffers from the decline of tourism, seasonal employment and a shortage of high-paid jobs.

Activities

2 Study Figure 23.
   a) List the human and physical features of this environment.
   b) How do these features compare to other seaside towns?
   c) Create a bi-polar survey that could be used to assess people's views about this environment. Test it on colleagues in your class.

Enquiry

Design an enquiry for Rhyl.

a) Create an over-arching enquiry question about place.
b) Describe how you would collect the qualitative data you need and design data collection sheets.

How do we manage our coasts?

The usual way to manage coastlines has been through a combination of hard and soft engineering strategies. **Hard engineering** means building structures that prevent erosion and fix the coastline in place. The concrete sea wall and boulders in Figure 1 are a typical example. Wide beaches soak up a lot of wave energy and are a natural defence against coastal erosion. **Soft engineering** strategies mimic this by encouraging natural deposition to take place along the coastline. In Figure 3 you can see that an artificial rock reef has been built parallel to the coastline. This encourages deposition on the beach behind.

▲ **Figure 1** The sea wall at Sea Palling, Norfolk is an example of hard engineering.

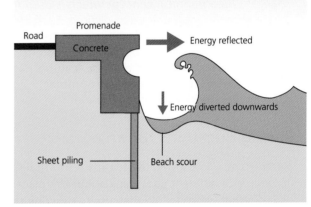

▲ **Figure 3** Sea walls can cause erosion of sediment from the beach.

Activity

1 a) Make a sketch of Figure 1.
   b) Label two hard engineering features on your sketch.
   c) Explain why boulders have been positioned at the top of the beach.

▲ **Figure 2a and b** There are a total of nine artificial reefs at Sea Palling. Notice how sand has been deposited behind the reef, joining it to the beach.

The importance of the inter-tidal zone

Estuarine landscapes, such as the one in Figure 4, contain many tidal creeks, salt marshes and mud banks. These features are exposed at low tide but at high tide they can store huge quantities of water. This is the **inter-tidal zone** and it acts as a natural buffer during storms – soaking up wave energy during a storm surge before the waves can reach more valuable land further inland.

Why is there a need for managed realignment?

There is a much narrower inter-tidal zone in the UK than there used to be:

- Many salt marshes were reclaimed in the past to create new farm land. Old earth embankments have kept the sea off these low-lying fields for centuries.
- Some salt marshes are being eroded by the sea. This is a particular problem along the Essex and Thames gateway coastlines where the land is subsiding so sea levels are rising faster than elsewhere in the UK.

Managed realignment can be used to create new inter-tidal zones of salt marsh. The process begins by punching holes through the old earth embankment. The invading sea water moves slowly across the land at high tide. As it flows in, it deposits mud. As it flows out, it creates tidal creeks like those in Figure 4. This process recreates natural mudflats and salt marshes that will store water and act as a buffer to erosion in future flood events.

▲ **Figure 4** The inter-tidal zone of the Lune estuary, Lancashire. Tidal creeks and mud flats, here at low tide, can store huge quantities of water and help prevent flooding and erosion.

Before

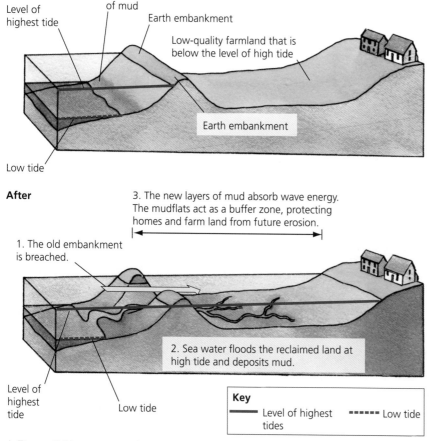

Narrow bank of mud

Level of highest tide

Earth embankment

Low-quality farmland that is below the level of high tide

Earth embankment

Low tide

After

3. The new layers of mud absorb wave energy. The mudflats act as a buffer zone, protecting homes and farm land from future erosion.

1. The old embankment is breached.

2. Sea water floods the reclaimed land at high tide and deposits mud.

Level of highest tide

Low tide

Key

⎯⎯ Level of highest tides   ------ Low tide

▲ **Figure 5** How managed realignment creates wide inter-tidal zones that act as natural stores for flood water at high tide.

Activity

2 a) Make a sketch of Figure 4.
   b) Annotate your sketch to explain why the inter-tidal zone is an important natural defence against erosion and flooding.

Enquiry

Should we create more inter-tidal zones along the UK's coastline? Outline the arguments for and against managed realignment.

Is everyone in favour of managed realignment?

Managed realignment is an example of 'retreating the line' which is an option available in all Shoreline Management Plans, but it is a controversial choice. In 2014 the UK's largest realignment sea defence scheme was completed at Medmerry, West Sussex. This scheme has effectively redrawn the coastline 2 km further inland! The scheme began with the destruction of the existing sea wall, allowing some land to flood naturally at high tide. The newly flooded area will be able to absorb the energy of the waves and will reduce the risk of coastal flooding. A new 7 km sea wall has been built further inland. The Environment Agency says homes are much better protected as a result. However, at £28 million, the scheme was not popular with everyone.

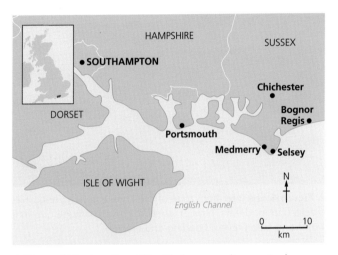

▲ **Figure 6** The location of the Medmerry realignment scheme.

The old sea defenses have been breached here to allow sea water to flood the land to the left and create new salt marshes.

▲ **Figure 7** Medmerry seen from the air.

Has the Medmerry scheme been successful?

During the winter of 2014–15, weeks of rain and fierce storms lashed the south coast. Allan Chamberlain, estate director at the adjacent Medmerry Holiday Village, was shocked by how successful the scheme was. 'It's the first winter in years we haven't had to deal with surface flooding. The rainwater drains into the new marsh beautifully.' The bonus for the Holiday Village and the nearby Bunn Leisure Homes complex is that the new nature reserve is attracting even more tourists. Bookings are up and the tourist attractions can stay open for longer now that the area is largely flood free. Other, somewhat unexpected gains relate to farming. Cattle will be grazed on the salt marsh. This produces a flavour of beef that is highly prized. It is worth more to farmers than the beef usually sold in supermarkets. Also, there are plans for a fish nursery in the new estuarine environment. This could boost the fishing economy in neighbouring Selsey.

> Once you give land back to the sea, there's no getting it back, so if this doesn't work, we will have given up that land for nothing. I would like to see the Environment Agency look at other alternatives such as constructing rock barriers out in the ocean in front of the coast to break wave energy.

Ben Cooper – a resident of nearby Selsey

> Three productive farms producing oilseed rape and winter wheat will have to be sacrificed to the sea. The UK is not self-sufficient in food. The idea of letting perfectly good agricultural land disappear into the sea is wasteful and short-sighted.

Local farmers

> We already have to close for a number of months each year due to coastal flooding. It could get even worse if the sea wall is breached.

Bunn Leisure Holiday Homes

> We have had to endure terrible flooding this winter and we are quite upset about the whole thing. Why is the Environment Agency spending £28 million on creating a coastal nature reserve at Medmerry when they could use the money to dredge rivers and reduce the risk of flooding where we live instead?

Somerset residents badly affected by floods in 2013/14

▲ **Figure 8** Opposition to the Medmerry scheme.

Activities

1 Use Figure 6 to describe the location of Medmerry.
2 Summarise the benefits of realignment at Medmerry for:
   a) local homeowners and businesses
   b) the environment including wildlife.
3 Explain why some local people may have opposed realigning the coast here.

Enquiry

How sustainable is the decision to re-align the coast at Medmerry?

Explain how the sustainability of this scheme could be measured over the next 50 years.

Shoreline Management Plans

Coastal communities expect the government to help protect them from erosion and coastal floods. However, managing the coastline is very expensive. Furthermore, there is no legal duty for the government to build coastal defences to protect people or their property. It is the responsibility of the local councils of England and Wales to prepare a **Shoreline Management Plan (SMP)** for their section of coast. In deciding whether or not to build new coastal defences (or repair old ones), the local council needs to weigh up the benefits of building the defences against the costs. They may consider factors such as:

- How many people are threatened by erosion and what is their property worth?
- How much would it cost to replace infrastructure such as roads or railway lines if they were washed away?
- Are there historic or natural features that should be conserved? Do these features have an economic value, for example, by attracting tourists to the area?

Option	Description	Comment
Do nothing	Do nothing and allow gradual erosion.	This is an option if the land has a lower value than the cost of building sea defences, which can be very expensive.
Hold the line	Use hard engineering such as timber or rock groynes and concrete sea walls to protect the coastline, or add extra sand to a beach to make it more effective at absorbing wave energy.	Sea walls cost about £6,000 per metre to build. Sea-level rise means that such defences need to be constantly maintained, and will eventually need to be replaced with larger structures. For this reason hard engineering is usually only used where the land that is being protected is particularly valuable.
Retreat the line	Punch a hole in an existing coastal defence to allow land to flood naturally between low and high tide (the inter-tidal zone).	Sand dunes and salt marshes provide a natural barrier to flooding and help to absorb wave energy. They adapt naturally to changing sea levels through a process of erosion at the seaward side and deposition further inland.
Advance the line	Build new coastal defences further out to sea.	This requires a huge engineering project and would be the most expensive option. The advantage would be that new, flat land would be available that could be used as a port or airport facility.

▲ **Figure 9** The options available to local councils when they prepare a Shoreline Management Plan.

◀ **Figure 10** Wooden groynes on Borth beach in 2008.

Activity

1 Use Figures 10 and 11.
   a) Describe these structures.
   b) Suggest how they have helped to protect Borth from erosion and flooding.

Management at Borth, Ceredigion

The village of Borth is built on the southern end of a pebble ridge, or spit, that sticks out into the Dyfi estuary. Sand is trapped on the beach by wooden groynes. The sand absorbs wave energy and prevents waves from eroding the pebble ridge. However, the groynes are in poor condition and are at the end of their working lives. What should be done?

The Ceredigion SMP divides the coast up into small management units (MU). Figure 13 shows the extent of five of these MUs.

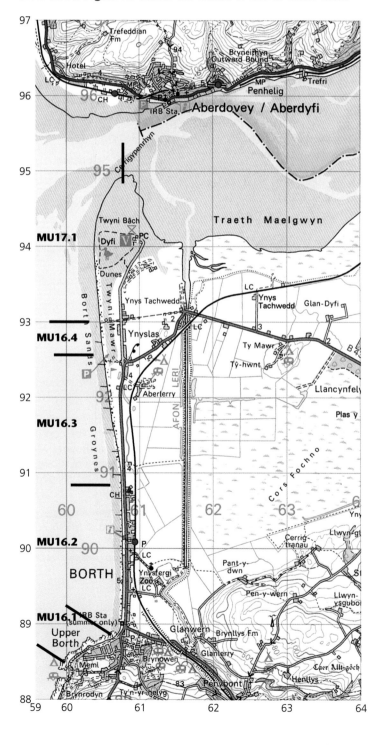

▲ **Figure 11** The wooden sea wall at the top of the pebble ridge (2010).

Activities

2 Work in pairs.
   Use Figure 12 to provide map evidence which suggests that this coast is worth protecting. Copy and complete the table below and add at least five more pieces of evidence.

Management Unit	
16.2	Railway station at 609901 would be expensive to replace
16.3	
16.4	The campsite in 6192 provides local jobs
17.1	

3 Which is the best SMP option for Management Unit (MU) 16.2? Use information from Figure 9 and evidence in Figure 12 to help you make your choice.

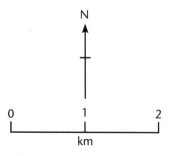

◄ **Figure 12** An Ordnance Survey extract of Borth, 1:50,000.

What coastal management is appropriate for Borth?

Ceredigion Council decided that there were two possible options for Management Unit (MU) 16.2 that needed further consideration. Read the points of view in Figure 14 before deciding what you would do.

Do nothing	Loss of property and economic loss in the short term. Change to Borth Bog.	Consider further
Hold the line	Current policy which protects property and businesses. Coastal processes disrupted with reduced longshore drift.	Consider further
Retreat	Retreat would affect homes that are immediately behind the existing line of defence.	Not considered further
Advance	No need to advance the line except to improve the tourist facilities.	Not considered further

▲ **Figure 13** The initial decision of the Ceredigion Council for MU16.2.

Sand from the southern end of the beach is gradually being eroded by longshore drift, moving it northwards. This process is happening faster than new sand is being deposited. The beach is getting thinner and is less able to protect the pebble ridge (on which Borth is built) from erosion. If the council does nothing then the pebble ridge will be breached by storm waves and the town of Borth, and Borth Bog (Cors Fochno) will be flooded by the sea. This could happen in the next 10 to 15 years. The peat bog at Cors Fochno will be covered in sea water at high tide and its existing ecosystem lost. Over the next few years erosion will punch more holes through the pebble ridge. A new spit of pebbles will eventually form further to the east. The sand dunes at Ynyslas will probably be cut off and form a small island.

Scientist

The beach and landscape of the spit, including the sand dunes at Ynyslas, are an important economic asset to the village. It's this natural environment that attracts thousands of holidaymakers each year. If the council does nothing then my home and many others will be flooded and local people will lose their livelihoods.

B&B owner

Scientist

The peat bog at Cors Fochno should be protected from flooding. It is a nationally and internationally important ecosystem. It has protection as a Special Area of Conservation and is also recognised by UNESCO. 'Do nothing' is an unacceptable option.

We calculate that property in Borth village is worth £10.75 million. On top of this there are many local businesses which would lose their income from tourism if we do nothing. The cost of holding the line is around £7 million. However, we are concerned that building new groynes will prevent longshore drift. We need to consider the impact of that. Currently the sediment moves to Ynyslas where it provides a natural defence to the whole estuary (including the larger village of Aberdyfi) from south-westerly storms.

Local councillor

▲ **Figure 14** Views on the future management of MU16.2.

Activities

1 Using a table, summarise the economic, social and environmental impacts of doing nothing or holding the line in Management Unit 16.2.
2 State which option you would recommend. Explain why you think your option is best for this stretch of coast.

Enquiry

Which is the best SMP option for Management Unit 17.1?

Analyse information from Figure 12 and evaluate the views in Figure 14 to help you justify your choice.

How will climate change affect coastal communities in the UK?

Rising sea levels will increase the rate of coastal erosion. More farmland will be lost and more expensive sea defences will be needed to 'hold the line' against erosion of our towns and cities. Climate change also means a warmer atmosphere, which means more storms like the devastating storm surges that flooded Jaywick in 1953 and 2013.

Year	2007	2032	2057	2082	2107
Rise in sea level (cm)	0	13	35	65	102

▲ **Figure 15** Predicted sea level rise at Jaywick, Essex.

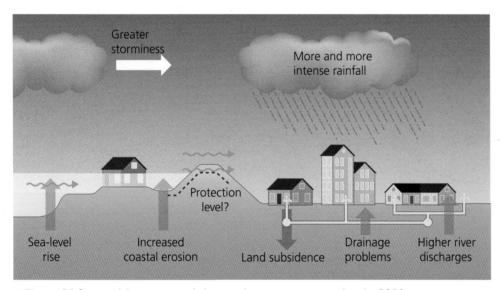

▲ **Figure 16** Some of the impacts of climate change on our coastline by 2050.

Key
Potential shoreline erosion:
- ☐ Low
- ☐ Moderate
- ☐ High
- ☐ Very high
- ■ Extreme

Activities

1 Use Figure 16 to describe five different impacts of sea-level rise on coastal communities in the UK.
2 Use Figure 17 and an atlas to name:
   a) five counties in England facing problems of extreme coastal erosion
   b) three counties in Wales facing very high rates of erosion.
3 a) Use Figure 15 to draw a graph of the predicted sea level rise at Jaywick.
   b) Give two reasons to explain why sea levels are rising here.

◀ **Figure 17** Coastal erosion if carbon dioxide emissions continue to increase and sea levels rise.

How could climate change affect London and the Thames Gateway?

One of the most vulnerable coastlines in the UK is the estuarine landscape of the River Thames to the east of London. This coastline, known as the Thames Gateway, is at risk from storm surges (like those in 1953 and 2013) that push sea into the narrow funnel-like coastline between Essex and Kent. This coastline has been sinking ever since the end of the ice age in the UK about 10,000 years ago – a process called postglacial rebound. As a result, the Thames Gateway is sinking at about 2 mm a year relative to current sea levels. Climate change means that sea levels in the Thames estuary are rising at about 3 mm a year. So the combined effect of sea level rise and postglacial rebound means that sea levels here are rising at 5–6 mm per year.

Year	Type of risk that caused closure		Total closures
	Tidal	River flood	
1983	1	0	1
1984	0	0	0
1985	0	0	0
1986	0	1	1
1987	1	0	1
1988	1	0	1
1989	0	0	0
1990	1	3	4
1991	2	0	2
1992	0	0	0
1993	4	0	4
1994	3	4	7
1995	2	2	4
1996	4	0	4
1997	1	0	1
1998	1	0	1
1999	2	0	2
2000	3	3	6
2001	16	8	24
2002	3	1	4
2003	8	12	20
2004	1	0	1
2005	4	0	4
2006	3	0	3
2007	8	0	8
2008	6	0	6
2009	1	4	5
2010	2	3	5
2011	0	0	0
2012	0	0	0
2013	0	5	5
2014	7	41	48

▲ **Figure 19** Closures of the Thames Barrier to protect against storm (tidal) surges (1983–2014).

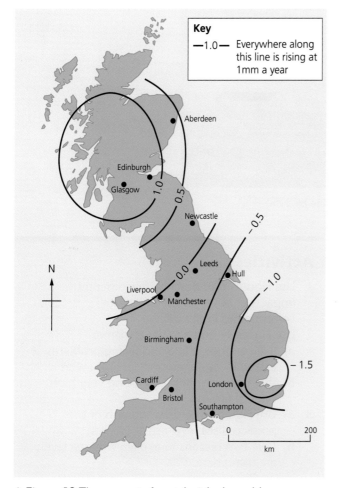

Key

—1.0— Everywhere along this line is rising at 1mm a year

▲ **Figure 18** The amount of postglacial rebound (mm per year). Positive numbers mean the land is rising relative to the sea and negative numbers mean the land is sinking.

Activities

1. Use Figure 18 to describe the parts of the UK where:
   a) land is rising fastest
   b) land is sinking fastest.
2. a) Use the data in Figure 19 to produce a graph of closures.
   b) Describe the trend of your graph.
   c) Explain why this graph could be seen to be more evidence for climate change.

Holding the line

The Thames flood barrier was completed in 1982. It is situated to the east of the City of London so protects large parts of London from tidal surges coming up the river from the North Sea. It protects 1.25 million people from tidal floods. However, it is now thought that the barrier is not large enough to protect London from future floods. The Thames Estuary 2100 Plan (TE2100) suggests that, by 2100, London needs to be protected from a possible flood that would be 2.7 metres higher than current flood levels.

The TE2100 Plan uses three strategies to protect London and the Thames Gateway:

- Continue to renew and replace existing embankments, sea walls and sluices in the Thames Gateway.
- Increase the amount of inter-tidal habitat in the Thames estuary by 876 hectares. These salt marshes will help to store flood water as it moves up the estuary during a tidal surge. These storage areas would be created by managed realignment projects like the one at Tollesbury, Essex.
- Consider building a new, larger barrier at Long Reach to the east of the existing barrier. The construction of this new barrier would cost between £6 billion and £7 billion.

Factfile: Property at risk of tidal flooding on the Thames floodplain

- Over 500,000 homes
- 40,000 commercial and industrial properties
- 400 schools
- 16 hospitals
- 35 tube stations
- Over 300 km of roads

Activities

3 Use Figure 20 to describe:
   a) the distribution of breaches
   b) the amount and value of flooded land.
4 Explain why the cost of flood damage in Essex would be lower than that in London.

Legend

☐	0 €/m²
☐	0 - 1 €/m²
☐	1 - 10 €/m²
▨	10 - 100 €/m²
▨	100 - 200 €/m²
▨	200 - 1000 €/m²
▨	1000 - 2000 €/m²
▨	2000 - 5000 €/m²
▨	5000 - 10.000 €/m²
▨	> 10.000 €/m²
●	Breach location

▲ **Figure 20** The cost of flood damage in 2050 after a flood similar to the 1953 storm surge if sea levels continue to rise and flood protection is not improved. Red dots show where coastal defences would be breached.

Enquiry

How should London and the Thames Gateway be protected in the future? Some people are sceptical about managed realignment. Justify why the TE2100 Plan proposes to combine a new flood barrier with managed realignment.

Why are some coastal communities more vulnerable than others?

A report by the Joseph Rowntree Foundation suggests that some of the most vulnerable people, living in isolated communities of the UK, will be the most affected by rising sea levels.

The report argues that poverty is a factor that makes some communities more vulnerable to sea level rise and coastal flooding than others. Poverty means that the local council has fewer resources available to reduce the threat of and the impacts of sea level rise.

The report suggests that vulnerability to coastal flooding increases where communities have:

- a higher proportion of people claiming benefits;
- a fast turnover of people through economic migration;
- a high proportion of poor-quality housing;
- an over-reliance on tourism, resulting in seasonal employment and low incomes.

▲ **Figure 21** Coastal floods in Great Yarmouth, December 2013.

Skegness, Lincolnshire

Skegness is one of the better-known seaside resorts in England. It is situated within the largely rural area of East Lindsey and has poor road and rail links. Skegness has one of the largest concentrations of caravan parks in Europe. Some static caravans are the permanent homes for retired residents and people on low incomes.

Great Yarmouth, Norfolk

Great Yarmouth is a medium-sized port and is an important seaside resort. It has a high proportion of elderly and retired residents. Unemployment rates are higher in Great Yarmouth than in the rest of the east of England. The economy of the port is in decline and the nearby North Sea gas fields have begun to reduce production.

GEOGRAPHICAL SKILLS

Interpreting population pyramids

Population pyramids are a specialist form of bar graph. Each bar represents males or females in a specific age category. The bars may represent actual population numbers or percentage figures. Interpreting the shape of a pyramid can tell you a lot about the structure of a population. Pyramids with a wide base have a youthful population and those with a wide top have an ageing population. Interpreting the structure is the first step in analysing possible issues that may be facing the population. For example, does an ageing population have sufficient health care and social services suitable for this age group?

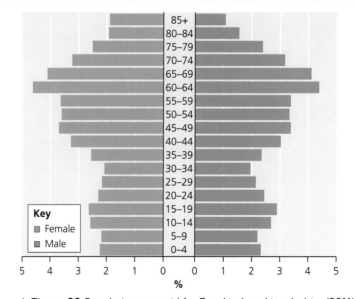

▲ **Figure 22** Population pyramid for East Lindsey, Lincolnshire (2011).

 www.ons.gov.uk/ons/interactive/uk-population-pyramid---dvc1/index.html

An interactive population pyramid for the UK showing change between 1971 and 2085.

Llanelli, Gwent

Unemployment in Llanelli is higher than the national average and the town has been particularly hard hit by the economic recession of 2008–9. Derelict industrial sites along the coastline are now the focus of several regeneration schemes. The town has a higher than average proportion of elderly residents. A high number of migrants from Eastern Europe have settled in the town.

Benbecula, Outer Hebrides

With a population of 1,200, the population and economy of this remote Scottish island have been in decline since the mid-1970s because of the closure of a military base. The lack of jobs for younger people has also contributed to the decline and to the ageing of the island's population. The island's coastal drainage system was built in the 1800s and is not very efficient. It struggles to cope with the combined effects of heavy rainfall and high tides.

Indicator	Skegness	Lincolnshire	England
% of working population in professional/ management jobs	14	18	23
% of working population claiming work-related benefits	18	13	13
% of adult population with no academic qualifications	33	26	22
% of the adult population who are in very good health	38	43	47

▲ **Figure 23** Socio-economic statistics for Skegness.

▲ **Figure 24** Skegness has a large concentration of static caravans.

In such communities, local people may lack the funds to make structural changes to their homes (e.g. to make them flood resistant). They may not be able to afford to move away. Coastal local authorities with areas of high deprivation may not be able to afford the resources for climate change preparation. Government policy means that there is an ever-increasing expectation that individuals and communities should help themselves to prepare for the likely increase in sea level rise. For disadvantaged residents, the threat of sea level rise is simply not a major issue at this moment in time. They have other things to focus on.

▲ **Figure 25** An extract (adapted) from the Joseph Rowntree Report summary statement.

Activities

1 Compare the four communities described on these pages. Describe three similarities that link at least two of these communities.
2 a) Describe the structure of the population structure for East Lindsey.
  b) Use the Weblink to compare this population structure to that of the UK.
  c) What does this suggest is needed in East Lindsey?
3 Explain why every local authority may not be able to afford the resources needed to prepare for sea level rise.
4 Use Figure 23 to:
  a) Identify the overall pattern shown in the table.
  b) The figures in the table date from the National Census in 2011. The worst impact of sea level rise is not expected to happen until 2050. Should the local authority use the data to appeal for additional outside help when planning for sea level rise? Justify your answer.

Enquiry

Who should be responsible for protecting communities in the UK from the effects of sea level rise?

'Government policy means that there is an ever-increasing expectation that individuals and communities should help themselves to prepare for the likely increase in sea level rise'. How far do you agree with this statement? Discuss this in groups.

How might climate change affect coastal communities around the world?

By 2030 it is estimated that 950 million people around the world will live in the **Low Elevation Coastal Zone (LECZ)** – that is, coastal areas that are less than 10 metres above sea level. Climate change presents a triple threat to people living in LECZs:

- Sea level rise increases the risk of coastal flooding at high tide.
- Heavier rainfall increases the risk of flash floods in urban areas with poor drainage (see page 174).
- More violent storms and hurricanes increase the risk of coastal erosion and storm surges.

The worst-affected coastal communities could be those living on the world's major river deltas. People living here are affected by subsidence of the soft land as well as by sea-level rise. Millions of people live on deltas in Bangladesh, Egypt, Nigeria, Vietnam and Cambodia.

In 2013 the World Bank identified 136 coastal cities that are at greatest risk from climate change. Mumbai, home to 18.4 million people, is one. Built on a low-lying island, much of Mumbai is only 10 metres above sea level. Other cities, like New York, Singapore and New Orleans, are also at risk. Many cities identified by the World Bank are in developing countries where the poorest members of society are at most risk of natural hazards. This is because the poorest neighbourhoods, like those in Figure 29, are often in low-lying areas and built alongside waterways or seafronts that are vulnerable to flooding. As sea levels rise, some people may have to leave their homes. They will become **environmental refugees**.

Activity

1 Use Figure 26 to describe:
   a) the distribution of SIDS
   b) the location of:
      i) the Maldives   ii) the Marshall Islands.
   c) Suggest why people living in isolated places like these are vulnerable to natural hazards.

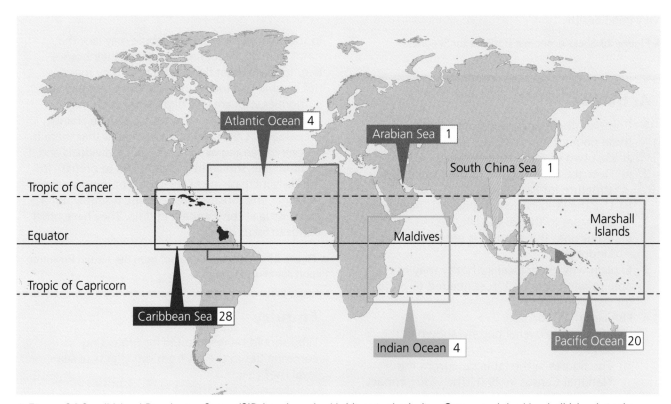

▲ **Figure 26** Small Island Developing States (SIDs) such as the Maldives in the Indian Ocean and the Marshall Islands in the Pacific are very low-lying. A 1 m rise in sea level by 2100 would flood up to 75 per cent of the land in each of these two nations.

Factfile: Small Island Developing States (SIDS)

- There are currently 58 SIDS with a combined population of 65 million people.
- Many SIDS are very small and some are located in remote and isolated parts of the world. Most

- SIDS are vulnerable to climate change and natural disasters.
- Standards of living among small islands differ widely, with GDP per capita ranging from $51,000 in Singapore to $830 in Comoros.

City	Population (%) at risk in LECZ	Land (%) at risk in LECZ	Population 2015	Population 2030
Cotonou, Benin	94.7	85.4	682,000	979,000
Warri, Nigeria	90.8	92.0	663,000	1,298,000
Alexandria, Egypt	85.1	68.8	4,778,000	6,313,000
Port Harcourt, Nigeria	64.4	61.9	2,344,000	4,562,000
Dakar, Senegal	61.6	47.6	3,520,000	6,046,000

▲ **Figure 27** Selected African cities in the low elevation coastal zone (LECZ).

▲ **Figure 28** Poor neighbourhoods in Cotonou, Benin are built on stilts along the waterfront.

Activities

2 Study Figure 28.
  a) Describe the housing carefully.
  b) Suggest why the poorest members of society live in neighbourhoods like this.
  c) Suggest how this community will be affected by climate change.
3 a) Calculate the actual number of people expected to be living in the LECZ in each of the cities in Figure 27.
  b) Using an atlas, suggest why each of the cities in Figure 27 is so vulnerable to climate change.

Enquiry

Analyse why it may be more difficult for the governments of SIDs to cope with climate change than a larger country like India.

Is it too late to save the Maldives?

The Republic of Maldives, in the Indian Ocean, is made up of 1,190 islands. It has a population of 350,000. Most of the islands are uninhabited, with over one-third of the population living in Malé, the capital city. Eighty per cent of the land area is under one metre above sea level. Nowhere is above 3 metres. No place on earth is more vulnerable and threatened by sea level rise. The GDP of the Maldives ranks the country as 165th out of 192 nation states (2013).

For more than three decades politicians from the country have tried to persuade world leaders to take climate change more seriously. In the 2015 Geneva Climate Change Conference, Dunya Maumoon, the minister of foreign affairs for the Maldives, asked the global community to take concrete action. He said, *'2015 should be remembered, not for stories about sea level rise, but ones about how we rose up together to stop it.'* The fact is, it's probably already too late.

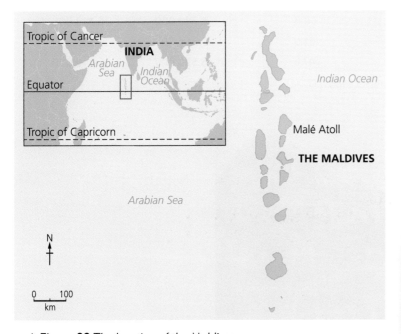

▲ **Figure 29** The location of the Maldives.

▲ **Figure 30** Is this the future for the Maldives?

Factfile: The effects of sea level rise on the Maldives

- A rise in sea level of 0.5 m by the year 2100 would mean that 77% of the land surface of the Maldives will be underwater.
- A rise in sea level of 1 m by the year 2100 would make the islands uninhabitable by 2085.

How is sea level rise affecting the islands?

Frequent flooding of the islands over the past 30 years has caused ongoing problems for the Maldives. Most of the problems occur when the highest spring tides coincide with storms across the northern India Ocean.

▲ **Figure 31** The capital city of the Maldives, Malé, is surrounded by sea.

The impact of flooding across the Maldives

Malé – a capital city surrounded by sea walls:
In 2008 Japan offered $60 million in aid to fund a 3 m sea wall for Malé. The sea wall has been completed and will hold back the advance of the sea for the medium term. All the other islands remain vulnerable. The sea wall needs constant repair, the cost has to be paid for through local tourist taxes.

Drinking water is in short supply:
Sea level rise is already beginning to put stress on the scarce freshwater resources of the Maldives; 87% of the population can currently be supplied by collecting rainwater. Groundwater sources across the chain of islands have been contaminated by salt-water intrusion and are now undrinkable. Bringing in supplies from abroad is unsustainable.

The tourist industry under threat:
Tourism is by far and away the most important industry. It accounts for 90% of government tax revenue. The damage caused by the 2004 tsunami-related sea surge destroyed many prize beaches and ruined some luxury resorts. For a year, tourist numbers dropped dramatically as the islands implemented a recovery programme. Tourist numbers have since recovered, but the industry may have been given a taste of what's to come.

▲ **Figure 32** The impact of flooding across the Maldives.

Islands that float

Floating islands will be moored to the seabed using cables to minimise environmental impact. This idea has been put forward by a Dutch company. One of the islands will be used to create an artificial golf course. Golfers will access the floating 'golf island' by a tunnel on the seabed. There will be a spectacular underwater clubhouse for golfers to relax in after their game. The artificial islands will be built in India or the Middle East and towed to the Maldives.

▲ **Figure 33** How might the Maldives develop tourism in the future?

Sea level rise forces castaways to move to Australia

The Maldivian President said his government was considering Australia as a possible new home if the Maldives disappear beneath rising seas. He explained that Maldivians wanted to stay but moving was an eventuality his government had to plan for. Australia may need to prepare for a mass wave of climate refugees, seeking a new place to live.

▲ **Figure 34** Sea level rise may create environmental refugees.

Activities

1. Describe the location of the Maldives.
2. Study the two newspaper headlines shown in Figures 33 and 34. Both were published in 2012. They offer very different radical solutions to the problems faced by the Maldives.
   a) Discuss how sustainable each idea would be.
   b) Discuss which is the most likely to be turned into reality.

Enquiry

What should the Maldives Government do?

a) List five different ideas for action – place your ideas in priority order.
b) Justify why you think ideas one and two need to be put into action as soon as possible.

Investigating global patterns of extreme weather

In March 2015, the Pacific island of Vanuatu was devastated by the destructive power of a **cyclone**. Homes and crops were destroyed by the extreme winds and rain. Eleven people lost their lives. At the same time in California, USA, farmers were managing limited water supplies during the third consecutive year of **drought**. The hot, dry weather caused wildfires that burnt out of control. How can such extremes of weather exist at the same time? What causes them?

Activity

1 Study Figure 1.
   a) Describe the location of cyclones that affect
      i)   Australasia
      ii) North and South America
      iii) South East Asia.
   b) Compare the direction of storm tracks in the northern and southern hemispheres.
   c) Name two countries that are at risk of both cyclones and drought.
   d) Describe the location of areas affected by drought in the northern hemisphere. How are these areas different to those that are vulnerable to cyclones?

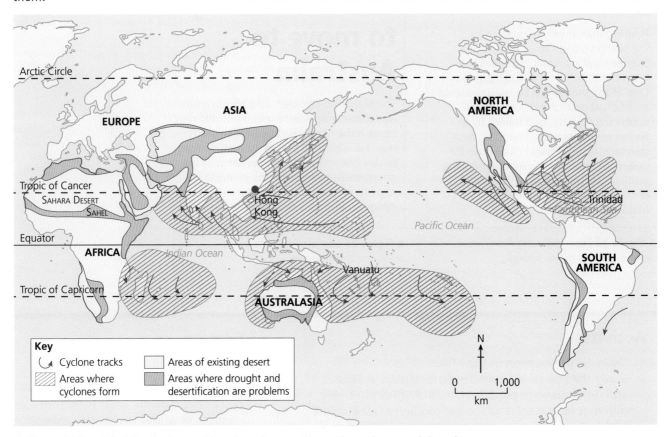

▲ **Figure 1** The global distribution and location of areas affected by cyclones and drought.

Activity

2 a) Make a copy of Figure 2 on page 173. Use the text boxes to annotate your diagram. Place your annotations in appropriate places on the diagram.
   b) Use your completed diagram to explain why there is rainforest at the Equator and desert at latitudes 30° to the north and south.

What is happening in our atmosphere to cause extreme weather?

We can begin to understand extreme weather by considering the intensity of the sun's heat on the ground at different latitudes on the Earth. The climate close to the Equator (within five degrees of latitude) is hot throughout the year. The Sun heats the Earth and the Earth heats the air above, which becomes **unstable** and rises. This creates a band of low pressure in the atmosphere, known as the intertropical convergence zone,

the **ITCZ**, which circles the equatorial region of the Earth. The position of the ITCZ is shown in Figure 3. Notice that its position varies throughout the year. This is because of the tilt of the Earth's axis. The northern hemisphere leans towards the Sun in June and July so the ITCZ is slightly north of the Equator. The ITCZ migrates to south of the Equator in December and January when the southern hemisphere leans towards the Sun.

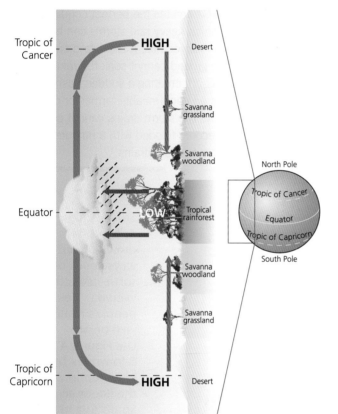

The Sun heats the Earth and the Earth heats the air above, which becomes unstable and rises creating an area of low pressure.

The air circulates back towards the equator in the lower atmosphere creating the trade winds.

At about 30 °N and 30 °S the air descends creating an area of high pressure. This air is dry. It seldom rains.

The air reaches a boundary layer in the atmosphere called the tropopause which is about 17 km above the equator. The air spreads outwards towards the poles.

◀ **Figure 2** How solar heating at the Equator creates the ITCZ.

Activity

3 a) Using Figure 3, describe the position of the ITCZ:
   i) Over the Pacific Ocean in January and July.
   ii) Over Central America in July.
  b) Compare the location and distribution of cyclones on Figure 1 to the position of the ITCZ in Figure 3. What conclusion do you come to?

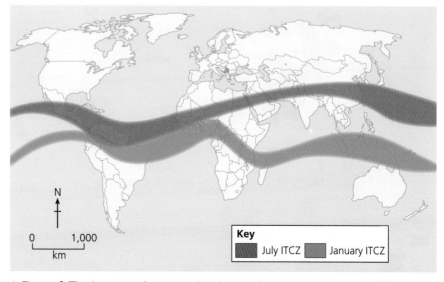

▲ **Figure 3** The location of equatorial and tropical low pressure systems (ITCZ).

How low pressure causes extreme weather

In late July 2015, India and Pakistan were badly affected by **monsoon** rains that caused flash floods and landslides. More than 120 people were drowned in India. It is thought that 116 people died in Pakistan and almost 1 million people had to leave their homes temporarily because of the floods. At the same time, West Bengal, Bangladesh and Myanmar were hit by flooding after a tropical storm caused heavy rainfall. Villagers in West Bengal said, 'We have seen floods, but never anything like this before. This year is the worst.' Why did these extreme weather events take place?

Why does South Asia have a monsoon season?

The flash floods of July 2015 were not the first time this region has suffered extreme weather. The monsoon rains occur each year across South Asia. These rains are formed as the ITCZ moves northwards across India during July (see Figure 3 on page 173). Figure 7 shows how the position of the ITCZ creates the perfect conditions for a month during which heavy rain storms can happen on any day. When the rain comes, it often falls on hard, dry-baked earth. The ground cannot soak the rainwater up fast enough so it runs-off, creating a sudden flash flood. In cities the rain falls on impermeable tarmac or concrete and cannot soak away. The storm drains cannot cope so the streets quickly become flooded with a mixture of rain water and sewage from the foul drains.

▲ **Figure 4** People struggle to get around after flash floods in Lahore, Pakistan.

Activities

1 Study Figure 4. Apart from drowning, list five ways floods of this sort could affect everyday life or people's health and well-being.
2 Use Figures 4 and 5 to write a brief news report about the floods across South Asia in July 2015. Make sure you describe:
    a) The location of the flooding.
    b) The cause and effects of the flooding.

Key
🌀 Tropical storm
◼ Areas affected by severe flooding
▨ Disputed territory

AFGHANISTAN Islamabad
Lahore
PAKISTAN New Delhi
NEPAL
RAJASTHAN
MADHYA PRADESH
GUJARAT
BANGLADESH
WEST BENGAL
Kolkata
Arabian Sea
Bengal Bay
Mumbai
INDIA
MYANMAR
Indian Ocean

N
0   500
km

◀ **Figure 5** Map of South Asia showing areas affected by flooding during July 2015.

Day	1	2	3	4	5	6	7	8	9	10	11	12	13	14	15	16
Rainfall (mm)	0	0	1.6	0	0	0	9	0	0	0.1	0.1	42	4	0.1	0	0
Day	17	18	19	20	21	22	23	24	25	26	27	28	29	30	31	
Rainfall (mm)	119	0.1	75	5	2	0.1	2	17	0.1	17	2	0	0	0	1	

▲ **Figure 6** Rainfall (mm) in Lahore for each day of July 2015.

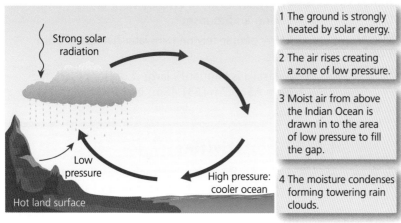

1 The ground is strongly heated by solar energy.

2 The air rises creating a zone of low pressure.

3 Moist air from above the Indian Ocean is drawn in to the area of low pressure to fill the gap.

4 The moisture condenses forming towering rain clouds.

▲ **Figure 7** Circulation of the atmosphere over South Asia during July.

Activities

3 a) Use the data in Figure 6 to draw a suitable graph.
   b) Use your graph to explain the flash floods you can see in Figure 4.

4 Make a copy of Figure 7. Annotate your diagram in appropriate places to show why the ITCZ's position creates such a large quantity of rainfall during the monsoon.

How do cyclones form?

Cyclones, known as hurricanes in America and typhoons in Asia, are more violent than tropical storms. They are seasonal events caused by extreme low pressure when the ITCZ is overhead. The destructive energy of a cyclone is created when warmth from the sea is transferred to the air above. Sea temperatures need to be at 27°C or above for several weeks before a cyclone will form. The warm water heats the air above it, which rises rapidly, creating an area of very low pressure in the atmosphere. This causes towering clouds to form and torrential rain to fall. At sea level, the rising air is replaced by more warm moist air coming in from the outside. As the air moves towards the centre of the low pressure, it spirals upwards into the atmosphere. The spiral effect comes from the rotation of the Earth, a process known as the **Coriolis Effect**.

	Jan	Feb	Mar	Apr	May	Jun	Jul	Aug	Sep	Oct	Nov	Dec
Vanuatu	29.1	29.5	29.5	29.3	28.4	27.7	27.0	26.5	26.6	27.0	27.4	28.2
Trinidad	27.6	27.3	27.3	27.6	28.1	28.2	28.3	29.3	29.4	29.0	28.4	27.9
Hong Kong	19.1	18.9	20.1	22.7	26.8	28.5	29.1	28.6	28.3	26.5	24.3	21.0
Cornwall, UK	10.4	10.0	9.7	10.6	12.0	14.2	16.5	17.1	16.5	14.8	13.2	11.7

▲ **Figure 8** Average sea temperatures for selected locations (°C).

Activity

5 Use Figure 8 to draw two graphs to represent average sea temperatures in Hong Kong and Cornwall. Use your graphs, and Figure 1, to explain why Hong Kong is at risk of cyclones but Cornwall is not.

Enquiry

Predict when cyclones are most likely to threaten each of the following islands. Use the information in Figures 1, 3 and 8 to justify your answer:

a) Trinidad
b) Vanuatu.

Cyclone Pam, March 2015

In March 2015, Cyclone Pam tore through the island chain of Vanuatu in the Pacific, causing a trail of destruction. Cyclones are placed in different categories according to the strength of the wind. These categories are described in Figure 10. Pam was a Category 5 cyclone. The cyclone was at full strength as it crossed several islands. Winds were at around 250 km per hour, with some gusts reaching 320 km an hour. Many homes were destroyed and crops flattened by the wind. The cyclone had been forecast and many people took shelter in evacuation centres. Eleven people lost their lives.

Factfile

- Vanuatu is a group of 83 volcanic islands in the Pacific Ocean.
- The population is 272,000.
- GNI is US$3,090, making Vanuatu one of the lower Middle Income Countries.
- The main forms of employment are farming, fishing and tourism.
- Many people rely on rainwater harvested from roofs.
- Australia is Vanuatu's largest donor of aid. It gave A$60.7m (£31.45m) in 2013/4.

Activities

1 Describe the track of Cyclone Pam. Use the North arrow and scale line.
2 Identify one social, one economic and one environmental problem faced by islanders.
3 Identify one social, one economic and one environmental problem caused by Cyclone Pam.

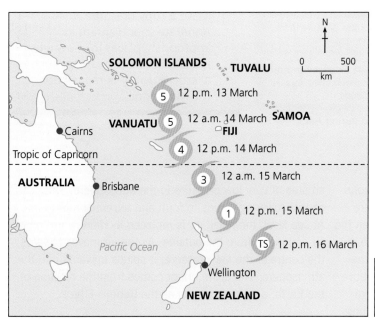

Key

⟲ Cyclone track

Numbers = cyclone strength

(TS) Tropical storm

▲ **Figure 9** The track of Cyclone Pam.

Category	Strongest gusts of wind (km/h)	Air pressure at the centre (millibars)	Typical damage
1	Less than 125	>980	Minimal damage to houses, but there is some damage to crops and trees. Some boats may drag their moorings.
2	125–164	965–980	Storm winds cause minor damage to houses but significant damage to road signs, trees and some crops. There is a risk of power failure. Small boats break from their moorings.
3	165–224	945–964	Very destructive winds cause damage to roofs. Many crops and trees are damaged. The risk of power failure is high.
4	225–279	920–944	Very destructive winds cause damage to roofs, walls and windows. Widespread power failures. Debris is blown by the wind, creating risk of injury.
5	More than 280	<920	Extremely destructive winds cause widespread damage to property and vegetation. Severe disruption to infrastructure such as roads, telephone lines and power lines.

▲ **Figure 10** Cyclone categories.

What were the effects of Cyclone Pam?

Villages in Vanuatu rely on two types of water supply:
- Rainwater is collected from streams or from the roofs of buildings and fed into overground tanks.
- Groundwater is collected from shallow wells.

Both types of supply were damaged by Cyclone Pam. The strong winds tore off roofs and blew down the storage tanks. Sea water from the storm surge flooded coastal areas and contaminated fresh water wells. It is estimated that 68 per cent of rainwater-harvesting structures and 70 per cent of wells were damaged.

The destructive winds damaged up to 90 per cent of homes on islands that lay directly in the path of the storm such as Erromango. In all, 90,000 people had their homes damaged. The winds also damaged hospitals and schools, affecting more than 35,000 pupils. The winds destroyed both up to 80 per cent of subsistence crops, such as vegetables, and cash crops such as coffee. Damage to farming was estimated to be US$2.5 million.

How did the world respond to the emergency in Vanuatu?

Australia, Fiji, France, New Zealand, Solomon Islands, Tonga and the United Kingdom all sent emergency aid using military aircraft and personnel. Vanuatu is a very remote group of islands. The steep volcanic slopes mean that there are very few long air-strips and the islands have very few harbours capable of taking large ships. Emergency aid was flown into Port Villa. The government then set up an 'air bridge' using smaller planes and boats to take the aid to where it was most needed.

▲ **Figure 11** United Nations personnel on board an RAF plane carrying emergency aid to Port Villa, Vanuatu.

21,000 people received supplies of safe drinking water

92,500 blankets

20 foreign medical teams

26,000 repairs made to water supply systems

95,000 people received medical care

153 temporary schools created

19,000 children vaccinated against measles

67,000 tarpaulin sheets

▲ **Figure 12** Emergency aid in numbers, by July 2015.

Activities

4 Explain why the government of Vanuatu would want to tackle each of the following problems urgently:
   a) Repairing water supplies
   b) Providing medical care
   c) Setting up temporary schools.

5 Suggest how countries, such as Australia, might provide effective long-term aid for the people of Vanuatu. Justify your ideas.

Enquiry

Analyse the impacts of extreme weather caused by low pressure. What are the main differences between the monsoon that affected South Asia in 2015 and the Cyclone Pam? Write a short report. Focus on:

a) causes
b) the scale of the event (area and people affected)
c) the duration of the event (length of time)
d) the social and economic impacts.

Heat wave and drought in California

In July 2015, wildfires in California hit the news headlines in the UK. In one fire, near Clear Lake, over 3,000 acres of land burnt out of control. People had to be evacuated from their homes. In another wildfire, shown in Figure 17, cars stuck in road works on Interstate 15 had to be abandoned as a wildfire swept across the road. What was causing this extreme weather?

The wildfires were a result of a three year-long drought that affected California between 2012 and 2015. A drought is when significantly less rain falls than usual over a prolonged period of time. During the period 2012–15, the winter rainfall totals in California were much lower than usual and it doesn't normally rain much in the summer months anyway. The result was a drought and dry vegetation that easily burns in the hot summer months.

Activities

1 Use Figure 13 to describe:
   a) the location of Los Angeles
   b) the distribution of states affected by exceptional drought conditions.

2 Suggest how the drought and wild fires might have affected farmers, consumers, homeowners and firefighters.

3 Use Figure 15 and an atlas.
   a) Forecast the weather in each of the following places. You should be able to comment on the temperature and precipitation.
      i)   Los Angeles
      ii) Ottowa
      iii) Mexico City.
   b) The jet stream has a wave-like motion as it swerves to the north and south, as shown in Figure 14. Explain why the winter weather of the USA would be different if the jet stream followed a more normal pattern.

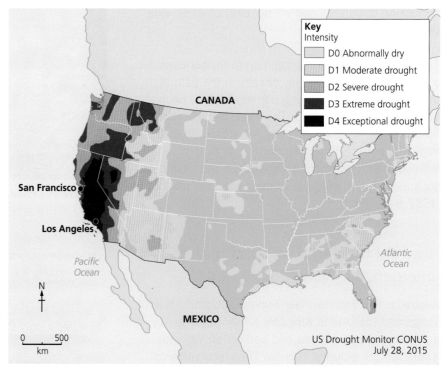

Key
Intensity
- D0 Abnormally dry
- D1 Moderate drought
- D2 Severe drought
- D3 Extreme drought
- D4 Exceptional drought

US Drought Monitor CONUS
July 28, 2015

▲ **Figure 13** The extent of the drought across the USA in July 2015.

What caused the drought in California?

The low winter rainfall has been caused by the position of the **jet stream**. The jet stream is a strong ribbon of winds that circle the globe between 9 and 16 km above the surface of the Earth. These winds separate the cold polar air masses to the north from the warmer tropical air masses to the south, as you can see in Figure 14. The jet stream usually curves further south than in Figure 14. It normally pushes rain-bearing low pressure air masses across California during the winter months. However, between 2012 and 2015, it was wrapped around a huge area of high pressure in the north-eastern Pacific. Dry air to the west of California had remained stationary for long periods of time. The United States Weather Service nicknamed this pressure system the 'Reluctant Ridge' of high pressure because of its reluctance to break down or move. Meanwhile, low air pressure and cold air from Canada was dragged down into the central and eastern areas of the USA, as you can see in Figure 15.

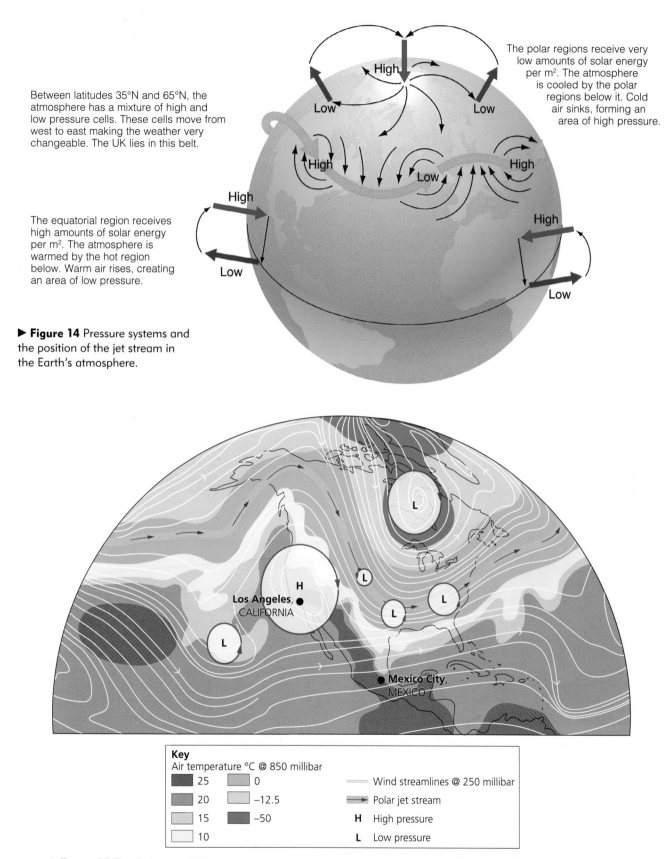

Between latitudes 35°N and 65°N, the atmosphere has a mixture of high and low pressure cells. These cells move from west to east making the weather very changeable. The UK lies in this belt.

The equatorial region receives high amounts of solar energy per m². The atmosphere is warmed by the hot region below. Warm air rises, creating an area of low pressure.

The polar regions receive very low amounts of solar energy per m². The atmosphere is cooled by the polar regions below it. Cold air sinks, forming an area of high pressure.

High
Low
Low
High
Low
High
High
Low

▶ **Figure 14** Pressure systems and the position of the jet stream in the Earth's atmosphere.

Los Angeles, CALIFORNIA
H
L
L
L
L
L
Mexico City, MEXICO

Key
Air temperature °C @ 850 millibar

25	0	═══ Wind streamlines @ 250 millibar
20	−12.5	➤ Polar jet stream
15	−50	H High pressure
10		L Low pressure

▲ **Figure 15** The Reluctant Ridge of high pressure in the eastern Pacific in mid-February 2015.

What have been the effects of the Californian drought?

Short-term impacts are easy to see. The amount of discharge in most rivers of California fell to much lower levels than usual. In August 2015, 44 per cent of rivers had flows that were just 10 per cent of their normal flow. In the summer heat, moisture from the soil is evaporated. Plants become withered and dry.

In these conditions a spark can easily trigger a wildfire. If the weather is windy then the fire can spread very quickly, endangering properties and lives. One way that firefighters use to tackle such a problem is to light deliberate fires between the wildfire and any property. The fire burns up any vegetation and is then put out. In this way, the wildfire has no fuel to burn when it arrives.

Farmers in Central Valley lost $810 m during 2015.

Homeowners were told to stop using water to wash down their driveways, or water gardens. Using a hose to wash cars was banned. Californians caught ignoring water restrictions were shamed on Twitter using the hashtag #DroughtShaming.

Most HEP dams stopped producing electricity.

[handwritten: Hydro-electric power]

Cracks appeared in buildings and roads due to subsidence. This happened because water was being pumped out of the ground faster than it was being naturally replaced.

▲ **Figure 16** How has the drought affected people and the environment?

California usually produces nearly half of the fruits and vegetables grown in the USA. Shortages meant that prices rose by 6% in the shops. More food was imported.

There was a 36% increase in wildfires. Property was damaged and wildlife killed. 31,000 acres of oak habitat burned.

The state government paid $687m of its savings to compensate farmers and homeowners who lost earnings or property. This money could have been used for other much needed projects.

Salmon and trout died in the San Joaquin River Delta. An increase in river temperature means the water carries less oxygen for fish.

The state lost 17,100 agricultural jobs due to the drought.

▲ **Figure 17** A wildfire destroyed several vehicles stuck in a traffic jam on Interstate 15, California, in July 2015. No one was injured.

Activities

1 Study the data in Figure 18.
   a) Use the data to draw a series of graphs.
   b) Compare the rainfall of 2014 to both the normal rainfall and the 1976 drought.
   c) Identify one strength and one limitation of this evidence and the way you have chosen to represent it.
2 Other than the physical cause of the drought, suggest three other factors that may have led to water shortages.

Rainfall: monthly figures in mm	Jan	Feb	Mar	Apr	May	Jun	Jul	Aug	Sep	Oct	Nov	Dec
Mean rainfall	78	95	45	30	18	3	3	12	8	25	40	105
The 1976 drought	37	42	32	22	0	0	0	4	5	12	19	33
The 2014 drought	25	28	30	2	0	0	1	2	0	9	15	22

▲ **Figure 18** San Francisco, like the rest of California, is experiencing record low rainfall.

What are the long-term impacts?

The long-term impacts of drought could be more serious to the economy and way of life in California. The drought means that groundwater is not recharged by rainfall soaking into the ground. So the water table drops as water is abstracted quicker than it is replaced. In the long term, this is unsustainable for water supplies and the important farming businesses that rely on the abstraction of ground water.

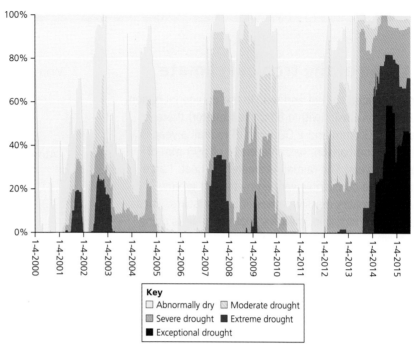

Key
- ☐ Abnormally dry
- ☐ Moderate drought
- ☐ Severe drought
- ■ Extreme drought
- ■ Exceptional drought

▲ **Figure 19** The percentage of California experiencing drought conditions (2000–15).

I had to introduce compulsory water restrictions. Every town and city must show how it will reduce water use by 25% compared to 2013 levels. Agricultural users must provide the State with frequent reports about their medium term plans to reduce water consumption. Those who install toilets, domestic washing machines and showers must only use modern, low-water technologies.

Jerry Brown, Governor of California

We have introduced a mixture of voluntary and compulsory water conservation programmes. Watering gardens, cars and driveways is banned. We will offer subsidies to people who want to change their toilets and washing machines for newer models. We have sent out millions of leaflets offering advice on how to conserve water in the home.

Harlan Kelly, General Manager of the San Francisco Water Utility

California needs to reduce the amount of electricity it gets from Hydro Electric Power. Reservoirs must be used for water supply not electricity supply. For the customer this will mean higher prices as we turn to natural gas in the short term. This will certainly mean adding more greenhouse gases into the atmosphere. In the longer term, Californians will need to get more serious about using solar and wind power.

An energy expert

Californians must realise that this problem will not go away. We must pay more for our water and put money into desalination plants that remove salt from sea water. We must encourage farmers to grow crops that are less thirsty, even if the profits are lower and more food is imported. We must hold back some water supplies to protect delicate ecosystems, to allow nature to have a fair chance of survival.

An environmentalist

▲ **Figure 20** The response to the drought.

Activities

3 Study Figure 16.
  a) Sort the impacts of the drought into social, economic and environmental effects.
  b) Use a diamond ranking technique (see page 108) to rank the impacts of the drought.
  c) Choose the three most serious impacts. Explain why you have chosen each one.
4 How should the people of California respond to the drought in the long term? Write a short report highlighting how the house building, farming and energy industries could respond.

Enquiry

How severe was the 2014–15 Californian drought? Study Figure 19. Use evidence from this graph to describe the severity of the 2015 drought. Consider both the length of the drought and the percentage of California that was affected, compared to previous years.

Features of the tropical climate

Tropical climates are hot and wet. In the equatorial region of the Amazon Basin (within 5° of the Equator) there is between 1,500 mm and 2,000 mm of rainfall a year. London, by comparison, has an average of 593 mm of rainfall each year. The rainfall is created by heat. Large air masses are constantly warmed by the hot ground below. This creates massive zones of low pressure. These air masses are **unstable**, meaning that warm air is rising within them. The unstable air rises and spreads away from the Equator, creating the **tropical rain belt** (or **ITCZ**) that circles the globe. You can see some of the clouds forming in the ICTZ in Figure 3.

There are three main types of wet tropical climate. Two have seasonal patterns to their rainfall. Figure 2 summarises the features of these climates. It also introduces the other main tropical climate type we will explore in this chapter, the hot semi-arid climate.

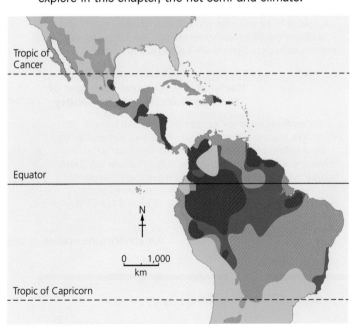

▲ **Figure 2** The distribution of the three main tropical climate types, and the hot semi-arid climate in Central and South America.

| Warm air rises within the unstable air mass |

| Tiny water droplets join together |

| Atmospheric molecules get further apart |

| Water vapour in the air condenses |

| The atmosphere is heated by the ground |

| Rainclouds form |

| The ground is heated strongly at the Equator by the Sun |

| Air pressure falls |

▲ **Figure 1** Atmospheric processes within the tropical rain belt.

Key	Climate type	Features
⬛	**Equatorial** (also known as the tropical rainforest climate)	All months have an average precipitation of at least 60 mm, often much higher. There are no seasons. It is hot and wet throughout the year.
▨	**Tropical wet** (also known as the tropical monsoon climate)	It is hot in every month with no real seasonal variation in temperature. Precipitation is seasonal, with some months having exceptionally high rainfall totals but other months having less than 60 mm of rainfall.
▨	**Tropical wet and dry** (also known as tropical savanna climate)	It is hot in every month but some months are a little cooler than others. There are very distinct wet and dry seasons. During the dry season monthly precipitation totals are below 60 mm. There is usually less total annual rainfall than a tropical wet climate and the dry season is drier and longer.
▨	**Hot semi-arid**	This is the most seasonal of the four tropical climates. It is extremely hot in the summer and mild in the winter. There is a short wet season and a long dry season. There is a lower annual precipitation total than in the savanna type of climate.

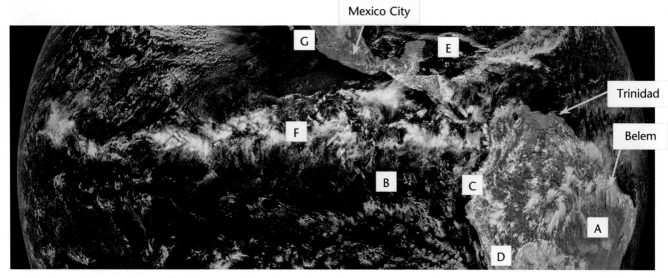

▲ **Figure 3** A satellite image of the tropical rain belt over the Pacific, Caribbean and Central America.

		Jan	Feb	Mar	Apr	May	Jun	Jul	Aug	Sep	Oct	Nov	Dec
Belem, Brazil	Average temp °C	26	26	27	27	27	26	26	26	27	27	27	27
	Average rainfall mm	318	358	358	320	259	170	150	112	89	84	66	155
Trinidad	Average temp °C	26	26.5	26	26.5	27	27	26.5	26.5	27	27	27	26
	Average rainfall mm	69	41	46	53	94	193	218	246	193	170	183	125
Mexico City, Mexico	Average temp °C	12	13	16	18	19	18.5	17.5	17.5	17.5	17.5	14	11.5
	Average rainfall mm	13	5	10	20	53	119	170	152	130	51	18	8

▲ **Figure 4** Three contrasting tropical climates (average 1961–90).

Activities

1 Study Figures 2 and 3 and, using an atlas:
   a) Name the countries A, B, C, D and E.
   b) Working in pairs, match the following label to letters F and G:
      ▪ The atmosphere is warmed by the hot region below. Warm air rises, creating clouds and an area of low pressure.
      ▪ Sinking air creates high pressure and cloudless skies.
   c) Explain why the clouds in Figure 3 indicate areas of low pressure.
2 Study Figure 2 and the phrases in Figure 1. Make a flow diagram that shows how large areas of low pressure are formed and how these create the tropical rain belt.

Enquiry

How and why does the tropical climate vary from one place to another?

a) Use the data in Figure 4 to create three tropical climate graphs (see page 185).
b) Use Figure 3 and an atlas to describe the location of each place.
c) Compare the rainfall patterns in all three locations. What type of climate does this indicate for each location?
d) Mexico City is 2,000 m above sea level. How does this fact help to explain the different climate here?

What are the features of the hot semi-arid climate?

Areas of hot semi-arid climate are found on the fringe, or outer edge, of arid areas. You can think of them as a transition zone, or a zone of change, between hot deserts and places with a seasonal tropical wet and dry climate. They are found largely between the Tropics of Cancer and Capricorn.

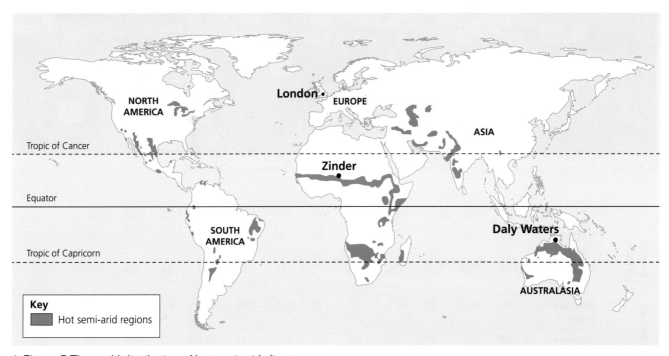

▲ **Figure 5** The world distribution of hot semi-arid climates.

What is the climate pattern like?

Temperatures vary throughout the year but, compared to the UK, remain high. The hot temperatures are due to the position of the Sun which remains high in the sky across the tropical belt throughout the year (see Figure 3 on page 284–285). The most striking feature of the climate is the low rainfall.

Hot semi-arid climates have low annual precipitation. Precipitation totals are lower than 600 mm per year. Precipitation falls only as rain. Snow never falls in this area except on the highest mountains, such as Kilimanjaro in Tanzania. The rainfall is seasonal. The dry period lasts for several months. Rainfall in the hot semi-arid zone is also unreliable. This means that, in some years, the usual rain storms of the wet season fail. The drought months are the result of stable descending air when air pressure remains high. This can be seen in Figure 2 on page 173. Even in the months when rainfall is higher, much of the water is quickly evaporated due to the relatively high temperatures.

▲ **Figure 6** A thunderstorm over Zinder, Niger.

Activities

1 Use Figure 5 to describe the location and distribution of the hot semi-arid climate zone.
2 Describe the vegetation in Figure 6. Suggest how this ecosystem might be affected by the climate of Zinder.

GEOGRAPHICAL SKILLS

Describing a climate graph

Climate graphs are a form of compound graph because they have at least two parts:

- Bars that represent the precipitation total each month.
- A line that represents average temperatures.

When you are asked to describe a climate graph, there are four features to consider. Study the graph and ask yourself:

1 What is the total annual rainfall? This is calculated by adding all of the values for the rainfall bars together.
2 Are there distinctive wet or dry seasons? If so, when are they, and how long does each last?
3 What is the annual temperature range? This is the difference in temperature between the hottest and coldest times of the year.
4 Does the temperature show a distinctive seasonal pattern? If so, at what time of year are the hot and cold seasons?

▲ **Figure 7** Climate graph to represent the hot semi-arid climate of Zinder, Niger.

	Jan	Feb	Mar	Apr	May	Jun	Jul	Aug	Sep	Oct	Nov	Dec
Average maximum daily temperature °C	6	7	10	13	17	21	23	22	19	14	10	7
Average monthly precipitation (mm)	78	59	61	51	55	56	45	51	63	70	75	79

▲ **Figure 8** Climate data for London, UK (average 1961–90).

	Jan	Feb	Mar	Apr	May	Jun	Jul	Aug	Sep	Oct	Nov	Dec
Average maximum daily temperature °C	36	36	35	34	31	29	28	32	35	38	39	38
Average monthly precipitation (mm)	125	150	60	15	10	0	2	0	1	17	52	92

▲ **Figure 9** Climate data for Daly Waters, Australia (average 1961–90). Daly Waters is in the southern hemisphere.

Activities

3 Use Figure 8 to draw a climate graph for London in the same style as Figure 7.
4 Use Figure 8 to compare the climate of Zinder with London. You should compare:
   a) The total annual precipitation
   b) If one or both have distinctive wet/dry seasons
   c) The annual temperature range
   d) If one or both have distinctive hot/cold seasons.

Enquiry

How do places with a hot semi-arid climate in the southern hemisphere compare to places like Zinder which is in the northern hemisphere?

Study Figure 9.

a) Draw a climate graph for Daly Waters in the style of Figure 7.
b) Daly Waters is also in the hot semi-arid climate zone.
   (i) Compare the climate data with Zinder. What are the similarities, what are the differences?
   (ii) Suggest reasons for the differences.

The temperate maritime climate of the UK

The UK has a temperate climate, that is mild, without extremes of temperature. The climate is **maritime** because it is strongly influenced by air masses and ocean currents crossing the Atlantic Ocean. A feature of the climate is its variability throughout the year. The UK has four distinct seasons.

The main factors that affect the UK's climate are:
- latitude
- the track of the jet stream and its effect on the movement of air masses
- the effect of ocean currents
- altitude and aspect.

London	Jan	Feb	Mar	Apr	May	Jun	Jul	Aug	Sep	Oct	Nov	Dec
Temperature °C	6	7	10	13	17	21	23	22	19	14	10	7
Precipitation (mm)	78	59	61	51	55	56	45	51	63	70	75	79

Oban	Jan	Feb	Mar	Apr	May	Jun	Jul	Aug	Sep	Oct	Nov	Dec
Temperature °C	8	8	8	10	13	14	16	16	15	12	10	8
Precipitation (mm)	195	142	155	84	69	83	105	123	174	189	185	197

▲ **Figure 10** Climate data for London in the south east of England and Oban in the north west of Scotland show how the UK's climate varies across the country.

Effects of aspect and altitude

The northern, central and western parts of the UK have upland landscapes. Upland areas are much colder than lowlands. Temperatures decrease by 1°C for every 100 m in height. **Aspect**, or the direction of a slope, is another factor that affects temperatures as it determines the amount of sun received. South-facing slopes tend to be warmer than north-facing slopes.

Activities

1. Compare the climate of London to that of Oban, making sure that you comment on the seasonality of both graphs.
2. a) Make a sketch of Figure 11.
   b) Complete and add the labels to the correct places on your sketch.

Flat valley floor

... will remain in shadow for most of the day in winter

... is warmed by early morning sunshine

North-west facing slope

... will remain in shadow until the Sun is higher in the sky so frost remains longer in the morning

South-east facing slope

▲ **Figure 11** A valley in the Lake District shows how aspect can affect temperature.

How does the maritime climate affect the UK?

Oceans contain flowing currents of sea water. These **ocean currents** circulate around the globe. They are able to transfer heat from warm latitudes to cooler ones. The Gulf Stream, and its extension the North Atlantic Drift, is one of these currents. It carries warm water from the Gulf of Mexico across the Atlantic, towards Europe. This warm water transfers heat and moisture to the air above it and influences the climate of the UK. It gives the UK a maritime climate which is warmer and wetter than other places at similar latitudes in **continental** parts of Europe.

▶ **Figure 12** Comparing temperatures in the maritime climate of the UK to the more continental parts of Europe.

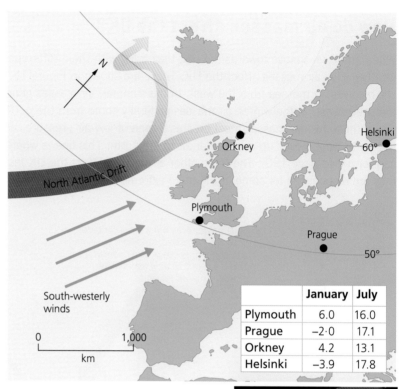

	January	July
Plymouth	6.0	16.0
Prague	−2·0	17.1
Orkney	4.2	13.1
Helsinki	−3.9	17.8

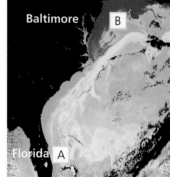

▶ **Figure 14** Satellite image of the Gulf Stream. The orange colours show warm water. Cold water is blue. Land is black.

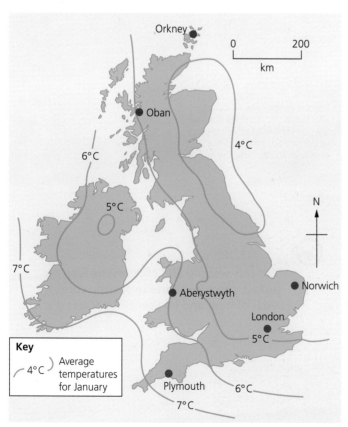

Key

⌒ 4°C ⌒ Average temperatures for January

▲ **Figure 13** Average temperatures for January. Lines of equal temperature are known as isotherms

Activities

3 Compare the temperatures that are at the same line of latitude in Figure 12. Explain why this pattern occurs.

4 a) Use Figure 13 to describe the January temperature in:
   i) Aberystwyth
   ii) Norwich
   iii) Orkney.

   b) Which parts of the UK have the lowest January temperatures?

   c) Draw a cross-section to represent the temperature change between Plymouth and Orkney.

5 a) Make a sketch of Figure 14. Label what is happening at A and B.

   b) Suggest how the ocean current at B will affect the climate of Baltimore.

How do air masses affect the UK?

When air masses move towards the UK, they bring with them different kinds of weather. Five air masses affect the UK. These are shown in Figure 15. Usually, the UK receives air masses from the west. In the summer, air masses generally come from the south-west. In the winter, air masses generally come from the north-west. The line where these two air masses meet creates a zone of low air pressure. Warmer air from the south-west moves up over colder air to the north. This line is where depressions can form (see page 190). The three other air masses affect the UK less often, but they are responsible for some of the more extreme weather we receive.

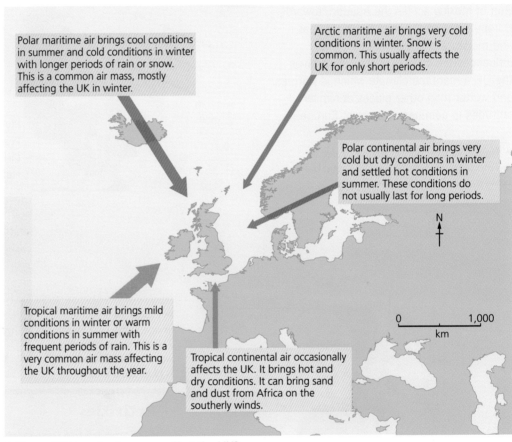

Polar maritime air brings cool conditions in summer and cold conditions in winter with longer periods of rain or snow. This is a common air mass, mostly affecting the UK in winter.

Arctic maritime air brings very cold conditions in winter. Snow is common. This usually affects the UK for only short periods.

Polar continental air brings very cold but dry conditions in winter and settled hot conditions in summer. These conditions do not usually last for long periods.

Tropical maritime air brings mild conditions in winter or warm conditions in summer with frequent periods of rain. This is a very common air mass affecting the UK throughout the year.

Tropical continental air occasionally affects the UK. It brings hot and dry conditions. It can bring sand and dust from Africa on the southerly winds.

0 ——— 1,000 km

▲ **Figure 15** How do air masses affect the UK?

Enquiry

Can you predict the weather?

Use the Weblink on this page to view the surface pressure chart for the next four days. Use the position of the high and low pressures to predict places across Europe that will have:

a) dry, settled weather
b) wet weather
c) the strongest winds.

www.metoffice.gov.uk/public/weather
Visit this website and click on the icon for surface pressure charts to see the current areas of high and low pressure across the UK.

How does the jet stream affect the UK's weather?

The jet stream (shown on page 179) is a strong ribbon of wind that circles the globe between 9 and 16 km above the surface of the Earth. It crosses over the UK, taking a sinuous course. It separates the cold polar air masses to the north from the warmer tropical air masses to the south.

When the jet stream takes a northerly track to the west of the UK, it tends to drag high pressure over the UK from the south. Areas of high pressure, also known as **anticyclones**, bring periods of dry, settled weather. The track taken by the jet stream tends to shift slightly over time. But if it stays in the same position for several weeks, then the UK will experience a long spell of similar weather. When high pressure becomes fixed over the UK in winter, the weather is sunny and dry but cold, and especially cold at night. During the summer an anticyclone brings hot dry weather. If the jet stream becomes fixed in this position it can cause problems such as heatwaves or drought. The UK's worst drought in recent years was in 2003 when an anticyclone stayed over western Europe for several weeks.

Key

1. Track that typically allows high pressure to settle over the UK like in summer 2003

2. Track that will bring unsettled weather conditions

3. Track that will bring a series of depressions across the UK like in winter 2013–14

▲ **Figure 16** Typical paths for the jet stream across the UK.

Activities

1 Use Figures 15 and 16 to explain:
   a) Why the more northerly route (track 1) of the jet stream will bring settled weather.
   b) Why the more southerly route (track 3) of the jet stream will bring unsettled weather.
2 Use Figure 17 and an atlas to describe:
   a) The location of the three zones of high pressure.
   b) The cold front.

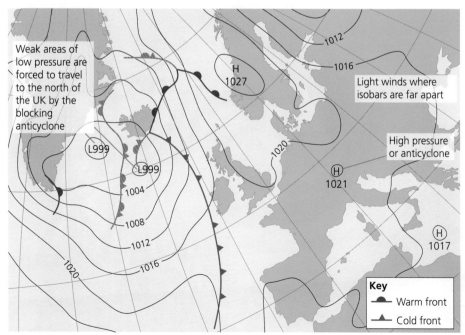

Weak areas of low pressure are forced to travel to the north of the UK by the blocking anticyclone

H 1027

Light winds where isobars are far apart

High pressure or anticyclone

H 1021

L999

L999

1004

1008

1012

1016

1020

H 1017

1012

1016

1020

Key

⏜ Warm front

▲▲ Cold front

◀ **Figure 17** A weather map showing an anticyclone in August 2003.

The effects of low pressure (or depressions)

Regions of low pressure in the atmosphere are formed when air lifts off the Earth's surface. It is common for several cells of low pressure, also known as **depressions**, to form in the North Atlantic at any one time. They then track eastwards towards Europe, bringing changeable weather characterised by wind, cloud and rain. Depressions are more likely to be deeper (have lower pressure) in the winter months. These weather systems can bring damaging gusts of wind and large waves onto the coast, as well as heavy rain like the storms that battered the UK in the winter of 2013–14. However, low pressure in the summer months is quite common: depressions during July 2012 caused flooding.

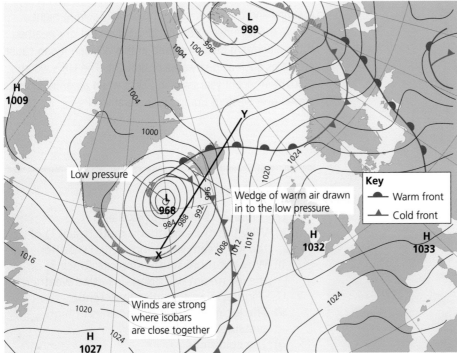

◄ **Figure 18** Weather map showing a deep area of low pressure in the North Atlantic (4 September 2003). A cross-section through the atmosphere along the line X–Y is shown in Figure 20.

► **Figure 19** A satellite image of the same area of low pressure off Iceland (4 September 2003).

Inside the depression there is a battle between huge masses of warmer and colder air. These air masses revolve slowly around each other in an anti-clockwise direction (in the northern hemisphere) as the whole system tracks eastward. As the warmer air rises and rotates, its moisture condenses, forming huge banks of cloud. Seen from above, these curving banks of cloud give the depression a characteristic shape.

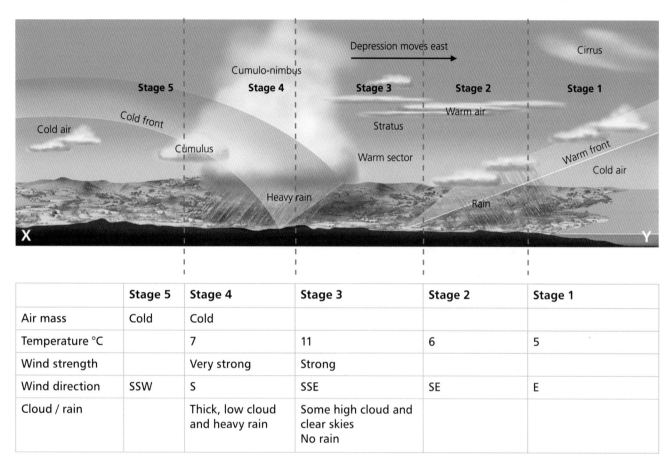

	Stage 5	Stage 4	Stage 3	Stage 2	Stage 1
Air mass	Cold	Cold			
Temperature °C		7	11	6	5
Wind strength		Very strong	Strong		
Wind direction	SSW	S	SSE	SE	E
Cloud / rain		Thick, low cloud and heavy rain	Some high cloud and clear skies No rain		

▲ **Figure 20** Weather that would have been associated with the easterly progress of the depression shown in Figures 18 and 19.

Feature	Cyclones or depressions	Anticyclones
Air pressure		High, usually above 1,020 mb (millibars)
Air movement		Sinking
Wind strength		Light
Wind circulation		Clockwise
Typical winter weather		Cold and dry. Clear skies in the daytime. Frost at night.
Typical summer weather		Sunny and warm

▲ **Figure 21** Comparing cyclones and anticyclones.

Activities

1 Use an atlas and Figures 18 and 19. Describe the location of the areas of high and low pressure.
2 a) Make a copy of the table in Figure 20. Use the evidence in Figures 18 and 19 to complete the missing sections.
   b) Imagine you are a weather forecaster working in north-east Iceland. Prepare a local weather forecast for the next few hours.
3 Make a large copy of Figure 21 and use the information on these pages to complete the blank spaces.

The winter storms of 2014

Between December 2013 and February 2014, the UK suffered its stormiest period for 20 years. Storms, created by extreme low pressure, battered the North Sea coastline during December 2013 (see pages 146–7). The coasts of Devon and Cornwall were badly damaged by a combination of fierce winds and huge waves. Much of Somerset, which had already been affected by flood water from earlier storms, received a further soaking. South-westerly winds reached speeds of 146 kmph on the exposed coast of Devon. Rainfall figures were well over twice the monthly average, with a high of 210 mm in Somerset.

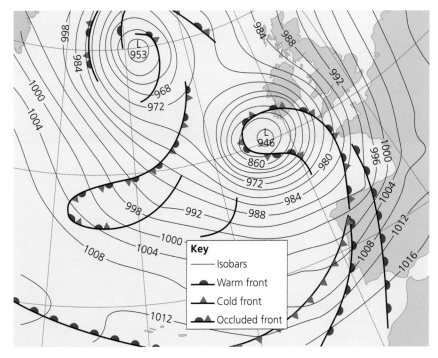

Key

— Isobars

⚫— Warm front

▲— Cold front

⚫▲— Occluded front

◀ **Figure 22** The weather map for 4th February 2014.

◀ **Figure 23** The coastal rail line at Dawlish was destroyed by the winter storms of 2014.

Activities

1 Study Figure 22.
   a) Describe the location of the area of low pressure.
   b) What do the isolines on this map tell you about the strength and direction of the winds?
2 Write a weather forecast for the southern half of the UK on 5 February 2014. Use Figure 19 to help you interpret Figure 22.

The short-term effects of the winter storms of 2014

Social impacts	Economic impacts	Environmental impacts
Hundreds of people were still in temporary accommodation for months after the flood levels went down. This disrupted family and school life.	Network Rail estimated that the cost of repairing the severed rail line near Dawlish was £35 million.	Conservationists have reported that 600 guillemots, puffins, razorbills and other birds have been killed in the storm.
The dirty secret of flooding is sewage. Homes and possessions were left with a coating of mud and raw sewage. Disease is a threat. Many homes are faced with needing new electrics and re-plastering.	The tourist industry was badly hit. The value of lost visitor days in January and February was thought to be £8m. Forward bookings went down by 20%. Spring and Easter are normally peak periods.	An ancient formation known as Pom Pom Rock has been destroyed by ferocious weather off Portland. The rock could not withstand the high winds and stormy seas.
During the floods, it was the most vulnerable groups who were at serious risk. The very young, the very old, the unwell, and people with disabilities found it difficult to move to higher floors as the water levels started to rise.	Some farmers lost as much as 95% of their land under water for many weeks. Livestock farmers had to evacuate animals. Instead of grazing the fields, sheep and cattle were fed with reserve stocks of animal feed.	Where embankments line rivers, floodwater that overtops the banks gets trapped for long periods of time. This lying water can drown all the worms and insects that live in the soil. These are vital food for birds like waders.

▲ **Figure 24** The short-term effects of the winter storms of 2014 in the Somerset Levels.

I think that concrete walls lining our river banks and coastlines are no longer the solution. A "back to nature" approach is needed to return water systems to the natural, slow systems they once were. Fields can be used as temporary ponds, and vegetation can soak up the water.

Academic researching flood protection in the UK

A huge amount of rain fell on the Somerset Levels, far greater than the river channel could ever cope with. We should simply stop building in flood prone areas.

Scientist at the Meteorological Office

Despite the thousands of homes being flooded during this record breaking winter, about one million homes and businesses have been protected by the defences that held out.

Officer at the Environment Agency

Attention needs to shift towards individual households being prepared for extreme weather. Measures can be simple from inflatable toilet bungs to stop sewage overflows, to slot-in door protectors. We can rewire electrical circuits nearer the ceiling. We can even build homes on stilts if they are in a flood prone area.

Government Minister

The government must reverse its spending cuts which target flood defence schemes. It is not cost effective to cut schemes that aim to reduce the impact of wild weather and then go on to make large compensation payments to those affected.

Local Councillor

▲ **Figure 25** Attitudes to the extreme weather of 2014.

Activity

3 Select one of each of the social, economic and environmental effects of the winter storms. Explain why you think your chosen effects are the most serious of the impacts shown.

Enquiry

What do you think is the most sustainable response to the threat of similar extreme weather events in the future?

a) Discuss the viewpoints in Figure 25.
b) Use these ideas, and your own, to suggest how the UK should respond to severe winter storms in the future.
c) Justify your answer.

How has climate changed during the Quaternary period?

The Quaternary, sometimes called the Pleistocene, is the most recent period of geological time. It is a period of Earth's history that has been dominated by cold climates and ice shaping the land. At the beginning of the Quaternary, the polar ice sheets were far bigger than they are today, as you can see in Figure 1. Throughout the 2.6 million years of the Quaternary, the climate has changed constantly. There have been periods, known as glacials, when the polar ice has reached much further south, covering large parts of the earth. At other times, known as inter-glacials, the polar ice retreated. Scientists have evidence of 60 different cycles of ice advance and retreat.

Are temperatures rising or falling?

With all the talk about global warming, Figure 2 may come as a bit of a surprise! The blue line shows the general trend of a cooling climate over the last 5 million years. The black lines show fluctuations around the general trend. Temperatures at the beginning of the Quaternary were much colder than they had been in the previous geological time period, known as the Tertiary. Since the Quaternary began, you can see that cooling has continued but that fluctuations have been much wilder. Evidence shows that the last 400,000 years have been a particularly unstable period, with very significant changes in temperature between glacial and inter-glacial periods. The ice sheets retreated about 10,000 years ago and the Earth is currently experiencing an inter-glacial period. However, the ice has not disappeared. Technically, we are living in an ice age!

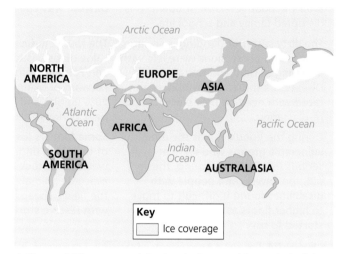

▲ **Figure 1** The extent of the ice during a colder period of the Quaternary period.

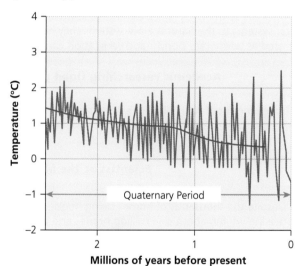

▲ **Figure 2** Climate change during the Tertiary and Quaternary.

Activities

1 Study Figure 1.
   a) Describe the amount and distribution of the ice sheets.
   b) Study the Mediterranean region carefully. Suggest why the Mediterranean Sea appears to be smaller than it is today.

2 Why does the surface temperature of the Earth change when the tilt of the Earth varies due to the natural 'wobble' and due to an eccentric orbit?

3 How does the information on pages 194–5 explain why some people remain sceptical about the threat from global warming?

What are the natural causes of climate change?

There is much debate about the cause of the change from glacial periods to inter-glacial periods. The most commonly accepted theory is based on the work of a scientist called Milankovitch. He suggests that the warmer and cooler periods are caused by a combination of two things:

- The natural wobble of the earth as it moves around the Sun. This affects the tilt of the Earth and the amount of energy it receives from the Sun.
- The fact that the Earth does not have a circular orbit around the Sun. The orbit is eccentric. It is sometimes closer to the Sun, sometimes it is further away.

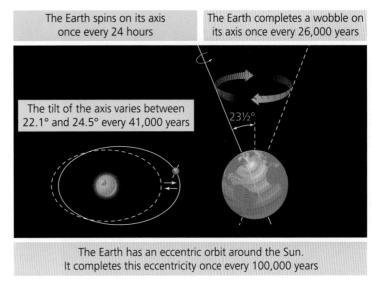

The Earth spins on its axis once every 24 hours

The Earth completes a wobble on its axis once every 26,000 years

The tilt of the axis varies between 22.1° and 24.5° every 41,000 years

23½°

The Earth has an eccentric orbit around the Sun. It completes this eccentricity once every 100,000 years

▲ **Figure 3** Why does the Earth's climate fluctuate?

So why worry?

In the last 150 years, records of world temperature change have become more accurate. Figure 4 shows changes in the average global temperature since 1860. Those who are sceptical about climate change argue that the increase in temperature is just part of the normal cycle of an inter-glacial period. Those who say the world needs to worry about climate change point to the fact that the change over time is now very fast. Indeed, since 1960, the rate of increase has been even greater.

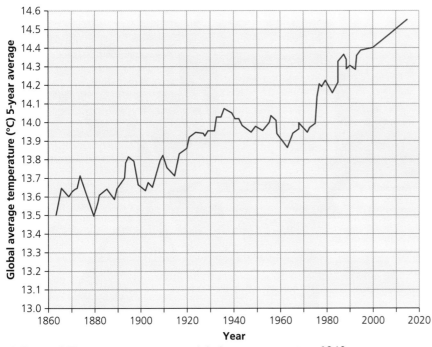

▲ **Figure 4** The increase in average global temperature since 1860.

Activity

4   Study Figure 4. How far does this graph suggest that the sceptics may be wrong to dismiss the threat of global warming? Use figures from the graph to support your answer.

Enquiry

To what extent are we still living in an ice age? Use an atlas or the internet to compare the amount and distribution of permanent ice today with that shown in Figure 1.

▲ **Figure 5** Wildfires in San Marcos, California (May 2014). 13,000 people had to be evacuated.

What is the greenhouse effect?

The greenhouse effect is a natural process of our atmosphere. Without it, the average surface temperature of the Earth would be −17° Celsius rather than the 15° Celsius we currently experience. At these temperatures, life would not have evolved on Earth in its present form and we probably wouldn't exist!

The greenhouse effect, shown in Figure 6, means that Earth's atmosphere acts like an insulating blanket. Light (short wave) and heat (long wave) energy from the Sun passes through the atmosphere quite easily. The Sun's energy heats the Earth and it radiates its own energy back into the atmosphere. The long-wave heat energy coming from the Earth is quite easily absorbed by naturally occurring gases in the atmosphere. These are known as **greenhouse gases**. They include carbon dioxide (CO_2), methane (CH_4) and water vapour (H_2O). Carbon dioxide is the fourth most common gas in the atmosphere. It occurs naturally in the atmosphere as a product of respiration from all living things. So carbon dioxide has existed in the atmosphere for as long as there has been life on Earth. Methane and water vapour have been in the atmosphere for even longer, so the greenhouse effect has been affecting our climate for thousands of millions of years.

Activity

1 Use Figure 6 to explain the greenhouse effect. Make sure that you use technical terms such as long-wave and short-wave energy in your answer.

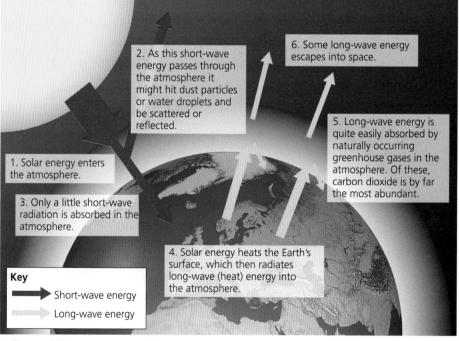

2. As this short-wave energy passes through the atmosphere it might hit dust particles or water droplets and be scattered or reflected.

6. Some long-wave energy escapes into space.

5. Long-wave energy is quite easily absorbed by naturally occurring greenhouse gases in the atmosphere. Of these, carbon dioxide is by far the most abundant.

1. Solar energy enters the atmosphere.

3. Only a little short-wave radiation is absorbed in the atmosphere.

4. Solar energy heats the Earth's surface, which then radiates long-wave (heat) energy into the atmosphere.

Key

→ Short-wave energy

→ Long-wave energy

▲ **Figure 6** The greenhouse effect.

How have people's actions affected the greenhouse effect?

Carbon is one of the most common elements in the environment. It is present in:

- all organic substances, i.e. all living things
- simple compounds such as CO_2, which exists as a gas in the atmosphere and is dissolved in the oceans
- complex compounds, for example, hydrocarbons found in fossil fuels such as oil, coal and gas.

Carbon is able to transfer from one part of the environment to another through a series of biological processes, such as respiration, and chemical processes such as solution. These transfers take place between parts of the environment that release carbon, known as sources, and parts of the environment that absorb the carbon over long periods of time, known as **carbon sinks**. The transfer between sources and sinks is shown in the carbon cycle diagrams, Figures 7 and 8.

At night photosynthesis stops. The tree continues to respire and it emits more CO_2 than it absorbs

Solar energy

While the tree is alive it absorbs more CO_2 from the atmosphere than it emits

When branches or leaves fall they transfer the carbon that is locked in the plant tissue into the soil

During the day the tree uses sunlight to convert carbon dioxide to plant sugars. This is **photosynthesis**

Organisms such as beetles and earthworms may digest the plant tissue. Their respiration adds CO_2 to air in the soil

Rainwater dissolves some of the carbon dioxide that has come from soil organisms. This water may carry the dissolved CO_2 into a river and eventually to the sea.

▲ **Figure 8** A simplified carbon cycle.

▼ **Figure 7** The carbon cycle, showing fast and slow transfers.

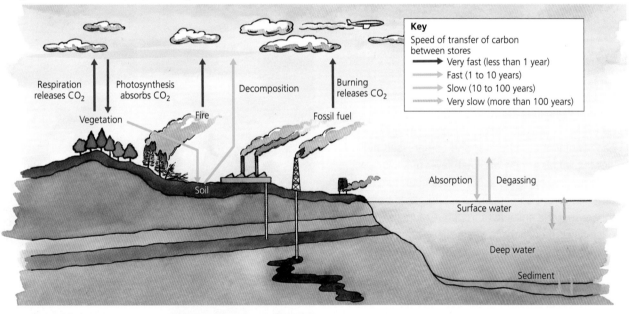

Key
Speed of transfer of carbon between stores
→ Very fast (less than 1 year)
→ Fast (1 to 10 years)
→ Slow (10 to 100 years)
→ Very slow (more than 100 years)

Respiration releases CO_2

Photosynthesis absorbs CO_2

Decomposition

Burning releases CO_2

Vegetation

Fire

Fossil fuel

Soil

Absorption   Degassing

Surface water

Deep water

Sediment

Activities

2 Study Figures 7 and 8.
   a) Describe the human actions that release CO_2 into the atmosphere.
   b) Explain the processes that allow forests to act as a carbon sink.
   c) Give two reasons why the burning of tropical rainforests will increase the amount of CO_2 in the atmosphere.

3 Use Figure 7.
   a) Describe the difference in the speed of transfer of carbon in the natural part of the cycle compared with the part of the cycle affected by human action.
   b) Explain what difference this makes to the amount of carbon stored in the atmosphere compared with the long-lasting carbon sinks. Explain why this is alarming.

How conclusive is the evidence for climate change?

In 1958 a team of scientists began to take regular measurements of carbon dioxide concentrations from the atmosphere. They realised that local levels of CO_2 could be higher if the sampling took place close to industry or traffic congestion, so they decided to conduct their tests on Mauna Loa, Hawaii. They thought that this would give them readings that would represent average CO_2 levels in the atmosphere. The sampling has been conducted regularly ever since and the graph, known as the Keeling Curve, is shown in Figure 9.

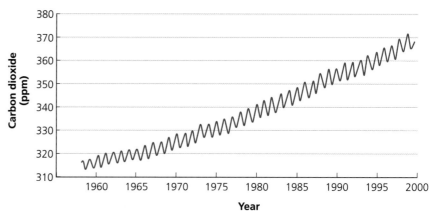

▲ **Figure 9** The Keeling Curve shows the rise of carbon dioxide in the atmosphere since monitoring began in 1958 (ppm = parts per million).

Evidence from the ice cores

We have already seen that scientific evidence from Hawaii proves that carbon dioxide levels have been rising steadily since 1958. However, can we be certain that this isn't part of a natural cycle? Perhaps carbon dioxide levels vary over long periods of time and the recent rise is part of one of those cycles.

Scientists working in both Greenland and Antarctica have been investigating information trapped in the ice to uncover evidence of past climate change. The snowfall from each winter is covered over and compressed by the following winter's snowfall. Each layer of snow contains chemical evidence about the temperature of the climate. Each layer also contains trapped gases from the atmosphere that the snow fell through. Gradually the layers turn to ice. Over thousands of years these layers have built up and are now thousands of metres thick. By drilling down into the ice, scientists can extract older and older ice cores. Chemical analysis of these ice layers and the gases they contain reveal a record of the climate over the last 420,000 years. This evidence suggests that the climate has indeed gone through natural cycles of colder and warmer periods known as glacials and inter-glacials. They also show that levels of carbon dioxide in the atmosphere have also gone up and down as part of a natural cycle.

▲ **Figure 10** Scientists taking ice core samples from the ice sheet in Iceland.

Activity

1 a) Describe and explain the trend of the Keeling Curve.
   b) Explain why the scientists chose Hawaii as a good place to collect their samples.

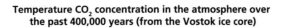

Temperature CO₂ concentration in the atmosphere over the past 400,000 years (from the Vostok ice core)

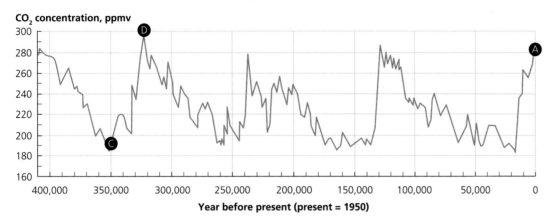

CO₂ concentration, ppmv

Year before present (present = 1950)

Temperature change from present, °C

Year before present (present = 1950)

▲ **Figure 11** Temperature and CO₂ concentration (ppm) in the atmosphere over the past 420,000 years.

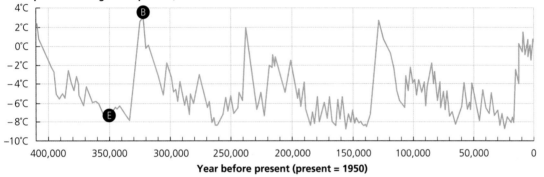

Carbon dioxide concentrations reached a maximum of 300 ppm in the warmest periods

Carbon dioxide concentrations dropped to 180 ppm during the coldest periods

Narrow peaks in the temperature record represent short warm episodes (interglacials)

Broad dips in temperature represent glacial periods

Carbon dioxide concentrations were at about 280 ppm in 1950

Activities

2 Use Figure 11.
   a) Match the five statements to the correct place on the graph shown by the letters A, B, C, D and E.
   b) Use the graph to copy and complete the following statement:
      The graph shows natural cycles of .... periods and .... periods. Average temperatures were higher than present on *three/four/five* occasions. These are known as .... periods. The current inter-glacial period appears to have lasted much *longer than/shorter than* previous periods.

3 Use your understanding of the greenhouse effect to explain why reduced levels of carbon dioxide in the atmosphere might be linked to cooler periods of climate.

4 Compare Figure 11 with Figure 9.
   a) How many times in the last 420,000 years have CO₂ levels been as high as in 2000?
   b) Based on the ice core data, do you think that the Keeling Curve fits into a similar natural cycle of carbon dioxide concentrations? Explain your answer fully.

Enquiry

How conclusive do you find the evidence for:
a) natural cycles of climate change over the last 420,000 years?
b) an unusual rise in carbon dioxide levels since 1958?

How is global warming affecting climate and ecosystems?

We have seen that some extreme weather events are being attributed to global warming. The theory is that pollution is causing heat to be trapped in our atmosphere. The extra heat energy may be causing:

- more violent storms such as Cyclone Pam that hit Vanuatu in 2015 (pages 176–7)
- more heatwaves, like the one in California in 2013–2015 (pages 178–81).

In addition, global warming is likely to affect global patterns of climate. Desert regions may become drier. The wet tropical regions which contain our rainforests may also receive less annual rainfall. That's why the media often refers to global warming as climate change. One region where there is evidence of climate change is the Arctic.

How is climate change affecting wildlife in the Arctic?

The polar bear is the world's largest land predator. There are about 20,000 polar bears living in the wild, but their numbers are falling. There are several possible reasons. One is chemical pollution. Bears are at the top of the Arctic food chain and can accumulate poisons in their bodies that they have taken in from the animals they have eaten. However, climate change is increasingly seen as the main reason for the decline in numbers.

There are 1,200 polar bears living in the region of Hudson Bay, Canada. This population of polar bears has been monitored by the Canadian Wildlife Service (CWS) for more than 40 years. Their results show that earlier thawing of sea ice in Hudson Bay is threatening the survival of polar bears.

Adult polar bears need the sea ice to remain frozen for a few weeks in the late spring so they can hunt for seals on the ice. Once the ice breaks up and melts, the seals become much harder to catch. CWS studies show that the ice now melts three weeks earlier than it did when studies began in the early 1970s. For each week that the thaw comes early, the bears have less chance to feed, and come on shore 10 kg lighter. Consequently, some polar bears do not have enough fat reserves to survive the summer months when food is harder to catch. The consequences of further climate change are worrying:

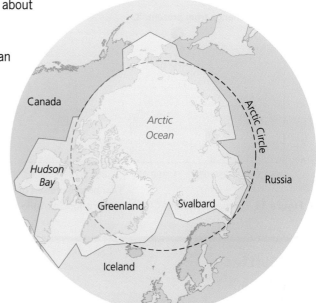

▲ **Figure 12** Distribution of polar bears and the location of Hudson Bay.

- More young bears and pups will starve over the longer summer.
- Females will be less fertile.
- Hungry bears are more likely to forage for food in towns where they come into conflict with people.

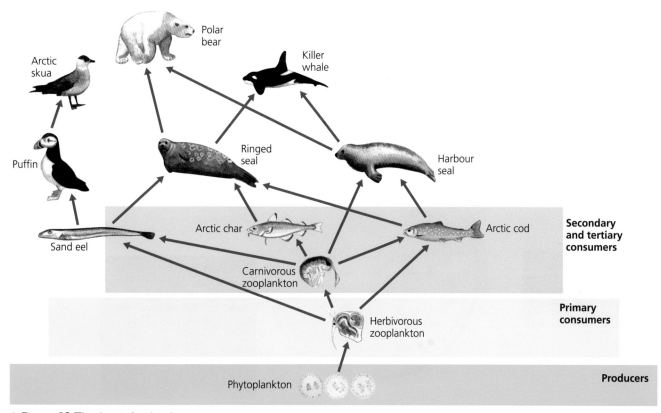

Polar bear

Arctic skua

Killer whale

Puffin

Ringed seal

Harbour seal

Arctic char

Arctic cod

Secondary and tertiary consumers

Sand eel

Carnivorous zooplankton

Herbivorous zooplankton

Primary consumers

Phytoplankton

Producers

▲ **Figure 13** The Arctic food web.

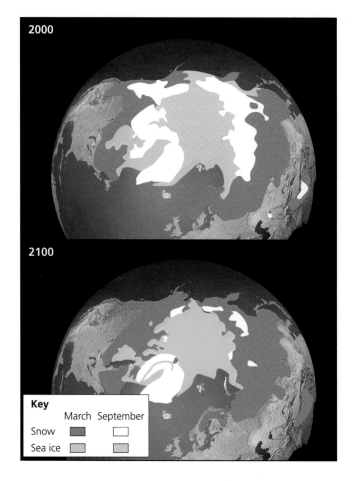

2000

2100

Key

	March	September
Snow		
Sea ice		

Activities

1 Study Figure 12.
   a) Describe the location of Hudson Bay.
   b) Describe the distribution of polar bears.
2 a) Use Figure 13 to draw a food chain which includes the polar bear.
   b) Explain what will happen to this food web if the polar bears are unable to catch enough ringed seals to survive the summer.
3 Look at Figures 12 and 14.
   a) Compare the distribution of polar bears to the sea ice in March 2000.
   b) Describe what is predicted to happen to the sea ice in March 2100.
   c) Compare the distribution of September sea ice in 2000 to 2100.

◄ **Figure 14** The extent of sea ice in 2000 compared with the predicted extent in 2100.

How do warmer temperatures affect the Arctic food chain?

We have seen that, as the Arctic warms, the sea ice breaks up and melts a little earlier in spring. This makes it harder for polar bears to catch seals. Figure 18 shows the average date at which the sea ice broke up in different parts of Hudson Bay.

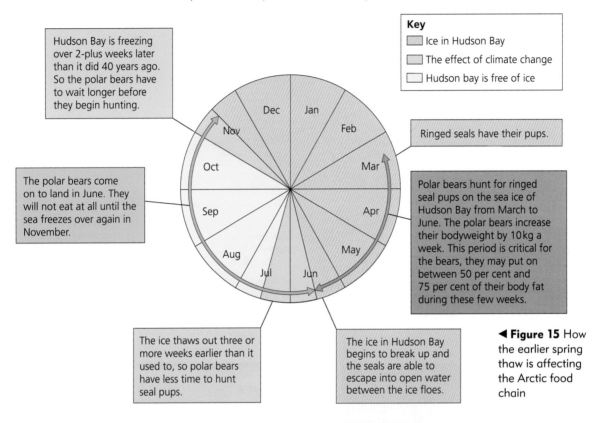

Key
Ice in Hudson Bay
The effect of climate change
Hudson bay is free of ice

Hudson Bay is freezing over 2-plus weeks later than it did 40 years ago. So the polar bears have to wait longer before they begin hunting.

Ringed seals have their pups.

The polar bears come on to land in June. They will not eat at all until the sea freezes over again in November.

Polar bears hunt for ringed seal pups on the sea ice of Hudson Bay from March to June. The polar bears increase their bodyweight by 10 kg a week. This period is critical for the bears, they may put on between 50 per cent and 75 per cent of their body fat during these few weeks.

The ice thaws out three or more weeks earlier than it used to, so polar bears have less time to hunt seal pups.

The ice in Hudson Bay begins to break up and the seals are able to escape into open water between the ice floes.

◀ **Figure 15** How the earlier spring thaw is affecting the Arctic food chain

▲ **Figure 16** Polar bear, with two cubs, hunting a seal on the sea ice.

The potential for fairly significant rises in temperature in Arctic regions seems to be quite high. And should that happen, especially over a time scale of decades, the possibility of marine mammals being able to adapt rapidly enough is very low.

▲ **Figure 17** The opinion of Dr Malcolm Ramsey, Professor of Biology at the University of Saskatchewan in Canada.

How do volcanic eruptions affect climate?

Large volcanic eruptions can eject dust and sulphur dioxide (SO_2) into the lower stratosphere – a layer in the atmosphere that is 15–25 km above the Earth. At this altitude, the jet stream is able to carry the volcanic material in a belt right around the globe. The mixture of dust and SO_2 form an **aerosol** – tiny droplets that scatter sunlight back into space. This can have the effect of reducing the amount of solar energy that reaches the Earth's surface, so average temperatures can be reduced slightly for a year or more.

The eruption of Mount Pinatubo in 1991 sent so much dust into the atmosphere that for the next year or so there was a temporary cooling of the whole planet by around 1°C. In 1992, when the polar bears came off the ice in July, they were heavier and more of their cubs survived than in the previous year.

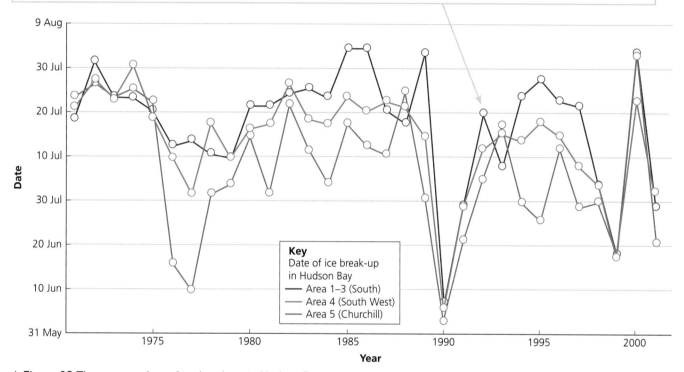

▲ **Figure 18** The average date of ice break-up in Hudson Bay.

Activities

1 Study Figure 18.
   a) What was the average date of the thaw between 1971 and 1975?
   b) What was the average date of the thaw in 1999 and 2001?
   c) Which of the two populations of polar bears will be more threatened by an earlier thaw? Justify your choice.
2 a) Use Figure 15 to help explain why polar bears are unable to adapt to climate change.
   b) Does it matter that polar bears might be threatened with extinction in the next few decades? Justify your point of view.

Enquiry

Why do changes in climate affect the polar bear population?

a) Describe the date of the thaw in the years between 1990 and 1993.
b) Explain why this happened and the effect it had on the bears.
c) How does this evidence support the view that climate change can have a direct effect on polar bear populations?
d) Draw a flow chart to show how climate change is affecting the polar bears.

How might climate change affect water supply and health in Africa?

Climate change is likely to have serious impacts on people and environments in Africa. More frequent extreme weather events, increased temperatures and more irregular patterns of rainfall will have effects on crop production. These, in turn, could damage some economies and cause food shortages. It is also likely that the mosquitoes that carry malaria will move into new regions and the number of people at risk of infection will increase. Perhaps the largest concern is that the number of people who suffer water stress (i.e. do not have access to enough fresh water) will increase. There are currently 1.7 billion people worldwide who suffer water stress. Most of these are in Africa. As the population grows and the climate changes, it is expected that this number will rise to 5 billion by 2025.

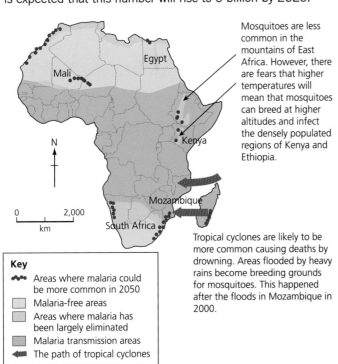

Mosquitoes are less common in the mountains of East Africa. However, there are fears that higher temperatures will mean that mosquitoes can breed at higher altitudes and infect the densely populated regions of Kenya and Ethiopia.

Tropical cyclones are likely to be more common causing deaths by drowning. Areas flooded by heavy rains become breeding grounds for mosquitoes. This happened after the floods in Mozambique in 2000.

Key
- ～ Areas where malaria could be more common in 2050
- ☐ Malaria-free areas
- ☐ Areas where malaria has been largely eliminated
- ☐ Malaria transmission areas
- ⬅ The path of tropical cyclones

▲ **Figure 19** How climate change could affect malaria by 2050.

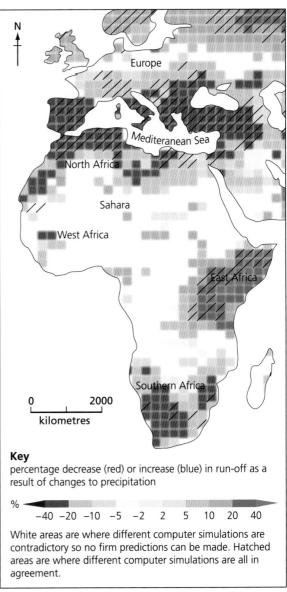

Key
percentage decrease (red) or increase (blue) in run-off as a result of changes to precipitation

% ▬▬▬▬▬▬▬▬▬▬▬▬▬▬
−40 −20 −10 −5 −2 2 5 10 20 40

White areas are where different computer simulations are contradictory so no firm predictions can be made. Hatched areas are where different computer simulations are all in agreement.

▲ **Figure 20** Future patterns of run-off in Europe and Africa in 2090–99 (compared with 1990–99).

Activities

1 Use Figure 20 to describe the distribution of countries which are expected to have:
   a) much less run-off
   b) much more run-off.
2 a) Explain how increased run-off might have positive and negative effects for people.
   b) Suggest why African countries might find it harder to cope with changes to run-off than European countries.

Enquiry

How is the risk of malaria likely to change?

a) Use Figure 19 to describe the zone of Africa which is currently at risk from malaria.
b) Describe how and why this zone is likely to change by 2050.

How might climate change affect Australia?

The Australian Bureau of Meteorology has predicted that Australia is likely to experience an increase in average annual temperature of 1.3°C by 2030 (compared with average temperatures recorded between 1986 and 2005). They predict more extreme droughts and less rainfall for southern regions of this vast country. They warn that average temperatures could rise by more than 5°C by 2090 if little global effort is made to cut the amount of greenhouse gases entering the atmosphere.

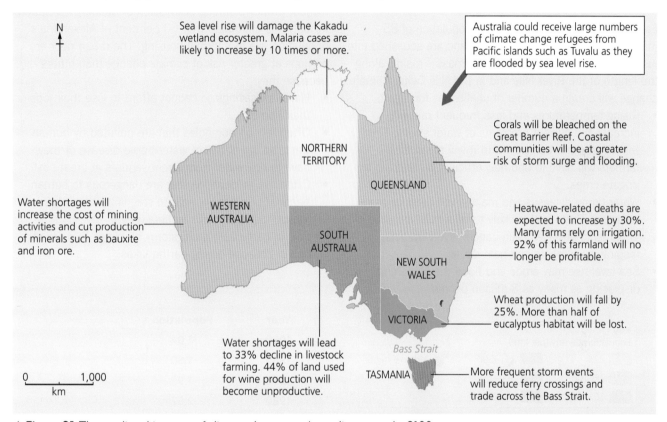

Sea level rise will damage the Kakadu wetland ecosystem. Malaria cases are likely to increase by 10 times or more.

Australia could receive large numbers of climate change refugees from Pacific islands such as Tuvalu as they are flooded by sea level rise.

Corals will be bleached on the Great Barrier Reef. Coastal communities will be at greater risk of storm surge and flooding.

Water shortages will increase the cost of mining activities and cut production of minerals such as bauxite and iron ore.

Heatwave-related deaths are expected to increase by 30%. Many farms rely on irrigation. 92% of this farmland will no longer be profitable.

Wheat production will fall by 25%. More than half of eucalyptus habitat will be lost.

Water shortages will lead to 33% decline in livestock farming. 44% of land used for wine production will become unproductive.

More frequent storm events will reduce ferry crossings and trade across the Bass Strait.

0   1,000
km

NORTHERN TERRITORY

WESTERN AUSTRALIA

SOUTH AUSTRALIA

QUEENSLAND

NEW SOUTH WALES

VICTORIA

Bass Strait

TASMANIA

▲ **Figure 21** The predicted impacts of climate change on Australian states by 2100.

Activity

3   Use Figure 21. Select three impacts and explain how climate change may cause these issues.

Enquiry

How serious is the threat of climate change in Australia?

a) Select five impacts of climate change in Australia and place them in rank order. The top-ranked one should be the most problematic or have the most serious impact.
b) Justify your ranking.
c) Suggest who should be responsible for trying to fix the most serious of these problems.

▲ **Figure 22** The Kakadu wetlands will be damaged by sea water.

How might climate change affect where people live?

The International Organization for Migration suggests that climate change will displace 200 million people by 2050. Rising sea levels, drought, food and water insecurity and increased health risks are the main reasons. Egypt is one country that could be affected.

Egypt is a desert country. It has a population of 85 million. Most urban areas and farmland are squashed into just 15 per cent of the nation's landmass – mainly along the length of the River Nile and in the Nile Delta. Climate change will create a number of challenges for Egypt:

- Rising temperatures and less frequent rain will increase the current problems of water stress. This will affect the urban poor and it will mean that farmers will have to find new efficient techniques to irrigate crops.
- Water-borne diseases and malaria will become more common. There is also likely to be a huge increase in parasitic diseases, skin cancer, eye cataracts, respiratory ailments and heat stroke
- Sea level rise may erode and flood the Nile Delta, displacing as many as 8 million people.

Alexandria, in the Nile Delta, is Egypt's second largest city. This Mediterranean port handles 80 per cent of Egypt's imports and exports. The wealth of the city attracts migrants. Natural population increase adds to pressure on space. Houses and flats are often built without proper planning permission or building regulation. In fact, it is estimated that 50 per cent of Alexandria's population live in informal housing. The urban poor are perhaps at greater risk of climate change than others because they:

- Have few savings so cannot afford to lose their jobs or their homes.
- Often rely on boreholes that are polluted by human waste so are at risk of water-borne disease or they have to buy water from street vendors at great cost.
- Often live in locations that are dangerous to human health. For example, near to stagnant water where mosquitoes that carry malaria breed.
- Live in badly built multi-storey buildings that are at risk of collapse during earthquakes.

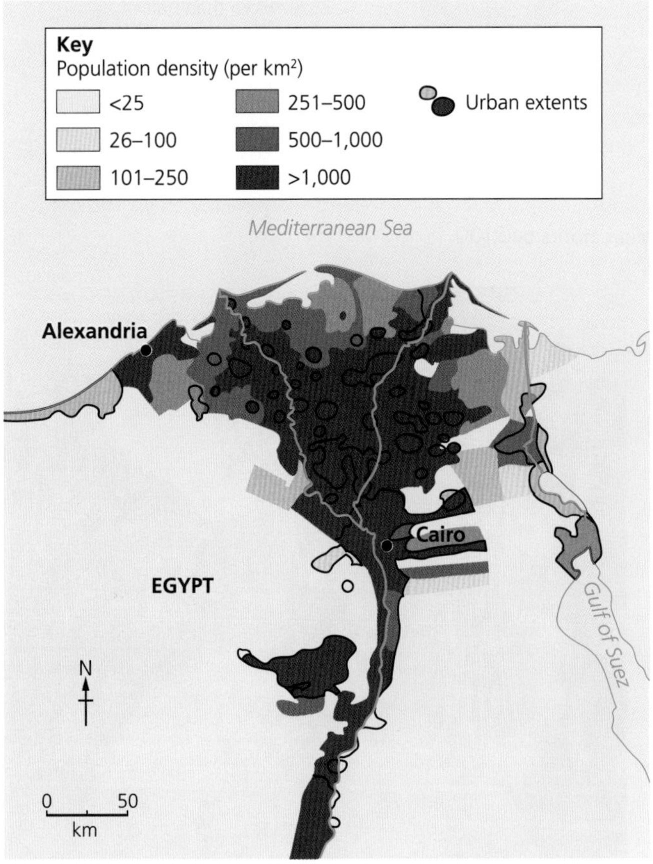

▲ **Figure 23** Population density of the Nile Delta.

Year	Population
1950	1.04
1960	1.50
1970	1.99
1980	2.52
1990	3.06
2000	3.55
2010	4.33
2020	5.23
2030	6.31

▲ **Figure 24** The population of Alexandria (millions). Figures after 2010 are predictions.

Alexandria is built on Egypt's Low Elevation Coastal Zone (LECZ) (see page 168) so is vulnerable to permanent flooding if sea levels rise. If this happens, Egypt will find it difficult to re-house the huge number of environmental refugees. Presumably, many people who currently live in informal housing in Alexandria will move into the poorest, most overcrowded districts of Cairo.

▲ **Figure 25** Illegally built flats in Alexandria, Egypt.

Mediterranean Sea

Damiette • Port-Said
Rosette
Alexandria
Mansourah

Actual sea level

4 million people affected
1,800 km² of land submerged
Mediterranean Sea

Damiette • Port-Said
Rosette
Alexandria
Mansourah

+50 centimetres

8 million people affected
5,700 km² of land submerged
Mediterranean Sea

Damiette • Port-Said
Rosette
Alexandria
Mansourah

N

0   50
km

+ 1.5 metres

▲ **Figure 26** Predicted changes to Egypt's coast-line as the sea level rises.

Activities

1 Describe the location of Alexandria.
2 a) Use Figure 24 to draw a line graph of population growth.
  b) Describe the trend of your graph.
  c) If this trend continues, what might be the population of Alexandria in 2040?
3 a) Outline three different problems that will be created for the people of Egypt by climate change.
  b) Explain why the urban poor are most at risk. Give two different reasons.
4 Describe the possible loss of land in the Nile Delta. How big is the potential environmental refugee problem?
5 a) Use Figure 23 to describe the distribution and density of Egypt's population.
  b) Why is this a significant problem for the Egyptian government if sea levels rise as predicted?

Enquiry

'Solving the problems caused by climate change refugees is the responsibility of all nations.' How far do you agree with this statement? Justify your answer.

How might climate change affect tourism?

For many countries, the income gained from tourism is the most important source of revenue. It pays for health services, schools and infrastructure projects like sewers and roads. Millions are employed in the tourist industry across the world. Climate is a key factor in the development of tourism, so the industry is vulnerable to the effects of climate change. This is especially true at:
* beach destinations such as in the Caribbean and Mediterranean;
* mountain tourist resorts or winter sports locations, such as in the Alps.
Very small changes to snow conditions in the Alps could severely damage the tourist industry.

On the other hand, warmer temperatures in Northern France might encourage French tourists to take a staycation rather than travel to the tropics in search of sun and sand.

How might climate change affect tourism in the Bahamas?

Tourism is vital to the economy of the Bahamas. In 2015, the income from tourism accounted for 40 per cent of gross domestic product (GDP) and earned the islands $1.3 billion in foreign exchange. It is estimated that half of the government's spending on health, education, sanitation, roads and airports comes from tourism. Climate change threatens to change the tourist industry for ever. The Bahamas is one of 58 Small Island Developing States (SIDS – see page 169) and is particularly vulnerable to the effects of climate change. These include:
* loss of beaches to erosion and inundation through sea level rise
* damage to freshwater aquifers due to salt water intrusion
* increasing stress on coastal ecosystems, particularly coral reefs, due to bleaching and sea temperature rise
* damage to infrastructure from increased frequency and intensity of tropical storms.

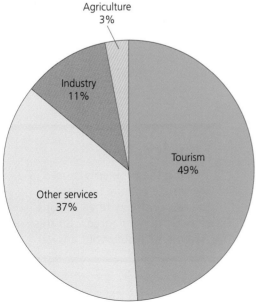

▲ **Figure 27** Labour-force in the Bahamas, by occupation (percentage figures).

▲ **Figure 28** A beach resort in the Bahamas.

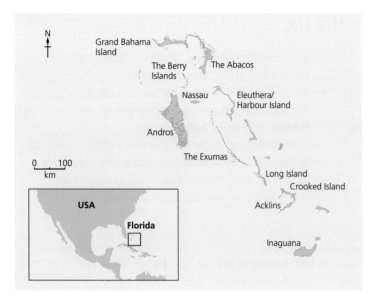

◀ **Figure 29** The islands of the Bahamas.

Short-term solutions	Difficulties to overcome
Building sea walls to reduce the problems of beach erosion through sea level rise and storm surges.	Sea walls are costly to build and maintain. They are visually unattractive and it is impossible to protect every island.
Invest in desalination plants and educate people and businesses about water conservation to make up for the loss of freshwater in aquifers.	Desalination plants are expensive. Rainfall totals may fall so water conservation is unlikely to be effective enough to meet demands.
Improve existing hurricane prediction and alert systems and construct more hurricane-proof buildings.	Hurricane-proof buildings are costly. They will not necessarily prevent damage by the strongest hurricanes.

▲ **Figure 30** Short-term solutions for the Bahama government to consider.

Activities

1 Describe the location of the Bahamas.
2 a) Explain why the economy of the Bahamas is more vulnerable to climate change than France, even though more tourists visit France.
  b) Identify six geographical factors that make the tourist industry in the Bahamas particularly vulnerable to climate change.
3 Discuss how far the Bahamian government should go in introducing short-term measures to reduce the immediate threat of climate change.

Enquiry

'The Small Island Developing States (SIDS) are more vulnerable to climate change than other, larger countries.' To what extent do you think this statement is true? Justify your decision.

▲ **Figure 31** Perry Christie, Prime Minister of the Bahamas, speaking in 2015 at the Paris International Climate Summit.

Attitudes to a low-carbon future in the UK

A low-carbon future could be achieved by combining three approaches:

- Using new technologies to reduce our dependence on fossil fuels for energy and transport.
- Better energy conservation and efficiency. This means changing our lifestyles so that each of us plays a part in reducing carbon emissions. For example, individuals can reduce energy consumption by insulating their homes, using low-energy appliances, using more public transport and taking fewer flights.
- Finding ways to remove carbon dioxide from the atmosphere and storing it in long-term sinks such as forests or in rocks underground.

Each of these approaches to the low-carbon future has advantages and disadvantages, and some may prove more popular than others. Figure 32 examines some different points of view on these low-carbon solutions.

▼ **Figure 32** Different attitudes towards a low-carbon future.

Energy conservation and efficiency

My husband has a low-paid job and I work part time. We don't have much money. I'm worried we don't have enough money to put the heating on this winter. The TV news calls this fuel poverty. Our house was built in the 1930s and it doesn't have much insulation. I know that it would be good to insulate the roof. It would cost a bit less to heat the house and eventually the savings I make would pay for the work. But, you see, I really have no money to spare. The insulation will just have to wait.

Young family

Liberal Democrat politician

Everyone should do their bit to help save energy. Simple things like insulating the roof and only boiling as much water as you need every time you use the kettle. We estimate that the CO_2 emissions from electrical items left on standby in the UK is the same as 1.4 million long-haul flights. That's the same as everyone in Glasgow flying to New York and back! And the number of TVs is growing fast. We think that by 2020 there will be 74 million TVs in the UK, that's more TVs than people!

We could capture carbon dioxide emissions from coal- and gas-fired power stations. The gas could then be turned to a liquid, pumped down into the ground and stored in sedimentary rocks. In fact, North Sea oil rigs that currently pump oil out of the ground could pump the CO_2 into the rocks when the oil has run out. Those rocks would make a perfect long-term carbon sink.

The process is not difficult but would be quite expensive to set up. Each person in the UK makes about 10 tonnes of CO_2 each year by their use of energy. We estimate that the cost for capture and storage of CO_2 in North Sea rocks is about £20 per tonne. So it will cost about £200 per person each year. Would people want to pay?

The government will have to find a way to make the power companies start to do this. The electricity generators have to capture the CO_2 and then transport it to a disposal site. The oil exploration companies will need to pay for the CO_2 to be stored deep underground. The government could threaten to tax these companies more unless they begin to capture and store the carbon.

Carbon capture and storage

Scientist

Nuclear power or renewables?

Some argue that nuclear power is a solution to climate change because it has no carbon emissions. But here at Friends of the Earth we oppose the building of any new nuclear power stations in the UK. We believe that nuclear power is dangerous for a number of reasons. Firstly, there is a security issue and power stations could be targets for terrorists. Secondly, there is the hazardous radioactive waste that will need careful management for generations. Finally, nuclear waste can be converted to be used in weapons.

We are in favour of green energy which is energy from renewables such as wind and solar. These technologies are a safer, cheaper and cleaner solution to the problem of climate change.

Spokesperson for Friends of the Earth

Biofuels

Industry spokesperson

There are a number of crops that produce oil that can be processed to make fuel for either cars or aircraft. The growth of these biofuels could reduce poverty in developing countries by creating jobs and wealth for farmers. At the same time people in the developed nations can continue to use their cars and take flights without the fear of oil shortages.

Biofuel crops are causing poverty and hunger in some developing countries. Farmers are being encouraged to grow biofuels instead of food so that we can drive our cars without feeling guilty about carbon emissions. But here at Oxfam we believe that in 2007 and 2008 this has been a factor in the rising cost of food. Using the World Bank's figures we reckon that rising food prices have pushed 100 million people worldwide below the poverty line.

Since April 2008, all petrol and diesel in Britain has had to include 2.5 per cent from biofuels. The European Union considered raising that target to 10 per cent by 2020. However it is now concerned that this could push food prices even higher.

Spokesperson for Oxfam

Forest sinks

Spokesperson for Greenpeace

Planting trees seems like a really a good solution to climate change. They soak up carbon from the atmosphere and store it. However, here at Greenpeace we don't think that planting trees is enough. People have got to actually reduce their carbon emissions in order to tackle climate change. So planting a tree to offset your emissions is just not good enough.

We have been raising awareness of some companies who plant trees to offset their carbon emissions. For example, there is a Japanese power company who wanted to offset their carbon emissions by planting trees. So they bought some land in Tasmania, Australia. They cut down the natural forest that was growing here so they could plant 3,000 hectares of fast growing eucalyptus trees to soak up the carbon. How crazy is that!

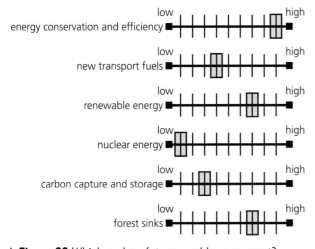

▲ **Figure 33** Which carbon future would you support?

Activities

1 Discuss the points of view shown in Figure 32. Outline some advantages and disadvantages of:
   a) energy efficiency and conservation
   b) biofuels
   c) nuclear power.
2 Explain why some environmentalists argue that planting forests is not a good enough option.
3 Working in pairs, study Figure 33.
   a) Imagine each slider represents the amount of effort and investment that could be made in the six possible solutions to climate change. Agree with your partner how each slider should be placed in your ideal low-carbon future. Be prepared to justify your decision.
   b) Team up with another pair. Each pair must give a short presentation to describe and justify their low-carbon future. Can you persuade the other pair to change their minds?

How can we create an alternative, low-carbon future?

Since 1990 representatives of governments from around the world have met periodically to discuss the issue of climate change. The Kyoto Protocol (1997) is an international agreement which commits countries to targets to reduce greenhouse gas emissions. The latest version of this agreement is the Doha Amendment to the Kyoto Protocol (2012). The Doha Amendment aims to limit global temperature increases to below 2°C. Countries that have signed this agreement, including the UK, are committed to it until 2020.

The Kyoto Protocol recognises that industrial countries like the USA, UK and Germany have been largely responsible for greenhouse gas emissions in the past and should make the biggest efforts to reduce emissions. There is an expectation that Newly Industrialised Countries (NICs) such as India and China will begin to reduce emissions once industrial growth in their economies has helped to reduce levels of poverty.

So how are the EU countries trying to reduce greenhouse gas emissions? Members of the EU have signed agreements to:
- Invest in renewable energy production using wind, solar and hydro-electricity.
- Source at least 10 per cent of their transport fuel from biofuel. Biofuel is the kind of fuel that is made from natural plant oils. It is considered to be **carbon-neutral** because these quick-growing crops absorb as much carbon from the atmosphere while they are growing as they give off when they are burnt as fuel.

◄ **Figure 35** The new solar furnace which provides electricity for the city of Seville, Spain.

Activity

1 a) Explain why biofuels are considered to be carbon-neutral.
   b) Suggest one disadvantage of growing biofuels.

Enquiry

How quickly should the international community reduce its greenhouse gas emissions?

a) Discuss Figure 34. Which model do you think the international community should be aiming for? Justify your decision
b) At what point do you think India and China should start reducing their emissions?

Model	Peak CO_2 level (ppm)	Year peak CO_2 is reached (year)	Change in CO_2 emissions in 2050 compared with 2000 (per cent)	Global average temperature increase compared with pre-industrial age (Celsius)	Global average sea level rise due to expansion of sea water but not taking ice melting into account (metres)
1	350–400	2000–2015	−85 to −50	2.0–2.4	0.4–1.4
2	400–440	2000–2020	−60 to −30	2.4–2.8	0.5–1.7
3	440–485	2010–2030	−30 to +5	2.8–3.2	0.6–1.9
4	485–570	2020–2060	+10 to +60	3.2–4.0	0.6–2.4
5	570–660	2050–2080	+25 to +85	4.0–4.9	0.8–2.9
6	660–790	2060–2090	+90 to +140	4.9–6.1	1.0–3.7

▲ **Figure 34** Computer models from the Intergovernmental Panel on Climate Change (IPCC), a highly respected group of climate scientists. Their computer models show that temperatures will rise even if we are able to control CO_2 concentrations below 400 ppm in the next five or so years. Model 1 would require the biggest and quickest cuts in CO_2 emissions, while model 6 allows countries to make smaller, slower cuts.

Can new renewable technologies help us achieve a low-carbon future?

Figure 35 may be a glimpse of a future, low-carbon Europe. A field of 600 steel mirrors reflect solar energy. They direct a beam of light and heat to the top of a 40 m tower where the energy is focused on to water pipes. The heat turns the water to steam which then turns a turbine to generate electricity. The whole system is computer controlled so that each mirror tilts at exactly the right angle. At the moment this **solar furnace** produces enough energy for 6,000 homes, but the plant is being extended and will eventually provide power for the whole of the city of Seville, Spain.

In the future it would be possible to build more solar furnaces in the Sahara desert and bring the electricity into Europe through a new 'super-grid' of cables. Scientists believe that all of Europe's electricity could be generated from just 0.3 per cent of the sunlight that falls on the Sahara. The cost of the super-grid alone would be around €45 billion. This would certainly reduce Europe's carbon emissions dramatically, but critics point out that Africa should also benefit from some of this clean energy.

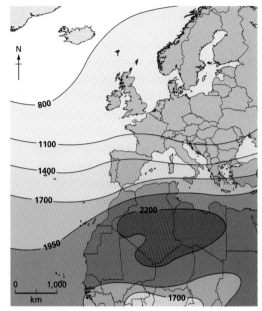

▲ **Figure 36** Patterns of solar energy across Europe and Africa (kilowatts/m²/year).

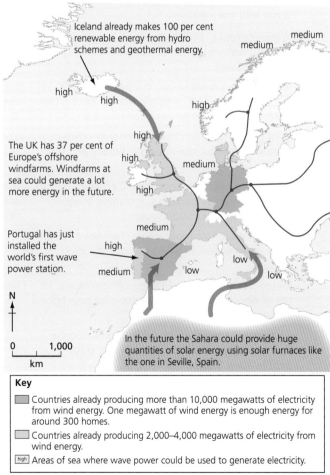

Iceland already makes 100 per cent renewable energy from hydro schemes and geothermal energy.

The UK has 37 per cent of Europe's offshore windfarms. Windfarms at sea could generate a lot more energy in the future.

Portugal has just installed the world's first wave power station.

In the future the Sahara could provide huge quantities of solar energy using solar furnaces like the one in Seville, Spain.

Key

Countries already producing more than 10,000 megawatts of electricity from wind energy. One megawatt of wind energy is enough energy for around 300 homes.

Countries already producing 2,000–4,000 megawatts of electricity from wind energy.

high Areas of sea where wave power could be used to generate electricity.

▲ **Figure 37** In the future an international grid of power cables could link the countries of Europe and North Africa so that renewable energy made in the Sahara could be fed into your home.

Activities

2 Use Figure 36 to describe the distribution of countries that have:
   a) between 1,100 and 1,400 kilowatts/m²/year
   b) more than 2,200 kilowatts/m²/year.
3 Use Figure 37 to describe the distribution of:
   a) countries currently producing more than 2,000 megawatts of wind energy a year
   b) countries that could use their seas to make high levels of wave power.

Enquiry

How should renewable energy be made in Europe?

Research and then make a poster about renewable energy in Europe. Focus on wind, wave and solar. Include facts and figures about how much renewable energy is made in at least one European country.

How can individuals and government reduce the risk of climate change?

The UK Government has an international role in combatting climate change. It is a signatory of the Doha Amendment (which is described on page 212) and the Paris Agreement (2015). The outcome of the Paris Agreement was a long-term aim to keep global warming to well below 2°C compared to pre-industrial levels. The UK Government also works at a national scale. It provides targets for local government and works with industry to reduce greenhouse gas emissions by:

- investing in low-carbon energy sources;
- improving fuel standards in cars;
- increasing energy efficiency in new buildings.

Councils must publish a policy statement on climate change by law.

Figure 38 describes some of the ways in which Bristol City Council is trying to meet its own climate change targets.

Activity

1 Study Figure 38.
   a) Explain why ideas 5 and 7 will help Bristol meet its climate change target.
   b) Make a diamond nine diagram (like the one on page 108) and place the strategies from Figure 38 in the diagram, putting those that you think are essential at the top of the diagram.
   c) Justify your choice of the top three strategies.

	What will they do?	Why it helps
1	Warmer homes. £105 million will be spent fitting external wall insulation to homes (including blocks of flats).	£3.5 million could be saved each year on heating bills. Possible 5 per cent reduction in the amount of gas used. 17,900 tonnes of CO_2 saved each year.
2	Install district heating (or heat networks). These will duct spare heat between the university, the hospital and buildings in the city centre.	Heating buildings and hot water use are two of the main reasons for CO_2 emissions in large cities. District heating uses energy efficient boilers.
3	Lead by example. Improve the energy efficiency of council offices, the museum, library and two schools.	£500,000 energy saving and 2,000 tonnes of CO_2 saved each year.
4	High energy performance. Install efficient boilers in all new council buildings, including schools, care homes and council housing.	It is cheaper in the long term to install energy efficient technologies when buildings are new rather than trying to modify older buildings.
5	Solar photovoltaic programme. Two solar farms were constructed in 2014 at a cost of £35.9 million.	
6	Metro-bus scheme. Build 6 km of new roads, 18 km of new bus lanes and purchase 50 new hybrid vehicles.	Shift passengers from car to bus will reduce congestion and CO_2 emissions from commuter traffic.
7	Sustainable transport. Invest in 10 km of cycle lanes and promote cycling and walking for people aged 8–80.	
8	Land use planning. Locating new homes to reduce the need for commuting and allow the use of district heating.	Future proof new housing developments by making them sustainable.
9	Improve mass transit. Spend £90 million improving suburban train services.	Improve air quality and transport safety. Reduce congestion and CO_2 emissions.

▲ **Figure 38** How Bristol City Council hopes to meet its targets to reduce CO_2 emissions.

GEOGRAPHICAL SKILLS

Collecting qualitative data

Some geographical data is easily quantified – meaning that it is easy to measure and record an actual number. Examples include pedestrian counts or the number of vacant shops in a high street. Other useful data is difficult to quantify; other people's opinions, for example, on their views about leading a low-carbon lifestyle. This is qualitative data and it can be collected in a number of ways:

- in a lengthy interview
- using a questionnaire
- with a quick survey such as a Likert scale.

If you are designing a questionnaire it is a good idea to have examples of both closed and open questions. Closed questions have set answers which you can tick.

For example: How do you get to school?

Walk [ ]   Cycle [ ]   Bus [ ]   Car [ ]

An open question is where people can give their own unstructured answer, e.g. How do you think the school could reduce its GHG emissions?

A Likert scale is where people are asked to use a scale when responding to a question.

Activities

1. Show one way you would represent each of the data sets from the survey. Justify your choice.
2. What conclusions can you draw from the responses given?
3. Suggest two other questions you could ask to investigate individual attitudes to climate change.
4. Explain why data representation and data analysis are easier if closed rather than open questions are asked in questionnaires.
5. Suggest an open question that you might ask. Explain why this open question would reveal useful information about how individuals feel about climate change.

Only offshore wind farms should be developed in future			
1	2	3	4
Agree	Slightly agree	Slightly disagree	Disagree

▲ **Figure 39** An example of a Likert scale.

Question, with responses measured on a Likert scale of 1–10 (1 = not at all seriously and 10 = very seriously)	Mean score
How seriously do you regard the threat of climate change?	7.5
How effective do you think that individuals can be in reducing the threat of climate change?	4.5

▲ **Figure 40** An example of a climate change enquiry.

A group of geography students were interested in investigating how people of different ages are responding to climate change. They set an enquiry question:

Are younger people more willing to change their lifestyles than older people?

As part of their enquiry, they used a Likert Survey with 100 people. They also asked the respondents to tick up to five things that they already do (as individuals) to help reduce the threat of climate change. The results are shown below.

Possible actions that individuals can take	Number of responses
Use low-energy bulbs	82
Choose energy-efficient goods	57
Improve insulation for the home	53
Recycle all plastics, glass, etc.	89
Lower the thermostat settings on the heating	23
Walk or cycle to avoid using the car	2
Use public transport	17
Buy locally produced food	11

▲ **Figure 41** Possible actions that individuals can take.

THEME 2

Chapter 8
Problem-solving exercise: How should the Red River be managed?

Introducing the Red River, southern USA

The Red River drainage basin is the second largest in southern USA. The Red River is heavily used and managed for a variety of purposes. In the **upper course** of the river, there is often not enough water and drought is an issue. In the **lower course**, flooding often impacts on human activity. In this chapter you will study the contrasting demands placed on the Red River and consider the priorities for its long-term management.

▲ **Figure 1** The Red River in drought, Texas.

▲ **Figure 2** The Red River in flood at Shreveport, Louisiana.

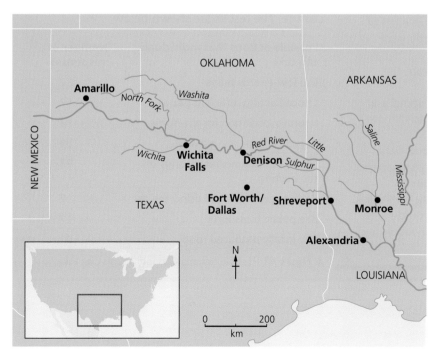

▲ **Figure 3** The drainage basin of the Red River.

Activity

1 Use Figure 3 to describe the course of the Red River.

How does climate affect the nature of the Red River drainage basin?

In its upper course, the Red River flows through high open grasslands and rough terrain known as the Great Plains. The cold semi-arid climate makes much of this region dry, with long periods of drought. As a result, river flow is intermittent. However, thunderstorms and tornadoes are common between April and August, leading to torrential downpours and flash flooding. Erosion levels can be very high during these storms, leading to large amounts of sediment being deposited in the river. This can severely reduce water quality, leading to silting up of the river channel.

In its middle and lower course, the Red River flows through mixed grasslands and forests and eventually through marshes and swamps, where the humid subtropical climate is warmer and wetter. Here the river meanders across its flood plain in a 300 m wide channel. When the river is in flood, it can widen to 2 km. The river is deep enough for shipping, but navigation is difficult. This is because of regular flooding that erodes banks, deposits sediment in the river and shifts the shape of the channel.

Cold semi-arid	Jan	Feb	Mar	Apr	May	Jun	Jul	Aug	Sep	Oct	Nov	Dec
Temp high (°C)	10.3	12.3	16.9	21.7	26.4	30.9	33	31.9	28.1	22.2	15.6	9.8
Temp low (°C)	-4.8	-3.1	0.7	5.3	11	16.1	18.4	17.9	13.6	7.1	0.3	-4.4
Precipitation (mm)	18	14	35	36	58	80	72	74	49	42	20	18

▲ **Figure 4** Climate data for Amarillo, Texas in the upper course of the Red River (average 1961–90).

Humid subtropical	Jan	Feb	Mar	Apr	May	Jun	Jul	Aug	Sep	Oct	Nov	Dec
Temp high (°C)	14.1	16.4	20.8	24.9	28.8	32.3	34.1	34.5	31.2	25.7	19.7	14.7
Temp low (°C)	2.3	4.3	7.9	12	17.1	20.8	22.6	22.3	18.7	12.6	7.3	3.2
Precipitation (mm)	107	121	105	106	125	137	93	69	80	126	115	121

▲ **Figure 5** Climate data for Shreveport, Louisiana, in the lower course of the Red River (average 1961–90).

Enquiry

Research five major world rivers and complete a copy of the table below.

River	Continent	Basin area (km²)	Length (km)	Mean discharge at mouth (cumecs)
Red River	North America	169,900	2,190	1,600
Rhine				
Nile				
Thames				
Yangtze				
Murray–Darling				

Compare the Red River to each of the other world rivers. Use sentence connectives such as 'whereas', and comparative words such as 'bigger' and 'most' in your response.

Activity

2 Study the data in Figures 4 and 5.
   a) Draw climate graphs for Amarillo and Shreveport.
   b) Describe four differences between cold semi-arid and humid subtropical climates.

Who manages the Red River?

The US Army Corps of Engineers (USACE) is responsible for managing all water resources in the USA. In the Red River Basin, USACE works closely with many regional and local organisations such as Texas Water Development Board, Red River Valley Association and Red River Water Commission to put water management strategies in place.

The neighbouring states of Arkansas, Louisiana, Oklahoma and Texas all use water from the Red River Basin. Under an agreement called the Red River Compact, these four states have agreed to work together to share the Red River water resources and to resolve any disagreements that may arise between them.

Conflicting demands on the Red River
Managing flood risk
Managing reservoirs and water supply
Hydro-electric power (HEP)
Leisure use such as fishing and sailing
Protecting the environment, fish and wildlife
Maintaining navigation for shipping

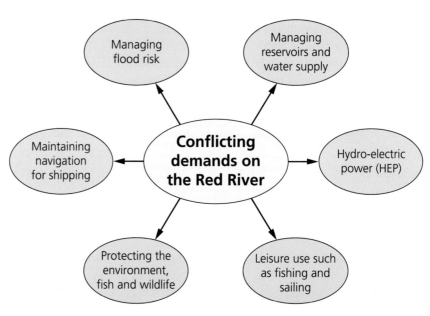

► **Figure 6** The work of the US Army Corps of Engineers (USACE).

Lower Red River: In the middle and lower courses through Arkansas and Louisiana, preventing large-scale flooding and maintaining navigation channels for shipping is a priority.
OKLAHOMA
ARKANSAS
Upper Red River: In the upper course through northern Texas and southern Oklahoma where drought is common, providing a clean and regular water supply is a major challenge.
TEXAS
LOUISIANA

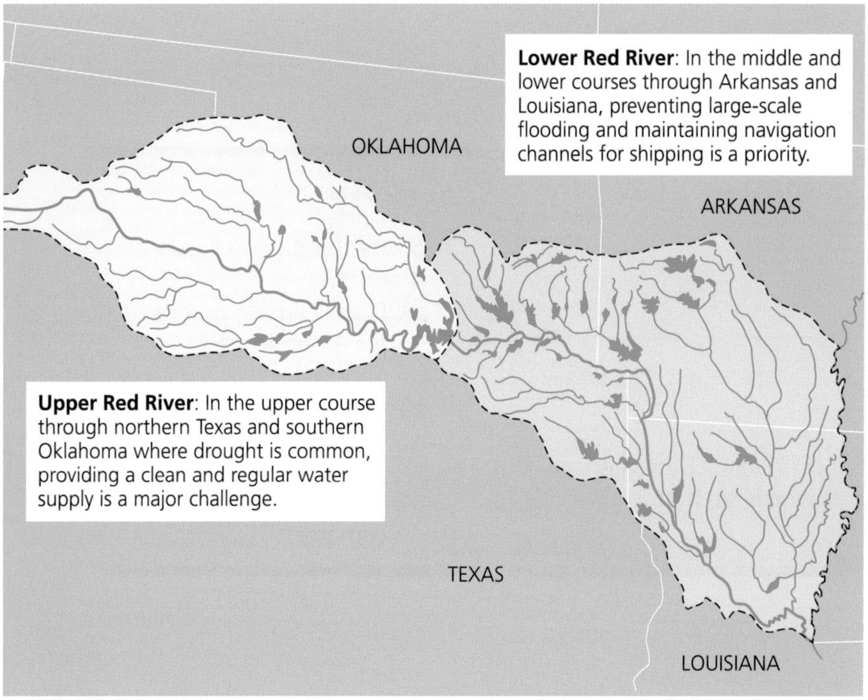

▲ **Figure 7** Major issues in the Red River drainage basin.

Activities

1. Use Figure 6 to identify two roles of USACE that may conflict with one another.
2. Study Figure 7.
   a) Explain why it is useful to divide the Red River drainage basin into Upper and Lower sections.
   b) Working in groups of four, use information from this page and your own research to discuss why the Red River Compact is needed. Select a spokesperson to feedback your conclusions to the rest of your class.

Enquiry

How important is USACE to the USA?

Use the internet to find out more about the river management work of USACE.

How is the Upper Red River managed?

The population of the USA is predicted to grow rapidly from 320 million in 2015 to 440 million people in the year 2050. Much of this growth will happen in cities in arid regions with limited water supplies. For example, the population of Fort Worth/Dallas in northern Texas is expected to rise from 7 million to 12 million by 2050. In a way, building dams on the Red River and its tributaries has encouraged urban growth in this arid region. For example, Lake Texoma, which is a reservoir formed by the Denison Dam, provides hydroelectricity (HEP), flood control, and water storage. This has encouraged people to move into the area to live and work. This and the other dams on the Red River also provide fantastic leisure opportunities such as boating, camping and hiking. As the population continues to grow, the demand for water supply and electricity will increase – will there be enough water in the future?

Each reservoir has a Drought Management Plan, but despite this, water levels are very low. Climate scientists warn that intense short-term droughts may be more common in this region as the climate changes, so experts are concerned that there will not be enough water to meet demand and to drive the turbines for hydro-electric power. In addition, the dams trap sediment being transported downriver, making the reservoirs shallower and not able to store as much water as they should. The sediment also makes the water salty which needs to be treated before it can be used.

◀ **Figure 8** Lake Texoma is at the heart of a National Park that attracts over 6 million visitors each year.

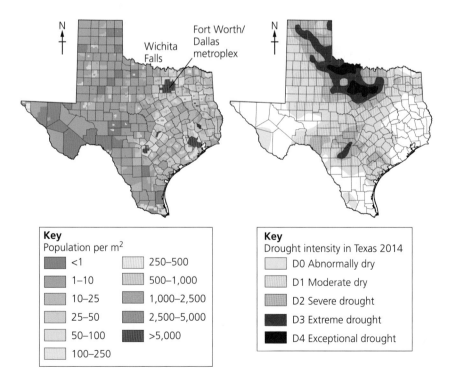

Key
Population per m²

<1	250–500
1–10	500–1,000
10–25	1,000–2,500
25–50	2,500–5,000
50–100	>5,000
100–250	

Key
Drought intensity in Texas 2014

- D0 Abnormally dry
- D1 Moderate dry
- D2 Severe drought
- D3 Extreme drought
- D4 Exceptional drought

▲ **Figure 9** Population density and drought intensity in Texas (2014).

Activity

3 a) Use the information in Figure 9 to compare similarities and differences in population distribution and drought intensity in Texas.

   b) Suggest what may happen to towns such as Wichita Falls and the surrounding countryside if short, intense droughts become more common.

How is the Lower Red River managed?

Over the course of late spring 2015, severe thunderstorms caused heavy rainfall across the Red River Basin, filling the Red River and its reservoirs. As the rainfall continued, the Red River eventually burst its banks and flooded large parts of the river basin in Arkansas and Louisiana. At Shreveport–Bossier City, river levels reached record heights, inundating hundreds of homes, businesses, roads and surrounding farmland.

A state of emergency was declared and the J. Bennett Johnston Waterway was closed to shipping.

However, according to some experts, the 2015 flood was not as damaging as it could have been because of the system of levees, flood control dams and spillways that had been put in place following previous flooding in 1945, 1957 and 1990.

◀ **Figure 10** Using sandbags to keep the floodwaters out at Shreveport, June 2015.

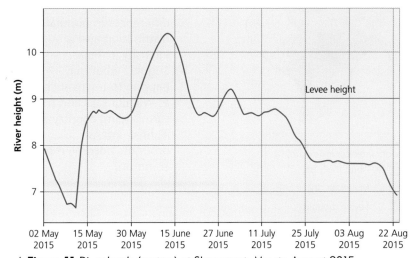

▲ **Figure 11** River levels (metres) at Shreveport, May to August 2015.

Activities

1 Study Figure 10. Describe the possible impacts of this type of flooding on:
   a) homeowners
   b) commuters
   c) elderly residents.
2 Study Figure 11. Describe the differences in river levels from May to August 2015.
3 Using your own knowledge of how water moves through a drainage basin, suggest reasons for differences in river levels during the Red River 2015 floods.

Challenges and options for the future

Managing the Red River and its valuable water resources can only become more difficult as conflicting demands for water increase and the climate changes. Study Figures 12 and 13 before considering how this drainage basin may need to be managed in the future.

Desalinisation: Chloride control programmes provide millions more litres of drinking water.

Groundwater is used for farming but can be treated for human usage.

Water reuse and recycling: Effluent could be treated and mixed with lake water to provide up to 35 million litres of drinking water per day.

More reservoirs have been built to provide extra water storage capacity.

Water-transfer from rivers and reservoirs outside of the Red River Basin along large pipes.

Wetlands are being built to store water and encourage wildlife in the river basin.

Non-conventional methods: Weather modification and evaporation suppression are being considered.

Water restriction: Wichita Falls City reduced consumption from 132 million litres per day to 41 million litres per day.

▲ **Figure 12** Strategies to provide a safe and reliable water supply in the Upper Red River.

Activities

1 Study Figure 12. With a partner, discuss each of the strategies. Which of these strategies might:
   a) provide short-term solutions?
   b) provide long-term solutions to the problems?
2 Explain your reasons.
3 Study Figure 13.
   a) In groups, discuss the advantages and disadvantages of each strategy, using criteria such as cost, scale, environmental impact.
   b) Carry out a diamond nine ranking activity (described on page 108), ranking the most effective strategy at the top of the diamond and the least effective strategy at the bottom of the diamond.
   c) Present your diamond nine to the rest of your class, justifying your ordering of the strategies. Do they agree?

Enquiry

How successful are 'non-conventional' strategies such as weather modification and evaporation suppression?

Research these non-conventional strategies. Evaluate the usefulness of these strategies in helping reducing drought in the Red River Basin.

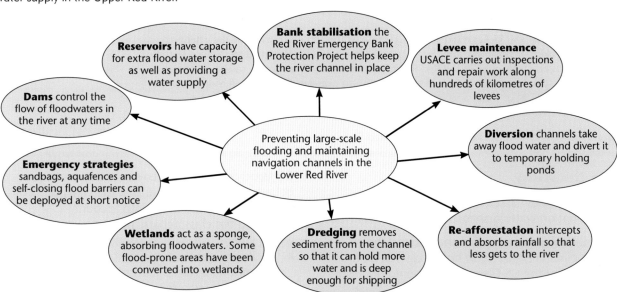

▲ **Figure 13** Preventing large-scale flooding and maintaining navigation channels in the Lower Red River.

What are the priorities for the longer-term management of the Red River?

Managing rivers such as the Red River is complex, with many competing demands and viewpoints, as outlined in Figure 14 below.

We need more water for our growing population. We have built more reservoirs and water treatment plants so that we can use more river water, groundwater and recycled effluent. We want to take more water from the Red River basin as well as creating wetlands as water stores. This whole programme will cost around $13 billion.

Texas Water Company representative

Six million people use Lake Texoma for recreation each year, bringing in money to the local economy. We are worried about droughts and floods restricting boating and fishing activities on the lake. Drought will also make the water saltier and kill fish - our business will suffer.

Lake Texoma Tourist Business representative

We receive $70 million per year from power generated by Denison Dam and other dams on the Red River. Much of this money is re-invested into managing the river. It is important that we have enough water in our reservoirs to generate this energy supply – otherwise we may not be able to pay for other flood and drought control projects.

United States Army Corps of Engineers

As the climate becomes drier, there will be less water stored in reservoirs. We need to look for alternatives to water energy such as wind power, which is much cheaper to produce. The high open grasslands in the upper Red River basin are ideal for this because of the strong, steady winds that blow all year round.

Energy Conservationist

We have dramatically reduced levee erosion through bank stabilisation schemes. Unless $19 million is spent every year continuing these schemes then the river will wash away all our good work, breaking through the levees and flooding the land behind. It would cost many more millions to repair the levees and clear up after the floods.

River scientist

Dams and levees make flooding worse as they trap sediment in the channel, making it shallower and pushing water levels higher. We need to remove dams and levees and let the Red River flood naturally. The money saved could be spent on creating wetlands and restoring grasslands which will reduce the amount of water and eroded sediment getting to the river in the first place.

Environmentalist

▲ **Figure 14** Different viewpoints on managing the Red River.

Your decision

Your class has been asked to advise the US Government on water management in the Red River.

1 Use the information in this chapter and the viewpoints in Figure 15 to hold a class debate on whether the US Government should prioritise drought management in the Upper Red River OR flood control in the Lower Red River. In your debate you should ensure that the viewpoints of all stakeholders are taken into account.

2 Following the class debate, present a report in which you:
   a) justify your chosen option, taking into account its advantages and disadvantages;
   b) explain why you rejected the other option.

▲ Canopy walkway through the tropical rainforest in the Kakum National Park, Ghana.

THEME 3

Chapter 1
How ecosystems function

What are ecosystems?

An **ecosystem** is a community of plants and animals and the environment in which they live. Ecosystems contain both living and non-living parts. The living part includes such things as insects and birds, which depend on each other for food. It also includes plants, which may also depend on insects and birds for pollination and seed dispersal. The non-living part of an ecosystem includes such things as the climate, soils and rocks. This non-living environment provides nutrients, warmth, water and shelter for the living parts of the ecosystem.

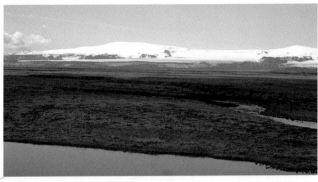

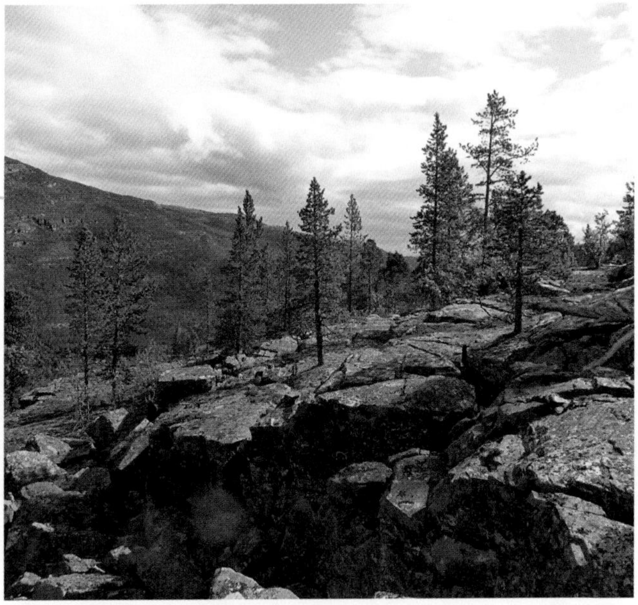

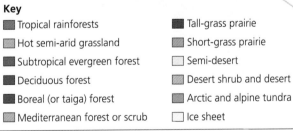

Key

- Tropical rainforests
- Hot semi-arid grassland
- Subtropical evergreen forest
- Deciduous forest
- Boreal (or taiga) forest
- Mediterranean forest or scrub
- Tall-grass prairie
- Short-grass prairie
- Semi-desert
- Desert shrub and desert
- Arctic and alpine tundra
- Ice sheet

▲ **Figure 1** Biomes of Africa and Europe.

▲ **Figure 2** Arctic tundra, Iceland.

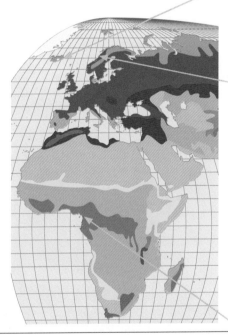

▲ **Figure 3** Boreal (taiga) forest, Norway.

▲ **Figure 4** Tropical rainforest, Gabon.

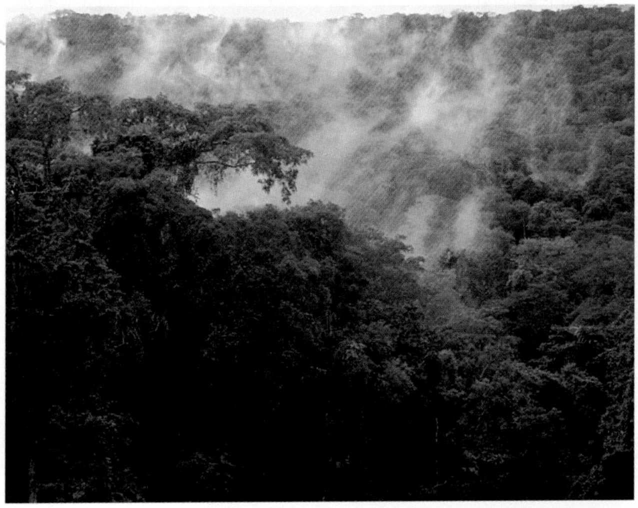

Activity

1 Use Figure 1 to describe the distribution of:
   a) tropical rainforests
   b) boreal (taiga) forests.

Global distribution of biomes

Climate is such an important factor in influencing the natural vegetation and wildlife of a region that **biomes** (the largest-scale ecosystems) broadly match the world's climate zones. **Tropical rainforests** grow in a band around the Equator where the equatorial climate is hot and wet (see page 182–3). The treeless **tundra** and forested **taiga** ecosystems exist where winters are cold and summers are short. The effect of latitude on temperature is explained by Figure 5.

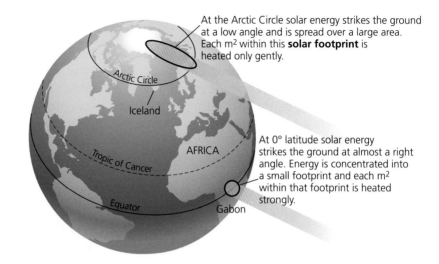

At the Arctic Circle solar energy strikes the ground at a low angle and is spread over a large area. Each m² within this **solar footprint** is heated only gently.

At 0° latitude solar energy strikes the ground at almost a right angle. Energy is concentrated into a small footprint and each m² within that footprint is heated strongly.

▲ **Figure 5** Solar heating of the Earth varies with latitude.

Month	Tundra moorland 64°N, Iceland Temperature (°C)	Precipitation (mm)	Boreal (taiga) forest 65°N, Norway Temperature (°C)	Precipitation (mm)	Tropical rainforest 0°N, Gabon Temperature (°C)	Precipitation (mm)
Jan	−0.5	145	−8.0	38	27.0	249
Feb	0.4	130	−7.5	30	26.5	236
Mar	0.5	115	−4.5	25	27.5	335
Apr	2.9	117	2.5	35	27.5	340
May	6.3	131	8.5	42	26.5	244
Jun	9.0	120	14.0	48	25.0	13
Jul	10.6	158	17.0	76	24.0	3
Aug	10.3	141	15.5	75	25.0	18
Sep	7.4	184	10.5	57	25.5	104
Oct	4.4	184	5.5	57	26.0	345
Nov	1.1	137	0	49	26.0	373
Dec	−0.2	133	−4.0	41	27.5	249

Figure 6 Climate data for three climate stations. There are tips on how to understand climate data and how to draw a climate graph on page 185.

Activities

2 Use the climate data in Figure 6 to complete a copy of the following table.
3 Suggest how the differences in climate might affect plant growth in the two forest systems.

	Tropical rainforest	Boreal forest	Tundra moorland
Temperature range			
Months above 10°C (length of growing season)			
Months below freezing			
Total annual rainfall			
Seasonal variation in rainfall			

Investigating the relationships between climate and ecosystems in the Arctic

The Arctic region of Northern Scandinavia and Iceland has cold winters and short, cool summers. These conditions have a major impact on plant growth. Plants have to survive the long, dark winters when temperatures fall well below freezing and when strong winds or snowfall can damage the branches of trees. In the summer, plants benefit from long hours of daylight but the growing season is very short. Plants therefore grow slowly.

The further north you go in Northern Norway and Finland, the smaller the plants become. South of the Arctic Circle, the ecosystem is taiga. This is a forest ecosystem of conifer trees and birches. As you travel north, the trees become shorter and grow further apart. Eventually, a little north of the Arctic Circle, the climate becomes too extreme for trees to grow and the treeless Arctic tundra takes over.

1. Temperatures are only above 10° C (the temperature at which most plants grow) for two or three months …	… plants grow close to the ground where they are less likely to be damaged.
2. Precipitation in the winter months falls as snow …	… plants have a short growing season.
3. Rocks weather (break down) slowly in the cold conditions which means soils have few nutrients …	… plants are extremely slow growing.
4. With few trees around there is little shelter from wind …	… plants have small leaves and so don't lose any moisture.

… so …

▲ **Figure 7** How the Arctic climate affects plant growth.

▲ **Figure 9** Reindeer grazing on lichen in Arctic Norway.

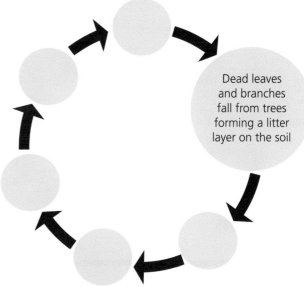

Dead leaves and branches fall from trees forming a litter layer on the soil

Leaf litter breaks down slowly in the cold conditions

Roots are shallow so they can take in nutrients near the surface

Decomposers such as beetles and fungi grow in the litter

Nutrients from leaf litter return to the soil

Plants use nutrients from the soil to help growth

▲ **Figure 10** Nutrient cycles in the taiga.

▲ **Figure 8** Lichens growing on a rotting tree stump, Arctic Norway.

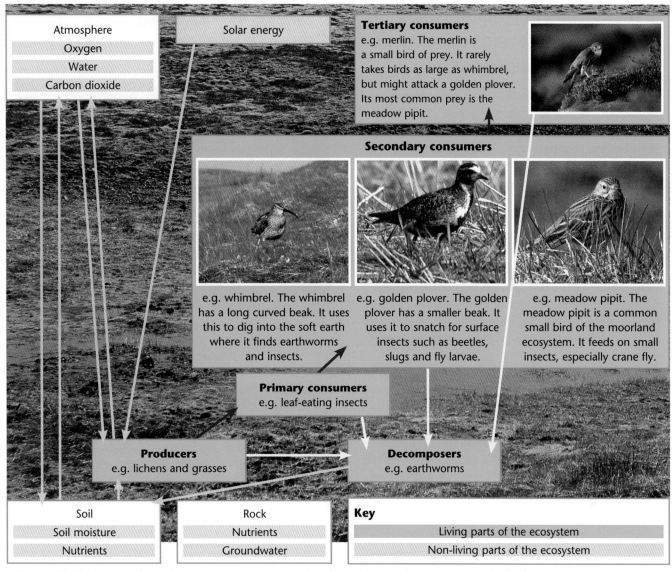

Atmosphere
Oxygen
Water
Carbon dioxide

Solar energy

Tertiary consumers
e.g. merlin. The merlin is a small bird of prey. It rarely takes birds as large as whimbrel, but might attack a golden plover. Its most common prey is the meadow pipit.

Secondary consumers

e.g. whimbrel. The whimbrel has a long curved beak. It uses this to dig into the soft earth where it finds earthworms and insects.

e.g. golden plover. The golden plover has a smaller beak. It uses it to snatch for surface insects such as beetles, slugs and fly larvae.

e.g. meadow pipit. The meadow pipit is a common small bird of the moorland ecosystem. It feeds on small insects, especially crane fly.

Primary consumers
e.g. leaf-eating insects

Producers
e.g. lichens and grasses

Decomposers
e.g. earthworms

Soil
Soil moisture
Nutrients

Rock
Nutrients
Groundwater

Key
Living parts of the ecosystem
Non-living parts of the ecosystem

▲ **Figure 11** The living and non-living parts (or components) of the treeless tundra ecosystem in Iceland.

Activities

1 Pair up the phrases in Figure 7 to make four sentences that explain the features of Arctic ecosystems.
2 Make a copy of Figure 10 and add the labels to the correct places to make a complete cycle.
3 Use Figure 11.
   a) Describe three non-living parts of the tundra ecosystem.
   b) Describe two ways that nutrients enter into the soil.
   c) Draw a food chain that includes meadow pipit.

Enquiry

How is the climate of the Arctic region affected by latitude? Do temperatures become more extreme as you travel north?

a) Research the climate and record the latitude of each of the following locations:
   i) Reykjavik, Iceland
   ii) Oulu, Finland
   iii) Murmansk, Russia
   iv) Churchill, Canada.
b) Apart from latitude, suggest one other factor that may explain these differences.

Investigating the relationships between climate and ecosystems in the tropical rainforest

The tropical rainforest biome has a climate that is hot throughout the year and has high annual rainfall totals. You can read more about this climate on pages 182–3. The heat and abundant rainfall allow rapid plant growth and trees can reach a height of 40 metres or more. This contrasts greatly with the very slow-growing plants of the tundra that never grow more than a few centimetres high. The differing growth rates of the plants in these contrasting biomes depend on latitude. Look again at Figure 5 on page 225 and how the angle made between the Sun and the ground varies with latitude. This is the basic reason for the difference in heat between the Equator and Arctic. The rate of plant growth in each of these biomes is controlled by factors such as the length of day and the amount of sunlight, warmth, and water.

Tropical rainforests contain a variety of habitats. In the basin of the River Amazon the **lowland tropical rainforest** is dominated by very tall trees and a continuous canopy of leaves. In more mountainous areas like Gabon (see Figure 4 on page 224), the temperatures are a little cooler and the trees are not quite so tall. The dominant ecosystem here is **cloud forest**. Figure 13 explains why it rains so frequently in this ecosystem.

There is plenty of sunlight overhead so plants grow straight and tall

In equatorial regions the temperature is constantly above 25°C so plants can grow all year and grow quickly

▲ **Figure 12** Tropical rainforest in Tobago.

There is plenty of water, sunshine and nutrients so a wide variety of plants are able to grow. This allows a wide diversity of insects, birds and animals

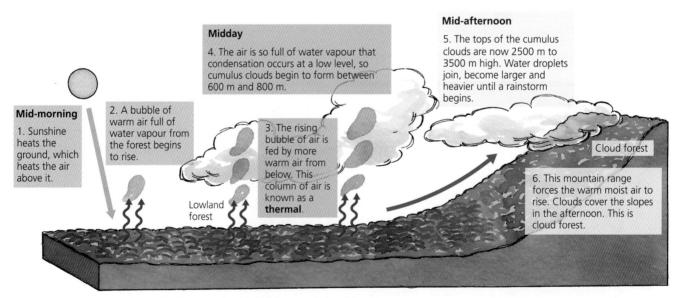

Mid-afternoon

5. The tops of the cumulus clouds are now 2500 m to 3500 m high. Water droplets join, become larger and heavier until a rainstorm begins.

Midday

4. The air is so full of water vapour that condensation occurs at a low level, so cumulus clouds begin to form between 600 m and 800 m.

Mid-morning

1. Sunshine heats the ground, which heats the air above it.

2. A bubble of warm air full of water vapour from the forest begins to rise.

3. The rising bubble of air is fed by more warm air from below. This column of air is known as a **thermal**.

Lowland forest

Cloud forest

6. This mountain range forces the warm moist air to rise. Clouds cover the slopes in the afternoon. This is cloud forest.

▲ **Figure 13** Convectional rainfall over lowland rainforest and cloud forest.

Nutrient cycles also depend on climate

Plants need minerals containing nitrogen and phosphates. These nutrients exist in rocks, water and the atmosphere. The plants take them from the soil, releasing them back into the soil when the plant dies. This process forms a continuous cycle.

Figure 14 represents nutrient stores and flows in the rainforest ecosystem. The circles represent **nutrient stores**.

The size of each circle is in proportion to the amount of nutrients kept in that part of the ecosystem. The arrows represent **nutrient flows** as minerals move from one store to another. The thickness of each arrow is in proportion to the size of the flow, so large flows of nutrients are shown with thick arrows while smaller flows are shown with narrow arrows.

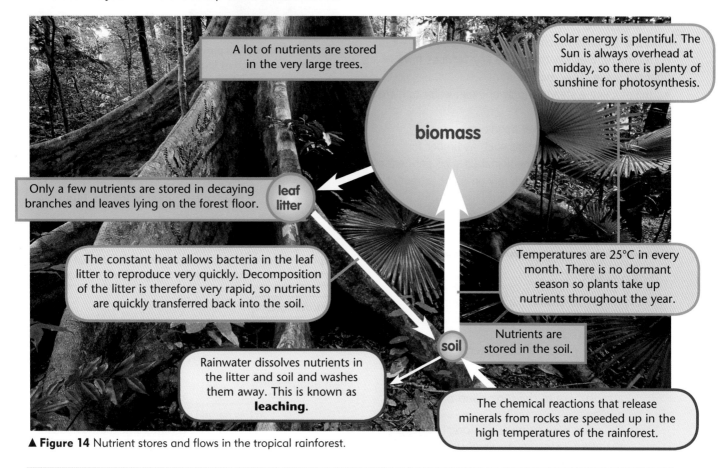

A lot of nutrients are stored in the very large trees.

Solar energy is plentiful. The Sun is always overhead at midday, so there is plenty of sunshine for photosynthesis.

biomass

Only a few nutrients are stored in decaying branches and leaves lying on the forest floor.

leaf litter

The constant heat allows bacteria in the leaf litter to reproduce very quickly. Decomposition of the litter is therefore very rapid, so nutrients are quickly transferred back into the soil.

Temperatures are 25°C in every month. There is no dormant season so plants take up nutrients throughout the year.

soil

Nutrients are stored in the soil.

Rainwater dissolves nutrients in the litter and soil and washes them away. This is known as **leaching**.

The chemical reactions that release minerals from rocks are speeded up in the high temperatures of the rainforest.

▲ **Figure 14** Nutrient stores and flows in the tropical rainforest.

Activities

1. Make a copy of Figure 13. Add the following labels to appropriate places on your diagram:

   Evaporation   Warm air rising
   condensation   Precipitation

2. Explain why the climate of the cloud forest is cooler and wetter than in the lowland forest.
3. a) Define what is meant by *nutrient stores* and *nutrient flows*.
   b) Describe three places where nutrients are stored in an ecosystem.
4. Study Figure 14.
   a) Describe two ways that nutrients can enter the soil.
   b) Explain why these two nutrient flows are rapid in the rainforest.
   c) Explain why these nutrient flows are likely to be much slower in the boreal forest and tundra.
5. Study Figure 14. Explain why nutrient cycle diagrams for the tundra and boreal forest would have:
   a) a larger circle for leaf litter than in the rainforest
   b) a thinner arrow for leaching
   c) a thinner arrow showing nutrient flows into the biomass.

Ecosystems provide key services

Sadly logging, oil exploration, intensive farming and over-fishing are all damaging natural ecosystems. But does it really matter if there are fewer forests and less wildlife? After all, farming and fishing provide us with food, jobs and wealth.

Scientists argue that ecosystems should be protected and not just for their scientific value. They argue that ecosystems provide people with a number of essential services which they describe as **key services**. Furthermore, they say that these key services have financial value. They include:

- maintaining a steady supply of clean water to rivers
- preventing soil erosion
- reducing the risk of river floods
- providing natural materials such as timber for building, or plants for medicinal use; 75 per cent of the world's population still rely on plant extracts to provide them with medication
- providing foodstuffs such as honey, fruit and nuts.

▲ **Figure 15** Bees provide a service to humans by pollinating our crops. Beetles also provide a key service. They digest waste materials such as leaf litter and dung.

Provide a safe environment for fish to spawn and juvenile fish to mature, so helping to maintain fish stocks

Tropical rainforests

Provide people with the opportunity to develop recreation or tourism businesses

Coniferous (boreal or taiga) forests

Support thousands of plants and wild animals that contain chemicals that may be useful to agriculture or medicine

Mangrove forests

Inspire a sense of awe and wonder in human beings

Peat bogs/moors

Act as natural coastal defences against storm surges, strong winds and coastal floods

Tropical coral reefs

Soak up rainwater and release it slowly, therefore reducing the risk of flooding downstream

Sand dunes

Act as huge stores of carbon dioxide, so helping to regulate the greenhouse effect

▲ **Figure 16** Key services provided by ecosystems.

Activities

1 Explain what would happen to our food production without bees and beetles.
2 Using Figure 17:
   a) List the places where water is stored in the rainforest.
   b) Explain how water flows from the atmosphere to the forest and back again.
3 a) Describe how tropical rainforests maintain a steady supply of water for local communities.
   b) Describe how damaging the structure of the rainforest could affect local people, and people in the wider region.
4 Discuss the six ecosystems in Figure 16. For each ecosystem identify at least one key service (the yellow boxes) that it provides.

Enquiry

Why should we conserve tropical forests?

Write a letter campaigning for the conservation of Gabon's cloud forest. Use information from Figures 16 and 17 to provide evidence of the real value of these key services.

Tropical rainforests regulate water supply

Figure 24 shows how rainforests play an essential role in the regional **water cycle** of tropical areas. The forest acts as a **store** for water in between rainfall events. After a rainstorm it is thought that about 80 per cent of the rainfall is transferred back to the atmosphere by evaporation and transpiration. This moisture condenses, forming rain clouds for the next rainstorm. So rainforests are a source of moisture for future rainfall events.

At least 200 million people live in the world's tropical rainforests. This includes the tribal groups, or **indigenous peoples**, of the rainforest. Many more people live downstream of the rivers that leave these forests. The forest maintains a constant and even supply of water to these rivers. If the rainforest water cycle were to be broken, then the water supply of many millions of people could be put at risk. The total amount of water flowing in the rivers would be reduced and the supply would become more uneven, with periods of low water supply punctuated by sudden flooding.

Conservationists argue that we need to place a greater value on these key services than on the value of the tropical timber alone. The benefit of a clean and regular water supply can be measured in financial terms. Rebuilding homes after a river flood can also be measured financially. The conservationists argue that these key services are more valuable in the long term than the short-term profits gained from logging.

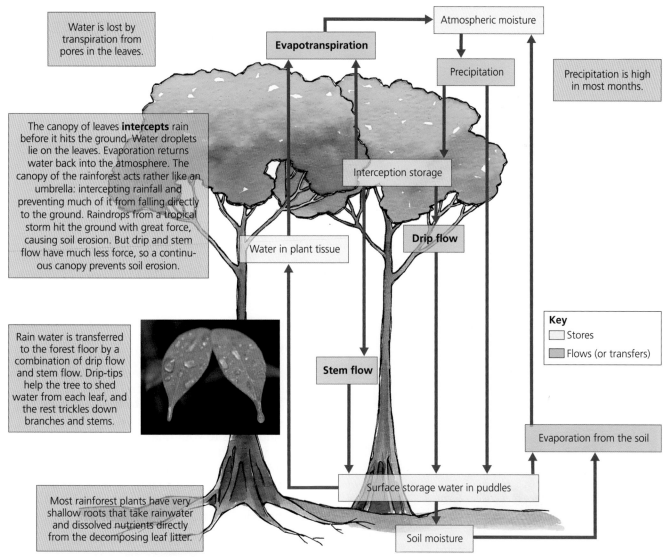

▲ **Figure 17** The water cycle in a tropical rainforest.

Characteristics of the hot semi-arid grassland biome

The global distribution of the hot semi-arid grassland biome is shown in Figure 18. This biome is a grassland ecosystem. It is sometimes known as savanna grassland and it forms a transition zone between tropical forests and deserts. This biome occurs in regions which have a tropical semi-arid climate. The climate pattern is one of marked wet and dry seasons with the rainfall concentrated in 5–6 months of the year, often in the form of heavy storms and high humidity. This is followed by months of drought with clear skies and fine sunny weather. The hot semi-arid climate is described in more detail on pages 184–5.

	Jan	Feb	Mar	Apr	May	Jun	Jul	Aug	Sep	Oct	Nov	Dec
Average Temp in °C	27	28	27	25	23	23	22	23	25	27	26	26
Precipitation in mm.	71	68	151	289	122	27	11	13	12	33	149	106

◀ **Figure 18** Climate data for Arusha, Tanzania.

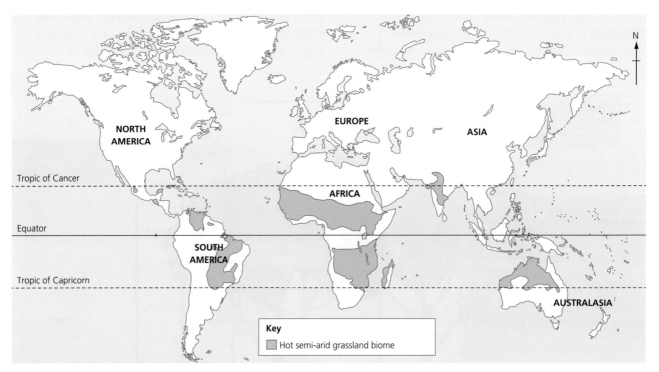

▲ **Figure 19** World distribution of hot semi-arid grassland.

▲ **Figure 20** Semi-arid grassland in Tanzania.

Activities

1 Use Figure 18 to describe the distribution of the semi-arid grassland biome.
2 a) Use the data in Figure 19 to draw a climate graph for Arusha in Tanzania.
  b) Add labels to your graph to show the wet season and dry season.
  c) What is the total annual rainfall in millimetres?
  d) Describe the annual range of temperature.
  e) Many people visit Tanzania to go on a safari holiday. What time of year would be the best time to go?

How does vegetation adapt to the hot, dry climate?

In hot semi-arid climates, the soils are porous which means they drain rapidly. The thin humus layer provides nutrients for plants. The typical vegetation is of scattered trees and drought-resistant bushes. The climate is too dry for thick forest to form because trees need a lot of water to grow and survive. Between the widely spaced trees and bushes there are also grasses that grow rapidly to 3–4 m in height in the wet season. In the dry season they turn yellow and die back, leaving the ground vulnerable to soil erosion. The baobab and acacia are examples of xerophytic (drought-resistant) trees found in this biome – this means they can survive long periods with very little rainfall during the dry season of the year. The baobab and acacia are adapted to survive drought in a number of ways – these are shown in Figure 21.

▶ **Figure 21** Adaptations of plants to the climate of the semi-arid grassland.

BAOBAB TREE

Grows over 30 m in height and 7 m in diameter. Can live for thousands of years.

Lots of shallow roots spread out from the tree. They collect water as soon as it rains.

Thick bark is fire-resistant.

Few leaves reduce water lost by transpiration.

Large barrel-like trunk stores up to 500 litres of water.

ACACIA TREE

Broad flat canopy reduces water loss. It provides shade for animals.

Thorns on branches deter animals from eating them.

Long tap roots reach ground water deep underground.

Small leaves with waxy skins reduce the amount of water lost through transpiration.

Grows up to 20 m in height and 2 m in diameter with whitish bark.

Activity

3 Study Figures 20 and 21.
   a) Describe the vegetation shown in each photograph.
   b) At what time of year do you think each photograph was taken? Give reasons for your answer.
   c) Draw a table like the one below. Use the information in Figure 21 to describe how these plants have adapted to the climate conditions.

	High rates of transpiration	Long periods of drought and high temperatures	Animals such as zebra eat the leaves
Acacia tree			
Baobab tree			

Enquiry

Australia has a large area of hot semi-arid grassland. Research the climate and ecosystems of East Kimberley, Australia. Hall's Creek is one of the only large towns in this region.

How do the climate and ecosystem of East Kimberley compare to the hot semi-arid grasslands of Africa that are introduced on these pages? What are the main similarities and differences?

How do ecosystem processes operate within hot semi-arid grasslands?

Within the hot semi-arid grassland ecosystem there are two main processes. These are the movement of energy (energy flows) and the recycling of nutrients.

Energy flows

The main source of energy for all living things is sunlight. This is absorbed by **producers** such as plants. They convert the light energy from the Sun into chemical energy by the process of photosynthesis. This energy is passed on to animals when they eat the plants. These animals are called herbivores or **primary consumers**. In turn, these are eaten by other animals called carnivores or **secondary consumers**. This is called a food chain. Energy flows up the food chain.

However, most producers and consumers are part of many different food chains. A food web shows the flow of energy through the whole ecosystem. A food web has many interconnecting food chains.

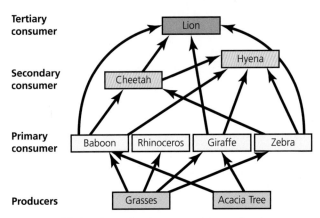

▲ **Figure 22** Food web for the semi-arid grassland ecosystem in Africa.

Nutrient cycles in the hot semi-arid grassland ecosystem

As well as energy, plants need essential chemical elements and compounds such as iron, phosphate and nitrogen. These nutrients are recycled through the ecosystem between the soil, biomass and leaf litter. When plants and animals die, they decompose and the nutrients are released and returned to the soil. This process is called the nutrient cycle.

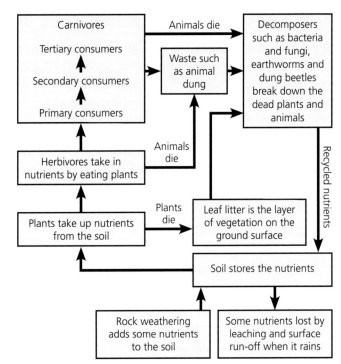

▲ **Figure 23** How nutrients are recycled in the semi-arid grassland ecosystem.

Activities

1 a) Draw a food chain by putting the following into the correct sequence.
      lion   grass   energy from the Sun   zebra
   b) Explain the difference between a food chain and a food web.
   c) Draw a table like the one below and add examples from the hot semi-arid grassland food web in Figure 22.

Biotic (living) part of the ecosystem	Examples
Producer	
Primary consumer	
Secondary consumer	
Tertiary consumer	

   d) Explain why the hyena is both a secondary and tertiary consumer.
   e) What would be the effect on the hot semi-arid grassland ecosystem if most of the lions were killed by people?
2 Study Figure 23.
   a) Explain why nutrients are important to this ecosystem.
   b) What role do decomposers play in the nutrient cycle?

Why is the biodiversity of Africa's grasslands under threat?

Hot semi-arid grasslands are under threat from both human activity and natural processes. During the dry season, fires are caused both by lightning strikes and by local farmers burning the grass to encourage new growth when the rains arrive. Grass can survive these fires, but young trees are destroyed.

This ecosystem contains a huge variety of plants, insects, birds, reptiles and mammals. This **biodiversity** – or range of living things – makes the grasslands of Africa a popular tourist destination. People come to see endangered species such as elephant, cheetah, lion and rhino. The safari industry is very important to the economy of countries like Kenya and Tanzania but it is difficult to create a sustainable balance between allowing visitor access to the natural scenery and wildlife, while protecting and conserving it. One of the greatest threats is hunting and poaching which has led to the illegal killing of over 40,000 animals each year in Kenya's Serengeti National Park. There were once over 100,000 black rhinos in Africa, now there are less than 2,700. They are killed for their horns which are used in traditional Asian medicines and sell for over five times the price of gold. Over 100,000 elephants were killed between 2013 and 2015 for the ivory in their tusks.

▲ **Figure 24** Conservationists remove the horn from a black rhino to discourage poachers from killing the rhino for its horn.

Enquiry

Poaching of wild animals is a serious problem in many parts of Africa. Rhino and elephant are key targets for poachers in the hot semi-arid grassland environments of Africa. Debate the following enquiry questions. You may want to do some research first.

- Why should we conserve elephant and rhino?
- How do these animals benefit the environment and people?
- What is the best way to protect these animals? Which of the following options might work best?
  - i) Dehorning the wild rhino
  - ii) Moving (translocating) wild rhino and elephant to National Parks
  - iii) Lifting the trade ban and exporting 'farmed' rhino horn and elephant ivory that has been reared sustainably.

Why are urban ecosystems important?

Not all ecosystems are in distant or exotic places. Several important ecosystems are literally on your doorstep. Parks, churchyards and public gardens all contain important habitats such as woodlands within our towns and cities. The biodiversity in churchyards can be particularly great because these green areas are not managed with chemical pesticides or fertilisers. Private gardens contain smaller habitats such as garden ponds, compost heaps and log piles. These gardens may be small, but it is estimated that an average of 13 per cent of the UK's urban land use is private garden. Hedgerows and the wooded spaces alongside rivers and canals act as **wildlife corridors** that link the separate ecosystems together. These corridors allow birds and mammals such as hedgehogs and foxes to move safely from one garden to another without being spotted by predators such as cats or birds of prey.

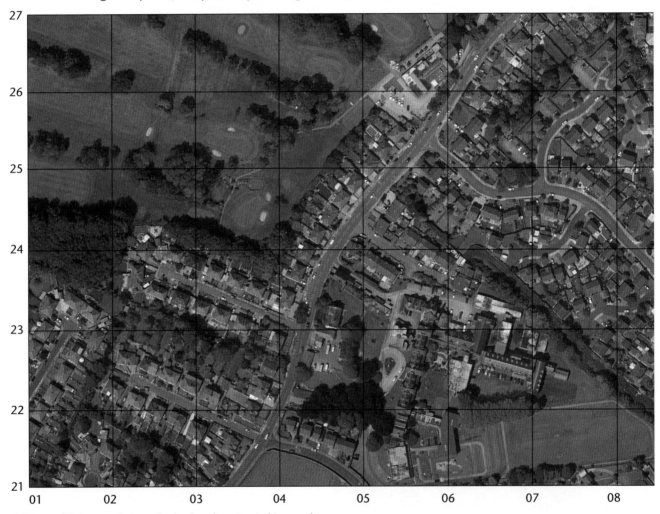

▲ **Figure 25** An aerial view of suburban housing in Liverpool.

Activities

1 Outline the different land uses you can see in Figure 25.
2 For each of the following ecosystems describe its scale, structure and main wildlife features:
   a) churchyard
   b) public, ornamental park
   c) playing fields
   d) garden pond.

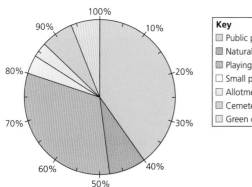

Key
- ☐ Public parks and gardens
- ☐ Natural and semi-natural greenspace
- ☐ Playing fields
- ☐ Small public greenspaces close to housing
- ☐ Allotments, community gardens and city farms
- ☐ Cemeteries and churchyards
- ☐ Green corridors

▲ **Figure 26** Public greenspace in Liverpool.

Activity

3 a) Use Figure 26 to describe the percentage of:
   i) churchyards
   ii) playing fields.
   b) Explain why churchyards have a much greater biodiversity than playing fields.

GEOGRAPHICAL SKILLS

Using transects to sample from a map or photograph

A transect is a line that is used to survey geographical features. Transects are commonly used in fieldwork (see page 242) but can also be drawn across a map or aerial photograph to survey land uses. By sampling land uses along a transect, we can estimate the actual proportion of land uses within an area without recording every single land use. Fieldwork transects can be of any length but long transects across an urban area can be time-consuming so you will save time and cover larger areas by using a photograph like Figure 25.

Step 1 Decide how many transects to use. More transects will mean greater accuracy but will take more time.

Step 2 Decide where to sample within the survey area. You could do this: systematically, e.g. every other vertical line on Figure 25, or randomly, e.g. by using random numbers to generate start and end points.

Step 3 Create a survey sheet with land use categories.

Step 4 Measure the length of each category of land use (in millimetres) along each line.

Step 5 Calculate the total length (mm) of each land use and then calculate these as percentages of the whole. For example:

If total length of all transects = 260mm and total length of private gardens = 65mm

(65/260) × 100 = 25%

Enquiry

How much greenspace is there in Figure 25?

a) Choose five grid lines (vertical or horizontal) across Figure 25.
b) Measure the length of each of the following land uses along each line:
  - gardens
  - housing
  - roads
  - parks
  - other.
c) Calculate the percentage of each land use.
d) How could you improve the accuracy of this survey?

Are urban ecosystems worth protecting?

Recent scientific studies have highlighted the importance of the UK's urban ecosystems. They contain an important diversity of wildlife, some of which, like bees, provide key services to us. Bees pollinate plants. Without urban bees we would have fewer flowers in our gardens and less crops in our fields. Urban ecosystems are good for people in other ways too:

- Living close to an urban park can improve your feelings of well-being and increase your home's value by an estimated 30 per cent.
- Public parks and playing fields give us places to enjoy outdoor leisure and keep fit.
- Parks and gardens soak up rain water and help to prevent the flash floods that might otherwise occur due to all of the impermeable surfaces in our towns and cities.
- Vegetation helps to remove pollution, such as the particulates emitted by diesel cars, from the air.
- Trees and hedges reduce noise from roads.
- Open spaces help to keep our urban areas cool in summer.

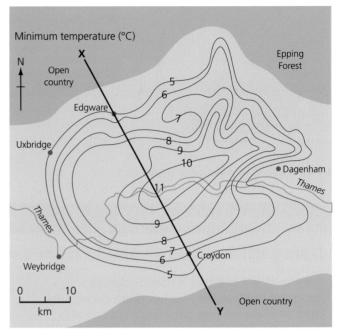

▲ **Figure 27** London's urban heat island. Night time temperatures in mid-May.

Urban heat island

The buildings and traffic in a large city influence the local climate, an effect known as **urban micro-climate**. One of the main impacts that a city has on the local climate is to create temperatures that are warmer than in the surrounding rural area. This is known as the **urban heat island**. The city acts like a massive storage heater, transferring heat from buildings and cars to the dome of air that covers the city.

- During the day, concrete, brick and tarmac absorb heat from the Sun. This heat is then radiated into the atmosphere during the evening and at night.
- Buildings that are badly insulated lose heat energy, especially through roofs and windows. Heat is also created in cars and factories and this heat is also lost to the air from exhausts and chimneys.

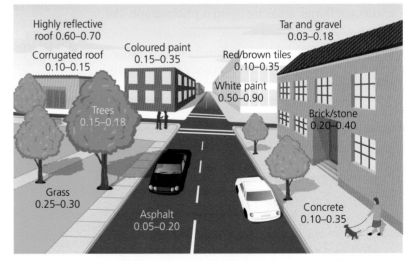

▲ **Figure 28** How the urban environment reflects the Sun's energy. The closer the number to 1.0 the more energy is reflected. Surfaces with very low numbers are absorbing more of the sun's energy. They then emit this heat at night.

City	Population (2011)	Total area (hectares)	Total area greenspace (hectares)
Newcastle-upon-Tyne	280,200	11,300	2,185
Northampton	212,100	8,076	1,403
Coventry	316,900	9,864	1,710
Liverpool	466,400	11,184	2,648

▲ **Figure 29** Amount of public open space in selected UK cities.

We need more homes in our cities. We shouldn't allow our cities to sprawl out into the countryside. It uses valuable farmland and increases the length of every commuter's journey. We should be allowed to build houses on some of our playing fields and open spaces.

Property developer

We need more green spaces. Parks reflect more of the sun's energy than concrete or tarmac. Out cities will become hotter as the climate changes. Greenspaces are a natural and sustainable way to combat the increased impact of the urban heat island. Vegetation can also help reduce noise and pollution in our towns and cities.

Climate scientist

Many homeowners are paving over their front gardens to create off-street parking. Surveys suggest that 3200 hectares of front gardens have been paved over in London in the last 30 years. This creates even more impermeable surfaces which increases the risk of flash floods during intense rainfall. Planning policies were changed in 2008 to try to reduce further losses of front gardens.

Town planner

▲ **Figure 30** Views on managing our green spaces.

Activities

1   Use Figure 27.
    a) Draw a cross-section of London's urban heat island along the transect line *x–y*.
    b) Describe the location of the area of highest temperatures in London.
    c) Describe the distribution of places with lower temperatures.
    d) Suggest reasons for the pattern shown on the map.

2   Study Figure 29.
    a) Choose a suitable method to represent the data in this table.
    b) Which city had the most amount of greenspace per person? Calculate the amount of greenspace available to every 1,000 people in each of these cities.

3   Use Figure 30 to explain how the creation of more parks, woodlands and lakes in our cities might:
    a) affect the urban micro-climate
    b) make urban areas more sustainable in the future.

Enquiry

How should we manage our urban green spaces in the future?

Discuss the views in Figure 30 before outlining the arguments for and against each of the following:

	Arguments for	Arguments against	Who might oppose this plan
Create more green spaces			
Build more urban homes on playing fields			
Pave over front gardens to create parking			

Investigating sand dune ecosystems

Many environments in the UK that appear to be natural are, in fact, heavily managed. However, sand dunes provide an example of a natural small-scale ecosystem that is commonly found in coastal areas of the UK. These distinctive coastal landscapes are constantly changing due to the power of the wind. As vegetation **colonises** the sand dunes, the plants themselves begin to influence the formation of the landscape. The result is **zonation** – distinctive bands or zones of vegetation that stretch across the dunes.

Embryo dunes

Sand is blown up the beach. The first obstacle it reaches is the **strand line** near the top of the beach. This is the pile of flotsam and jetsam – driftwood, washed up seaweed and plastic rubbish – which has been dropped at the high tide mark. The strand line slows the flow of air over the beach and some sand is deposited by the wind so small dunes begin to form. Only specialised plants that can tolerate the salty conditions, like sea rocket, can grow here.

Mobile (or yellow) dunes

As time passes, the tough marram plant with its long flexible leaves colonises. It can tolerate the strong wind. The plants slow the wind speed and more sand is deposited. Piles of sand grow larger and ridges of sand several metres high are formed. But there are gaps between the plants and on windy days the sand is easily eroded on the **windward** side of each ridge. Sand tends to be deposited on the **leeward** side where wind speeds are lower. So, the first two or three ridges of the sand dune system are mobile because their position is changing.

Fixed dunes

Further inland the conditions for plant life are not quite so harsh. It is less windy and there is less salt spray. The dunes here have a wider variety of plants including a narrow leaved grass called fescue. With more roots to bind the soil there is less chance for sand to be eroded on a windy day so the dune ridges become fixed in position. Rainfall soaks through the sandy ridges and comes to the surface in the dips between the ridges. These are the **dune slacks** – a habitat that may be flooded with fresh water during the winter months.

▲ **Figure 31** Three zones within the sand dune ecosystem.

Fixed dunes Wind speeds are lower and there are more nutrients in the soil because plants have been growing and dropping leaf litter for several years. A wider variety of flowering plants, shorter grasses and shrubs colonise this area.

Mobile dunes Marram grass grows on the dune ridges. Marram has large fibrous roots that hold the sand together. The tall leaves slow the flow of air causing it to deposit more sand so the ridges build in height.

Embryo dunes A few specialised plants that are tolerant of salt spray live here, taking advantage of the nutrients from the decomposing strand line.

▲ **Figure 32** Ynyslas sand dunes, at the north end of Borth spit, are in the foreground of this aerial photograph.

Activities

1 Match the following descriptions to labels A–D on Figure 32.
   - Sand travels down the length of the spit by longshore drift.
   - Prevailing wind direction.
   - An erosional feature called a blow-out.
   - Wind erodes sand from the beach.
2 Use Figure 32 to identify one way that people have tried to manage this coastline.
3 Use Figures 31 and 32 to describe three ways that the sand dunes change as you walk from the beach through each zone. Focus on:
   a) the landscape
   b) the vegetation
   c) the factors that affect plant growth.

Enquiry

How does the sand dune ecosystem change over time?

Use the information on these pages to explain how the colonisation of plants helps to change the shape of the landforms in the sand dunes.

Investigating sand dunes

A transect is an imaginary straight line drawn across or through a geographical feature. Transects are used to collect data across a geographical feature. Observations can be taken at regular (systematic), random or stratified intervals along the length of the transect (see page 45 for these sampling strategies).

Step one: Design your enquiry

A fieldtrip to the sand dunes allows you to see how the plant life and growing conditions vary as you walk through this ecosystem from the strand line to the dune slacks. How quickly do the zones change? What factors cause these changes? Does your sand dune system follow the typical pattern seen at Ynyslas on page 241? You could use a hypothesis to organise your enquiry, for example:

The variety of plants increases with distance from the strand line.

Activities

1 Study Figures 34, 35 and 36. Describe two adaptations to:
   a) strong winds experienced in the yellow dunes
   b) the lack of nutrients in the sandy soils.
2 Using evidence from Figure 33, suggest why each plant:
   a) needs long roots
   b) has adaptations to reduce evapotranspiration from the leaves.

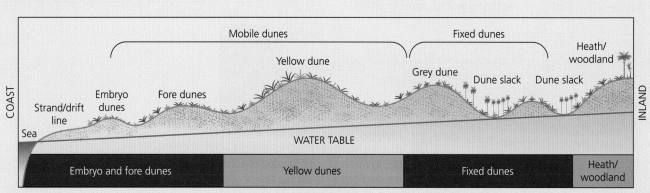

▲ **Figure 33** Cross-section through the zones of a sand dune ecosystem.

▲ **Figure 34** Sea rocket is a pioneer plant. It grows in the embryo dunes. The waxy outer surface of the leaf helps to reduce water loss by evapotranspiration. Shallow roots take nutrients from decaying material on the strand line.

▲ **Figure 35** Marram grass is the main plant of the yellow dunes. Strong leaves bend in the wind without breaking. Long tap roots find water. Burial by sand stimulates new shoots to grow from surface roots.

▲ **Figure 36** Restharrow is a low growing flowering plant of the yellow dunes. Sticky hairs on leaves reduce water loss by evapotranspiration. Nodules on the long roots are able to take nitrogen from air and turn it into nutrients that are useful for plant growth.

Step two: Starting and ending your transect

Sand dunes are formed when the wind frequently blows in the same direction. The dunes make ridges that are roughly parallel to the coast and at right angles to the prevailing wind direction. So, your transect should be at right angles to the beach so that it samples each zone within the sand dune system – like in Figure 33. You will need to start on the beach at the strand line. It will end when you have sampled data in each zone. If the dunes are managed (like the ones at Ynyslas) you may be asked to use a specific line for your transect.

Collect your data

If your enquiry is about zonation then you will need to record the percentage of plants at each sample point along the transect using a quadrat. You may want to record other variables that could affect the growing conditions in each zone. If so, you could record:
- wind speed
- soil pH
- soil colour (as an indication of the amount of organic material providing nutrients)
- evidence of trampling or management.

	Distance (m) from embryo dunes											
	0	50	100	150	200	250	300	350	400	450	500	550
Sea rocket	20	10	0	0	0	0	0	0	0	0	0	0
Sea spurge	0	10	10	10	10	0	0	10	0	0	0	0
Marram	0	40	60	70	60	70	50	30	30	20	0	0
Restharrow	0	0	0	0	10	10	20	10	0	0	0	0
Fescue	0	0	0	0	0	10	30	50	60	50	30	70
Bramble	0	0	0	0	0	0	0	0	0	0	70	0
Others	0	0	0	0	0	0	0	0	10	30	0	30
Bare sand	80	40	30	20	20	10	0	0	0	0	0	0

▲ **Figure 37** Percentage of each type of vegetation in each quadrat.

Present the data

The percentage of each plant type along the transect is best shown using a kite diagram like Figure 38. The axis of this graph represents the length of the transect. The vertical axis is divided by two so that half of the total percentage is displayed on each side of the horizontal axis.

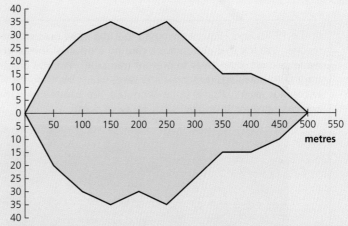

▲ **Figure 38** Kite diagram for marram drawn using data from Figure 37.

Enquiry

How might you design an enquiry to investigate the effects of wind speeds on sand dune zonation? Use Figure 32 and 33 when you consider the following points.

a) What questions can you pose?
b) How should you sample along your transect? Would regular, random or stratified sampling be best? How many sample points should you use? Do you need a control?
c) How would you design your data collection sheets?

Activity

3 a) Use the information in Figure 37 to draw a series of kite diagrams.
   b) What conclusions can you reach about?
      i) The plants that commonly grow in each zone.
      ii) How nutrient levels must change as you travel along the transect.

Changing styles of conservation management at Ynyslas sand dunes

Conservation management of the sand dunes at Ynyslas began in 1969 when the area was designated as a National Nature Reserve. During the 1960s some parts of the dune system had been damaged by off-road vehicles. In some places the marram grass, the roots of which help to bind the loose sand, had been destroyed by people driving into and parking in the dunes. The wind had then eroded huge hollows in the **windward** slopes of the dune system creating ugly scars known as **blow-outs**. The management strategies used by wardens at Ynyslas have gradually changed since 1969. These changes are summarised in Figure 39.

▶ **Figure 39** The changing style of management at Ynyslas.

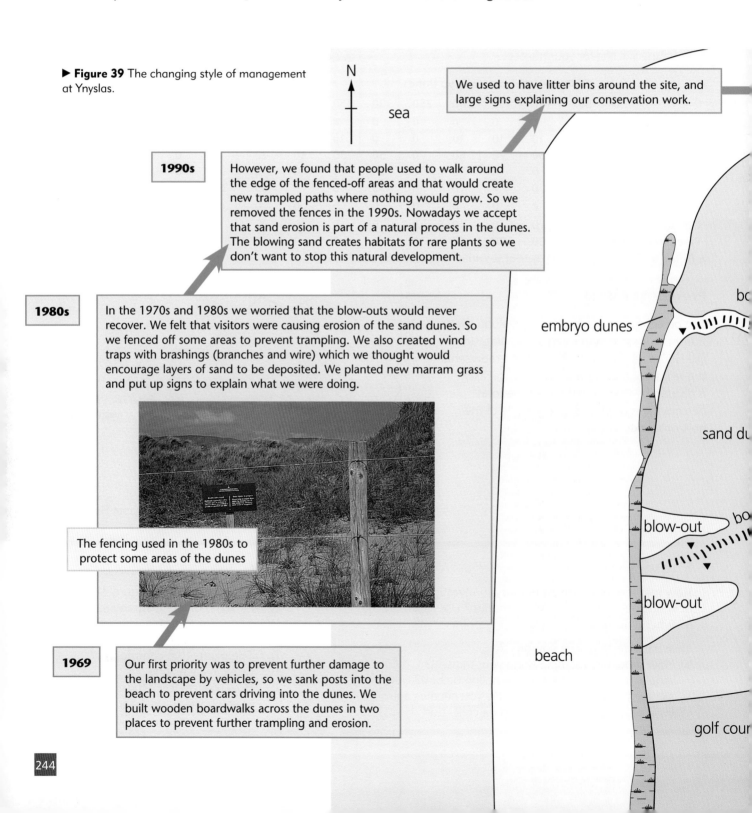

N

sea

We used to have litter bins around the site, and large signs explaining our conservation work.

1990s

However, we found that people used to walk around the edge of the fenced-off areas and that would create new trampled paths where nothing would grow. So we removed the fences in the 1990s. Nowadays we accept that sand erosion is part of a natural process in the dunes. The blowing sand creates habitats for rare plants so we don't want to stop this natural development.

1980s

In the 1970s and 1980s we worried that the blow-outs would never recover. We felt that visitors were causing erosion of the sand dunes. So we fenced off some areas to prevent trampling. We also created wind traps with brashings (branches and wire) which we thought would encourage layers of sand to be deposited. We planted new marram grass and put up signs to explain what we were doing.

The fencing used in the 1980s to protect some areas of the dunes

1969

Our first priority was to prevent further damage to the landscape by vehicles, so we sank posts into the beach to prevent cars driving into the dunes. We built wooden boardwalks across the dunes in two places to prevent further trampling and erosion.

embryo dunes

bo

sand du

blow-out

bo

blow-out

beach

golf cour

Activities

1 Study Figure 39. Use it to complete the following table. You should be able to identify at least four issues.

Issue	Management strategy	Evaluation of strategy
1		
2		

2 Produce a short report on management at Ynyslas. In it, you must identify:
a) Why people visit.
b) The two main aims of the wardens.
c) How and why management strategies have changed.
d) How you think management of the dunes should change in future.

We found that the litter bins used to overflow and rubbish blew about, so we got rid of all the bins.

2000s

A lot of rabbits live in the dunes. They keep the grass short and stop it from choking the less competitive flowering plants. The rabbit dung makes the soil much more fertile and as many as 40 different species of flowering plants can grow in just 1 square metre. Also some birds nest in the abandoned rabbit burrows. So we like to have a healthy population of rabbits. However, our neighbour is the golf course. They don't want too many rabbits burrowing into the putting greens and creating damage. So we erected a rabbit-proof fence along our southern boundary. The problem is that this fence now has holes in it and will be costly to maintain.

Lots of song birds live in the dunes including linnet, stonechat, skylark and meadow pipit. We have one area where ringed plovers breed. These small birds nest on the ground and are easily disturbed. So we have fenced off the shingle area where they nest.

parking area

posts to prevent cars driving into the dunes

In recent years we have enlarged and improved the visitor centre and the boardwalks. Now anyone can easily cross the site to get to the beach. Wheelchair users can access the visitor centre along the boardwalks.

visitor centre

The boardwalk and visitor centre

caravan park

One of our biggest management problems today is dog fouling. People are banned from walking their dogs in the summer months on Borth beach to the south. So they come up to Ynyslas to walk their dogs. The problem is that there are very few bacteria in the sandy soil so the dog excrement does not bio-degrade. It lies around for ages and is a nuisance for other visitors.

2016

Human use of ecosystems

People have always made use of the environment for their own needs, to grow food or produce fuel. There are very few natural ecosystems left anywhere in the world where there has been no human intervention. Most of the UK's ecosystems are heavily modified and managed by people. Forest clearance and farming have changed our natural landscape for 100s if not 1,000s of years. What appears to be a natural landscape in Figure 1, for example, is in fact, artificial. These hills in mid Wales would be covered in oak and ash forests if not for the sheep that graze the fields and eat every tree sapling as it tries to grow.

However, as people continue to change what is left of the world's ecosystems, scientists have come to realise that natural ecosystems provide people with a wide range of economic and cultural benefits. Some of these benefits are suggested in Figure 3. They provide us with reasons for conservation.

▲ **Figure 1** The 'natural' landscape of mid Wales is actually created by sheep.

◄ **Figure 2**
An oak sapling. This field in mid Wales has not been grazed for 10 years. This oak sapling, now 50 cm tall, is a sign that woodland would be the natural ecosystem here.

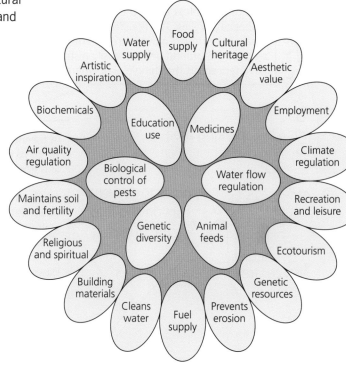

▲ **Figure 3** Benefits provided by ecosystems.

Activities

1 Describe how each of the following activities might affect an ecosystem.
   a) How a tropical rainforest would be affected by cutting down and burning trees.
   b) How a wetland might be affected by spraying crops with pesticides on a nearby farm.
   c) How UK woodlands were affected by the introduction of non-native species such as the grey squirrel.

2 Make a Venn diagram and use Figure 3 to add examples of the environmental, economic and social benefits of ecosystems.

3 Some of the benefits provided by ecosystems are described as key services (see page 230). Select five benefits in Figure 3 that could be described as key services. Explain your choice.

How might the production of renewable energy affect ecosystems?

In 2014 a new solar furnace opened called the Ivanpah Solar Electric Generating System. It is located in the Mojave Desert in California, 64 km south-west of Las Vegas. Sunlight is focused by 173,000 heliostat mirrors, each measuring 7 m^2, onto three 138 m high solar power towers. The heat from the Sun generates steam to drive turbines that generate enough electricity for 140,000 homes. The project cost $2.2 billion and covers 360,000 hectares of land. Environmental campaigners have expressed their concerns over the impact of this project on the fragile desert ecosystem. Vegetation had to be removed during construction, leading to the destruction of rare plants. Birds are confused by the mirrors, mistaking them for water and are also killed by flying into the concentrated rays. Groundwater is used to wash the mirrors. The habitats of the golden eagle and bighorn sheep have been destroyed, and over 130 desert tortoises have been killed or displaced.

As part of the need to reduce the use of fossil fuels, there has been an increase in the number of solar farms in the UK. Until recently there were government grants available if people were prepared to set these up on their land. Solar farms in the UK use photovoltaic (or solar) panels to produce electricity.

▲ **Figure 4** The Ivanpah Solar Electric Generating Station in the Mojave Desert, USA.

Soil may dry out and blow away

Birds and bats are confused

No noise or air pollution

Farmers may still be able to crow crops and graze sheep

Wildlife may return and biodiversity increases

Less land used to grow crops

▲ **Figure 5** Impact of solar panels in the UK.

Activities

4 Do you think that the benefits of the Ivanpah Project outweigh the impact it might have on the environment? Give detailed reasons for your answer.

5 Make a larger copy of the table below and then add the statements in Figure 5 to explain the impact of solar panels in the UK. Try to add your own extra elaboration statement for each one.

Statement	Elaboration	Extra elaboration
Lack of moving parts, so		
Most panels are raised above the ground, so		
Panels may reduce infiltration, so		
Famers may make more money from solar panels, so		
Brownfield sites such as old airfields can be used, so		
Panels may look like water from the air, so		

Enquiry

Should more solar farms be built in the UK? What are the arguments for and against? If one was proposed near to your school, how would local people feel?

a) Design a questionnaire that could be used to investigate the viewpoints of local people on the development of solar farms.

b) Suggest how you might sample people's views. What sampling strategy would you use and why have you chosen this method?

Are there enough fish in the North Sea?

'Fish and chips' is a popular UK take-away food. Traditionally, the fish was cod or haddock caught in the North Sea – an example of a marine ecosystem. But in recent years, cod has been replaced with other fish such as coley or pollock as cod has been in short supply. Why has this happened?

Over-fishing is not sustainable because, when too many young fish are caught, there are not enough fish left in the sea to breed and replace the fish stocks. This is shown in Figures 7 and 8. It can take up to four years for cod to become mature enough to breed, so fish stocks have to be managed to give them a chance to survive. It is illegal in the UK to land a cod fish that is less than 35 cm long. These fish have not yet bred and if caught they must be thrown back into the sea.

How can cod be protected?

The EU manages the fish stocks around Europe, including the North Sea, by imposing quotas. This is where a limit is put on the number of fish that can be caught by member states in certain sea areas. They also limit the number of days in a month when the fishermen can go out to fish. The quota system has angered UK fishermen. They have argued that the restrictions have been too severe. Quotas mean they catch less fish so they earn less money and some fishermen have gone out of business. There was also criticism of how quotas were allocated to different member states of the EU. Catching too many or small fish leads to hefty fines, so fish are sometimes thrown back into the sea, dead or alive. A minimum net size should mean that small fish can swim back out of the net and escape.

▲ **Figure 6** Cod for sale at the market in Peterhead, Scotland. Peterhead is the UK's largest fishing port.

Activity

1. a) Describe the overall trend of Figure 7.
   b) Suggest how changes to the catch affected people working in the North Sea fishing industry.
   c) What proportion of the cod catch was discarded (thrown back) in 2008?

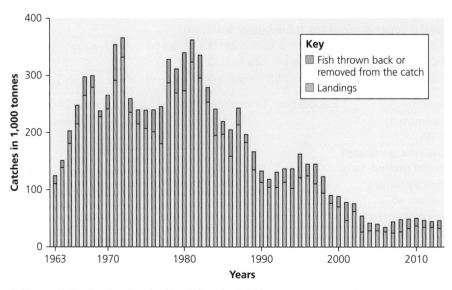

Key
- Fish thrown back or removed from the catch
- Landings

▲ **Figure 7** Catch of cod in the North Sea (in 1,000s of metric tonnes).

Has the cod been saved?

Figures released in September 2015 show that stocks of North Sea cod are beginning to increase (see Figure 9). Preventing over-fishing has allowed the cod to breed and increase in number. The fishing industry is now much smaller than it was in the 1990s, with fewer smaller family businesses still working. So is it okay for consumers to eat cod again? Scientists warn that the cod is not yet out of danger.

> Quotas don't go far enough. We need to stop fishing over-exploited stocks altogether for one year. Then stocks would be restored to a fully sustainable level in four years.

Scientist

> We need to look at how we catch the fish. Trawlers use dragnets and catch more fish but damage the sea bed. Gillnets are vertical nets which catch less fish with less waste. We need to fish responsibly.

Environmental campaigner

> We need to protect our fishing industry. If we set quotas as low as the scientists would like, our fishing industry would collapse. We have set quotas low enough to conserve fish stocks but high enough to keep people in jobs.

Government minister

> I like cod, but we have a responsibility to conserve the world's resources. If I have to buy other sustainable types of fish for a while, so be it.

Consumer

> This town relies on the fishing industry. People work on the boats, in the fish market and in the boat repair yard. When the government limits the amount of fish we can catch then the whole town suffers.

Fish and chip shop owner in Peterhead

▲ **Figure 8** Views on fishing.

Activities

2 a) Compare the trend of Figure 9 to Figure 7.
   b) At what date might scientists have asked for fishing quotas to be introduced?
   c) Explain why fishermen and scientists might disagree about the meaning of the final three years of this trend line.
3 Discuss the views shown in Figure 8. Give one reason why it is important to:
   a) protect the ecosystem of the North Sea
   b) protect jobs in the fishing industry.
4 Suggest two different ways that UK consumers could help conserve the North Sea ecosystem and support the fishing industry.

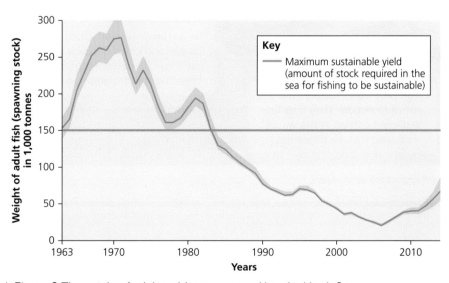

▲ **Figure 9** The weight of adult cod (spawning stock) in the North Sea.

Is shrimp farming sustainable?

Mangrove forests grow on tropical coastlines. The trees of the mangrove tolerate flooding by both fresh and salt water, so this is both a forest and a wetland, and it supports a very wide range of fish, insects and animals.

Mangroves help to absorb wave energy during storms so they help to protect coastal communities. Despite this, big business regards mangroves as useless wasteland. Trees are cut down and the swampy land redeveloped for tourism or **aquaculture**. Over 25 million hectares of mangrove forest are estimated to have been destroyed in the last 100 years. The fastest rates of destruction have been in Asia during the late 20th century. Globally, around 150,000 hectares of mangrove are destroyed every year which is equal to about 1 per cent of the global total. Only 6.9 per cent of mangrove forests are protected. One of the most common reasons for the destruction of mangroves has been the rapid growth of shrimp (or prawn) farming. Mangroves are cleared away to make space for artificial ponds. These ponds are flooded with salt water and used to rear the shrimp.

Shrimp is low in fat and high in protein. Most consumers are in Europe, North America and Japan. Around 55 per cent of all shrimp we eat is farmed. The rest is caught from our oceans, largely from tropical waters such as the Bay of Bengal where large trawlers catch wild shrimp in nets. Over-fishing wild shrimp damages the food web of the marine ecosystem. A smaller quantity is caught in cold waters such as in the North Atlantic around the coast of Iceland.

Most shrimp aquaculture is in China, Thailand, Indonesia, Brazil, Ecuador and Bangladesh. Shrimp farming is carried out by both big business and many small farmers. Some argue that shrimp farming has helped poor farmers to diversify their income and reduce poverty. The global shrimp industry is thought to be worth US$12–15 billion.

Shrimp aquaculture is an **intensive** form of farming. It takes between three and six months to rear shrimp so farmers produce two to three crops a year. The shrimp are treated with pesticides and antibiotics. Organic waste, chemicals and antibiotics escape from the ponds polluting fresh groundwater supplies that local communities use for drinking.

The forest acts as a natural coastal defence. The roots hold the mud together, protecting the land from erosion and reducing the force of large storm waves.

The forest ecosystem supports a range of animals including howler monkeys, deer and armadillo. The canopy provides safe nesting sites for birds.

The wetlands support crocodiles, snakes and crabs. Tropical fish use these sheltered waters as a breeding ground and nursery.

Large prop roots support the tree above high tide. They trap fine sediment carried in the water, causing it to be deposited.

▲ **Figure 10** Why mangroves are important ecosystems.

Activities

1 Describe how mangrove forests provide benefits for wildlife and people.
2 Do you think shrimp farming is a sustainable use of this ecosystem? Explain your point of view.

Activities

3 a) Use a suitable technique to represent the data in Figure 12.
   b) Describe the trends shown by your graph.
   c) What percentage of shrimp production came from aquaculture in:
      i) 2008
      ii) 2014?
4 Study the points of view in Figure 13.
   a) What are the long-term benefits of shrimp farming and who gets these benefits?
   b) What problems does shrimp farming create for:
      i) people
      ii) the environment?
   c) Discuss what consumers in the UK can do to help ensure that ecosystems (either mangroves or other ecosystems) are used sustainably.

▲ **Figure 11** A shrimp farm in Bangladesh.

Shrimp production (1,000s of metric tonnes)							
	2008	2009	2010	2011	2012	2013	2014
Wild	3,217	3,269	3,263	3,442	3,568	3,541	3,591
Aquaculture	3,400	3,532	3,629	4,046	4,168	4,320	4,581

▲ **Figure 12** Global shrimp production (2008–2014) in 1,000s of metric tonnes.

Enquiry

'Mangroves are a swampy wasteland. There is nothing wrong in clearing them away if it means jobs are created and poverty reduced.'
To what extent do you agree with this statement? Justify your point of view.

Local people lose out because they can no longer use the timber or other resources available in the mangrove forest. Local fishermen have noticed a fall in the number of fish they catch. This may be because the mangroves are a nursery ground for young fish. Shrimp farming releases a lot of fertilisers and other chemicals into the environment. Fresh-water wells are polluted by these chemicals. These are problems that are likely to affect coastal communities for many years after the farms have been abandoned.

A local fisherman

People make quick profits from shrimp farming. However, after a few years ponds are abandoned because of disease and pollution. In Asia there are approximately 250,000 hectares of abandoned, polluted ponds where healthy forests once grew. This boom–bust cycle is about to be repeated in Latin America, Africa and the Pacific where shrimp farming is growing in popularity.

Economics expert

The biggest consumers of shrimp are the USA, Canada, Japan and Europe. Perhaps consumers will be able to influence what happens to mangroves if we demand to know more about how our food is produced. Then we might decide to only buy shrimps or other fish that have been farmed sustainably.

Consumer in the UK

▲ **Figure 13** Views on whether the use of mangroves for shrimp farming is sustainable.

How are tropical rainforests used for food production?

▲ **Figure 14** The Borneo orang-utan.

Global resources

Malaysia and Indonesia are Newly Industrialised Countries (NICs). Their economies have grown as they have traded their natural resources and developed manufacturing industries. They have cashed in on the global demand for produce such as timber, fuel and food. Borneo's rainforests provide much needed timber, but at what cost? In 1985, 73.3 per cent of Borneo was covered in forest. By 2005, only 50.4 per cent was left. Many areas of rainforest have been cleared, destroying the homes of indigenous people, and the habitat of animals such as the orang-utan.

As the rainforest is cleared, it is replaced with crops such as palm oil. Global production of palm oil doubled between 1997 and 2008. Palm oil is a healthier alternative for other fats used in food and cooking. The desire to find greener fuels has led to palm oil being grown to produce biofuel. Palm oil plantations are a form of monoculture with a much lower biodiversity than the rainforest they replace.

Percentage	Use
71	Foods, e.g. margarine and processed foods such as cake, biscuits, chocolate
24	Consumer products, e.g. cosmetics and detergents
5	Fuel

▲ **Figure 15** How palm oil is used.

Borneo is an island in South East Asia, divided between Malaysia, Brunei and Indonesia. It has 1 per cent of the world's land area but 6 per cent of the world's species of wildlife. This makes Borneo an important biodiversity hotspot. The rainforest is thought to be 140 million years old and contains many thousands of species of plants and animals, some of which are now endangered, like the Borneo orang-utan.

▲ **Figure 16** The island of Borneo and the 'Heart of Borneo'.

Activity

1 a) Represent the data in Figure 15.
   b) Explain why palm oil production creates benefits for Malaysia and Indonesia.
   c) Outline the environmental and social problems created by palm oil production.

Enquiry

How much palm oil is in your home?

a) Design a survey that could be used to investigate the food ingredients and cleaning products that are commonly used in the UK that contain palm oil.
b) As part of your design, consider how you might question people about:
   i) their awareness of the issue
   ii) their willingness to change their consumer behaviour.

Is palm oil good for Borneo?

Palm oil has higher yields and lower production costs than other oilseed crops, such as soybean and sunflower. It requires less fertiliser and pesticides and can be grown on small farms as well as large plantations.

Country	Metric tonnes
Colombia	1,100,000
Indonesia	35,000,000
Malaysia	21,000,000
Nigeria	970,000
Thailand	2,200,000
Others	4,895,000

▲ **Figure 17** Estimated world palm oil production 2015–16 (values in metric tonnes).

What about the rainforest?

Clearing the land and putting in infrastructure, such as roads and electricity supply, provides jobs and incomes, but often these go to migrant workers, and not the local communities. Many indigenous people, who rely on the rainforest for their food and homes, have been displaced. Animals can become isolated living in the fragments of habitat that are still intact between the oil palm plantations. The rapid decline in areas of the rainforest, especially through illegal logging, is a threat to many species of plants and animals. The loss of the rainforest can even change local weather patterns.

In 2007, the three countries of Malaysia, Brunei and Indonesia, along with NGO support, declared to conserve and manage the forest resources that are still largely undamaged in the central part of Borneo. This is the 'Heart of Borneo' and you can see the location of this forest in Figure 16. NGOs such as WWF and Greenpeace have campaigned to raise public awareness of the deforestation. They have encouraged multinational companies to support sustainable use of land for palm oil production. In 2015, 18 per cent of palm oil is produced using sustainable methods. In 2015, Colgate-Palmolive and Procter & Gamble both pledged to responsibly source primary commodities such as palm oil that are used in their products.

▲ **Figure 18** Plantations of oil palms. Sabah, Borneo Island, Malaysia.

▲ **Figure 19** Greenpeace Protect Paradise campaign.

Activities

2 Use Figure 17 to calculate the percentage of global palm oil production in:
   a) Malaysia
   b) Indonesia
3 a) Use an atlas to locate the countries listed in Figure 17. Describe their distribution.
   b) Explain why most palm oil production is located in these countries.
4 a) Suggest why the palm oil plantations are not a suitable habitat for orang-utans.
   b) Suggest why tropical monocultures have much lower biodiversity than tropical rainforests.

How do human activities change processes in the tropical rainforest ecosystem?

Study Figure 20. It shows the continuous **canopy** of the rainforest which acts rather like a giant umbrella. Raindrops from a tropical storm can hit the ground with great force, causing soil erosion. By intercepting rainfall, the canopy prevents much of it from falling directly to the ground. Water then drips from the leaves with much less force.

In Figures 21 and 24 the canopy has been removed. Where the canopy has been removed by human activities, such as logging or forest clearance for palm oil plantations or other agriculture, there is an increased risk of soil erosion. The soil is washed into local rivers where it reduces the capacity of the river channel. This can lead to flooding problems.

m
50
40
30
20
10
0
Emergent
Continuous canopy
Under canopy
Trees of different ages and sizes
Shrub layer
Little light so few shrubs

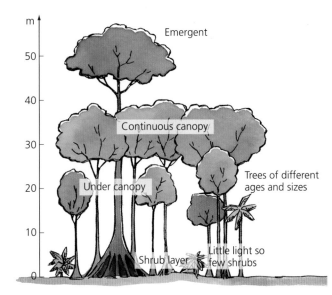

▲ **Figure 20** Typical structure of the tropical rainforest.

The forest in the foreground was burnt a few months ago. The stumps and roots of larger trees have helped to retain soil. What was once the forest floor (and therefore starved of direct sunlight) is now open to sunlight and weeds have quickly colonised. Seeds from trees in the background could blow into this area and the forest could regrow in around 40 years (creating what is known as a secondary rainforest).
This fragment of forest is now an ecological island, and animals here are separated from animals in other remnants of the forest. This forest has probably been selectively felled: trees such as teak and mahogany have already been cut for their timber. The use of heavy machinery in such a confined space will have damaged many other trees and shrubs. This process opens up holes in the canopy. It also deprives insects of a food source (some of which only feed on selected trees) so begins to damage the food chain.
The forest here has been clear felled and recently burnt. The entire structure of canopy, under-canopy and shrub layer has been destroyed. The soils are vulnerable to erosion, especially on this slope. Obviously, since the canopy has been removed, the nutrient cycle has been broken.

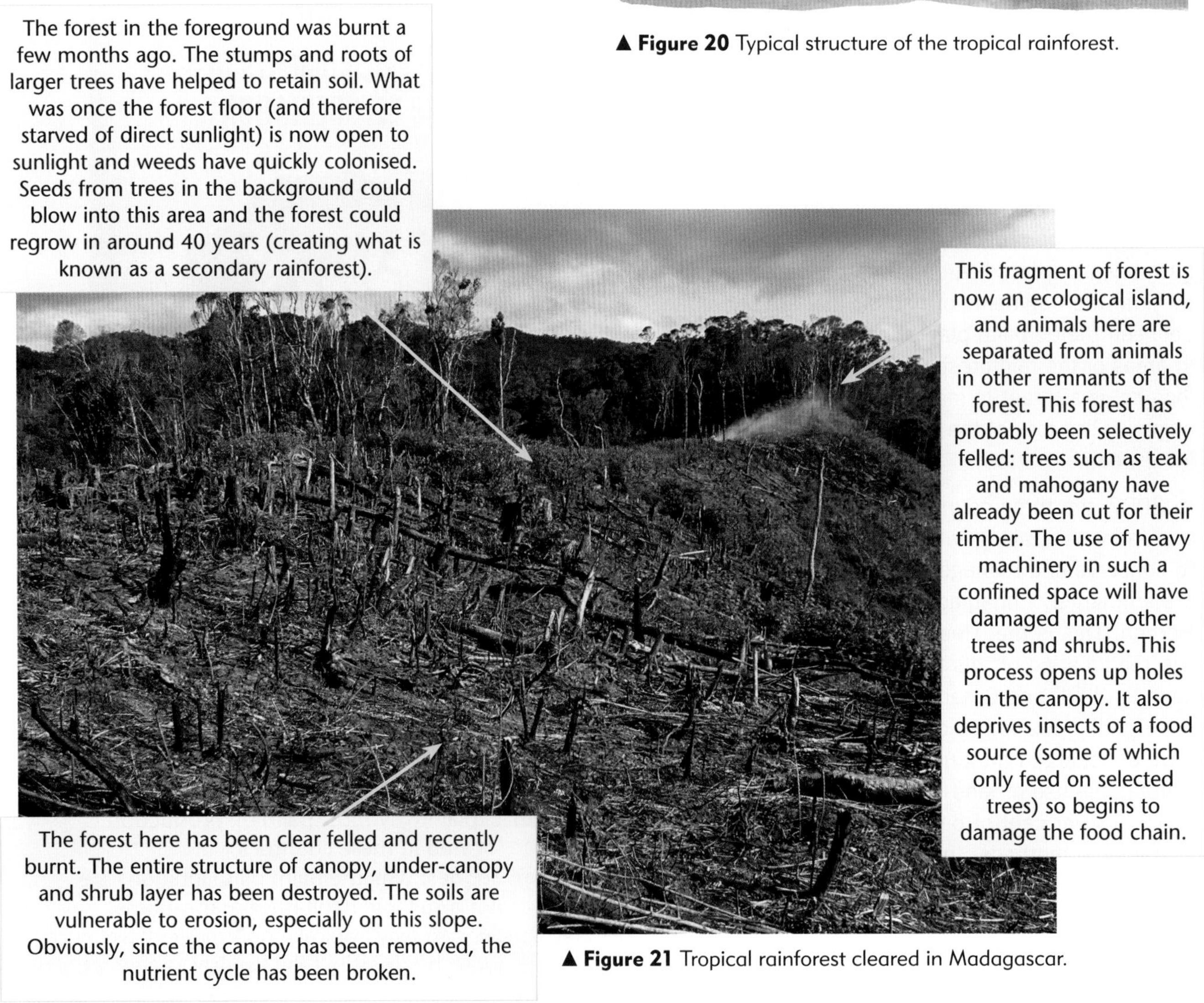

▲ **Figure 21** Tropical rainforest cleared in Madagascar.

Forest type	Location of study	Percentage intercepted and evaporated from canopy
Sitka spruce (conifer)	Scotland	28
Douglas fir (conifer)	Oregon, USA	19
Beech (deciduous)	England	15
Tropical rainforest	Indonesia	21
Tropical rainforest	Dominica	27
Tropical rainforest	Malaysia	27

▲ **Figure 22** Interception and evaporation of water from different forest canopies.

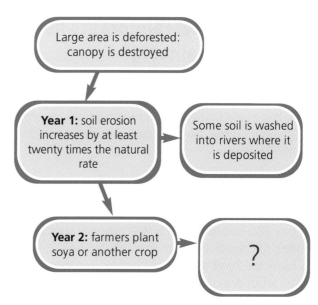

▲ **Figure 23** The consequences of deforestation.

Large area is deforested: canopy is destroyed

Year 1: soil erosion increases by at least twenty times the natural rate

Some soil is washed into rivers where it is deposited

Year 2: farmers plant soya or another crop

?

A

B

C

▲ **Figure 24** Logging next to a river in Borneo.

Activities

1 Explain how the canopy of the rainforest reduces the risk of soil erosion.
2 Study Figure 22.
   a) Choose a suitable method to create a graph to represent this data.
   b) Calculate the mean interception rates for
      i) coniferous forest
      ii) deciduous forest
      iii) tropical rainforest.
   c) Suggest why the deciduous forest has significantly lower figures.

Enquiry

How does human activity affect water stores and flows in the tropical rainforest?

a) Using Figure 23 as a starting point, create a flowchart or spider diagram to explain the links between deforestation, soil erosion, silt deposition in rivers, and river floods.
b) Write suitable annotations to fill the boxes on Figure 24.

How can tropical rainforests be managed sustainably?

Virunga was Africa's first National Park. It was established in 1925 in the Democratic Republic of Congo. It is now a UNESCO World Heritage site, covering 7,800 km^2 of tropical forest, savanna, wetland and active volcanic mountains.

Why is Virunga so important?

Virunga is the most biodiverse National Park in Africa, with over 700 bird species and 200 mammal species, including the rare okapi which is only found here. It is also home to 220 of the critically endangered mountain gorillas, about one-quarter of the global population. More than 100,000 people depend directly on the Park and in the past it has been affected by poaching, civil unrest, poverty and a lack of investment in infrastructure.

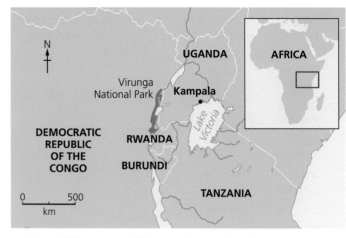

▲ **Figure 27** Location of Virunga National Park.

▲ **Figure 25** The endangered mountain gorilla which lives in the tropical rainforest of Virunga.

◀ **Figure 26** The rare okapi. Although it has striped markings like a zebra it is actually related to the giraffe.

Factfile: Sustainable management strategies in Virunga

- 40,000 saplings have been planted to create a forested buffer zone for the gorillas.
- Electric fences have been set up to reduce conflict between wildlife and people.
- Bloodhounds have been trained to track poachers.
- Hydro-electric plants have been built to provide schools and hospitals with free electricity and power for over one million people.
- Over 60,000 new jobs will be created in agriculture and industry by 2020.
- The Mikeno Luxury Lodge has been built to encourage high-end tourism with overnight accommodation and opportunities for gorilla trekking.

Activities

1 Use Figure 27 to describe the location of Virunga National Park.
2 Choose three of the strategies outlined in the Factfile and explain why each is an example of sustainable management.

Planning a sustainable future

The Virunga Alliance is a project designed to protect the Park's ecosystems and wildlife while allowing economic development and stability to the local communities. Investments in infrastructure such as roads and schools will benefit local communities and figures for some of these improvements are shown in Figure 29. A three-stage development plan of investment from both private and public (state) sectors will run from 2008–20.

- Phase 1 – Experimental 2008–12
- Phase 2 – Development 2013–15
- Phase 3 – Consolidation 2016–20

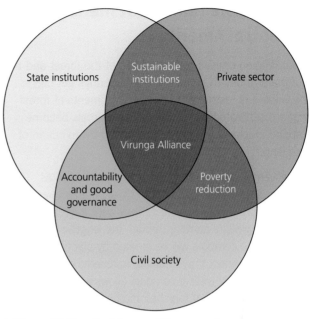

▲ **Figure 29** How the Virunga Alliance works.

Number of new schools	Number of new health clinics	Number of kilometres of roads improved	Number of people with access to clean water
64	23	320	145,000

▲ **Figure 28** Planned improvements to social infrastructure in Virunga National Park.

Threats to Virunga's future

Deposits of oil have been discovered in Virunga National Park. The government of the Democratic Republic of Congo (DRC) is considering changing the boundaries of the National Park to allow for oil exploration. DRC is one of the poorest countries in the world and the government is keen to develop its natural resources so that the economy can grow. This would involve seismic tests, forest clearance, drilling and the building of new roads and pipelines.

Activities

3 Use the information in Figure 28 to explain how the quality of daily life of the people living in Virunga National Park would be improved.
4 There is a scheme called Sponsor a Gorilla for $10 a month to raise awareness globally and fund an orphan mountain gorilla centre. Suggest how people participating in this scheme in the UK could help to protect the species in Virunga.

Enquiry

Should the Democratic Republic of Congo be allowed to redraw the boundaries of the Virunga Park to allow oil exploration? UNESCO have said that oil exploration activities are incompatible with World Heritage Status.

a) With a partner, discuss the costs and benefits of allowing oil activities in or near the National Park.
b) Draw up a list and produce either a written report or a PowerPoint presentation to summarise your findings.

Sustainable rainforest management in Central America

Deforestation causes fragmentation of the forest and this is a major problem for wildlife. As clearings get bigger, the wildlife is restricted to isolated fragments of forest that are separated by farmland. The animals become trapped in islands of forest surrounded by an ocean of farmland.

The governments of Central America (also known as Mesoamerica) are co-operating with each other in an ambitious conservation project. They want to create a continuous **wildlife corridor** through the length of Central America. The corridors will be created by planting strips of forest to connect the remaining fragments of forest together. Creating wildlife corridors allows animals to move freely from one area of forest to another without coming into conflict with people. It means that animals can find new sources of food. It also allows them to find mates in other forest areas, so helping to maintain healthy genetic

diversity. The project is called the Mesoamerican Biological Corridor (known by its Spanish initials, CBM) and involves all seven governments of Central America, plus Mexico.

Debt-for-nature swap

Mesoamerica is a **biodiversity hotspot**. It only amounts to 1 per cent of the world's land surface, but it is estimated to contain 7 per cent of the world's terrestrial (land-based) species. Western governments are encouraging conservation in this region by offering **debt-for-nature swaps**. Under these arrangements, the Central American governments agree to spend money conserving ecosystems and wildlife. In return, the Western governments agree to reduce the amount of money that is owed to them. One such debt-for-nature swap was made between Costa Rica and the USA. In 2010 Costa Rica agreed to spend $27 million on conservation projects. Such agreements help governments of HICs meet their own targets for supporting conservation and tackling climate change.

▲ **Figure 31** Satellite image of the Mesoamerican Biological Corridor (CBM) project. The red dots show where forest fires are burning.

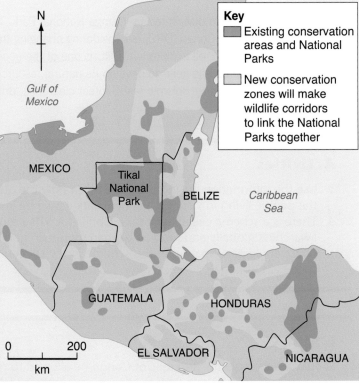

▲ **Figure 32** Protected areas (including forest reserves) in Central America and Mexico and the proposed wildlife corridors.

Ecotourism in Costa Rica

The government and businesses in Costa Rica have also encouraged the growth of **ecotourism**. These are small-scale tourist projects that create money for conservation as well as creating local jobs. It is estimated that 70 per cent of Costa Rica's tourists visit the protected environments. By 2024 Costa Rica's economy is expected to earn £6.2 billion from tourism. One successful example of ecotourism is the creation of a canopy walkway through a small, privately owned part of the Monteverde reserve. Tourists are charged $45 to climb up into the canopy and walk along rope bridges, the longest of which is 300 m long.

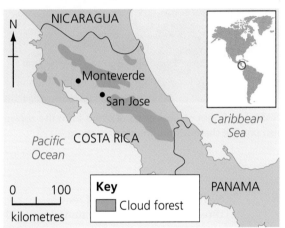

◀ **Figure 33** The location of Monteverde reserve.

Country	Protected land as % of total area
Belize	47.5
Costa Rica	23.4
El Salvador	2.0
Guatemala	25.3
Honduras	20.8
Mexico	5.0
Nicaragua	21.3
Panama	19.5

▲ **Figure 34** Protected areas (including forest reserves) in Central America and Mexico.

▲ **Figure 35** The canopy walkway allows visitors to see the birds and other wildlife that live in the canopy of the tropical rainforest.

Activities

1   Study Figures 31 and 32.
    a) Describe the location of Tikal National Park.
    b) Describe the distribution of forest fires. Do many appear to be burning in conservation areas?
2   Working in pairs, draw a spider diagram to show how fragmentation of the rainforest affects wildlife. Consider the likely impacts of fragmentation on:
    ▪ food chains
    ▪ success of mating
    ▪ predator/prey relationships
    ▪ pollination and seed dispersal.
3   Explain how the new wildlife corridors will help to conserve wildlife.

Enquiry

How good is Costa Rica's record on conservation compared with that of its neighbours?

a) Study Figure 34. Calculate the average amount of land that is protected in Central America and Mexico.
b) Present the data in graphical form – include a bar for the mean.
c) What conclusions can you reach?

The global threat to coral reefs

Coral reefs are a marine ecosystem located in regions that have a tropical climate (see pages 182–3 for details of this climate). Coral reefs develop in clear, warm tropical water which has a minimum water temperature of 18°C. A reef is made of millions of tiny animals called coral polyps, which live in colonies and feed by reaching out tentacles to catch plankton. They secrete a skeleton of calcium carbonate, which protects them and builds up over time to form a reef. Coral has a symbiotic (two-way) relationship with algae called **zooxanthellae** which live in the polyp and provide food in return for shelter and compounds the algae need for photosynthesis.

Why are coral reefs so important?

Coral reefs are important to coastal communities. Reefs soak up wave energy so act as a buffer against damaging ocean waves. They reduce wave energy by up to 97 per cent, which reduces coastal erosion and damage to coastal settlements. This is especially important during tropical storms or cyclones.

Coral reefs are important to the global environment because they contain the greatest biodiversity of species of any marine ecosystem. Reefs provide a very important habitat for fish to spawn. They provide a nursery environment for juvenile fish where they can be relatively safe from predators. As such, reefs are a major source of commercial fish species. They are also a popular tourist attraction for activities such as reef walking and scuba diving.

▲ **Figure 36** The bright colours of coral come from the zooxanthellae which also provide them with nutrients and energy.

Region	% of reef threatened by 2011	% of reef threatened by 2030
Atlantic	75	90
Australasia	14	90
Indian Ocean	66	88
Middle East	65	88
Pacific Ocean	48	89
South East Asia	94	99
Global	61	92

▲ **Figure 37** The percentage of the world's reefs that are at risk.

How are coral reefs affected by global warming?

Coral reefs are a very fragile ecosystem because they are very sensitive to change. Coral reefs are highly complex structures which are vulnerable to the effects of warmer air and ocean surface temperatures. The main effects are:

- Coral bleaching caused by higher than normal sea temperatures. This results in the zooxanthellae leaving the coral tissue, turning them white. Bleached corals are unhealthy and vulnerable to diseases such as blackband and white plague. Climate change is causing bleaching to occur more often and the reefs take longer to recover.

- Much of the carbon dioxide entering our atmosphere is dissolved in the oceans and as this increases, so the pH of the water becomes more acidic. Ocean acidification means corals are not able to absorb as much calcium carbonate so the reef becomes unhealthy and may dissolve.
- Rising sea levels caused by melting ice and thermal expansion of the ocean can make the water too deep for corals to receive adequate sunlight.
- Scientists are predicting an increase in the frequency of tropical storms, which may further damage the already fragile coral reefs.

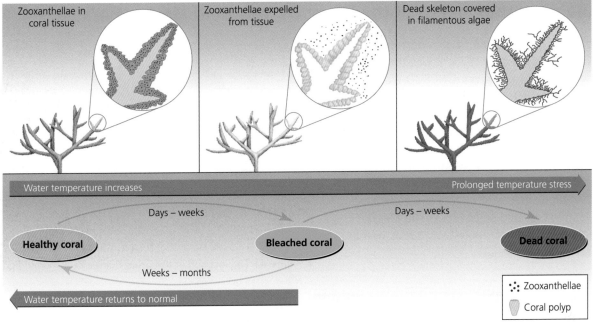

▲ **Figure 38** Stages in the process of coral bleaching.

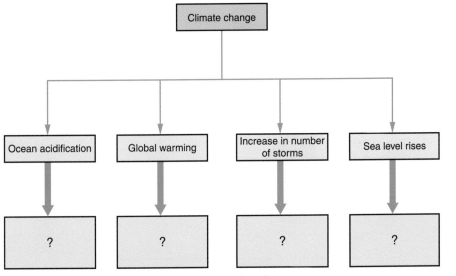

▲ **Figure 39** Impact of climate change on coral reefs.

Enquiry

Why are tropical coral reefs important to both local communities and globally?

Make a list of at least three reasons why coral reefs are important to local communities and at least one reason why they deserve global protection. Make sure you refer to the key services provided by reefs.

Activities

1 Describe what a coral reef is.
2 Choose a suitable graphical technique to show the data in Figure 37. You could add proportional symbols to an outline world map.
3 Study Figure 38 and write a detailed description of how climate change causes coral bleaching.
4 Make a copy of Figure 39 and add the labels to the right in their correct places to complete the diagram summarising the effects of climate change on coral reefs.

Higher sea temperatures cause coral bleaching which weakens the structure

Deeper water leads to reduced amounts of sunlight and poorer water quality

Acidified water has lower pH levels which means less calcium carbonate is absorbed so coral skeletons dissolve faster

Delicate reef structures are damaged by heavy rain and run-off from the land

Sustainable management of the Great Barrier Reef Marine Park

The Great Barrier Reef Marine Park in northern Australia was established in 1975. It was the first coral reef ecosystem to be given UNESCO World Heritage Status in 1981. It is now considered to be one of the best managed marine ecosystems in the world. As well as being important for its biodiversity, protection is given to more than 70 Aboriginal and other groups whose traditions and culture are under threat from development. The area also has many places of historical significance including lighthouses and shipwrecks. The Marine Park attracts over 2 million tourists a year as well as 5 million recreational users.

▲ **Figure 41** The location of the Great Barrier Reef Marine Park.

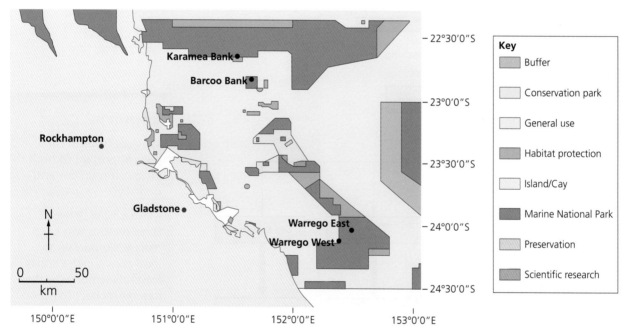

Zone	What is and isn't allowed
Preservation	No one can enter without written permission.
Marine National Park	Fishing and oyster collecting are not allowed. Boating, swimming, snorkelling and sailing are allowed.
Scientific research	For scientific study. Members of the public are usually not allowed.
Buffer	Some fishing is allowed. The public are allowed to enjoy the natural environment in this zone.
Conservation park	Only a limited amount of fishing is allowed.
Habitat protection	Sensitive and vulnerable habitats are protected from damaging activities.
General use	Trawling is not allowed. Crabbing, boating, diving, photography, line fishing and trawling are all allowed.

▲ **Figure 40** Zones of the Great Barrier Reef Marine Park to the east of Gladstone.

How is the park managed?

The Great Barrier Reef Marine Park has been divided into different **management zones**. A zoning plan identifies which activities are permitted in each zone. The aim is to separate uses of the ecosystem that might conflict with each other. The level of protection increases from General Use Zone up to the most restrictive Preservation Zone. At honeypots like Cairns and the Whitsunday Islands, there are special management plans. Boat length and visitor group size are restricted to prevent overcrowding of these vulnerable locations. There is also a joint programme of education and enforcement with the Queensland Parks and Wildlife Service. Every five years the Great Barrier Reef Outlook Report is published and from this, a detailed management plan is produced. Reef 2050 is the latest long-term sustainability plan.

Is zoning effective?

Zoning the reef protects the unique marine animals, plants and habitats, as well as threatened species like the green turtle and dugong. Industries that rely on the reef, such as fishing and tourism, can continue. This provides social and economic benefits to local communities and the national economy. Wider benefits include opportunities for recreational, cultural, educational and scientific research into coral reef ecosystems. Research from the latest report has shown that fish numbers and average size are increasing. Coral trout is now 50 per cent more abundant. Bigger fish mean more eggs, and increasing numbers in closed areas mean the fish population can spill into other zones.

▲ **Figure 42** The dugong, a large marine mammal sometimes known as the sea cow.

▲ **Figure 43** The green turtle is threatened by habitat loss, the wildlife trade, fishing for its meat and accidental drowning in fishing nets.

Activities

1 Why do you think the Great Barrier Reef Marine Park was given World Heritage Status?
2 Explain why it needs to be managed.
3 a) Describe how the Marine Park zoning system works.
   b) Explain why the system is an example of sustainable management.
4 Describe the advantages and disadvantages of the zoning system for each of the following groups of people:
   a) fishermen
   b) research scientists
   c) divers and tourists.

Enquiry

Do you think that such a zoning system would work in a National Park in England and Wales such as the Lake District or Norfolk Broads?

Weigh up the benefits and problems of such a system. Support your answer by referring to a particular National Park in the UK.

How much water do we use?

Everyone needs water. It is essential for healthy life. We also use vast quantities of water to grow food and in many industrial processes. However, the total amount of water used varies greatly from one country to another. For example, the average American family uses 1,300 litres of water a day, whereas the average African family uses only 22 litres of water a day. Generally, much more water is used per person in the richer nations of the world than in the poorest. This may be because:

- Water **abstraction** is expensive – it requires huge investments to build dams and water-transfer schemes.
- Wealthier people tend to use more water in non-essential ways, such as watering gardens, washing cars or filling swimming pools.

However, the global pattern of water use is not quite as simple as that. Some countries have higher rainfall totals than others and many countries have major rivers which bring water into their territory. These countries have the opportunity to use a lot of water for agriculture. Pakistan is an example. Rivers that are fed by snow melt in the Himalayan Mountains flow into Pakistan. This water is taken, or abstracted, and used to irrigate crops. So, even though Pakistan is a Middle Income Country it uses a lot more water per person than the UK which has a much higher gross national income (GNI).

Country	Annual water use by agriculture (km³/year)	Annual water use per capita (m³/inhab/ year)	GNI per capita, PPP (current international $)*
Cambodia	2.05	158.9	2,260
Egypt	59	1,000	6,160
Ghana	0.65	49.63	1,820
India	688	615.4	3,620
Malawi	1.17	98.95	870
Niger	0.66	69.28	720
Nigeria	7.05	89.07	2,300
Pakistan	172.4	1,024	2,880
UK	0.99	1,71.8	35,940
USA	192.4	1,575	48,890

▲ **Figure 1** How much water is used by selected countries.

Activities

1 a) Working with a partner, make a list of all the ways that you use water every day.
   b) How many of these uses are essential and how many could you live without?
2 a) Use data in Figure 1 to represent the per capita water use in the UK and the two poorest nations in the table.
   b) Suggest five reasons why families in richer countries like the UK use more water than families in the world's poorest countries.

▲ **Figure 2** An extravagant use of water? A desert golf course in USA.

Some groups of people have very poor access to water. Many people in rural regions of sub-Saharan Africa have to collect water and carry it some distance from their home. Collecting water is time-consuming and heavy work. In Africa, 90 per cent of the work of collecting water and firewood is done by women and children. A piped supply to the home would not only be safer, it would save time. A study in Tanzania showed that reducing the distance to a source of water from 30 to 15 minutes increased girls' attendance at school by 12 per cent. Having piped water also gives families privacy and dignity. Imagine how unhappy children must feel if they have nowhere private to wash.

In sub-Saharan Africa, people living in urban areas are twice as likely to have access to safe, piped water as people living in rural areas. However, even within urban areas, there are massive differences between the way that rich and poor have access to water. In the informal settlements of Africa's cities, many people do not have access to piped water and cannot afford to drill a borehole. They are forced to buy water from street vendors like in Figure 3. As a result, people who live in the shanty towns of some African cities can pay up to 50 times the amount for water as people living in European cities.

▲ **Figure 3** Street vendor selling water in Nigeria.

– BUT WHAT WILL WOMEN DO IF THEY DON'T HAVE TO CARRY WATER FOUR HOURS A DAY?

▲ **Figure 4** African women of the Sahel (see page 284) spend a lot of time doing work that does not contribute directly to family or state income.

Long working days are the norm for women in the **Sahel**. Women work up to a total of 16 hours per day in the growing season, of which about half is spent on agricultural work. Time allocation studies from Burkina Faso and Mali show women working one to three hours a day more than men. In rural areas, the lack of basic services such as reliable water supplies, health centres, stores (shops) and transport adds considerably to the time women must also spend on household chores. Shortage of time constrains women's attendance at activities to benefit them, the time and attention they can pay to productive activities, and visits to health facilities.

▲ **Figure 5** Extract from a World Bank report.

Enquiry

How close is the connection between a nation's wealth and its water use?

a) Study Figure 1. Suggest a hypothesis that links wealth and water use.

b) Draw a scatter graph to investigate the possible relationship between these sets of data.

c) What conclusions can you draw?

d) How could you improve this enquiry?

Activity

3 Study Figures 4 and 5.

a) Give three reasons why women in Sahel countries such as Mali have such long working days.

b) Suggest a number of ways in which the lives of rural African women and children would be improved if they had access to a clean and safe water supply close to their home.

c) Suggest how women in Mali might use four extra hours a day.

What is your water footprint?

Every day each of us drinks between 2 and 4 litres of water a day. You use a lot more water through washing, bathing and flushing the toilet. For example, you will use about 95 litres in a five-minute shower. However, even this is only a small fraction of the total amount of water you will use in a day. Our food and clothing contain **embedded** water. This is water that has been used to grow our food and make our clothes. Each of us uses 2,000–5,000 litres of embedded water every day. So, as consumers we each have a **water footprint** – the impact of our water use on the planet. Our water footprint is a measure of our individual water use and our impact on this vital resource.

Other footprints	Litres
T-shirt and pair of jeans	10,000
Pizza	1,260
100 g chocolate	1,700
A dozen bananas	1,920
1 kg beef	13,500

▼ **Figure 6** Water footprints for selected items.

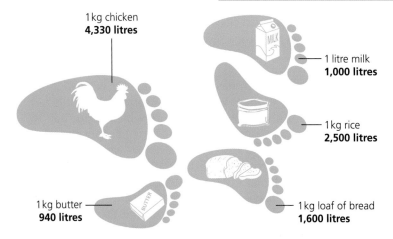

1 kg chicken
4,330 litres

1 litre milk
1,000 litres

1 kg rice
2,500 litres

1 kg butter
940 litres

1 kg loaf of bread
1,600 litres

Activities

1   Present the data in Figure 6 as five pictograms. Try to make your pictograms roughly proportional so that larger water footprints are shown using larger pictures.
2   Explain why drip irrigation is more suitable for farming in hot semi-arid climates than other forms of irrigation.

Water is not delivered to where plants are not growing.

Small pipes deliver drips of water to the roots of each individual plant.

Some water will evaporate from the damp soil.

▲ **Figure 7** Drip irrigation reduces the amount of water lost by evaporation. The system was invented in Israel where water supply is an issue.

Water for food

Globally we use about 70 per cent of our water to grow food, 20 per cent to supply industry and just 10 per cent to give us a safe domestic water supply. There are 7 billion people in the world today and the world's population is expected to rise to 9 billion by 2050. To feed these extra people, and overcome poverty and malnutrition, we need to produce 60 per cent more food by 2050.

This won't be a problem in regions which have an equatorial climate where high quantities of rainfall provide water for farming without the need for irrigation. However, in regions where rainfall totals are low, water is withdrawn or abstracted from the ground or reservoirs so that it can be used to irrigate crops. In these regions farmers will need to adopt techniques that use less water to produce more food. Figure 7 shows one example of these techniques.

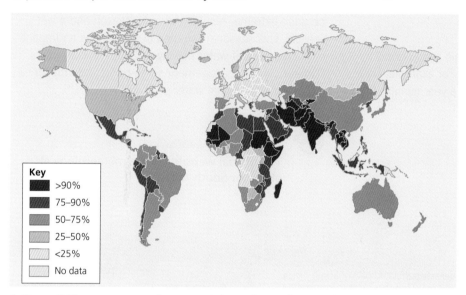

Key
- >90%
- 75–90%
- 50–75%
- 25–50%
- <25%
- No data

▲ **Figure 8** The percentage of water withdrawn for use by agriculture.

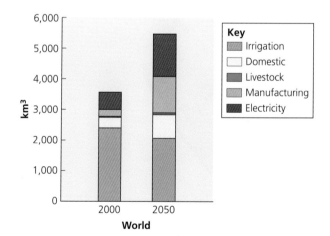

Key
- Irrigation
- Domestic
- Livestock
- Manufacturing
- Electricity

▲ **Figure 9** Global water demand in 2000 and 2050.

	Agriculture	Industry	Domestic
Cambodia	94.0	1.5	4.5
Egypt	86.4	5.9	7.8
Ghana	66.4	9.7	23.9
India	90.4	2.2	7.4
Malawi	85.9	3.5	10.6
Pakistan	94.0	0.8	5.3
UK	9.2	32.4	58.5
USA	40.2	46.1	13.7

▲ **Figure 10** The percentage of water, withdrawn for each sector, in selected countries.

Activities

3 Use the data in Figure 9 to compare global water use in 2000 and 2050.
4 Study Figure 8.
   a) Describe the location and distribution of countries that use more than 90 per cent of water withdrawals for agriculture.
   b) Suggest one way that this style of map could be improved to make it more effective.

Investigating patterns of water supply in South Africa

On average, South Africa has about half as much rainfall as the UK. But rainfall is not distributed evenly over South Africa. The east coast receives a lot more rain than the west (see Figure 11). This is because moist air comes in from the Indian Ocean, forming rain clouds over the highlands of eastern South Africa and Lesotho. Lesotho is a small mountainous country that is entirely surrounded by South Africa.

Geographical patterns of rainfall in this region don't match the distribution of population. For example, parts of Lesotho receive 1200 mm of rain a year (similar to mid Wales) but Lesotho has only a low population. This is good for Lesotho because it can sell its excess water to parts of South Africa where the population is higher but rainfall is lower.

The amount of precipitation also varies through the year. For some regions in South Africa, this difference can be quite extreme, resulting in a dry season and a wet season. This seasonal variation in rainfall has an impact on the amount of water flowing in South Africa's rivers. Without careful management some parts of South Africa would suffer seasonal water shortages.

www.weathersa.co.za

The official website for the meteorological office for South Africa.

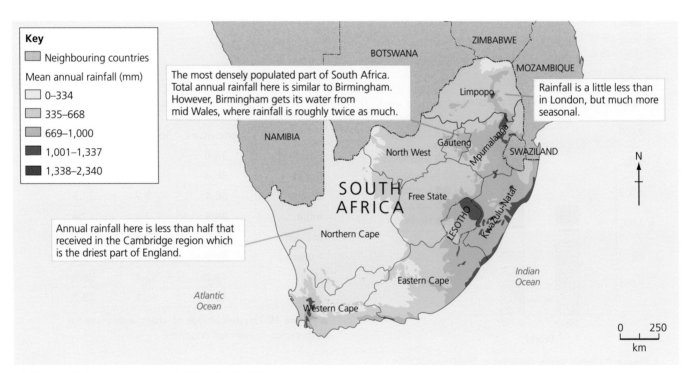

▲ **Figure 11** Average annual rainfall in South Africa.

	Jan	Feb	Mar	Apr	May	Jun	Jul	Aug	Sep	Oct	Nov	Dec	Total
Western Cape	8	4	11	24	40	41	47	45	24	12	12	10	278
Gauteng	125	90	91	54	13	9	4	6	27	72	117	105	713

▲ **Figure 12** Rainfall (mm) for selected regions of South Africa.

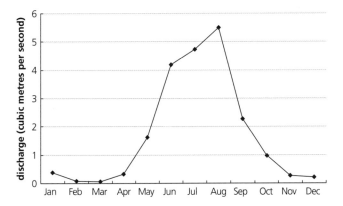

▲ **Figure 13** Hydrograph for the River Dorling, Western Cape Province, South Africa. The catchment area of the River Dorling before this station is 6900 km².

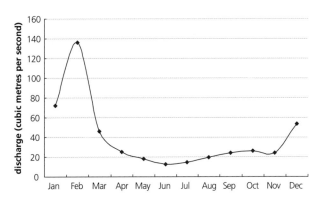

▲ **Figure 14** Hydrograph for the River Vaal, Gauteng Province, South Africa. The catchment area of the River Vaal before this station is 38,560 km².

▲ **Figure 15** Relief rainfall patterns in South Africa and Lesotho.

Activities

1   Use Figure 11 to describe the distribution of rainfall in South Africa.
2   Explain why Lesotho is able to sell water to South Africa and why South Africa wants to buy it.
3   a) Use Figure 12 to draw a pair of rainfall graphs.
    b) Compare your rainfall graphs with Figures 13 and 14.
    c) At which times of year do these two regions face possible water shortages?
4   Use Figure 15 to explain why Lesotho has so much more rainfall than Free State in South Africa. Describe what is happening at each point (1–6) on the diagram.

Investigating a major water-transfer scheme

The Lesotho Highlands Water Project (LHWP) is an example of a large-scale water-transfer scheme. Dams collect water in the mountainous areas of Lesotho to supply water to areas of water deficit in the neighbouring country of South Africa. It is the largest water-transfer scheme in Africa, diverting 40 per cent of the water in the Senqu river basin in Lesotho to the Vaal river system in the Orange Free State of South Africa via 200 km of tunnel systems. The River Vaal then carries the water into Gauteng Province.

The first phase of the project, started in 1984, is complete. Two dams, the Katse and the Mohale, have been built. The LHWP transfers 24.6m³ of water per second to South Africa. A second phase of construction has just begun with the building of the Polihali Dam. This development will deliver an extra 45.5m³ per second of water to South Africa. The new dam will also generate 1,000MW of electricity for Lesotho. Phase two will cost $1 billion and be completed by 2020. There are plans for two more dams to be built in later phases of the LHWP.

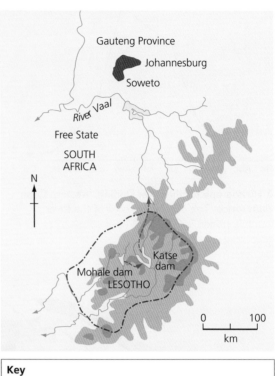

Key

`·-►` Pipe transferring water into the River Vaal catchment

▨ Land over 3,000m ▨ Land over 2,000m

▶ **Figure 16** A map of the Lesotho Highlands Water Project water management and transfer scheme.

Year	Urban areas			Rural areas		
	Improved supplies			Improved supplies		
	Piped in home (%)	Other improved (%)	Unimproved (%)	Piped in home (%)	Other improved (%)	Unimproved (%)
1990	85.9	12.2	1.9	24.0	42.3	33.7
2000	87.5	11.0	1.5	27.9	42.7	29.4
2010	90.3	8.9	0.8	34.5	43.3	22.2
2015	91.7	7.9	0.4	37.7	43.7	18.6

▲ **Figure 17** Improved and unimproved water supplies in urban and rural areas of South Africa.

Year	Urban areas			Rural areas		
	Improved supplies			Improved supplies		
	Piped in home (%)	Other improved (%)	Unimproved (%)	Piped in home (%)	Other improved (%)	Unimproved (%)
1990	26.3	66.3	7.4	2.3	72.6	25.1
2000	39.4	53.7	6.8	2.9	72.6	24.5
2010	61.3	32.8	5.9	3.9	72.5	23.5
2015	70.0	24.5	5.4	4.3	72.6	23.0

▲ **Figure 18** Improved and unimproved water supplies in urban and rural areas of Lesotho.

What are the advantages and disadvantages of the LHWP?

Lesotho is one of the world's poorest countries. It has few natural resources so selling water to South Africa provides 75 per cent of Lesotho's income. However, many people in Lesotho do not have access to improved water sources. A new dam, the Metlong Dam is being constructed to supply lowland areas of Lesotho with water. The project is costing US$31.80 million – money that Lesotho has borrowed and will have to pay back. The dam is finished and the pipes and tunnels to transfer the water should be completed by 2020. Until then, many people in rural areas of Lesotho will spend many hours fetching and carrying water.

▼ **Figure 19** Impacts of the LHWP.

Roads have been constructed in the highlands to gain access to the dam sites.

Farmland is flooded to create the reservoirs. About 20,000 people were displaced when the Katse Dam was built.

Compensation is paid to families who lose land during construction of the dams. Many families have complained that the compensation is too little and too late.

Phase two dams will generate 1,000 megawatts of electricity for Lesotho.

Phase one created around 20,000 jobs. Many workers moved to shanty towns on the construction sites. Alcoholism and HIV/AIDs became significant problems in the shanty towns.

▲ **Figure 20** A family in Lesotho collecting water.

Activities

1 Summarise the aims of the Lesotho Highlands Water Project.

2 Use the text on these pages to complete a copy of the following table. You should find more to write in some boxes than in others.

Country	Short-term advantages (+) and disadvantages (–) of LHWP	Long-term advantages (+) and disadvantages (–) of LHWP
Lesotho	+	+
	–	–
South Africa	+	+
	–	–

3 Summarise what each of the following groups of people might think about the LHWP:
   a) a farmer in the Lesotho Highlands
   b) a government minister in Lesotho
   c) residents in Johannesburg, South Africa.

Enquiry

How much progress have Lesotho and South Africa made in providing improved water supplies?

Use the evidence in Figures 17 and 18 to:

a) Compare progress in urban and rural areas.
b) Compare progress in South Africa and Lesotho.
c) What conclusions can you draw about the benefits of the LHWP?

Are there alternative ways to manage South Africa's water?

South Africa has 539 large dams, which is almost half of all the dams in Africa. But despite this, there are still a large number of South Africans without access to clean drinking water. Many of these people live in rural, remote parts of South Africa. They are too isolated to become part of the big projects such as the LHWP and they are too poor to drill boreholes to tap into groundwater supplies. Instead they have to rely on cheap, small-scale methods of rainwater harvesting.

Sustainable water management on a small farm

Ma Tshepo Khumbane is a South African farmer who teaches rainwater harvesting techniques. Her management strategies (shown in Figure 21) are affordable and practical for families, no matter how small the farm is or how little money they have. They use ways that are cheap, practical and easy to maintain using appropriate technology. They are commonly used in rural areas of Limpopo that do not have piped water. They are designed to:

- collect and use rainwater, for example, by collecting water from the roof of the farm
- maintain soil moisture by encouraging as much infiltration as possible. In this way groundwater stores are recharged.

Rainwater harvesting techniques and soil moisture conservation are examples of sustainable water development. They benefit people now without doing any lasting damage to the environment or using up valuable resources. These methods of water management are not usually big enough to have negative impacts on the surrounding drainage basin – unlike the big dam building schemes used by governments.

Vegetable beds are filled with organic matter such as leaves and manure. This helps to retain water.

The edges of some beds are reinforced with stone to prevent erosion.

Water is collected from the roof and paving around the house. This is grey water and an average of 503 m³ is collected per year. It is stored in large water butts and in an underground concrete tank.

A trench along the contour catches run-off.

A treadle pump can be used to pump grey water up to the vegetable plots.

Rainwater slowly flows along a network of channels.

If it rains too much the extra water goes through a hole in the **bund** to prevent the vegetable plots flooding.

Fruit trees are planted on the lower side of a trench where the roots can find water.

The water is collected in a small pool.

▲ **Figure 21** Rainwater harvesting techniques used by Ma Tshepo Khumbane.

Activities

1 Choose five techniques shown in Figure 21. For each technique describe how it either collects rain water or recharges groundwater.
2 Explain why the type of management shown in Figure 21 is sustainable.

Enquiry

Should South Africa invest in big schemes like LHWP or small-scale sustainable water management schemes?

a) Contrast the impacts of this type of water management with the building of large dam and water-transfer schemes like the LHWP.
b) Which would you prioritise? Explain your answer.

Could South Africa harvest water from fog?

Fog has been 'harvested' to provide clean drinking water to isolated rural communities since 1987 when a scheme was set up in Chungungo, Chile. Since then, similar systems have been used successfully in Peru, Ecuador, Tenerife, Ethiopia and South Africa. It is another form of appropriate technology because it is relatively cheap to install and maintain. To collect water from fog, a simple system of fine-mesh nylon nets are suspended vertically between tall poles. The fog condenses on the net and drips into a gutter below. It then passes through sand before being piped to where it is needed.

Fog harvesting works best in upland regions (at least 400 m above sea level) that experience moist air being blown from the coast. As the air rises it condenses to form fog. So would fog harvesting work in Limpopo in South Africa? Most of Limpopo is over 1,000 m above sea level. Moist air from the Indian Ocean is blown inland by prevailing easterly winds. The first fog harvesting scheme was built at Tshanowa Primary School in Limpopo. All 130 school children used to bring bottled water to school every day. Now they drink pure water collected from fog.

▲ **Figure 22** Fog collectors in Tenerife. The nets, which look like giant volley ball nets, trap moisture as it condenses from the air.

It is not foggy every day.

The nets and poles are relatively cheap to buy.

Repairs are essential. Nets are easily torn in the wind.

Repairs are easy to make and require little training.

Ground water is contaminated.

Fog harvesting technology does not need any electrical energy.

Many rural areas do not have a piped supply from a reservoir.

Some of the foggiest sites are some distance from rural communities.

▲ **Figure 23** Advantages and disadvantages of fog harvesting in Limpopo.

Activity

3 a) Use Figure 23 to sort the advantages and disadvantages of fog harvesting.
   b) Based on the evidence in Figure 23, explain why fog harvesting may be considered to be an appropriate technology for a poor rural community.

Enquiry

Research the fog harvesting systems in Chungungo and Tshanowa by typing the names into an internet search engine. To what extent has each scheme been a success?

 http://www.weathersa.co.za
This is the website of the South African weather service. Click on the Limpopo link to find out how foggy it will be in the next five days. Or, scroll to the bottom of the home page to find recent rainfall maps.

273

What problems are caused by over-abstraction?

Lake Chad is in the Sahel region of Africa. In the last 50 years, Lake Chad has shrunk dramatically. The reasons are complex. They include overgrazing and deforestation in the lake's drainage basin which have resulted in a drier climate – a process known as **desertification**. However, a more significant reason may be the over-abstraction of water from the rivers that supply Lake Chad. Since 1970 a large number of dams have been built in both the Komodougou-Yobe river basin and Chari-Logone river basin. Some water is abstracted for domestic supply in cities like Kano. The rest is used in irrigation projects which grow crops such as onions, tomatoes, chilli peppers and rice. It is thought that only 5–10 per cent of the water in the Chari-Logone river now flows into Lake Chad. The rest evaporates or is abstracted and used. Twenty dams have been built in north-eastern Nigeria since the construction of the Tiga Dam in 1974. This leaves only about 2 per cent of the water in Komodougou-Yobe river basin to flow into Lake Chad.

▲ **Figure 24** The drainage basin of Lake Chad is shown by the pale green area.

Country	Total area of the country (km²)	Area of the country within the basin (km²)
Nigeria	923,770	179,282
Niger	1,267,000	691,473
Algeria	2,381,740	93,451
Sudan	2,505,810	101,048
Central Africa	622,980	219,410
Chad	1,284,000	1,046,196
Cameroon	475,440	50,775
Total area of Lake Chad basin		2,381,635

▲ **Figure 25** The drainage basin of Lake Chad.

Activities

1 Study Figure 24.
   a) Describe the location of Kano
   b) Describe the drainage pattern within the Lake Chad drainage basin.
   c) Use your understanding of tropical climates (page 182) to explain why Lake Chad has this drainage pattern.
2 Study Figure 25.
   a) How could this information be adapted to make it easier to use?
   b) What percentage of Nigeria is within the Lake Chad drainage basin?

▲ **Figure 26** People harvest chilli peppers on a farm that is irrigated with water from the River Yobe in northern Nigeria. Chilli peppers are an essential part of Nigerian cooking and fetch a good price but have a very high water footprint.

How has the shrinking lake affected people and the environment?

This is a very poor part of Africa. There are 40 million people living in the drainage basin of Lake Chad and 60 per cent of them live on less than $2 a day. Over-abstraction means that:

- Some people rely on lake water for human and animal supply. This is not safe for human health and is a source of cholera and polio.
- Soils have suffered from **salinisation**. This process occurs when too much water is used to irrigate crops. Water evaporating from the soil leaves behind harmful minerals.
- The wetland ecosystems surrounding the lake have dried out. Wetland bird populations and fish stocks have declined. Less lake fish has meant declining incomes for fishermen.
- Poverty has increased, leading to increased migration to cities like Kano. Increased poverty has also led to a rise in support for extremist groups such as Boko Haram.

Can Lake Chad be saved?

Thirty years ago an ambitious plan was announced to save Lake Chad. It was proposed that the Transaqua Project would transfer water from the Democratic Republic of Congo (DRC). A 2,400 km canal would transfer 100 billion m³ of water every year from the River Congo to the River Charri. Few people have taken the project seriously until now. The governments of India, China and Brazil see this project as an opportunity to invest in Africa – a continent that is rich in resources that would help support the growth of rapidly growing NIC economies. This infrastructure project would provide water for agriculture, industry and electricity production. It would create job opportunities and water security. This peace-through-development approach to tackling poverty may also reduce extremism and violence in the region.

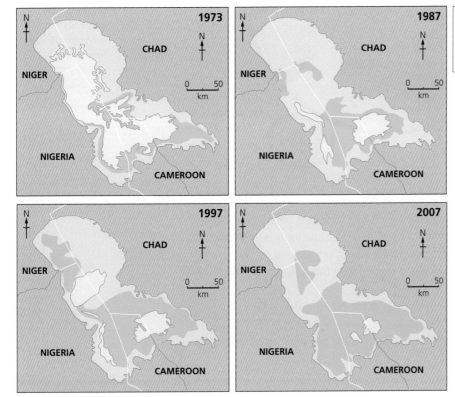

▲ **Figure 27** The shrinking of Lake Chad.

Enquiry

Should the Transaqua Project be built? Justify your decision by considering the possible social, environmental and economic benefits.

Activities

3 Use Figure 27 to describe the changes in shape and size of Lake Chad between:
   a) 1963 and 2007
   b) 1987 and 1997
   c) Suggest reasons why Lake Chad has reduced in size so erratically.

4 Outline the impacts of over-abstraction on the people, economy and environment of the region.

What is water security and why is it important?

We have seen that we need water to maintain water supplies, provide hygiene, grow food and supply industrial processes. Without sufficient water our health and the development of our economies could suffer. For a country to have **water security** is an important aim. It means having enough water to keep the population healthy and fed, and for the economy to develop sustainably – without damaging the prospects for future generations. Achieving water security creates enormous benefits, as shown in Figure 28.

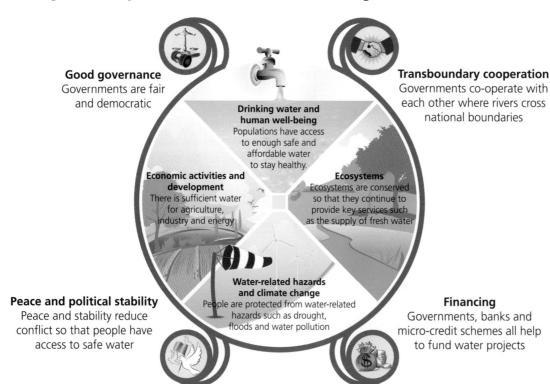

◀ **Figure 28** UN definition of water security (2013). The central part of the diagram describes the features of water security. The outer part of the diagram describes how water security can be achieved.

What happens when there is water insecurity?

The north-eastern part of Nigeria is in the Sahel region of Africa (see page 284). This region suffers from water insecurity. There are a number of reasons for this problem:

- The region has a hot, semi-arid climate which has a long dry season.
- The rainy season is unreliable. In many years since 1965 there has been below average rainfall.
- The Nigerian government has failed to provide enough piped water supply or sanitation to fast-growing cities, such as Kano.
- Poverty and drought have led to political instability and the rise of an extreme Islamist group called Boko Haram.

Activities

1 Study Figure 28. List the benefits of water security for people, the economy and environment. Record your answer in a Venn diagram.
2 Study the information about water insecurity in Kano State and Kano City.

a) Make a list of the physical and human causes.
b) Use Figure 28 to help give at least four reasons why Kano is at huge risk of water insecurity.
c) Use this example to explain why water security can only be achieved if political leaders work hard.

Water insecurity and health in Kano

Kano City is Nigeria's third-largest city. Its population continues to grow quickly, partly because of rural to urban migration from the surrounding rural areas where low rainfall and poverty are push factors. Kano's water supply comes from the Tiga Dam (completed in 1974) and the Challawa Gorge Dam (completed in 1992). The Tiga Dam also supplies water to the Kano River Irrigation Project which uses water to grow food for Kano. However, Kano has no sewerage system or sewage treatment plants. People living in high-density shanty towns in the city use pit latrines. Poor sanitation means that people are at risk of diseases such as

cholera and polio. Polio attacks the nervous system and can cripple its victims. But polio can be eradicated by immunising young children.

Between 2003 and 2004 local Muslim religious leaders and the state government of Kano decided to oppose any future vaccination of children in Kano State. The state government now supports the vaccination programme but some people have remained violently opposed to it. In February 2013, extremists opened fire on two polio clinics in Kano, killing nine health workers. The state government and UNICEF have led a huge programme to educate local people about the benefits of the polio vaccine. It is now hoped that polio can be eradicated from Nigeria by 2018.

◀ **Figure 29** Immunisation campaign worker Hassan Makama keeps count while Riskat Giwa, UNICEF officer of social mobilisation, vaccinates children against polio in Kano, Nigeria.

1970	1975	1980	1985	1990	1995	2000	2005	2010	2015	2020	2025	2030
0.54	0.86	1.36	1.86	2.06	2.34	2.60	2.90	3.22	3.59	4.17	5.11	6.20

▲ **Figure 30** Population of Kano (millions).

Year	Number of polio cases in Nigeria
2001	56
2002	202
2003	355
2004	782
2005	830
2006	1,122
2007	285
2008	798
2009	388
2010	21
2011	62
2012	122
2013	53
2014	6

▲ **Figure 31** Polio cases in Nigeria.

Activities

3 a) Use Figure 30 to draw a line graph showing population growth of Kano City.
   b) Describe the trend of your graph.
   c) Outline two main reasons for this trend.
4 a) Use Figure 31 to draw a line graph of polio cases in Nigeria.
   b) Explain the factors that have influenced the shape of this graph.

Enquiry

How can water security be brought to the Lake Chad drainage basin?

Outline five steps that need to be made to bring water security to the Lake Chad drainage basin.

A trans-boundary water issue

Many rivers cross from one country into another on their long journey to the sea. The River Mekong, for example, flows through six countries between its source in Yunan province in China and its mouth in the South China Sea. Each country relies on the river for water supply and for food. For example, fishermen in Cambodia catch about 2 million tonnes of fish a year from the river. It is thought that no other country on Earth relies so much on wild protein in its diet. But the fishermen in Cambodia are unhappy. They say that they catch fewer fish each year and that the fish that are caught are smaller. They blame a series of dams under construction in China since 1990.

Cambodia, in South East Asia, has a tropical climate with a seasonal pattern of rainfall. Spring has low rainfall and drought and food shortages are possible. Then late summer is dominated by low pressure that usually brings heavy rainfall known as the monsoon (see page 174–5 for a description of this weather system). The heavy rain regularly causes flooding on the River Mekong. The worst floods in recent years in Cambodia were in 2000 when 347 people were killed, 80 per cent of whom were children. However, seasonal floods can also bring benefits. Floods deposit fertile silt onto the flood plain and many farmers rely on these floods to water their rice crops. About 80 per cent of the rice production in the countries of the lower Mekong basin relies on these natural flood events.

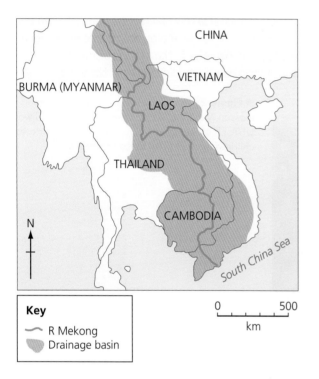

Key
⌒ R Mekong
▨ Drainage basin

◀ **Figure 32** The location of the River Mekong and its river basin.

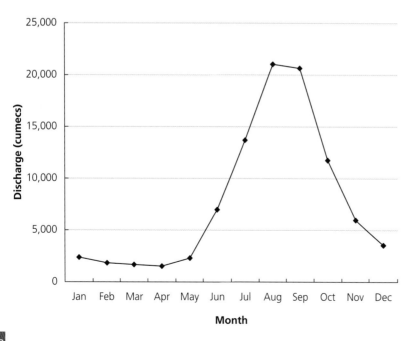

◀ **Figure 33** Hydrograph for the River Mekong, Cambodia (discharge in cubic metres per second).

Year	Drought and flood events
September 2015	Heavy rain led to dangerously high water levels in a Chinese-built HEP dam. Water was released to avoid a collapse of the dam. This water flooded homes of 1,571 families. No one was killed.
August 2014	Severe flooding on the River Mekong in the eastern part of Cambodia caused 45 deaths. At the same time, drought in the north and south meant that farmers did not have enough water to irrigate crops.
October 2013	Heavy rainfall led to flooding in the north-west and south-east. 188 people were killed and 145,000 had to be evacuated because of the floods. 377,000 people were at risk after the floods because of the lack of clean water and poor sanitation in evacuation centres.
October 2011	The worst floods since the year 2000 killed 247 people and destroyed 200,000 hectares of rice fields – almost 10 per cent of the entire harvest. 34,000 homes had to be evacuated and 1,000 schools damaged.

▲ **Figure 34** Recent drought and flood events in Cambodia.

▲ **Figure 35** The River Mekong in this photo is brown because it is full of sediment. Many boatmen have noticed that sediment banks in the river are increasing in size. Some larger boats, such as ferries, are struggling to cross the river without running aground. Are dams in China responsible for this change?

Activities

1 Name the six countries that share the River Mekong.
2 a) Describe the pattern of river discharge on the River Mekong in Cambodia.
   b) In which months are floods most likely?
   c) Explain why building dams on the River Mekong in China could affect this discharge pattern.
3 'Low- to medium-sized floods are beneficial to living conditions in the region. Floods of higher magnitude cause devastation.' Explain the beginning of this government report.
4 a) Use Figure 34 to describe how flooding in Cambodia affects people and the economy.
   b) Use evidence from Figure 34 to suggest two ways that dams occasionally cause floods.

Are dams the answer or the problem?

Dams certainly have benefits. The dams in China have been built to generate hydro-electric power (HEP) to feed power into China's fast-growing economy. Dams also reduce the risk of flooding during heavy rainfall. The dams built on the Mekong have evened out its flow and should help to reduce the size of the annual floods suffered in Cambodia and Vietnam. However, dams also have disadvantages. For example, 25,000 people in China were forced to move when the creation of the reservoir behind the newly completed Manwan dam (completed in 1993) flooded their homes. So large dam projects create conflict between people who benefit and people who lose out when they are built. And dams on international rivers, like the Mekong, can create conflict between the different countries that are dependent on the water. Building a dam in one country alters the flow of water, causing problems for people who live further downstream. So as more water is used in China, less arrives in Cambodia and farmers are fearful that there will be insufficient water for a good rice harvest.

The Cambodian government feels that, as the country that is furthest downstream, it is most vulnerable to changes made to the river by other countries. It feels that river management upstream is affecting the frequency of floods, rates of sediment deposition and the fish population. The dams prevent fish migration and the number of fish making their annual journey downstream has been cut. The fishermen need the seasonal rise and fall in the river's flow because the fish spread out into the lakes and ponds of the flood plain during the flood season, where they are caught. The massive dams are evening out the seasonal ups and downs in the Mekong's pattern of discharge and reducing the overall size of the flood.

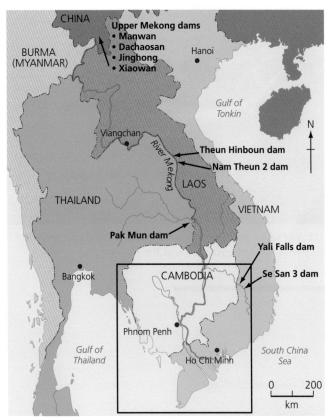

▲ **Figure 36** Major dam projects built or under construction on the River Mekong (the area of Figure 37 is shown by the box).

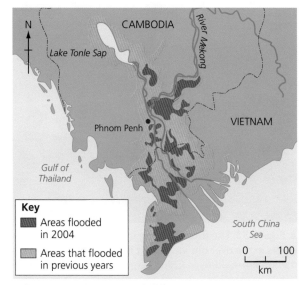

▲ **Figure 37** Flooding in Cambodia and Vietnam on the Mekong in 2004. 30,000 people had to leave their homes during the floods, which lasted for 59 days.

How should the river be managed in the future?

Only Phnom Penh is protected by flood embankments. Most other towns are unprotected and rural families live in houses built on stilts. The government is considering a range of options (shown in Figure 38) in order to reduce the risk of both drought and flood.

a) Fund a flood control centre to collect data and issue forecasts

b) Assess flood risks in each community

c) Produce advice to householders on how to protect themselves

d) Build flood walls and embankments

e) Build small dams to hold back floodwater

f) Better land use planning so that homes are not built on flood plains

g) Start to talk to neighbouring governments about river management

h) Set up an annual flood conference where guests are invited from neighbouring countries

i) Assist neighbouring countries with aid during emergencies

▲ **Figure 38** Strategies used in Cambodia to reduce flood and drought risk.

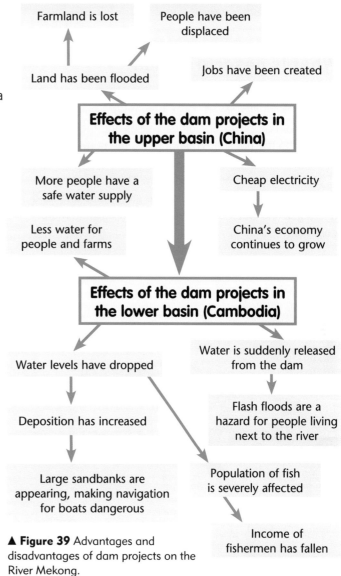

▲ **Figure 39** Advantages and disadvantages of dam projects on the River Mekong.

Activities

1 a) Describe the location of the floods in 2004.
  b) Suggest how building more dams in Cambodia might reduce the risk of flooding.
  c) Look again at Figure 34 on page 279. Is there any evidence that China's dams are reducing the size of the worst floods in Cambodia?
2 Study Figures 36 and 39.
  a) What are the advantages of building more dams on the Mekong?
  b) Explain why some countries benefit from these dams more than others.
3 Discuss Figure 38.
  a) Sort the strategies into short-term and long-term responses.
  b) How many of these do you think will help Cambodia deal with the international dimension of its problem?
  c) Suggest how international co-operation between the six countries on the Mekong could reduce the risk of flooding:
    i)   in the short term
    ii) in the long term.

Enquiry

Do you think Thailand should build more dams on the River Mekong? Justify your decision by explaining the possible advantages and disadvantages in Thailand and Cambodia.

What is desertification?

Desertification is the process by which dry environments become more like desert. Over a period of years, the amount of natural vegetation decreases and the soil is exposed to the hot sun. When it rains, the rainwater runs over the surface of the soil, rather than soaking down into it, and the soil can be washed away. The soil becomes degraded or worn out. It's harder to grow crops and food shortages and water shortages may both become more common.

Desertification is a serious issue that affects over 1 billion people around the world. It affects large parts of North America, Africa, Central Asia and Australia, so it affects people in countries at different levels of economic development. However, its most serious effects are on those people who already live in poverty, because desertification makes it even harder for them to make a living from the land. It is estimated that 90 per cent of the people who are affected by desertification live in the world's poorer countries and that US $42 billion worth of income is lost due to desertification every year.

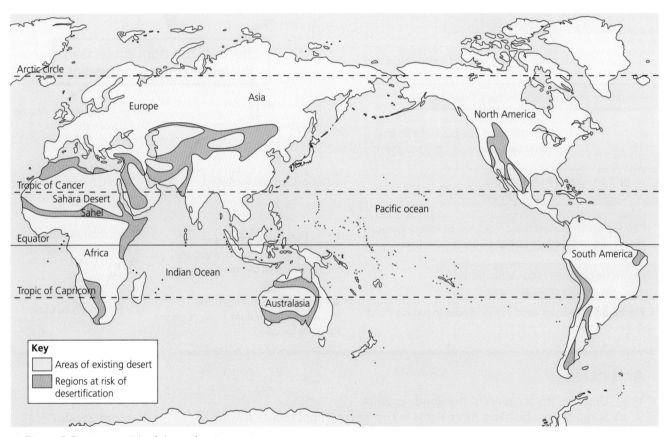

▲ **Figure 1** Regions at risk of desertification.

Activity

1 Study Figure 1.
   a) Describe the location of the Sahel.
   b) Describe the distribution of other regions at risk of desertification.
   c) Name two wealthy countries at risk of desertification.

 www.wateraid.org.uk
A number of non-governmental organisations (NGOs), such as WaterAid, work in Mali to try to improve the amount of fresh water available.

Unpredictable patterns of rainfall

Regions that have low rainfall totals each year are at most risk from desertification. The **Sahel** region of Africa is one such region. The Sahel has a long dry season of nine months, followed by a wet season of rainfall for three months. The total amount of rainfall over these three months is similar to the total amount of rainfall in Cambridge in a year. However, these wet seasons have become unpredictable, with short periods of heavy rainfall running off the land and failing to soak down into the soil where it is needed to recharge the soil moisture and rock **aquifers**.

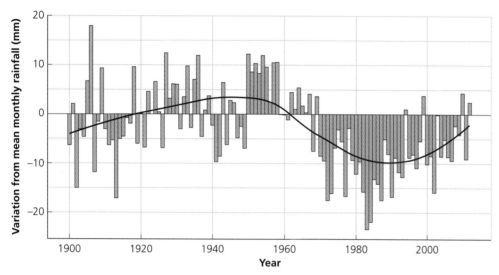

▲ **Figure 2** Variation from the mean monthly rainfall in Sahel countries 1900–2013. Each bar represents whether the average rainfall in each month of the rainy season was above or below average (when compared to the average rainfall during the period 1950–79). The line shows the trend.

Activity

2 Use Figure 2.
   a) How many years between 1900 and 1960 had:
      i) above-average monthly rainfall of 5 mm or more?
      ii) below-average monthly rainfall of 5 mm or less?
   b) How many years between 1960 and 2013 had:
      i) above-average monthly rainfall of 5 mm or more?
      ii) below-average monthly rainfall of 5 mm or less?
   c) Using evidence from Figure 2, compare rainfall patterns in the Sahel before 1960 with the period from 1960 to 2013.

Enquiry

How can we support communities that face water insecurity?

Use the internet link to WaterAid, opposite, to research how this charity is helping to solve problems of water shortages in Africa. From the home page, click on the drop-down menu under the heading 'Where we work'. Select Mali and then Ethiopia.

a) Prepare a short report that focuses on:
   ■ a comparison of the water problems facing the two countries
   ■ how WaterAid and other NGOs are tackling problems in urban or rural areas in the two countries.
b) Use the website to:
   ■ suggest how water and sanitation are linked to disease and poverty
   ■ explain why WaterAid thinks it is essential to involve women in their projects.

Seasonal rainfall patterns in the savanna

The regions that suffer from desertification have a hot, semi-arid climate (see pages 184–5). In Africa, the Sahel region has a short rainy season which coincides with the movement of the ITCZ across Africa (see pages 172–3). Figure 3 shows how rain falls in the Sahel between June and October when the ICTZ moves north of the Equator. The dry season in the Sahel occurs when the ITCZ moves to the south of the Equator. However, the movement of the ITCZ is not perfectly regular so the rainy season is shorter in some years and that's why some years have less rainfall than others (as shown in Figure 2 on page 285).

Signs of desertification	% of people in survey
Poor rainfall	27
Less trees in the landscape	22
Less shade from trees and shrubs for animals	20
Poor harvest	16
Streams and ponds drying up	2

▲ **Figure 4** What farmers in Ghana had noticed about the changing environment in a 20-year period.

▶ **Figure 3**
The seasonal movement of the tropical rain band (ITCZ) across Africa.

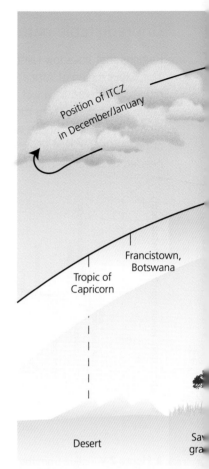

City	Latitude	Jan	Feb	Mar	Apr	May	Jun	Jul	Aug	Sept	Oct	Nov	Dec
Bamako, Mali	12°N	0	0	3	15	74	137	279	348	206	43	15	0
Tamale, Ghana	9°N	3	3	53	69	104	142	125	196	226	99	10	5
Kumasi, Ghana	6°N	61	291	479	560	546	598	302	311	390	361	89	42
Francistown, Botswana	21°S	107	79	71	18	5	3	0	0	0	23	56	86

▲ **Figure 5** Annual rainfall totals in selected cities.

Activity

1 a) Draw a series of rainfall graphs for the four cities in Figure 5.
   b) For each graph, describe:
      i)   the total amount of annual rainfall
      ii) the length of the rainy season.
   c) Use Figure 3 on page 173 and Figure 3 above to explain why the tropical rain belt moves during the year.
   d) Use Figure 3 to predict the seasonal rainfall pattern of Lilongwe, Malawi (location is at latitude 14°S).

  www.wateraid.org.uk
A number of non-governmental organisations (NGOs), such as WaterAid, work in Mali to try to improve the amount of fresh water available.

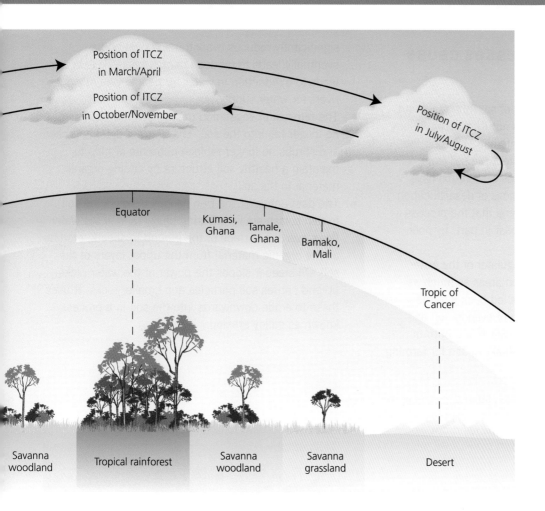

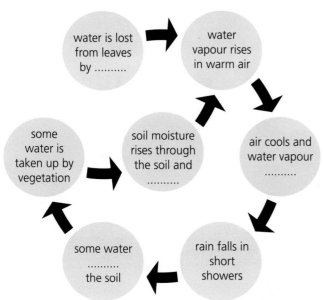

▲ **Figure 6** Convectional rainfall during the wet season.

Activities

2 a) Make a copy of Figure 6. Complete the diagram by adding the correct words below:
   evaporates   condenses
   transpiration   infiltrates
   b) Predict what would happen to the amount of rainfall if lots of trees were cut down.
3 a) Produce a graph or graphs to represent the data in Figure 4.
   b) Suggest how each of these 'signs of desertification' could have affected people, their health, their livestock or the natural environment.

What physical processes cause desertification?

Desertification occurs in regions of savanna grassland. The trees are scattered. They do not form a continuous canopy like that of a tropical rainforest. However, the trees, shrubs and grasses all protect the soil from erosion. In regions where the trees and shrubs have been cut down or burnt, the process of desertification has been rapid. Therefore, it seems that the process of desertification is caused, at least in part, by poor management of the land:

- Vegetation is an important regulator of the water cycle. In more heavily forested areas as much as 80 per cent of rainfall is recycled back into the atmosphere by a combination of evaporation and transpiration from the leaves. Slash and burn of savanna trees and bushes to make space for farming significantly reduces evapotranspiration and so eventually leads to reduced rainfall totals. This in turn leads to a reduction in water for people who rely on rivers for water supply.
- The removal of vegetation means that leaf litter can no longer fall into the soil. The nutrient cycle is broken and shrubs no longer replace nutrients or help to maintain a healthy soil structure by adding organic material to the soil.
- The destruction of the tree canopy exposes the soil to rain splash erosion. During heavy rainfall the water flows over the surface of the ground in sheets, eroding all the organic material from the upper layers of the soil. On steeper slopes the power of the water picks up and carries soil particles and smaller rocks. It uses these to erode downwards into the soil in a process known as **gulley erosion**.

The dense canopy of leaves intercepts rainfall. From here it falls gently to the ground by dripping from leaf tips. Without this interception, the raindrops would strike the soil and their force can erode small soil particles.

The surface of the soil becomes baked in the heat. Moisture in the soil is drawn upwards and evaporates from the surface.

The canopy of leaves provides shade. Air temperatures in the shade can be 20°C cooler than in the open, so the soil stays cooler.

Roots help to bind the soil together and prevent gulley erosion.

▲ **Figure 7** Interactions between vegetation, soils and climate.

▲ **Figure 8** Gulley erosion is a common problem in areas suffering from desertification. This farmer is placing large stones across the width of the gulley.

Farmers allow their goats to overgraze shrubs, and vegetation is killed

Annual rainfall totals are gradually falling

Trees and shrubs are burnt to clear land for farming or urbanisation

Trees are cut down for firewood for cooking

The rain in the wet season is unpredictable and can be very heavy, causing soil erosion

Commercial farms use the land so intensively that the soil is quickly worn out

Less vegetation means less water is returned to the atmosphere by evapotranspiration

▲ **Figure 9** Physical and human factors that may cause desertification.

Activities

1   Sort the causes of desertification listed in Figure 9 into physical and human factors.
2   Study Figures 7 and 8. Use the information to write an explanation of what will happen if …

Farmers allow goats to overgraze	Effect on vegetation	
	Effect on soils	
	Effect on climate	

3   Explain why the farmer is placing rocks across the gulley in Figure 8.
4   a) Use pages 286–7, and the Glossary, to make sure you understand the following key terms:
    infiltration   interception   overland flow   evaporation of soil moisture   transpiration   gulley erosion
    b) Predict whether each of the processes in question 4a will increase or decrease during desertification.
    c) Write a short news report about the issue of desertification. Make sure you use each of the key terms from question 4a in your report.

Is poor land management the cause of desertification in Africa?

Farming in the savanna grasslands of Africa is a mixture of arable (crop-growing) and pastoral farming (animal grazing). Farmers keep goats and cattle for both their milk and meat. Crops are grown using a traditional bush fallow system. Scrub vegetation is removed by slashing and burning. Crops such as maize, root crops and vegetables are grown for between one and three years. The land is then abandoned for between 8 and 15 years. This is known as the **fallow period**. During this fallow period, the natural shrubs grow back. Leaves from the shrubs decompose in the soil, replacing organic fibre and nutrients that have been taken out by farming. This system is sustainable as long as the fallow period remains long enough. However, in some villages the fallow period is now only two to three years. This does not give the soil enough time to recover. It loses its organic content and its structure becomes dusty. This means that the soil is at risk of erosion from both wind and rainfall.

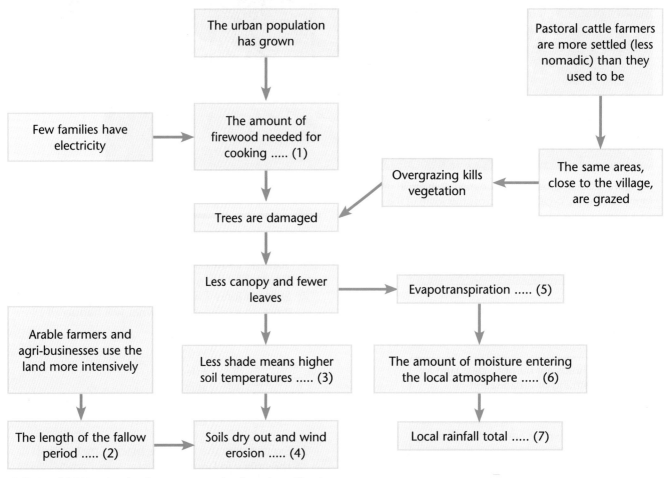

▲ **Figure 10** How poor land management leads to desertification.

Activities

1 Copy and complete the following description of the bush fallow system:
   Natural vegetation is cleared using slash and .... techniques. Crops are grown for one to .... years. The land is then allowed to rest for at least .... years in between crops. This is known as the .... period. During this time .... are returned to the soil.

2 Explain why:
   a) the traditional bush fallow system is sustainable
   b) reducing the length of the fallow period has degraded the soil.

3 Make a copy of Figure 10. Complete the boxes numbered 1–7 by adding the word *decreases* or *increases*.

Can drought-resistant crops help solve the problem?

Ghana is a tropical country in West Africa. Northern Ghana has a hot semi-arid climate with a dry season that can last up to eight months of the year. Trees are used for firewood and shrubs are over-grazed so soil erosion has become a serious issue in the Northern, Upper West and Upper East regions. Farmers are also concerned about the impacts of climate change. Rainfall patterns seem to be increasingly unpredictable. Crop failures and the death of livestock lead to economic losses for farmers, food shortages and higher food prices. According to UNICEF, one in five children in Ghana is stunted because they are suffering from chronic malnutrition. In the Northern region it is thought that 37 per cent of children are stunted due to malnourishment.

Drought-resistant crops may help this region produce food even when rains are poor. These are crops that can grow well even if rainfall totals are low. Crops like chickpea, pigeonpea, groundnut, millet and sorghum can all grow in hot semi-arid regions and are all suitable for growing on smallholdings. The Ghanaian government is encouraging

farmers to use four new varieties of maize that have been developed with the help of the Nippon Foundation which is a non-government organisation (NGO). Local farmers, however, have complained that the new seeds are more expensive than the usual varieties that they grow.

▲ **Figure 12** Clementia Talata cooking banku, a staple made from maize, at a local 'chop bar' (simple restaurant) using water from a Safe Water Network distribution point.

Natural vegetation is savanna grassland. The risk of soil erosion in the Northern and Upper West regions is classified as Moderate to Very Severe.

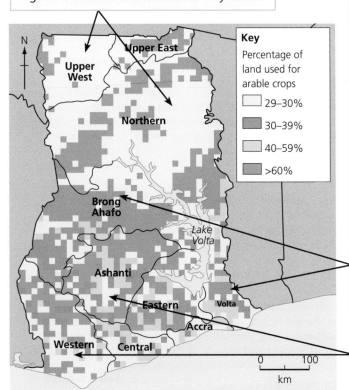

Key

Percentage of land used for arable crops

- 29–30%
- 30–39%
- 40–59%
- >60%

Natural vegetation is savanna woodland. The risk of soil erosion in Brong Ahafo and Volta is classified as Slight to Moderate.

Natural vegetation is tropical rainforest. The risk of soil erosion in Ashanti and Western regions is classified as Moderate to Severe.

▲ **Figure 11** Arable farming and the risk of soil erosion.

Is commercial farming to blame for desertification and food shortages?

In recent years, many large European agricultural businesses (known as **agri-businesses**) have either bought or leased land in Africa to grow crops. This means that land is converted from the traditional bush fallow system to grow huge fields of a single crop. Some agri-businesses grow biofuel crops, such as jatropha shown in Figure 13. These are processed for their natural oils and then used in biofuels that replace diesel in European cars. These agri-businesses can make quick short-term profits because there is a huge demand for biofuels in Europe. Biofuels are seen as carbon-neutral because the plants take carbon dioxide from the atmosphere when they are growing. This means they have less impact on climate change than other fuels such as diesel.

▲ **Figure 13** Jatropha is a crop grown for its oil content.

A large number of foreign MNCs, including Agroils (Italy) and ScanFuel (Norway) have been buying or leasing land in Ghana over the last ten years. It is estimated that 5 million hectares (an area the size of Denmark) is now used for commercial farming by foreign agri-businesses in this way and that as much as 37 per cent of all of Ghana's cropland is now used to grow jatropha.

Some see this as an important way for Ghana to earn foreign income. In the past, Ghana earned most of its income from the export of tropical timbers. This led to a rapid loss of tropical rainforest during the period 1950–80. Growing commercial crops such as jatropha should be more sustainable.

> The European Union needs to tackle climate change. One way to achieve this is to reduce our use of petrol and diesel in Europe. We have therefore set a target of 10 per cent of transport fuels to come from renewable sources by 2020. There isn't enough space in Europe to grow all of the biofuels we need, so some has to be grown in Africa.
>
> **An EU spokesperson**

> Small farmers like me, especially women farmers, are being pushed from our communal land by large commercial farms who are growing jatropha. I used to sell the fruit and nuts from my shea nut and dawadawa trees in the local market. But all of these different trees have been cleared away to make space for fields of jatropha. What will local people eat if we stop growing our own food?
>
> **A Ghanaian farmer**

> Too much land is being grabbed by foreign companies to supply Europe with biofuels. The situation is out of control. Jatropha is not a wonder crop. It uses valuable water resources and needs expensive pesticides. In some regions food crops have been cleared to plant jatropha so local farmers have no source of food.
>
> **A spokesperson for Friends of the Earth**

> I think that growing large fields of crops like jatropha puts too much strain on land that is at risk of desertification. The bush fallow system allows the soil to recover between crops. Commercial farms use the land more intensively. Some scientists believe that, without careful management, the soils will become worn out by commercial farming and then be at risk of erosion.
>
> **Soil scientist**

▲ **Figure 14** Stakeholder views on the growth of Jatropha in Ghana.

How can local communities manage the problems of desertification?

The twin problems of lack of water and soil erosion can be managed and the future of Sahel countries can be sustainable. What is needed is a combination of low-technology **rainwater harvesting** and soil conservation strategies, similar to those used in the drier regions of South Africa as shown on pages 272–73.

These include:
- tree-planting schemes
- building small rock dams
- collecting rainwater from the roofs of buildings
- building terraces on steeper slopes
- building stone lines on gentle slopes
- planting grass strips along the contours of gentle slopes.

How do bunds help?

One strategy that has been used successfully in crop-growing regions of Burkina Faso and Mali is the construction of low stone lines known as bunds. The so-called 'magic stones' are placed along the contours on gentle slopes. Sometimes the bunds are reinforced by planting tough grasses along the lines. The stones and grass encourage rainwater to infiltrate the soil and reduce the amount of rainwater that is lost by run-off. They also prevent soil erosion.

Run-off is slowed by the bund, giving more time for infiltration.

Rainwater infiltrates and recharges soil moisture.

Bunds are placed 10 to 25 m apart.

Any soil that has been eroded by run-off is trapped by the bund. Topsoil and organic matter (e.g. leaf litter) is deposited here.

▶ **Figure 15** How bunds, or 'magic stones', work.

Activity

1 Explain how stone lines are able to:
   a) reduce soil erosion
   b) increase soil moisture
   c) increase the amount of grain grown.

Enquiry

Should farmers in the Sahel grow biofuel crops?

a) Who benefits from planting crops such as jatropha?
b) What are the arguments for and against allowing agri-businesses to grow biofuel crops in Africa?
c) What do you think should be done and why?

The Great Green Wall (GGW) of Africa

The Great Green Wall is one example of an initiative where countries are working in partnership with one another. Eleven countries signed an agreement in 2010 to begin planting this 'wall'. The plan is to plant a 15 km-wide strip of land with trees and shrubs across the width of Africa. It is hoped that this wall of vegetation will help prevent further soil erosion from the Sahel and improve incomes.

The plan is to encourage local communities to plant a mixture of native trees. These will include fruit and nut trees. Small fields between the trees can be planted with food and cash crops – a type of farming called **agro-forestry** because it combines farming and forestry.

▲ **Figure 16** Fields of millet growing between native shrubs and trees in Zinder, Niger.

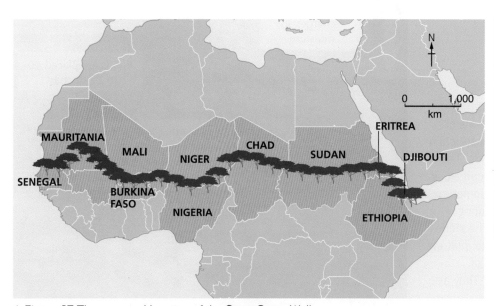

▲ **Figure 17** The proposed location of the Great Green Wall.

Activities

1 a) Describe the environment in Figures 16 and 19.
2 Use Figure 17.
   a) Describe the location of the Great Green Wall.
   b) What is its approximate length?

Reduce soil erosion during the rainy season	Diversity farm incomes by growing fruit trees
Improve soil fertility by using leaves as a mulch	Increase the ability of communities to cope with climate change
Increase the amount of fodder (plant food) for livestock	Trees will provide shade for crops and increase their yield
Reduce the amount of time women spend collecting firewood	Grow medicinal plants
Increase biodiversity	

▲ **Figure 18** Benefits of the Great Green Wall.

How successful is the GGW?

Huge progress has been made by Niger. But Niger had a head start. It began its tree-planting programme 25 years before the 2010 international agreement was signed. Five million hectares of land in the Zinder region of Niger have been planted with trees since the mid-1980s. Senegal has also made good progress. Eleven million trees have been planted across 27,000 hectares of land. The Senegal government wants local communities to develop ecotourism in the newly planted areas to take advantage of the larger number of bird species that live in these new forests.

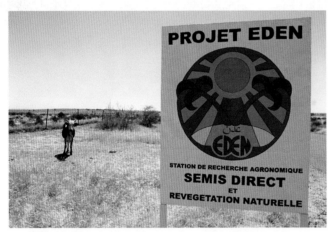

▲ **Figure 19** The Project Eden Research station in Niger. Project Eden is a Swedish NGO. It funds research into plants that will grow in semi-desert conditions without the use of fertilisers or irrigation.

Activities

3 a) Discuss the benefits of the Great Green Wall shown in Figure 18.
   b) Classify each benefit as economic, social or environmental. Do any of the benefits fit into more than one category? Explain why.
   c) Make a copy of the diamond nine ranking diagram (page 108) and place each of the benefits into your diagram.
   d) Explain why you have chosen your top three benefits.

4 Suggest why some people may be suspicious of top-down development.

The Food and Agriculture Organization (FAO) of the United Nations claims that tree-planting in these two countries has been a success:

- crop yields have increased
- livestock is better fed
- the trees are providing medicines and firewood.

Progress has been slow in the other nine countries who signed the agreement. This may be because some local communities do not feel as though they have been involved in the decision-making process and they feel suspicious. This is an example of a 'top-down development' and some communities are disappointed because they have not been consulted. They cannot imagine how their own community might benefit.

Enquiry

How do changes in climate over time affect spatial patterns (i.e. change over a map) in the environment?

Figure 20 uses isohyets to show spatial patterns of rainfall. Every place along an isohyet has an equal amount of rainfall over the year.

a) Use the isohyets on Figure 20 to explain the change in ecosystems as you travel south to north through Niger.

b) Use Figure 2 (page 283) to state whether the rainfall in 1961 and 1985 were similar to average or below average.

c) Use evidence from Figure 20 to explain why relatively small changes in rainfall can have significant impacts on people and the environment.

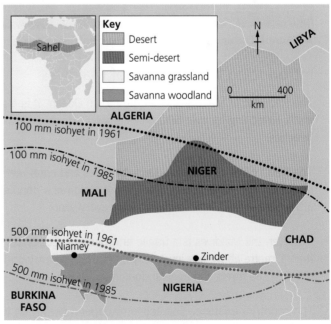

▲ **Figure 20** Ecosystems and the location of the Great Green Wall in Niger.

<table><tr><td>THEME

3</td><td>Chapter 5
Problem-solving exercise: How should
coral reefs be managed?</td></tr></table>

How are coral reef ecosystems managed in the Maldives?

▲ **Figure 1** The underwater beauty of the coral reef ecosystem.

Introducing the Republic of Maldives

The Republic of Maldives lies in the Indian Ocean. It is a group of 1,190 islands and **atolls** stretching for over 500 miles among extensive coral reefs and white sandy beaches.

The warm climate, shallow waters, beaches and coral reefs form an idyllic setting for relaxation and water sports, making the Maldives a popular tourist destination that attracts over 600,000 holiday-makers every year.

However, the Maldives is a fragile environment. Eighty per cent of the country is less than 1 metre above sea level. It is the flattest country on Earth and extremely vulnerable to rising sea levels and coastal flooding.

The country's existence and economy depend heavily on tourism and fisheries. Both of these activities have the potential to seriously harm the coral reef ecosystem and surrounding marine environment.

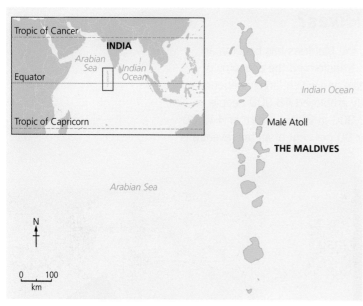

▲ **Figure 2** The location of the Republic of Maldives.

The Maldives' coral reef ecosystem

The unique geographical location of the Maldives has created a rich and complex coral reef ecosystem with some of the highest levels of biodiversity on the planet.

The 26 atolls that comprise the Maldives are formed along a narrow submerged mountain range where the ocean bed is much closer to the surface than the surrounding deep ocean, creating shallower and warmer waters.

Reef-building corals thrive in these conditions, where the average water temperature is between 30–32°C and there is abundant sunlight for plants to photosynthesise and support the coral reef ecosystem.

The clear waters are plankton-rich and are home to thousands of species of brightly coloured fish, corals and other marine life.

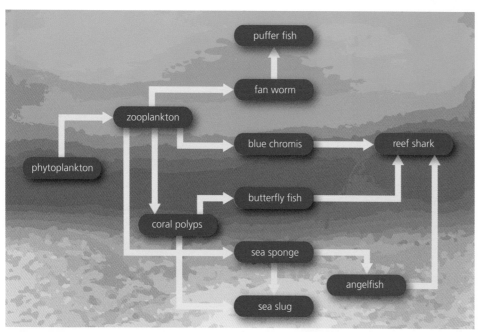

▲ **Figure 3** A coral reef food web.

Activities

1   Use Figure 2 to describe the location of the Republic of Maldives.
2   Study Figure 3.
   a) Name one primary producer in the food web.
   b) Describe one food chain in the coral reef.
   c) Suggest what would happen to this food web if there were no butterfly fish in the coral reef.

How has tourism affected the Maldives?

Since the beginning of cheaper air travel in the 1970s, the Maldives has become an established 'sun and sand' tourist destination. This has transformed the economy of the Maldives. A country that was dependant on fishing is now one which largely depends on tourism for its largest source of income. Tourism directly employed 48,000 people in the Maldives in 2015 and this is expected to rise to 52,000 in 2025. A further 44,000 jobs are created indirectly by the tourism industry. Over 90 per cent of all tax revenue is generated by tourist activities.

▲ **Figure 4** The Hawksbill turtle is an endangered species and a national emblem of the Maldives.

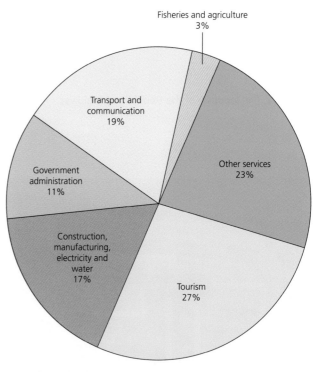

▲ **Figure 5** The GDP of the Maldives in 2013.

Factfile: Resort Islands

'Resort Islands' are hotel complexes that are built on uninhabited islands or atolls in the Maldives.

They play a key role in the government's strategy to further develop tourism under its One Island, One Resort policy.

Most Resort Islands are built and owned by large foreign tourist companies. They are self-sufficient, rarely interacting with nearby island communities, and usually bring in their own employees from abroad who live and work on site.

Resort Islands are subject to strict governmental planning regulations and environmental controls.

▲ **Figure 6** A typical Maldives Resort Island with 'house reefs'.

Enclave tourism

Hotels often sell 'all-inclusive' packages. This means that tourists pay one price and get all their food, drink and entertainment from the hotel. Cruise ships offer the same kind of deal. In either case, their customers have no real need to leave the hotel or cruise ship. A consequence of enclave tourism is that tourists do not visit or spend money in locally owned bars or restaurants. If they did, less money spent by tourists would leak away from the local economy.

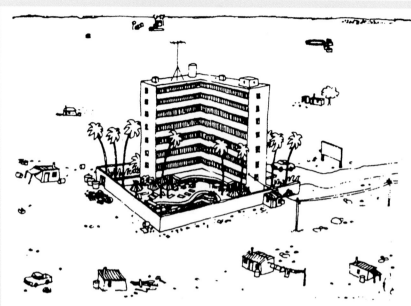

"Dear George, here we are in the middle of things having a great time. We feel we're really getting to know this exotic country . . ."

▲ **Figure 7** Enclave tourism.

Activities

1 Use Figure 5 to compare differences in the GDP of the Maldives.
2 Study Figure 8.
   a) Choose a suitable technique to represent the trend of this data.
   b) Describe patterns in your graph, using summary statements.
3 Study Figure 7.
   a) Suggest a new caption for this cartoon.
   b) Justify the view that enclaves are bad for both tourists and local people.
4 Suggest the advantages and disadvantages of tourism for the economy and environment of the Maldives by completing a table like the one below:

	Advantages	Disadvantages
For local people		
For the economy of the Maldives		
For the local environment		

Year	Tourist arrivals
2005	395,320
2006	601,923
2007	675,889
2008	683,012
2009	655,852
2010	791,917
2011	931,333
2012	958,027
2013	1,125,000
2014	1,204,857

▲ **Figure 8** Tourist arrivals to the Maldives 2005–14.

Enquiry

How sustainable are Resort Islands?

a) Use Egan's Wheel (page 17) to consider ways in which Resort Islands are sustainable.
b) Suggest why Resort Islands may not be welcomed by some Maldivian communities.

Managing the coral reef ecosystem

Despite strict planning regulations and environmental controls, the growth of tourism in the Maldives continues to pose a serious threat to the coral reef ecosystem.

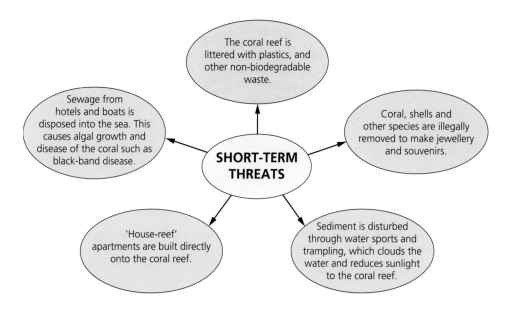

▲ **Figure 9** Tourist activity threatens coral reef ecosystems.

Longer-term threats

Coral reefs are extremely sensitive to changes in sea temperature and sea levels which can seriously damage and kill off large areas of coral. An example of this is the bleaching event in 1998 from which some coral reefs in the Maldives are still recovering. Pages 260–1 describe coral bleaching in more detail.

The Maldives has no energy resources of its own and so imports fossil fuels to generate electricity. The tourist industry is already the biggest user of energy in the Maldives, and this demand for energy is likely to increase if more Resort Islands and transport networks are built.

The Maldives government is extremely concerned about climate change, which could lead to more bleaching events and further increase the country's vulnerability to rising sea levels. If sea levels rise as predicted, 77 per cent of the land surface of the Maldives could be submerged by the year 2100. This will threaten coral reefs, the tourist industry, and the entire existence of the Republic of the Maldives as a nation.

Factfile: Over-fishing in the Maldives

The coral reef fish of the Maldives have always been an important food resource for Maldivians.

Over 70 different species of fish are caught for both local and overseas markets, with increasing numbers being caught as the demand from the local tourist industry and from around the world grows.

At least 120 species of fish are collected and exported for the global aquarium trade, often illegally.

This growing demand is placing additional strains on the health of the coral reef ecosystem.

▲ **Figure 10** Fishing provides food and income for local communities.

Activities

4   Study Figure 9. Work with a partner to explain how each threat impacts on the health of the coral reef ecosystem.
5   Draw a simple labelled diagram to show how the burning of fossil fuels may threaten coral reefs in the future.

Enquiry

What should be done to protect coral reefs from wildlife trafficking?

a)   Use the Factfile and the internet to investigate the collection of coral reef fish species for the global aquarium trade.
b)   Suggest what should be done to protect the wildlife of coral reefs and who should do it.
c)   Present your findings as a blog or webpage.

Sustainable approaches to managing the coral reef ecosystem in the Maldives

The government of the Republic of Maldives has developed two key environmental policies to conserve the long-term biodiversity of the coral reef ecosystem:

- To establish the entire country as a **biosphere** reserve, with protected marine and land zones.
- To become a **carbon-neutral** country by 2020, with a focus on affordable and efficient green energy technology.

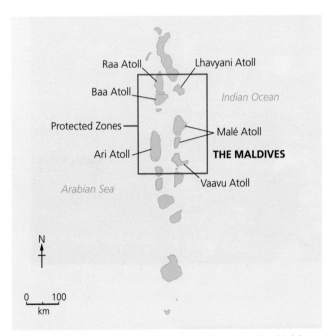

▲ **Figure 10** Protected marine and land zones in the Maldives.

Biosphere reserve

The government wants all of the country to become a protected biosphere. For every island that's developed into a resort area, one other island must be kept undeveloped. Environmental management plans are now compulsory for all new developments, including Resort Islands, with strict building and environmental controls.

The government expects Resort Islands to play their part in developing the biosphere by protecting the coral reef ecosystem and adapting to meet the challenge of climate change. Resort Islands must:
- be contained on a single island
- only take up 20 per cent of the island space
- generate their own green and affordable energy and water supply
- be responsible for managing their own sewage and solid waste
- limit the number of tourists on any one island
- carry out guest and staff coral reef-awareness programmes.

Carbon-neutral country

The government wants to replace the use of fossil fuels with reliable and affordable energy from renewable resources such as solar, wind, sea, biomass and bio-gas. All buildings will have to develop energy-saving measures such as using energy-efficient equipment, minimising air conditioning, and maximising the use of daylight hours.

The use of anchors by boats and ships

The dumping of sewage or other types of waste from boats and buildings

BANNED in the protected marine zones:

Commercial fishing, although traditional pole and line fishing is allowed

Removing fish, marine animals or any living creatures from the ocean

Coral mining and sand removal from reefs, beaches, lagoons

▲ **Figure 11** Strategies in the protected marine and land zones in the Maldives.

▲ **Figure 12** Solar power is used to generate electricity in some resorts in the Maldives.

The government of the Maldives wants to increase tourist arrivals to over 1.6 million by 2020. There are already over 100 Resort Islands and planning permission has been given for a further 71 islands to be developed as Resort Islands. This could have a significant impact upon the long-term survival of the coral reef ecosystem. The views of differing groups of people are given in Figure 13.

Environmentalist

We already have enough Resort Islands – how can we maintain the biosphere if we allow more? Coral reefs are too fragile an ecosystem to support a huge tourist industry – some of the marine protected zones have been so badly managed that the ecosystem hasn't been protected at all. We have noticed that the fish caught by local fishermen are getting smaller and younger so we will have to bring in more restrictions on fishing to protect the biodiversity of the reef.

Government official

Tourism brings in vital money – we are trying our best to manage tourism through the restricted zones and strict planning regulations. If we can protect the coral reef ecosystem whilst generating income and collecting taxes, then we can help our country to develop. Eighty-nine per cent of our population think that tourism is good for our country.

Local fishermen

Tourism is good for local fishermen – we are making more money than we did before. But I have noticed that most jobs in the tourist industry go to the foreign workers that the foreign hotel owners bring in to run their Resort Islands. I am also worried about further restrictions on fishing. Restrictions mean less fishing, less work and lower incomes.

Local cultural leader

Tourism is harmful to our society. We don't like the way some foreign tourists behave and dress when they come to our country – they don't respect our values and beliefs, our culture and religion. The foreign businesses are not interested in our people and both they and the tourists are polluting and destroying our environment and coral reef ecosystem.

Resort island company

We are keen to stay here and built more resorts, as this is a popular tourist destination. Our hotel complexes and house reefs are already well managed and we lead the way in environmental management and conservation in the Maldives – we are making money as well as conserving the coral reef ecosystem.

▲ **Figure 13** Conflicting views on future management of tourism in the Maldives.

Your decision

1 Make use of the opinions in Figure 13 to complete a copy of the following table.
2 Discuss with a partner the arguments for and against further development. Share your findings with other pairs in your class.
3 Are coral reef ecosystems safe in the Maldives? Present a report to the government of the Republic of Maldives in which you justify your decision.

	Arguments for further development of Resort Islands	Arguments against further development of Resort Islands
Economic		
Environmental		
Social		

GLOSSARY

Abrasion – Erosion, or wearing away, of the landscape caused by friction. Abrasion occurs when rivers or waves are carrying sand or pebbles. The water uses these materials to do the work of erosion.

Abstracted – When water is taken from a river, reservoir or underground source to be used it is abstracted.

Aerosol – Tiny particles of dust, volcanic ash and gas in the atmosphere that can reflect the Sun's energy back into space.

Ageing population – A country which has a high proportion of people aged over 65 is said to have an ageing population.

Agri-businesses – Farming that is organised by large businesses – often by multinational companies.

Agro-forestry – A type of farming in which a mixture of crop, shrubs, fruit trees and nut trees are grown.

Air mass – A large parcel of air in the atmosphere. All parts of the air mass have similar temperature and moisture content at ground level.

Annual regime – The way in which a river's discharge varies throughout the year.

Anticyclone – A high pressure system in the atmosphere associated with dry, settled periods of weather.

Apartheid – A political system which was used in South Africa which separated people by their skin colour or race.

Aquaculture – The commercial farming of fish and shellfish.

Aquifers – Rocks in the ground that are capable of holding large quantities of water.

Aspect – The direction in which a slope or other feature faces.

Atolls – Islands that are made of coral. Atolls are usually surrounded by a shallow lagoon of water and a circular coral reef.

Attrition – A type of erosion where rocks smash against each other making them smaller and more rounded.

Backwash – The flow of water back into the sea after a wave has broken on a beach.

Biodiversity – The variety of living things.

Biodiversity hotspot – A region with a particularly great variety of organisms. Central America (or Meso-America) is one such hotspot.

Biomes – Very large ecosystems e.g. tropical rainforests or deserts.

Biosphere – The parts of the Earth that contain living things.

Birth rate – The number of children born in one year for every 1,000 people in a country's population.

Bivariate data – Two sets of numbers that are linked by some kind of relationship.

Blow-outs – Erosional features of sand dunes. Blow outs are often caused when too many people trample through the dunes. This kills the plants and allows wind to erode the sand.

Braided – A river pattern made when a shallow river has deposited gravel islands so that the river is split into several smaller channels. From above the river looks a little like plaited (or braided) hair.

BRICs – Brazil, Russia, India, China, Mexico. Large and growing economies that contribute to global patterns of trade and interdependence.

Brownfield site – A development site where older buildings are demolished or renovated before a new development takes place.

Capacity – The ability of a group of people to withstand a problem such as a natural disaster. Capacity is the opposite of vulnerability.

Canopy – The upper layer of a forest. The canopy receives most sunlight so contains many leaves, flowers and fruit.

Carbon sinks – Places where carbon is stored over very long periods of time, for example, in fossil fuels.

Carbon-neutral – An activity in which any carbon dioxide emissions are equal to carbon being stored.

Carrying capacity – The ability of a landscape or ecosystem to absorb the activity of people without any lasting damage. Some ecosystems have larger carrying capacities than others.

Catchment area – The area a river collects its water from. This is also called a drainage basin.

Central Business District (CBD) – The area of a town or city in which most shops and offices are clustered together.

Chawl – The name for a type of flat or tenement building found in many Indian cities.

Cloud forest – A type of tropical rainforest that grows in upland regions.

Colonises – The process by which plants or animals move into a place where they have not lived before. Some plants, for example, are specially adapted to be the first to colonise sand at the top of the beach.

Comparison goods – Items in your shopping that are bought less often, such as washing machines and TVs.

Consumers – A name used to describe people in wealthy economies who buy and use food, resources, energy and other stuff.

Continentality – The climatic condition of large land masses heating up and cooling down very quickly.

Convenience goods – Items in your shopping that are bought regularly, such as bread and milk.

Coriolis Effect – The way in which the rotation of the Earth deflects the movement of objects such as airplanes or hurricanes.

Corrosion – The wearing away of the landscape by chemical processes such as solution.

Counterurbanisation – The movement of people and businesses from large cities to smaller towns and rural areas.

Cove – A coastal landform that takes the form of a small, rounded bay.

Cumecs – An abbreviation of cubic metres per second – which is a measure of the discharge of a river.

Cyclone – A low pressure system in the atmosphere associated with unsettled weather, wind and rain.

Debt-for-nature-swap – An agreement between poorer nations that owe money to richer nations. The poorer nation agrees to spend money on a conservation project. In exchange the richer country agrees to cancel part of the debt of money that it is owed.

Dependent variable – A set of data whose values depend on another set of data which is the independent variable. The relationship may be tested in a scatter graph.

Deposition – The laying down of material in the landscape. Deposition occurs when the force that was carrying the sediment is reduced.

Depression (weather) – A weather system associated with low air pressure. Depressions bring changeable weather that includes rain and windy conditions.

Desertification – When the climate of a dry region becomes even drier. Vegetation dies or is eaten by grazing animals and the soil becomes vulnerable to soil erosion.

Development aid – Help which is given to tackle poverty and improve quality of life over the long term to improve education or health care.

Direct employment – Jobs that are created within a business. For example, direct employment is created for baggage handlers if a new airport is constructed. See indirect employment.

Discharge – The amount of water flowing through a river channel or out of an aquifer. Discharge is measured in cubic metres per second (cumecs).

Diversify – Where a much wider variety of new business opportunities and jobs are created in a region.

Drainage basin – The area a river collects its water from. This is also called a catchment area.

Drought – A long period of time with little precipitation.

Drought-resistant – Plants that are able to survive periods with below average rainfall.

Dune slacks – Low-lying areas of a sand dune that are prone to flooding during the winter.

Ecosystem – A community of plants and animals and the environment in which they live. Ecosystems include both living parts (e.g. plants) and non-living parts (e.g. air and water).

Ecotourism – Small-scale tourist projects that create money for conservation as well as creating local jobs.

Embedded – The amount of water or energy that is required to make a product.

Emergency aid – Help that is given urgently after a natural disaster or a conflict to protect the lives of the survivors.

Emerging middle class – The growing number of people in developing countries who are well educated and reasonably well paid.

Environmental refugees – People who have to flee their homes because of a natural disaster such as coastal floods, drought or climate change.

Fertility rate – The average number of children born to each woman in a country. If the fertility rate is greater than two, the population will grow.

Fetch – The distance over which wind has blown to create waves on the sea. The greater the fetch, the larger the waves.

Flash floods – Flooding caused by a sudden downpour of rain. The rain falls so quickly it cannot soak into the ground.

Floodplain – The flat area beside a river channel that is covered in water during a flood event.

Foreign direct investment – An investment of money by a company in a development, such as a new factory, located in another country.

Formal occupations – Jobs that receive a regular wage and which are recognised and controlled by the state.

Free trade – When countries trade without any limits to the amount of goods that can be exported and imported.

Garden cities – New, planned urban areas (towns) that have village-like communities and plenty of space for private gardens and public open space.

Glacials – Cold periods in the Earth's history when glaciers have advanced and ice sheets increased in size.

Global cities – Cities that are well connected by the process of globalisation. For example, global cities are usually important transport hubs with major airports and ports. They often have headquarters for multi-national companies.

Globalisation – Flows of people, ideas, money and goods are making an increasingly complex global web that links people and places from distant continents together.

Globalisation of culture – The process by which art, architecture, music, literature and theatre are influenced by cultures from other parts of the world.

Globalisation of consumer products – The process by which the stuff we buy (including food, clothes and cars) is increasingly similar to the stuff bought in all other countries of the world.

Gorge – A steep-sided, narrow valley. Gorges are often found below a waterfall.

Green belt – A government policy used to prevent the spread of cities into the countryside. It is very difficult to get planning permission for new homes in a green belt.

Greenfield site – A plot of land that has not been used before for building.

Greenhouse gases (GGs) – Gases such as carbon dioxide and methane that are able to trap heat in the atmosphere.

Gross National Income (GNI) per person – The average income in a country. It is also known as Gross National Product (GNP) per person.

Groundwater (store) – Water in the ground below the water table.

Groundwater flow – The flow of water through rocks.

Guest workers – People who move to another country in search of work. Guest workers are a type of economic migrant.

Gulleys – Narrow, V-shaped channels cut by running water on steep slopes.

Hard engineering – Artificial structures such as sea walls or concrete river embankments.

Highly skilled – Workers who have high levels of qualification or technical ability and training. See unskilled workers.

Honeypot site – A place of special interest that attracts many tourists and is often congested at peak times.

Host countries – Countries that receive investment from multi-national companies.

Human Development Index (HDI) – A measure of development that takes into account a country's level of education, its wealth and average life expectancy.

Hydraulic action – Erosion caused when water and air are forced into gaps in rock or soil.

Hypothesis – An idea or theory that can be investigated.

Impermeable – Soil or rock which does not allow water to pass through it, such as clay.

Import duty – A tax placed on goods brought into a country to make them more expensive.

Imports – The purchase of goods from another country.

Independent variable – A set of data whose values stand alone and are not altered by other sets of data. See dependent variable.

Indicators – Data or evidence that can be used to measure the economic or social development of a country.

Indigenous peoples – Tribal groups who are native to a particular place.

Indirect employment – Jobs that come as a result of the investment by a business but not within the business itself. For example, indirect employment is created for existing taxi drivers if a new airport is constructed.

Infiltration – The movement of rain water or snow melt into the soil.

Informal sector (informal jobs) – The sector of the economy that includes many types of irregular jobs as well as work such as household chores, child care, and studying.

Infrastructure – The basic structures and services needed by any society such as water supplies, sewage systems, roads or bridges.

Intensive – Farming that needs the input of a lot of labour and food stuffs, pesticides or fertilisers.

Inter-glacials – Warmer periods in the Earth's history when glaciers have retreated and ice sheets have decreased in size.

Interlocking spurs – A feature of V-shaped valleys where the river meanders from side to side so that the hillsides interlock rather like the teeth of a zip.

Intermediate technology – Technology that is appropriate for use in a developing country because it does not need expensive parts or high-tech repairs.

Intertidal zone – The part of the shoreline that is between high tide and low tide.

Jet stream – A strong wind that circulates around the Earth.

Knowledge economy – Jobs that require high levels of education or training.

Lateral erosion – The process by which a river can cut sideways into its own river bank.

Leeward side – The side of a hill or mountain that is sheltered from the wind.

Legacy – Future benefits created by an investment. For example, hosting a major sporting event such as the Olympic Games creates a legacy of first class venues that can be used by younger athletes.

Line of best fit – A line that represents the trend through the points plotted on a scatter graph.

Load – The sediment carried by a river.

Long shore drift – A process by which beach material is moved along the coast.

Low Elevation Coastal Zone (LECZ) – Flat, low-lying land close to the sea that could be at risk of coastal flooding or sea level rise.

Lower course – The section of a river that is closer to its mouth. The lower course of a river is often across low lying land. See upper course.

Lowland tropical rainforest – A type of forest that grows at lower altitudes in the tropics. The Amazon rainforest is an example.

Management zones – Within an area of conservation, such as a National Park, different activities will be permitted within the area or zone.

Mangrove forests – A type of tropical forest that grows in coastal regions.

Manufactured goods – Items that have been made in a workshop or factory.

Maritime climate – The climatic condition of land close to sea. The sea moderates temperatures meaning that there are only small variations in temperature.

Mass movement – When soil, rocks and stones slip, slide or slump down a slope. Some mass movement is very slow, for example, soil creep. Other mass movements are very rapid, for example, a rock fall.

Mass transit – A type of transport system that is able to move large numbers of people through a city, for example, an underground rail system.

Meander – A river landform. A sweeping curve or bend in the river's course.

Mega-cities – Urban areas (cities) that have a population greater than 10 million people.

Micro-credit – Where small loans are given to businessmen and women who are too poor to qualify for traditional bank loans.

Monoculture – A type of agriculture (farming) in which only one crop is grown over very large areas of land.

Monsoon – A seasonal pattern of high rainfall caused by low pressure.

Multi-national companies (MNCs) – Large businesses such as Sony, Microsoft and McDonalds, who have branches in several countries. Multi-national companies are also known as trans-national companies.

Multiplier effect – An upward spiral of the economy and its benefits on employment. Positive multipliers are often triggered by a large investment, for example, the opening of a new factory.

Natural increase – A population increase which is due to there being more births than deaths.

Net immigration – When more people move into a region than leave it.

Newly Industrialised Country (NIC) – Newly industrialised countries such as India, Thailand or Indonesia have a large percentage of the workforce working in the secondary (manufacturing) sector.

NIMBY – Not In My Back Yard. People who object to a development because they live close by are said to be NIMBYs.

Nutrient flows – The movement of minerals from one store to another.

Nutrient stores – A part of an ecosystem in which nutrients are kept.

Ocean currents – Predictable flows of water through the seas and oceans. Some currents are flows of relatively warm water, like the Gulf Stream. Other currents are relatively cold, like the Labrador.

Offshore bar – A feature on the sea bed formed by the deposition of sand.

Open cast – A type of mining that occurs at the surface.

Outsourcing – To get a product or service from a supplier that is outside of the company.

Over-abstraction – When water is abstracted at a faster rate than it is recharged, leading to a store of water decreasing in size.

Overland flow – The flow of water across the ground surface.

Oxbow lake – The loop of an old meander that is no longer connected to the river channel by flowing water.

Pavement dwellers – People who live in make-shift homes on the footpaths of some developing cities, especially in Indian cities.

Permeability – The ability of a rock to allow water to pass through it.

Permeable – A rock which allows water to pass through it, such as limestone.

Plunge pool – The pool of water found at the base of a waterfall. Plunge pools are erosional features created by abrasion and hydraulic action of the plunging water.

Point bar – A river beach formed of sand and gravel that is deposited on the inside bend of a meander.

Porosity – The ability of a rock to store water in tiny air spaces (pores).

Porous – A rock which has many tiny gaps within it (pores) that allow it to store water, such as chalk and sandstone.

Postglacial rebound – An adjustment in the level of the Earth's crust. The crust was depressed by the mass of ice lying on it during glacial periods of the ice age. Since the end of the last glacial period the crust has been slowly rising back to its original level.

Poverty line – A level of income. If someone earns less than this amount they are said to be poor.

Primary commodities – Raw materials which have not been processed. Coal, minerals and unprocessed food stuffs are all examples.

Primary consumers – Animals that eat vegetation (producers) in the food chain. These animals may be eaten by secondary consumers.

Producers – Plants that are able to create starch from the Sun's energy. Producers are at the bottom of the food chain.

Pull factors – Reasons that attract migrants to move to a new home.

Purchasing Power Parity (PPP) – A way of comparing the average wealth of a country by taking the cost of living in those countries into account.

Push factors – Reasons that force people to move away from their existing home.

Quotas – Restrictions on the amount of particular goods that can be imported each year.

Ragpicker – Someone who collects, sorts and sells rubbish for recycling.

Rainwater harvesting – The collection and storage of rain water, for example, from the roof of a house.

Range – The distance that a consumer is willing to travel to purchase a particular product. Low value items such as groceries have a shorter range than high value goods such as cars.

Raw materials – Materials such as timber, stone or crude oil that have not been processed or refined.

Reafforestation – The planting of large areas with trees.

Recharge – Water that enters an aquifer and refills a groundwater store.

Remittances – The return of money sent by migrant workers to support their families who have remained at home.

Retreat – The gradual backward movement of a landform due to the process of erosion. The coastline retreats due to the erosion of a cliff and a waterfall retreats towards the source of a river as it is eroded.

Re-urbanisation – The recent trend for the population of city centres to grow.

Rural to urban migration – The movement of people from the countryside to towns and cities.

Sahel – The semi-arid region of North Africa to the south of the Sahara desert. Sahel means 'shore' in Arabic.

Salinisation – A process by which soluble salts such as calcium, sodium and magnesium build up in the soil. Salinisation occurs when too much water is used to irrigate fields. It reduces soil fertility.

Sea arches – Natural arch-shaped features in cliffs on the coastline that are formed by the erosion of a cave in a headland.

Secondary consumers – Animals that are higher up the food chain and that eat primary consumers.

Self-help – Improvement projects carried out by ordinary people rather than by businesses or governments. Compare this to top-down development.

Shoreline Management Plan – The plan that details how a local authority will manage each stretch of coastline in the UK in the future.

Soft engineering – Alternative method of reducing floods by planting trees or allowing areas to flood naturally.

Soil erosion – The loss of soil due to either wind or heavy rain. Gulley erosion is a major cause of soil erosion in countries that have a seasonal wet and dry climate.

Solar furnace – A renewable technology that uses the Sun's energy to heat water. The resulting steam is used to turn a turbine and generate electricity.

Spit – A coastal landform formed by the deposition of sediment in a low mound where the coastline changes direction, for example, at the mouth of a river.

Squatter homes (slums) – Homes where the householders have no legal rights to the land i.e. they do not have legal housing tenure. Informal settlements are commonly known as shanty towns or squatter homes. They are referred to as slums in India.

Stacks – Natural features of an eroded cliff landscape. Stacks are formed by the collapse of a sea arch.

Staycation – Taking a holiday at home or in your own country rather than travelling abroad.

Storm surge – The rise in sea level that can cause coastal flooding during a storm or hurricane. The surge is due to a combination of two things. First, the low air pressure means that sea level can rise. Second, the strong winds can force a bulge of water onto the shoreline.

Strand line – The high tide mark on a beach. The strand line is marked by a collection of seaweed and litter.

Subsidy – A payment that a country makes to its own farmers and businesses so that their goods can be sold at a lower price to consumers.

Subsistence farmers – A type of economic activity where very little money is used. In subsistence farming the farmer only produces enough food to feed the family. There is very little surplus that can be sold for cash.

Surface stores – Places where water is found on the surface such as lakes and rivers.

Sustainable community – A community which is designed to have minimum impact on the environment. Such communities may make use of energy efficiency, renewable technologies and local services in order to reduce transport costs.

Swash – The flow of water up the beach as a wave breaks on the shore.

Taiga – Natural forest ecosystems found in the cold climates of Northern Europe and America.

Tariffs – A type of tax that may be charged on goods as they enter a country.

Throughflow – The downhill flow of water through soil.

Top-down development – When decisions about development are made by governments or officials rather than by ordinary people. Compare this to self-help schemes.

Tor – A natural pile of stones found on top a low hill.

Trade blocs – Trading partnerships between different countries. The European Union is one example.

Transport – The movement of material through the landscape.

Tributary – A smaller river which flows into a larger river channel.

Tropical rain belt (ITCZ) – A zone between the Tropics of Cancer and Capricorn that has a lot of rainfall.

Tropical rainforest – Large forest ecosystems (or biomes) that exist in the hot, wet climate found on either side of the equator.

Tundra – An ecosystem largely found in the Arctic region. The tundra is treeless because the growing season is short and the average monthly temperature is below 10¬[thin]°C.

Unskilled workers – Workers who have low levels of qualification or little technical ability and training. See skilled workers.

Unstable – Warm air that is rising may be described as unstable. Unstable air causes clouds to build up and form rain.

Upper course – The section of a river that is closer to its source. The upper course of a river is often in upland areas. See lower course.

Urban heat island – When a city has temperatures that are warmer than in the surrounding rural area.

Urban micro-climate – The small-scale, local climate of a large city which is influenced by its buildings and traffic.

Urbanisation – The physical and human growth of towns and cities.

Variables – Sets of data. See dependent variable and independent variable.

Vertical erosion – When the force of water, that is wearing away the landscape, is concentrated downwards. Vertical erosion is common in steeply flowing streams and also in gulley erosion.

Vulnerable – To be exposed to a risk such as a natural disaster. Some groups of people in society are more vulnerable to risk than others. Vulnerability can be overcome by building capacity.

Water cycle – The continuous flow of water between the Earth's surface and the atmosphere – also called the hydrological cycle.

Water footprint – The amount of water used to make an item of food or a product such as an item of clothing.

Water security – When a society has enough water to ensure that everyone has clean water, sanitation and good health and the economy has enough water to grow food and make things.

Water stress – When there is a shortage of water which creates risk for individuals, farmers or industries.

Wave-cut notch – A slot with overhanging rocks that has been cut into the bottom of a cliff by wave action.

Wave-cut platform – A coastal landform made of rocky shelf in front of a cliff. The wave cut platform is caused by erosion and left by the retreat of the cliff.

Wholesale clearance – The demolition of a large quantity of old unfit housing and the redevelopment of new, better homes.

Wildlife corridor – Strips of habitat that allow wild animals to migrate from one ecosystem to another, for example, hedgerows.

Windward – The side of a mountain that faces into the wind.

Zonation – The distribution of plants and animals in distinct areas or zones. Zonation occurs in sand dunes with distance from the sea. Zonation also occurs on mountains where the zones depend on altitude.

Zooxanthellae – Algae that live symbiotically within the cells of other organisms. This relationship creates the coral polyps that we see in coral reefs.

ACKNOWLEDGEMENTS

The Publishers would like to thank the following for permissions to reproduce copyright material:

Photo credits: p.1 © Shoults/Alamy Stock Photo; p.4 © Commission Air/Alamy Stock Photo; p.16 © Raf Makda/View Pictures/Rex Features; p.21 © Peter Macdiarmid/Getty Images News/Getty Images; p.24 © Greg Balfour Evans/Alamy Stock Photo; p.31 © Dead Shot Keen/Alamy Stock Photo; p.43 www.naturalengland.co.uk p.45 © Tony Watson/Alamy Stock Photo; p.49 www.visitwales.com p.50 © ZUMA Press, Inc./Alamy Stock Photo; p.52 t © Robert Gray/Alamy Stock Photo; bl © vdbvsl/Alamy Stock Photo; br © Jeffrey Blackler/Alamy Stock Photo; p.54 © Atmotu Images/Alamy Stock Photo; p.58 © dbimages/Alamy Stock Photo; p.59 © Dinodia Photos/Alamy Stock Photo; p.62 t © Zuma Press, Inc./Alamy Stock Photo; b © Galit Seligmann/Alamy Stock Photo; p.63 © Saifee Burhani Upliftment Trust; p.64 © Punit Paranjpe/AFP/Getty Images; p.67 © Roger Parkes/Alamy Stock Photo; p.68 © Zuma Press, Inc./Alamy Stock Photo; p.69 © ZUMA Press, Inc./Alamy Stock Photo; p.70 l © Panos Pictures/Christien Jaspars; p.76 t © Raveendran/AFP/Getty Images; m © Danita Delimont/Alamy Stock Photo; b © Peter Parks/AFP/Getty Images; p.77 © Stuart Freedman/Panos Pictures; p.81 © Janine Wiedel Photolibrary/Alamy Stock Photo; p.83 © Thomas Imo/Photothek/Getty Images; p.84 © Simon Stirrup/Alamy Stock Photo; p.86 t © Kav Dadfar/Alamy Stock Photo; b © Karen Robinson/Panos Pictures; p.87 © Raveendran/AFP/Getty Images; p.88 © Duncan Chard/ArabianEye/Getty Images; p.89 © Courtesy of Zaha Hadid Architects; p.90 © Sport In Pictures/Alamy Stock Photo; p.91 © Commission Air/Alamy Stock Photo; p.92 © Flip Schulke/Corbis; p.93 © Ulrich Doering/Alamy Stock Photo; p.96 © Bloomberg/Getty Images; p.97 © Panos Pictures/Karen Robinson; p.99 © Joerg Boethling/Alamy Stock Photo; p.101 © Unmeer/Alamy Stock Photo; p.102 © Hemis/Alamy Stock Photo; p.104 © Majority World/Universal Images Group/Getty Images; p.107 © Press Association Images; p.108 © Practical Action; p.109 © Stefan Heunis/AFP/Getty Images; p.111 © Terry Whittaker/Alamy Stock Photo; p.115 © MSP Travel Images/Alamy Stock Photo; p.117 © Copyright Andrew Lane – www.alanephotographic.co.uk 2016; p.121 © Robert Morris/Alamy Stock Photo; p.126 © Travelib Prime/Alamy Stock Photo; p.131 © SWNS/Alamy Stock Photo; p.132 t © Paul Glendell/Alamy Stock Photo; b © JMF News/Alamy Stock Photo; p.134 t © Richard Stanton/UPPA/Photoshot; p.146 © Jon Gibbs/Alamy Stock Photo; p.150 t © Billy Stock/Alamy Stock Photo; p.155 © robertharding/Alamy Stock Photo; p.158 © Environment Agency; p.166 © Stephen Pond/Getty Images News/Getty Images; p.167 © Mark Richardson/Alamy Stock Photo; p.169 © Irene Abdou/Alamy Stock Photo; p.170 tl © Kamensky/Marian/Cartoon Stock; b © PhotographyTTL/iStock/Thinkstock; p.174 © Xinhua/Alamy Stock Photo; p.177 © epa european pressphoto agency b.v./Alamy Stock Photo; p.180 © Press Association Images; p.183 © NASA/Image Courtesy GOES Project Science Office; p.184 © Prisma Bildagentur AG/Alamy Stock Photo; p.186 © Ashley Cooper/Alamy Stock Photo; p.187 © Nasa; p.190 © http://visibleearth.nasa.gov/view_detailphp?id=6204; Jacques Descloitres, MODIS Rapid Response Team, NASA/GSFC 6204; p.192 © Toby Melville/Thomson Reuters; p.196 © US Marines Photo/Alamy Stock Photo; p.198 Arctic Images/Alamy Stock Photo; p.202 © Arco Images GmbH/Alamy Stock Photo; p.205 © Hemis/Alamy Stock Photo; p.207 © JTB Media Creation, Inc./Alamy Stock Photo; p.208 © Christopher P. Baker/Lonely Planet Images/Getty Images; p.209 © Alain Jocard/AFP/Getty Images; p.212 © Eduardo Abad/epa/Corbis; p.216 l © Stephen Saks Photography/Alamy Stock Photo; r © Jonathan Bachman/AP/Press Association Images; p.219 © Ken Hurst/Alamy Stock Photo; p.220 © Jonathan Bachman/AP/Press Association Images; p.223 © Eitan Simanor/Alamy Stock Photo; p.224 b © Martin Harvey/Alamy; p.227 t © FLPA/Paul Hobson; p.228 © FLPA/Tui De Roy/Minden Pictures; p.229 © FLPA/Tui De Roy/Minden Pictures; p.230 l © Ben Cranke/The Image Bank/Getty Images; r © Brad Simmons/Beateworks/Corbis; p.231 © FLPA/Gerry Ellis/Minden Pictures; p.232 © Val Davis; p.233 © Val Davis; p.235 © Images of Africa Photobank/Alamy; p.236 Image from Getmapping PLC, getmapping.com; p.241 © Janet Baxter Photography; p.245 t © KBImages/Alamy Stock Photo; p.247 © Jim West/Alamy Stock Photo; p.248 © Simon Price/Alamy Stock Photo; p.252 © YAY Media AS/Alamy Stock Photo; p.253 t © Age Fotostock/Alamy Stock Photo; b © Greenpeace; p.254 © Photoshot License Ltd/Alamy Stock Photo; p.255 © blickwinkel/Alamy Stock Photo; p.256 t © Aurora Photos/Alamy Stock Photo; b © Martin Harvey/Alamy Stock Photo; p.258 © NASA/Goddard Space Flight Centre; p.259 © Celia Mannings/Alamy Stock Photo; p.260 © WaterFrame/Alamy Stock Photo; p.263 t © ImageBroker/Alamy Stock Photo; b © Steffen Binke/Alamy Stock Photo; p.264 © Gary Whitton/Alamy Stock Photo; p.265 t © Ton Koene/VWPics/Alamy Stock Photo; b © The International Women's Tribune Centre; p.266 © Dieter Telemans/Panos Pictures; p.271 © Friedrich Stark/Alamy Stock Photo; p.273 © Desiree Martin/AFP/Getty Images; p.274 © Jacob Silberberg/Panos Pictures; p.277 © Zuma Press, Inc./Alamy Stock Photo; p.279 © Richard T. Nowitz/Corbis; p.286 © Ian Nellist/Alamy Stock Photo; p.287 © Neil Cooper/Alamy Stock Photo; p.289 © Nyani Quarmyne/Panos Pictures; p.290 © Joerg Boethling/Alamy Stock Photo; p.291 © Mark Newham/Eye Ubiquitous/Hutchinson; p.292 © Prisma Bildagentur AG/Alamy Stock Photo; p.293 © Ullstein Bild/Getty Images; p.294 © WaterFrame/Alamy Stock Photo; p.296 t © WaterFrame/Alamy Stock Photo; b © Hemis/Alamy Stock Photo; p.299 © Horizons WWP/TRVL/Alamy Stock Photo; p.300 © Courtesy of Gili Lankanfushi.

Text acknowledgements: p.5 © Crown copyright 2016 Ordnance Survey. Licence number 100036470; p.12 © Crown copyright 2016 Ordnance Survey. Licence number 100036470; p.18 Data from Danny Dorling, 'Average house prices in Oxford "become least affordable in Britain"', www.dannydorling.org; p.18 Data from Oxford City Council; p.19 Screenshot from Environment Agency (www.gov.uk); p.31 Data from The Local Data Company; p.32 t Data from Office of National Statistics; m and b Data from Google; p.35 t Data from Office of National Statistics; p.43 tl Data from Shropshire Hills Area of Outstanding Natural Beauty Visitor Survey 2007; tr Shropshire Hills Area of Outstanding Natural Beauty Management Plan 2014–2019; b Natural England; p.48 Data from Ernst & Young LLP, The Economic Impact of Rugby World Cup 2015; p.51 all Data from United Nations Department of Economic and Social Affairs, Population Division, World Urbanization Prospects: The 2014 Revision; p. 53 b Data from United Nations Department of Economic and Social Affairs, Population Division, World Urbanization Prospects: The 2014 Revision; p.54 b Data from United Nations Department of Economic and Social Affairs, Population Division, World Urbanization Prospects: The 2014 Revision; p.57 all Data from Australian Bureau of Statistics; p.60 Data from Census of India; p.61 t Data from National Sample Survey Organizations; m Data from Census of India; p.65 Data from http://blogs-images.forbes.com/niallmccarthy/files/2014/09/Bollywood_2.jpg; p.70 Colm Regan, Man thinking about car and woman thinking about shoes, cartoon, *Thin Black Lines: Political Cartoons & Development Education* (Teachers in Development Education, 1988); p.71 Map created by Tina Gotthardt and Benjamin Hennig with data from United Nations Human Development Report 2014; p.73 Colm Regan, Man eating the world that someone else is holding, cartoon, *Thin Black Lines: Political Cartoons & Development Education* (Teachers in Development Education, 1988); p.79 l Data from Nike.com; r Estimates based on *Washington Post*, 1995 and http://answers.yahoo.com/question/index?qid=20100225152454AACzaIP; p.83 l Zafar Sobhan, 'Progress and Globalization in Bangladesh: The Tazreen Fashions Garment Factory Fire', 2 December 2012, Vice.com; r www.globallabourrights.org/campaigns/factorycollapse-in-bangladesh; p.87 Data from www.hindustancoca-cola.com; p.92 Data from World Trade Organization Statistics Database; p.49 Map from COVAMS Newsletter, No. 1, 29 May 2009; p.103 t Data from Statistics South Africa; m Data from World Weather Online; b Data from Statistics South Africa; p.107 Open letter from Moses Mudau to The Hon Edna Molewa, MP (http://www.minesandcommunities.org/article.php?a=11319&l=1); p.116 © Crown copyright 2016 Ordnance Survey. Licence number 100036470; p.127 © Crown copyright 2016 Ordnance Survey. Licence number 100036470; pp.128–129 Plan of the Boscastle flood defences designed by the Environment Agency, reproduced by permission of Cornwall Council; p. 130 b Data from the National River Flow Archive; p.136 Screenshot from Environment Agency (www.gov.uk); p.137

Map from Department for Business, Information and Skills; p.141 Screenshot from Check My Flood Risk (www.checkmyfloodrisk.co.uk); p.143 Screenshot from ArcGIS (www.arcgis.com); p.147 *b* Graph from Met Office; p.148 Map data from British Geological Survey; p.154 *b* Data from Gerd Masselink, Plymouth University; p.161 © Crown copyright 2016 Ordnance Survey. Licence number 100036470; p.164 *r* Data from Environment Agency; p.165 Map from 'Safecoast – trends in flood risk', www.safecoast.org (July 2008), reproduced by permission of Rijkswaterstaat-Centre for Water Management; p.166 Graph from 2011 Census Population Estimates: East Lindsey; p.167 *tl* Data from Office for National Statistics; *mr* Extract from Joseph Rowntree Foundation, Summary of 'Impacts of climate change on disadvantaged UK coastal communities' (6 March 2011); p.168 Map from http://www.scidev.net/global/water/feature/ocean-science-development-sids-facts-figures.html; p.169 Data from UN Habitat, State of the World's Cities 2008/2009; p.178 © 2015 National Drought Mitigation Center; p.181 Graph from The National Drought Mitigation Center; p.182 Map based on M. C. Peel, B. L. Finlayson and T. A. McMahon, World Map of Köppen-Geiger Climate Classification (2007); p.184 Map based on M. C. Peel, B. L. Finlayson and T. A. McMahon, World Map of Köppen-Geiger Climate Classification (2007); p.192 Map from Analysis chart 1800 GMT 4 February 2014, Met Office; p.198 Arctic Images / Alamy Stock Photo; p.202 Dr Malcolm Ramsay, © Jim Metzner Productions, Inc.; p.206 *l* © 2008, United Nations Environment Programme; p.207 Map based on Otto Simonett (UNEP/GRID, Arenday and Nairobi), Potential Impact of Sea Level Rise: Nile Delta; p.219 Map data from City of Wichita Falls Status of Water Resources, Water Supply Summary (10 November 2014); p.220 Data from U.S. Geological Survey; p.248 © ICES – All Rights Reserved; p.249 © ICES – All Rights Reserved; p.251 Table data from Food and Agriculture Organization of the United Nations, 2014, Fishery and Aquaculture statistics, URL: http://www.fao.org/3/a-i5716t.pdf; p.252 *b* Data from www.palmoilextractionmachine.com; p.253 Data from www.worldpalmoilproduction.com; p.259 *ml* Data from Earthlands/Institute of Environmental Awareness; p.260 Data from L. Burke, K. Reytar, M. Spalding, A. Perry, Reefs at Risk Revisited 2011; p.261 *t* © 2006 Great Barrier Reef Marine Park Authority; p.262 *b* Map from Dr P. J. Doherty, 'Assessing the effects of changes in Great Barrier Reef Marine Park Zoning plans on southern mid-shelf shoals (MTSRF Project 4.8.2)', eatlas.org.au; p.264 Data from Aquastat; p.267 *t* Map from Aquastat; *bl* Data from The United Nations World Water Development Report 2015, Water for a Sustainable World; *br* Data from Aquastat; p.275 Maps from United Nations Environment Programme, Vital Water Graphics: An Overview of the State of the World's Fresh and Marine Waters (2008); p.276 UN Water; p.278 *br* Data from Center for Sustainability and the Global Environment; p.295 *b* Information from discoverthecoralreef.weebly.com; p.296 Data from Maldives Ministry of Tourism yearbook 2014; p.297 Data from www.tourism.gov.mv; p.300 Map from Fourth Tourism Master Plan (2013–2017), Ministry of Tourism Arts and Culture, Republic of Maldives September 2013.